MW01069541

SONG HONGBING

CURRENCY WARS I
Currency Warfare

Song Hongbing

Song Hongbing (born in 1968) is a young economic researcher who emigrated to the United States. He worked there as a consultant for the American pension funds Freddie Mac and Fanny Mae that will disappear during the financial crisis of 2008.

貨幣戰爭 – *Huòbì zhànzhēng*

CURRENCY WARS I
Currency Warfare

Translated from Chinese and published by
Omnia Veritas Limited

www.omnia-veritas.com

© Omnia Veritas Ltd – 2021

PREFACE

In the summer of 2006, just as the U.S. real estate bubble was hitting its stride, I was already deeply concerned about the impending financial tsunami, and it was out of this unease and anxiety that the book Currency Wars was born. In my view, the root cause of the 2008 global financial crisis is the fatal flaw in the dollar system since 1971, which is that the world's monetary edifice is in fact built on the debt beach of the United States, and that the dollar's debt position is neither stable nor sustainable, and as the world economy's gross tonnage grows, the foundation of the dollar is sinking, and with it, the crisis of the edifice tipping.

Money, by its very nature, is a claim to wealth, and people hold money, the equivalent of a receipt for holding wealth. What is wealth? What form of wealth is used to issue money as collateral determines the nature of the currency. The most widely accepted form of wealth is currency. Wealth, but also currency, is the fruit of human labour. The commodity property of the commons is, in essence, the property of labour. Over the 5,000 years of human civilization, more than 2,000 commodities have taken on the role of currency, and the market has evolved to phase out other currencies, eventually choosing gold and silver as the ultimate representatives of wealth. No matter what region, no matter what civilization, no matter what religion, gold and silver formed the currency as the most widely accepted form of wealth. The gold and silver at this time is both the claim to wealth and the wealth itself.

Paper money, originally used as a receipt for gold and silver, came into being mainly to facilitate transactions. The ultimate purpose of the people in holding the paper money was not to have the receipt, but to have the gold and silver that the receipt could claim, and ultimately the other wealth that gold and silver could freely and equivalently exchange. Such a monetary system was in operation until 1971, and the United States dollar was its representative. Previously, the real reason people felt grounded with dollars in hand was that dollar bills could eventually be exchanged for gold. Over time, people even forgot that the dollar was merely a receipt for wealth, and never wealth itself, and the dollar was gradually portrayed as the ultimate wealth that was as good as gold.

Even though people have gradually forgotten the gold behind the paper money receipts in the long process of being brainwashed, gold, after all, restricts the over-issuance of receipts, because when there are too many receipts, sooner or later people will be interested in the gold that these receipts can claim. Bankers, as the rule makers of the money game, did not like gold as collateral for paper money, either because it was not enough to satisfy the inflation of paper money desires, or because it did not generate interest income. The idea that bankers would prefer to replace gold with an asset that would never run out and would be viable is a tempting one, and after 1971, the demonetization of gold was in fact an unequal treaty unilaterally imposed on others by the rule-makers of the money game. Thus, we were introduced to an entirely new form of money – sovereign credit money.

It is an attempt to issue money with the debt of a sovereign as collateral asset, and the ultimate wealth that paper money, a receipt, can claim is no longer gold, but national debt! Is national debt a wealth with labor attributes? Maybe. Because the national debt is a future commitment of the taxpayer to pay taxes, but this future tense introduces an element of uncertainty, and that is time. Gold is the fruit of completed labor, and it's all there whether you look at it or not. The national debt, on the other hand, is the fruit of unfinished labour, the wealth of the future, which is always at risk of default. When a national debt becomes the ultimate claim on a monetary receipt, it amounts to an overdraft of future wealth. At the same time, another serious side effect of debt money in circulation is the double interest cost, where people not only have to pay interest on the borrowed money, but also have to pay interest again on the collateral of the money. Under the debt-money system, money becomes a burden on economic development.

Paying interest costs to a few for the use of public money, deadlocking the national debt to the currency, is a design that cannot be logically convincing, and a monetary system that has a "cancerous" message in its DNA. The larger the currency issue, the larger the debt, the higher the interest costs and the greater the pressure on the population to be "indebted". Since interest is only related to time, monetary expansion presents an endogenous rigid demand, with a natural tendency to devalue the currency, and inflation becomes the ultimate corollary. The "invisible hand" of inflation, which leads to the redistribution of wealth in society, is responsible for the worldwide polarization of the rich and the poor.

If monetary and credit expansion and its interest costs continue to increase faster than economic growth, it will inevitably lead to a "lagoon" effect of debt accumulation throughout the economy, which is the increasing ratio of the size of total debt to GDP (gross domestic product). When this ratio reaches a certain level of severity, economies will be overburdened with debt and will default on a large scale. This is where the roots of the financial crisis that swept the world in 2008 lie.

The world currency status of the dollar has widened the scope and intensified the intensity of the crisis. The issuance of global trade and reserve currencies collateralized by United States treasury bonds will inevitably result in a serious mismatch between the size of the United States treasury debt and its fiscal revenues, as well as a deteriorating trend in the total debt-to-GDP ratio of the United States economy, the inevitable result of which is a crisis in the sovereign credit of the dollar.

It is based on the above judgment that in 2006, in "Currency War", I put forward the following inferences: 1, the outbreak of financial crisis will be inevitable, it will originate from the United States, but affect the whole world; 2, the subprime mortgage crisis in the United States is by no means an isolated, controllable and non-spreading small problem, but the first domino to fall; 3, Fannie Mae and Freddie Mac, the financial hubs of the real estate industry, the worst asset bubble in the United States, will become the trigger of the financial crisis; 4, in order to save financial institutions, the United States will have to issue a large amount of additional currency, thus triggering the dollar sovereign credit crisis; 5, while the dollar crisis worsens, gold will rise sharply, so it is suggested that China should increase gold reserves on a large scale.

The sudden changes in the world economic situation over the past five years have and are validating these inferences.

The subprime mortgage crisis of 2007 intensified, leading to the financial tsunami of 2008.

> (a) The successive bankruptcies of Two Houses and Lehman Brothers in September 2008.

(b) In 2009 and 2010, the United States twice started printing money and engaging in so-called quantitative easing of money.

(c) The European debt crisis and the euro crisis, which began in 2010 in the five southern European countries, are still worsening.

(d) In July 2011, the price of gold surged to $1,600 per ounce, three times what it was in early 2006.

On July 19, 2011, the U.S. Congress was hotly debating the need to raise the ceiling on U.S. Treasuries, and if no compromise is reached by August 2, the U.S. will have an unprecedented crisis of treasury default. Although the national debt ceiling will eventually be raised again, the hidden crisis of the national debt caused by the danger of the severe fiscal and balance-of-payments deficits of the United States has been revealed to the world.

Why on earth did the United States, and indeed the world, adopt such a debt-money system that was bound to lead to a crisis? Why didn't the currency opt for institutional arrangements with no interest costs and serving the population at large? What kind of special interest groups are really swaying the establishment and evolution of the monetary system? And how did they wrest the power to issue money from the government?

It is in the course of these intensely questionable explorations that the quest for The Currency War slowly begins. From the United States to Europe to China, the series has gradually developed a research style of "Currency Wars", which is to interpret and restore major historical events and look forward to the future with a monetary vision, a global perspective and a historical perspective.

In 2006, when I was writing my book "Currency War", I did not expect that just a few years later, "currency war", a term that had been ridiculed as a "nonsense", would become an international hot topic of widespread concern among dignitaries and scholars around the world.

History has proven the immense power of money. The fate of the currency will eventually become the fate of the nation as well. China's future development is also bound to be closely tied to the currency.

Author: July 19, 2011 in Fragrant Hill

Will the sailing of China's economic aircraft carrier be smooth sailing?

Written on the fifth anniversary of China's accession to the WTO (World Trade Organization), the full opening up of finance to foreign investment

Cho Yuk-kun

In 2006, U.S. Treasury Secretary Paulson noted in an interview with CNBC (Consumer News & Business Channel) on the eve of his visit to China that, as an economic powerhouse, "they are already a leader in the global economy and the rest of the world will not give them much more time." There is no doubt that this "they" is China.

Clearly, China today is transforming itself into a significant part of the global economy at an alarming rate. A series of economic data and indications suggest that the huge Chinese economic carrier, has taken off.

If the Politburo invited a few scholars to Beijing three years ago to lecture on the history of the rise of great powers, it was only to prepare for China's foreseeable development, then the change from "rise" to "development" is enough to see the adjustment of China's self-confidence and the speed of China's economic development, even faster than the filming of the CCTV documentary called "Rise of Great Powers".

The world has set its sights on China: "The 21st century will be the century of the Chinese", "Around 2040, China's economic power will catch up with that of the United States", and the list goes on and on, as if China is set to become the world's number one economic power.

However, will the Chinese economic aircraft carrier that set sail be smooth sailing? Will China's economy be able to maintain its current "speed" and move forward in the crucial next 50 years? What are the unpredictable factors that may affect the course, course, and voyage?

According to conventional analysis, the most challenging voyage for China's giant aircraft carrier in the coming decades will be its safe passage through the "Taiwan Strait" and its acquisition of sea control in the relevant East Asian waters. However, in my opinion, whether China can become a real power in the world economy in the middle of the 21st century, the most important hidden danger is more likely to come from an invisible battlefield, that is, the potential threat of "financial war". The danger of this threat is increasing with the expiration of five years of China's WTO membership and the full opening of the financial sector to foreign investment.

China's financial industry, which will soon be fully open to foreign investment, has sufficient resilience, including practical experience, to prevent "long-range precision strikes" on a range of financial instruments such as financial derivatives?

Let's take the naval battle: 10 years ago, Chinese submarines drove back the USS Nimitz carrier, and at the end of October 2006, Chinese Song-class submarines again approached the USS Kitty Hawk battle group five miles closer. China has developed a corresponding strategy to contain the U.S. carrier group by virtue of its submarine tactical characteristics, given the reality that its military power is temporarily unable to compete with the U.S. military. Likewise, today, with China's rapid development, there is no guarantee that some countries that believe that China is strong to the detriment of their own interests will not use the "nuclear submarine" of financial warfare to attack China, an economic carrier that has already set sail, to change the course and course of its economic development. China's emergence as a world power in the mid-21st century is currently a routine forecast and does not include an assessment of the potential disruption and obstruction caused by major unexpected events, such as financial wars.

To make an inappropriate analogy, the risks of opening up finance to foreign investment may even be greater than the risks of having all U.S. carrier formations drive into China's adjacent waters. Because military attacks destroy at most construction facilities and wipe out human bodies, conventional warfare is almost impossible to cause complete damage to China's economic lifeblood, given the country's vast frontiers. And the stealthy nature of financial warfare and the brutality of no war cases to draw on and no live drills are a huge challenge for China's national defense. Once the economic order of the country as a whole is struck by financial warfare, it can quickly lead to internal instability, with "internal unrest" triggered by "external problems".

History and reality are equally grim: the disintegration of the Soviet Union, the devaluation of the ruble; the Asian financial turmoil, the "four little dragons" ceased to exist; the Japanese economy was as if it had been dosed with ecstasy. Have we thought carefully: is it all just chance or coincidence? If not, who are the real pushers behind the scenes? Who could be the next target of assassination? Has the assassination of one former Soviet agents and energy moguls and European bankers after another in recent months had anything to do with the collapse of the former Soviet Union? Was the most important factor in determining the breakup of the Soviet Union a political reform or a financial blow?

This cannot help but worry about the defensive capacity of China's financial system and, by extension, the future of its economic development. Even if we put aside the RMB exchange rate and 1 trillion foreign exchange reserves for the time being, then what kind of situation China is in when it comes to the game of political hot money at the national level and between countries, which is out of sight of the normal financial order, must be the most important concern. Can the kindness and patience of Chinese civilization, and the concept of "peaceful development" repeatedly expressed by China, withstand the financial invasion of the "new Roman Empire", which is always subversive and aggressive? On a practical level, does China currently have such a pool of professionals that it can effectively guard against potential financial attacks, both in theory and in practice? If we encounter invisible financial "nuclear blackmail" or even "nuclear attack", will there be such national pillars as Qian Xuesen and Deng Xiaoxian among the Chinese "turtles" distributed in the world financial field?

Paulson will be in China for a "strategic economic dialogue" and Bernanke will accompany him. What is the meaning behind this out-of-the-ordinary move by the US Treasury Secretary and the Fed Chairman arriving in Beijing at the same time? Apart from the exchange rate of the RMB, how else are there "competitions" between countries that are not known to the outside world? In an interview with CNBC, Paulson stressed that the two-day dialogue will focus on the long-term challenges posed by China's rapid economic rise.

So, does this so-called "long-term challenge" include a possible "financial war"?

The purpose of this book is to expose the masterminds behind the world's major financial events since the 18th century, to replay, observe, experience, compare, and summarize the strategic aims and tactics of these people, to predict their future major attacks against China, and to explore China's counter-measures.

The war has begun, though the smoke is invisible!

CHAPTER I

The Rothschilds: The World's Richest "Avenue of the Invisible"

> *"Give me control of a nation's money supply, and I care not who makes its laws."*[1]
>
> Mayer Rothschild.

While the international media is speculating that Bill Gates, who is worth $50 billion, has been crowned the world's richest man, if you believe the truth, you've fallen for it. You won't find the "invisible" super-rich on the familiar list of the so-called billionaires, because they have already tightly controlled the major Western media.

As the saying goes, the Rothschilds are still running the banking business today, but if we ask 100 random Chinese people on the streets of Beijing or Shanghai, 99 of them might know about Citibank and not one of them knows about Rothschild Bank.

Who exactly is Rothschild? A person in finance who has never heard the name "Rothschild" is just as unbelievable as a soldier who doesn't know Napoleon and a person who studies physics who doesn't know Einstein. Strangely but not surprisingly, the name is very foreign to the vast majority of Chinese people, yet its impact on the past, present and future of the Chinese people and the world at large is so great, yet its popularity is so low that its ability to remain invisible is breathtaking.

How much wealth does the Rothschild family actually have? It's a world of fascination. The conservative estimate is $30 trillion![2] How on

---

[1] G. Edward Griffin, *The Creature from Jekyll Island* (American Media, Westlake Village, CA 2002), p218.

[2] Note: Morton (1962) noted that the Rothschild wealth was estimated at over $6 billion US in 1850. Not a significant amount in today's dollars; however, consider the potential future value compounded over 156 (2006) years! Taking $6 billion (and assuming no

earth did the Rothschilds manage to make such an amazing fortune? That's the story this chapter is going to tell you.

Tight family control, completely opaque black-box operations, clockwork precision coordination, access to information always ahead of the market, downright ruthless reasoning, a never-ending desire for gold power, and a deep insight into money and wealth based on it all, as well as genius foresight, have allowed the Rothschilds to build one of the largest financial empires in human history to date, in the brutal whirlpool of finance, politics, and warfare that has swept the world for over two hundred years.

Napoleon's Waterloo and Rothschild's Arc de Triomphe

Nathan was the third son of the old Rothschilds and the most daring of the five brothers, and in 1798 he was sent by his father from Frankfurt to England to open up the Rothschilds' banking business. Nathan is a deep-town, decisive banker who has never really understood his inner world. With astonishing financial prowess and godlike means, by 1815 he had become the premier banking oligarch in London.

Nathan's eldest brother, Amschel, ran the Rothschild family bank at Frankfurt (M. A. Rothschild and Sons), his second brother, Solomon, established another branch of the family in Vienna, Austria (S. M. Rothschild and Sons), his fourth brother, Karl, established another in Naples, Italy, and his fifth brother, James, also had a bank in Paris, France (Messieurs de Rothschild Frères). The banking system created by the Rothschild family was the world's first international banking group. At this time the 5 brothers were closely watching the European battle of 1815.

This is an important war that concerns the fate and future of the European continent. If Napoleon had achieved the ultimate victory, France would have become undoubtedly the master of the European continent. If Lord Wellington defeats the French, then Britain will dominate the great power parity in Europe.

---

erosion of the wealth base) and compounding that figure at various returns on investment (a conservative range of 4% to 8%) would suggest the following net worth of the Rothschild family enterprise.

Long before the war, the Rothschilds were very far-sighted in establishing their own strategic intelligence gathering and courier system. They have built up a vast network of secret agents, known as "children", who resemble strategic intelligence spies. These men were stationed in all the capitals of Europe, in the great cities, in the important centres of trade and commerce, and all sorts of commercial, political and other intelligence passed back and forth between London, Paris, Frankfurt, Vienna and Naples. The efficiency, speed and accuracy of this intelligence system are breathtaking, far exceeding the speed of any official information network and beyond the reach of other commercial competitors. All this puts Rothschild Bank at a distinct advantage in almost all international competition.[3]

> "Rothschild Bank carriages rode down the (European) highways, Rothschild Bank ships crossed the channel, Rothschild Bank spies spread across the (European) city streets, carrying large amounts of cash, bonds, letters and news, and their latest scoop was swiftly circulated through the stock and commodity markets, but all without the precious results of the Battle of Waterloo."[4]

The Battle of Waterloo, which took place on June 18, 1815, near Brussels, Belgium, was not only a battle of life and death between the two armies of Napoleon and Wellington, but also a huge gamble by thousands of investors, with the winner gaining unprecedented wealth and the loser losing heavily. The air in the London stock exchange was tense to the highest degree, and all were anxiously awaiting the final outcome of the Battle of Waterloo. If the UK loses, the price of British public debt (Consols) will fall into the abyss; if the UK wins, British public debt will crash into the clouds.

Just as the two armies were fighting to the death, Rothschild's spies were nervously gathering information from within the two armies on the progress of the various battle situations as accurately as possible. More spies were in charge of relaying the latest battlefield intelligence to the nearest Rothschild intelligence staging area. By evening, Napoleon's defeat was final, and a Rothschild express messenger named Rothworth, who had witnessed the battle, immediately galloped

---

[3] Des Griffin, *Descent into Slavery* (Emissary Publications 1980), Chapter 5.

[4] Des Griffin, *Descent into Slavery* (Emissary Publications 1980), p. 94.

on a fast horse towards Brussels, and then turned towards Port Ostend. It was late at night when Rose Woods hopped aboard a Rothschild Express ship with a special pass. By this time the wind was blowing high in the English Channel, and after paying a fee of 2,000 francs, he finally found a sailor to help him cross the channel[5] overnight. When he arrived at the shore in Folkestone, England, early on the morning of June 19, Nathan Rothschild himself was waiting there. Nathan quickly opened the envelope, skimmed through the headlines of the battle report, and then galloped straight to the London Stock Exchange.

When Nathan quickly entered the stock exchange, the anxious and excited crowd waiting for the battle report immediately fell silent, and all eyes were on Nathan's expressionless and inexplicable face. At this point, Nathan slowed down and walked to his own throne known as the "Pillar of Rothschild". At this moment, the muscles on his face were as if they were stone sculptures without the slightest emotional flutter. By this time the trading floor was completely free of its former bustle, and everyone was pinning their riches and glory on Nathan's eyes. After a moment, Nathan passed a deep wink to the Rothschild family traders who were around the ring, and everyone immediately rushed to the trading table without a word and began selling British bonds. There was an immediate commotion in the lobby, some people began to talk to each other, and many more people remained at a loss for words. At this point, the equivalent of hundreds of thousands of dollars of British public debt was thrown violently into the market, and the price of public debt began to fall, and then the even larger throwing of the order went more violently than the tide.

At this point Nathan remained expressionlessly leaning against his throne. Someone in the trading floor finally let out an alarmed cry,

> *"Rothschild knows!" "Rothschild knows!" "Wellington is defeated!"*

All the people immediately looked back like they had been electrocuted, and the sell-off finally turned into a panic. When one violently loses one's mind, following the actions of others becomes a self-imposed act. Everyone wanted to get rid of the already worthless British public debt in their hands at once, and keep as much of what was

---

[5] Eustace Mullins, *The Secrets of the Federal Reserve* – Omnia Veritas Ltd, www.omnia-veritas.com Chapter 5.

left as possible. After a few hours of frenzied tossing, UK public debt has become a pile of junk, with only 5% of its face value left.[6]

At this point Nathan remained as indifferent to the situation as he had been at the beginning. His eyes flickered slightly in a way that no one without long training could ever read, but this time the signal was completely different. The numerous traders around him immediately pounced on their respective trading desks and began to buy every single British bond they could see in the market.

At eleven o'clock on the evening of June 21, Henry Percy, Lord Wellington's messenger, finally arrived in London with the news that Napoleon's army had been utterly defeated after eight hours of bitter fighting, with a loss of 1/3 of its men, and that France was finished!

This information was a whole day later than Nathan's information! And Nathan wildly made 20 times as much money in that one day, more than Napoleon and Wellington had ever made in decades of warfare combined![7]

The Battle of Waterloo made Nathan the largest creditor of the British government in one fell swoop, thus dominating later British public debt issuance, with the Bank of England under Nathan's control. Britain's public debt is the proof of future government taxation, and the obligation of the British people to pay all kinds of taxes to the government becomes a disguised tax on the whole population by the Rothschild Bank. The British government's financial outlays were financed by the issuance of public debt, in other words, the British government had to borrow money from private banks to spend because it did not have the right to issue money, and paid about 8 percent interest, all of which was settled in gold coins. While Nathan held the overwhelmingly large amount of British public debt in his hands, he effectively manipulated the price of the public debt, swaying the entire

---

[6] Des Griffin, *Descent into Slavery* (Emissary Publications 1980), Chapter 5.

[7] Ignatius Balla, *The Romance of the Rothschilds*, (Everleigh Nash, London, 1913). Note: the *New York Times*, April 1, 1915 reported that in 1914, Baron Nathan Mayer de Rothschild went to court to suppress Ignatius Balla's book on the grounds that the Waterloo story about his grandfather was untrue and libelous. The court ruled that the story was true, dismissed Rothschild's suit, and ordered him to pay all costs.

British money supply, and the economic lifeblood of Britain was tightly pinched in the hands of the Rothschilds.

The smug Nathan made no secret of his pride in conquering the British Empire.

> *I don't care what kind of English puppet is put on the throne to rule this vast sunset empire. Whoever controls the money supply of the British Empire controls the British Empire, and that person is me![8]*

Rothschild's beginnings in the era

> *"The few who can understand the system (check money and credit money) are either so interested in the profits it generates, or so dependent on the system's handouts (politicians), that this class of people will not oppose us. On the other hand, the vast majority of the people are intellectually inadequate to understand the enormous advantages of capital derived on the basis of this system, and they will be oppressed without complaint or even the slightest suspicion that the system has harmed their interests."[9]*
>
> —The Rothschild Brothers, 1863.

The old Rothschild grew up during a time when the Industrial Revolution was rapidly growing in Europe and the financial industry was booming like never before, with entirely new financial practices and ideas radiating from the Netherlands and England to all of Europe. With the establishment of the Bank of England in 1694, a far more complex concept and practice of money than in the past was created by a large group of adventurous bankers.

The concept and form of money changed profoundly during the 100 years of the 17th century, from 1694 to 1776, when Adam Smith's Wealth of Nations came out, and for the first time in human history the amount of paper money issued by banks exceeded the total amount of

---

[8] Eustace Mullins, *The Secrets of the Federal Reserve* – Omnia Veritas Ltd, www.omnia-veritas.com, Chapter 5.

[9] The Rothschild Brothers of London in a letter sent in 1863 to New York Bankers in support of the then proposed National Banking Act.

metal money in circulation.[10] The unprecedented demand for financing in emerging industries such as railroads, mines, shipbuilding, machinery, textiles, military industry, and energy, generated by the industrial revolution, has created an increasingly strong contradiction with the ancient inefficiencies and extremely limited financing capabilities of traditional goldsmith banks. The emerging bankers, represented by the Rothschilds, seized this historically important opportunity to fully dominate the historical course of modern finance in the way that was most advantageous to them, while the fate of all others had to be determined, or was unwittingly determined, by this system.

Two civil wars and political turmoil since 1625 had left the English treasury empty, and when William I entered England in 1689 (a throne he had won by marrying Mary, daughter of King James II) he was faced with a mess, which, combined with his ongoing war with His Holiness Louis XIV, had left him begging for money and nearly starving for food. At this point, bankers led by William Paterson proposed to the king a new concept learned from the Netherlands: the creation of a privately owned central bank, the Bank of England, to finance the king's enormous expenses.

This private bank provides the government with £1.2 million in cash as the government's "Perpetual Loan" with an interest rate of 8% per annum and an annual management fee of £4,000, so that for £100,000 per year the government can immediately raise £1.2 million in cash and never have to pay back the principal! Of course, the government had the added "benefit" of allowing the Bank of England to issue nationally recognised bank notes exclusively.[11]

It has long been known that the most profitable thing about the Goldsmith Banker was the issuance of bank notes, which were actually receipts for gold coins deposited by depositors with the goldsmith. Since it was very inconvenient to carry large amounts of gold coins, everyone started trading with receipts of gold coins and then redeeming the corresponding gold coins from the goldsmith. Over time, people did not feel the need to always go to the goldsmith to access the gold coins,

---

[10] Glyn Davis, *History of Money from Ancient Times to the Present Day* (University of Wales Press, 2002), p257, p258.

[11] Eustace Mullins, *The Secrets of the Federal Reserve* – Omnia Veritas Ltd, www.omnia-veritas.com, Chapter 5.

and later these receipts gradually became currency. The wise goldsmith bankers gradually found that only a few people came to collect gold coins every day, and they began to quietly increase the number of receipts to lend money to those who needed it and charge interest, and when the borrowers paid off the debts with interest, the goldsmith bankers recovered the debts and destroyed them quietly, as if nothing had happened, but the interest went steadily into their own money bags. The wider the circulation and acceptance of a goldsmith bank's receipts, the greater the profit. And the extent of circulation and acceptance of bank notes issued by the Bank of England is far beyond the reach of other banks, and these nationally recognised bank notes are the national currency.

The Bank of England's cash share capital is recruited to the community and those who subscribe to over £2,000 are eligible to become directors of the Bank of England (Governors). A total of 1330 people became shareholders of the Bank of England and 14 became directors of the bank, including William Paterson.[12]

In 1694, King William I issued the Royal Charter for the Bank of England, and the first modern bank was born.

The Bank of England's core philosophy is to convert the private debts of kings and royalty into permanent national debt, secured by universal taxation, with the Bank of England issuing the national currency based on the debt. In this way, the king has money to fight or enjoy, the government has money to do what it loves, the bankers give out the huge loans they daydream about and get substantial interest income, and it seems to be a happy situation for all, with only the people's taxes as collateral. Thanks to such powerful new financial instruments, the deficit of the British government skyrocketed, and from 1670 to 1685 the British government's coffers were £24.8 million. Government revenue more than doubled from 1685 to 1700 to £55.7 million, but British government borrowing from the Bank of England skyrocketed more than 17 times from 1685 to 1700, from £800,000 to £13.8 million.[13]

---

[12] *Ibid.*

[13] Glyn Davis, *History of Money from Ancient Times to the Present Day* (University of Wales Press, 2002), p. 239.

Even better, the design deadlocks the issuance of the national currency and the permanent national debt. To add new currency would require an increase in the national debt, and to pay off the national debt would be to destroy the national currency, and there would be no money in circulation in the market, so the government would never be able to pay off the debt. As the need to repay interest and economic development inevitably leads to a greater demand for money, which has to be borrowed from the banks, the national debt will only grow forever, and the interest income from these debts will all go into the bankers' pockets, while the interest payments will be covered by the people's taxes!

Sure enough, since then, the British government has never paid off the debt, by the end of 2005, the British government's debt from 1.2 million pounds in 1694 increased to 525.9 billion pounds, accounting for the British GDP.[14]

It would seem that for such a large sum of money, it would be worth taking the risk of beheading a king or assassinating several presidents if anyone dared to stand in the way of a privatized national bank.

Old Rothschild's First Bucket of Gold

On February 23, 1744, Meyer A. Bauer was born in the Jewish ghetto of Frankfurt, where his father, Moses, was an itinerant goldsmith and moneylender who spent his years earning a living along the Eastern European continent. When Meyer was born, Moses decided to settle down in Frankfurt. From an early age, Meyer displayed an amazing intellect, and his father devoted a great deal of his life to him, carefully coaching him and systematically teaching him about the business of money and lending. A few years later, Moses died, and at the age of thirteen Meyer, encouraged by relatives, came to Hanover as a banking apprentice at the Oppenheimer Family Bank.[15]

Meyer, with his great perception and diligence, quickly mastered the specialized skills of banking operations, and for seven full years he

---

[14] UK National Statistics.

[15] Des Griffin, *Descent into Slavery* (Emissary Publications 1980), Chapter 5.

absorbed and digested like a sponge the whims of the financial industry from the United Kingdom. For his outstanding work, Meyer was promoted to junior partner. During his time at the bank, he met some very well-connected clients, including General von Istvor, who was instrumental in his later development. It was here that Meyer realized that lending money to the government and the king was much more profitable and insured than lending it to individuals, not only with much larger loans, but with government taxes as collateral. This new financial concept from the UK has given Meyer's mind a new lease of life.

A few years later, the young Meyer returned to Frankfurt to continue his father's lending business. He also changed his surname to Rothschild (Rothschild, Rot is the German word for red and Schild is the German word for shield). When Meyer learned that General von Istvor had also returned to Frankfurt and was working at Prince William's court, it immediately occurred to him to make good use of the relationship. General von Istvor was also very happy when he saw Meyer again. The general himself is a numismatic collector, and Meyer's research on numismatics has been handed down from generations of ancestors, and the talk of ancient numismatic coins is so familiar that the general's eyebrows danced. Even more to the general's delight, Meyer was willing to sell a few rare gold coins to the general at a very low discount, and soon General von Istvor took Meyer as a confidante. The scheming Meyer quickly became acquainted with important people at court. At last one day, after being introduced by General von Istvor, Prince William summoned Meyer, who, it turned out, was himself a collector of gold coins, and by the same means Meyer soon had the Prince in his favor.

On 21 September 1769, Meyer inscribed his signboard with the royal coat of arms, next to which he wrote in gold letters: "M. A. Rothschild, appointed agent of His Royal Highness Prince William."[16] Over time, Meyer's credibility skyrocketed and business became increasingly red-hot.

Prince William himself was historically a man of fortune, famous in 18th century Europe for "leasing armies" to other countries to "keep the peace". He was close to various European royals, and particularly liked to do business with the British crown – Britain, with many

---

[16] Ibid.

overseas interests, often needed to use its own troops, and with its own army in short supply, and with Britain putting out more money and rarely defaulting on it, was a match for Prince William. Later in the American War of Independence, Washington dealt with more German soldiers than British soldiers. Prince William thus amassed the largest royal estate in European history, equivalent to about $200 million. No wonder people call him "the coldest loan shark in Europe".[17]

After committing himself to Prince William's account, Meyer worked diligently to do every errand to the best of his ability, and thus gained the prince's trust. Soon the French bourgeois revolution (1789–1799) broke out and the wave of revolution gradually spread from France to the surrounding monarchies. Prince William became anxious and increasingly worried that the revolution would resonate in Germany and that the mob would loot his wealth. Contrary to what the prince thought, Meyer was very happy about the French Revolution, as the panic caused his gold business to soar. When the revolution was aimed at the Holy Roman Empire, trade between Germany and England was interrupted, the price of imports soared, and the trafficking of goods from England to Germany made Meyer a fortune.

Meyer has been a very active leader in the Jewish community.

> *"Every Saturday evening, when the synagogue service was over, Meyer would always invite some of the wisest Jewish scholars to his home, and they would gather together while slowly sipping wine and discussing in detail the order of doing something late into the night."*[18]

Meyer famously said, "A family that prays together will come together." Later on, people never understood what kind of power made the Rothschilds so insistent on conquest and power.

By 1800, the Rothschilds had become one of the wealthiest Jewish families in Frankfurt. Meyer also received the title of "Imperial Agent of the Holy Roman Empire" from the Holy Roman Emperor that year. This title enabled him to pass through the various regions of the Empire, exempting him from the various taxes imposed on other Jews, and allowing his company's personnel to be armed.

---

[17] Frederic Morton, *The Rothschilds* (Fawcett Books, 1961), p40.

[18] *Ibid.*, p. 31.

In 1803, Meyer's growing relationship with Prince William brought Meyer's power to a great leap forward. Here's the thing, one of Prince William's cousins was the King of Denmark, and he approached Prince William to borrow a sum of money, which Prince William was reluctant to agree to for fear of showing his wealth. When Meyer learned of this, and thought it a good opportunity, he proposed a solution to the prince, in which the prince would pay the money, and Meyer would negotiate a loan to the king of Denmark in the name of Rothschild, with interest Meyer could take. The prince thought about it carefully and thought it was a good way to lend and collect money without showing his wealth. For Meyer, lending money to the king was something he dreamed of, not only a steady return, but a great opportunity to improve his reputation. As a result the loan was a great success. Immediately afterwards, six more loans from the Danish royal family were closed through Meyer. Rothschild rose to fame, especially as his close ties to the royal family began to be known in Europe.

After Napoleon came to power, he tried to pull Prince William to his side. Prince William was unwilling to choose a side before the situation became clear, and finally Napoleon announced "to remove Hess Kaiser (Prince William's family) from the list of European rulers", then the French army pressed against the border, Prince William went into exile to Denmark in a hurry, before fleeing, handed over a cash worth 3 million dollars to Meyer to keep.[19] It was this $3 million in cash that brought Meyer unprecedented power and wealth, becoming the first bucket of money Meyer had forged his financial empire.

Meyer has far greater ambitions than establishing a Bank of England! When he got this huge sum of money from Prince William, he began to mobilize his troops. His five sons shot like five sharp arrows into the five heartlands of Europe. The oldest, Amschel, kept the Frankfurt headquarters, the second, Solomon, went to Vienna to open a new battlefield, the third, Nathan, was sent to England to preside over the big picture, the fourth, Karl, went to Naples, Italy, to establish a base and acted as a messenger between the brothers, and the fifth, James, took charge of the Paris business.

A financial empire, unprecedented in human history, was unveiled.

---

[19] Des Griffin, *Descent into Slavery* (Emissary Publications, 1980), Chapter 5.

Nathan dominates London Financial City

> *"They (the Rothschilds) are the masters of the world's money market, and of course of almost everything else. They actually had assets pledged against the coffers of the entire southern Italian region, and the kings and ministers of all (European) countries were listening to their teachings."[20]*
> —Benjamin Disraeli, British Prime Minister, 1844.

The Financial City of London, a mere square kilometre in the heart of Greater London, has been the financial centre of Britain and the world since the 18th century, with an independent judicial system, similar to the Vatican, and rather like a country within a country. It is the place where the world's major financial institutions, including the Bank of England's headquarters, create 1/6th of the UK's GDP today, and whoever dominates the Financial City of London dominates the UK.

Nathan's initial arrival in England coincided with the Franco-British confrontation and mutual blockade. British goods sold at high prices in Europe, and Nathan began teaming up with his brother James, who was in France, to smuggle the goods from England to France and change hands, making a lot of money from it. Later Nathan befriended John Harris, an officer in the British Treasury, and inquired about the plight of British troops in Spain. The British army, commanded by the Duke of Wellington, was ready to attack the French army, and the only difficulty was the lack of pay. The Duke of Wellington, despite being guaranteed by the British government, had difficulty in persuading the Spanish and Portuguese bankers to accept the bank notes he produced, and the Duke of Wellington's army was in dire need of gold.[21]

Nathan had a bright idea and was determined to make a killing on the matter. He asked around for gold supplies, it just so happened that the East India Company had a batch of gold just shipped from India, ready to sell, and the British government also wanted to buy, just felt that the price was too high, wanted to wait for the gold price to come

---

[20] Benjamin Disraeli, *Coningsby* (New York: Alfred A. Knopf, originally published in England in 1844), p225.

[21] G. Edward Griffin, *The Creature from Jekyll Island* (American Media, Westlake Village, CA 2002), p. 224.

down before buying. Nathan gauged the situation and immediately bet all of Prince William's three million dollars in cash, which he had brought to Britain to fight, and the large sums he had earned from smuggling British goods, seized the opportunity to deal with the East India Company, purchased £800,000 of gold,[22] and then immediately raised the price of gold. The British government saw that the price of gold could not be lowered, and the military situation in front of the 100,000 urgent, only to buy from Nathan at a high price. The deal made Nathan a fortune.

But Nathan continued his serial ploy, and he offered to escort the gold to the Duke of Wellington's army. At the time, France had a tight land blockade against Britain, which was so risky that the British government was willing to pay a high price to transport the gold. After taking this errand, Nathan asked his 19-year-old brother James to inform the French government that Nathan wanted to ship gold to France, which the British government would probably be furious about, as the flow of gold to France would greatly weaken Britain's financial capacity. When the French side heard that there was such a good thing, why not strongly support the reason, immediately ordered the French police to protect along the way, all the way through. Individual French officials, who have been bribed heavily, have also been deafened and silenced.

So Nathan and others escorted the gold, with the support of the British and French governments, entered the bank in Paris in a big way, Nathan attended the welcome banquet of the French government, while quietly sent someone to exchange the gold into gold coins acceptable to the Duke of Wellington, and then unwittingly transported through the Rothschild transport network to the British army in Spain, the method of the subtlety of the modern Hollywood movie plot.

A Prussian diplomat in Britain put it this way:

> *"Rothschild's influence on financial affairs here (in London) is staggering. They completely dictate the price of forex trading in the Financial City of London. As bankers, their power is mind-boggling. The Bank of England shuddered when Nathan got angry."*

---

[22] Frederic Morton, *The Rothschilds* (Fawcett Books, 1961), p. 45.

On one occasion, Nathan took a cheque drawn by his brother Amschel from the Rothschild Bank in Frankfurt to the Bank of England and asked for cash, which the bank refused on the grounds that it would only exchange checks from this bank. Nathan was furious, and early the next morning he led his own nine bank clerks with a large number of Bank of England cheques demanding gold, which in just one day caused the Bank of England's gold reserves to fall significantly. The next day Nathan brought more cheques, and a senior bank executive asked Nathan in a trembling voice how many more days he had to cash them, to which Nathan coldly replied, "The Bank of England refused to accept my cheque, why did I want it?" The Bank of England immediately called an emergency meeting, and then the senior director of the bank very politely informed Nathan that the Bank of England would be honoured to cash all Rothschild Bank cheques in the future.

Nathan took control of the financial city of London in one fell swoop at the Battle of Waterloo, thus holding the economic lifeblood of Britain. Since then, crucial decisions, including currency issuance and gold prices, have remained in the hands of the Rothschilds.

James conquered France

> *"When a government depends on the money of the bankers, it is the bankers, not the leaders of the government, who control the situation, because the hand that gives money is always higher than the hand that takes it. Money has no homeland, financiers don't know what is patriotic and noble, and their only purpose is to make a profit."* [23]
>
> —Napoleon, 1815.

James, the fifth son of the old Rothschild, traveled mainly between London and Paris during Napoleon's reign, establishing a family transport network to smuggle British goods. James made a name for himself in France after helping Wellington ship gold and the Battle of the British National Debt buyout. He founded the Rothschild Paris Bank and secretly financed the Spanish Revolution.

After the defeat of Waterloo in 1817, France lost a large part of its territory from the Napoleonic wars, was politically besieged and its

---

[23] R. McNair Wilson, *Monarchy or Money Power* (Omnia Veritas Ltd – www.omnia-veritas.com), p68.

national economy became increasingly depressed. Louis XVIII's government went around borrowing money in hopes of gradually gaining a foothold financially. James was indignant that a French bank and the British Bank of Bahrain had received a huge number of government-financed projects, while the prestigious Rothschild Bank had fallen into disrepute.

By 1818, as the government bonds issued the previous year were rising in Paris and other European cities, the French government got a taste of the sweet spot and wanted to raise money from these two banks again. The Rothschild brothers went to great lengths to get no semblance of profit. It turns out that the French aristocrats, proud of their illustrious origins and noble bloodlines, felt that the Rothschilds were nothing more than a bunch of peasant mobsters and were unwilling to do business with them. Despite his wealth and luxury in Paris, James was not of high social standing, and the arrogance of the French aristocracy infuriated James.

James and a few other brothers immediately began plotting to subdue the French nobility. The arrogance of the French aristocracy, however, was not intelligent, and underestimated the Rothschild family's strategic and tactical excellence in finance and its ability to plan a victory, no less than Napoleon's military mastery.

On November 5, 1818, the French bonds, which had been steadily appreciating, suddenly began a rather unusual decline in value. Soon, other government bonds began to take a hit, with prices falling to varying degrees. Investors in the market are starting to talk about it. Instead of getting better, the situation got worse as time went on.[24] The talk on the exchange gradually turned into gossip, with some saying that Napoleon might come to power again, others saying that the government coffers were not collecting enough money to pay back the interest, and others fearing a new war.

The atmosphere within Louis XVIII's court was also quite tense, and if bonds continued to plummet, there would be no way to raise money for future government spending. The faces of the noblemen were also piled with sadness, and everyone was worried about the future of

---

[24] Des Griffin, *Descent into Slavery* (Emissary Publications, 1980), Chapter 5.

this country. There were only two people watching coldly from the sidelines, and they were James and his brother Carl.

Thanks to the British antecedents, slowly some people began to suspect that the Rothschilds were manipulating the public debt market. That is exactly what happened. Beginning in October 1818, the Rothschilds began to back it up with their considerable wealth, quietly eating into French bonds in the great cities of Europe, which gradually appreciated in value. Then, starting on November 5, they suddenly released simultaneous sell-offs of French bonds across Europe, causing great panic in the markets.

Watching the price of his bonds slide like a free fall into the abyss, Louis XVIII felt his crown go with him. At this point, the agent of the Rothschild family at court approached the king and said, "Why don't you let the rich Rothschild bank try to save the situation?" The distraught Louis XVIII, no longer in a position of royalty, immediately summoned the James brothers. The atmosphere at the Elysée Palace has changed, with the long-lost James brothers surrounded by smiling faces and respect.

Sure enough, the James brothers stopped the collapse of the bonds as soon as they struck, and they became the center of attention in France, which they saved from the economic crisis after its military defeat! The praise and flowers enchanted the James brothers, and even the style of their clothes became a popular fashion style. Their banks became places where people competed for loans.

As a result, the Rothschilds took complete control of French finance.

> "James Rothschild's wealth reached 600 million francs. There is only one man in France who has more wealth than him, and that is the King of France, whose wealth is 800 million francs. The wealth of all other French bankers combined is still 150 million francs less than James. Such wealth naturally conferred on him an undeserved power, even to the extent that it could bring down a government cabinet at any time. For example, it is well known that the Tyrian government was overthrown by him."[25]

---

[25] David Druck, *Baron Edmond de Rothschild* (Privately printed).

Solomon's Quest for Austria

"In their eyes (the Rothschilds) there is no war or peace, no slogans or declarations, no sacrifice or honour, and they ignore those things that confuse the eyes of the world. There are only stepping stones in their eyes. Prince William was one, Metternich was next."[26]

—Frederick Morton.

Solomon was the second in line of the Rothschilds and spent many years shuttling between major European cities, acting as a coordinator between the family's various banks. Among his brothers, he had a great deal of diplomacy, was well-spoken and complimentary. A banker who dealt with Solomon once commented, "No one leaves him not refreshed." It was for this reason that the brethren publicly proclaimed him to Vienna to open up banking in the heart of Europe.

Vienna was the political center of Europe at the time, and almost all European royals were inextricably linked to the Habsburg dynasty of Austria. The Habsburg dynasty ruled for over 400 years as the royal family of the Holy Roman Empire (dissolved in 1806), including what is now Austria, Germany, northern Italy, Switzerland, Belgium, the Netherlands, Luxembourg, the Czech Republic, Slovenia and eastern France, making it the oldest and most authentic royal lineage in Europe.

Although the Napoleonic Wars crushed the Holy Roman Empire, its successor, Austria, still held itself out as the leader of Central Europe, arrogant to the rest of the royal family. In addition, its orthodox Catholic doctrine is much more rigid than that of Protestant countries such as England and France, and dealing with such noble families is much more noble than dealing with Prince William. Although the Rothschilds have tried several times in the past to establish business relations with the Habsburgs, the result has always been to keep the royal family out of the loop and out of the door.

When Solomon knocked again at the gates of Vienna after the Napoleonic Wars, the situation was all different. The Rothschild family has become a prestigious family in Europe, with the courage to conquer Britain and France, and a lot of courage. In spite of this, Solomon did not dare to do business directly with the Habsburgs, but found a

---

[26] Frederic Morton, *The Rothschilds* (Fawcett Books, 1961).

"stepping stone" in the form of the Austrian Foreign Minister, Klemens von Metternich, who was a great influence in 19th century European politics.

In Europe after Napoleon's defeat, the Vienna system, led by Metternich, sustained the longest period of peace in 19th century Europe. Metternich has put the essence of checks and balances to good use in the face of Austria's waning fortunes and strong enemies. He used the remaining royal orthodoxy of the Habsburgs' appeal in Europe to pull neighbouring Prussia and Russia into a sacred alliance, both to contain the resurgence of France and the restlessness of Russian expansion, and to form a joint mechanism for suppressing the wave of nationalism and liberalism in the country, ensuring that the multi-ethnic divisions in Austria would not get out of hand.

The Aachen Conference of 1818 was an important meeting to discuss the future of Europe after Napoleon's defeat, with representatives from Britain, Russia, Austria, Prussia, and France deciding such issues as French war reparations and the withdrawal of Allied troops. Both Solomon and his brother Carl attended this meeting. It was at this meeting, introduced by Metternich's right-hand man, Gentz, that Solomon made Metternich's acquaintance and quickly became intimate friends with Metternich without words. On the one hand, Solomon's clever and appropriate praise made Metternich extremely useful, on the other hand, Metternich also very much wanted to borrow the Rothschild family's strong financial power, the two men immediately hit it off, Solomon and Kings is even more inseparable from each other.

At the strong recommendation of Metternich and King, and with Rothschild's close business relations with Prince William and the Danish crown, the tall walls of the Habsburg were finally crossed by Solomon. In 1822, the Habsburg royal family conferred the title of Baron on the four Rothschild brothers (except Nathan).

Europe from 1814 to 1848 is known as the "Metternich era", but it was the Rothschild Bank that actually controlled Metternich.

In 1822, three brothers, Metternich, King and Solomon, James and Carl, attended the important Verona Congress. After the meeting, the Rothschild Bank received a lucrative offer to finance the first Central European railway project. In 1843, Solomon acquired the Vítkovice Consolidated Mining Company and the Austro-Hungarian Smelting

Company, both of which were among the ten largest heavy industry companies in the world at the time.

By 1848, Solomon had become the master of Austrian finance and economy.

Germany and Italy under the Rothschild Coat of Arms

Since Napoleon's withdrawal from Germany, Germany has merged from the past 300 or so small, loosely feudal states into 30 or so larger nations and formed the German Confederation. Amschel, the Rothschild boss who remained in Frankfurt, was appointed Germany's first finance minister and was made a baronet by the Austrian emperor in 1822. The Rothschild Bank in Frankfurt became the center of German finance. Since Amschel had no children at his knees, and had a lifelong regret, he was devoted to the rising star. One of the young men who was beloved by Amschel was Bismarck, the iron-blooded German chancellor who later became famous in modern world history.

Amschel was a father and son to Bismarck, and after Amschel's death, Bismarck remained in close contact with the Rothschild family. Samuel Bleichroder, the banker behind Bismarck, was also an agent of the Rothschild family.[27]

Old Fourkar was the most mediocre of the five Rothschild brothers, serving as the family's main messenger, traveling to and from Europe to pass on information and assist other brothers. After helping his fifth brother's glorious victory in the Battle of the French National Debt of 1818, Karl was sent to Naples, Italy, to establish a bank by Nathan, the third brother in charge of the family. In Italy, however, he demonstrated an ability that exceeded the expectations of his fellow brothers. Karl not only financed the army that Metternich sent to Italy to suppress the revolution, but also, with remarkable political sleight of hand, forced the local Italian government to bear the cost of the occupation forces. He also helped his friend Maddich plan and recapture the key position of Chancellor of the Treasury of Naples. Carl gradually became the financial backbone of the Italian court and his influence spread across the Italian peninsula. He also established business dealings with the Vatican, and when Pope Gregory XVI saw

---

[27] Des Griffin, *Descent into Slavery* (Emissary Publications, 1980), Chapter 5.

him, he made an exception and extended his hand for Karl to kiss, instead of extending his foot as is customary.

Rothschild Financial Empire

> *"No bank in the world can compete with you, hurt you, or profit from you as long as you are brothers together. Together you will have more power than any other bank in the world."*[28]
> —Letter from Davidson to Nathan, June 24, 1814

Before his death in 1812, Rothschild Sr. made a solemn will and testament.

(1) All important positions in family banks must be held by members of the family and never by outsiders. Only male family members are able to participate in family business activities.

(2) Family marriages can only be performed between cousins to prevent the dilution and outflow of wealth. (This provision was strictly enforced in the early days and later relaxed to the extent that intermarriage with other Jewish banking families was allowed.)

(3) There is absolutely no public disclosure of property.

(4) Absolutely no lawyer is allowed to intervene in the inheritance of property.

(5) The eldest son of each family, who is the head of each family, may choose a second son to succeed him only with the unanimous consent of the family.

Anyone who violates the will loses all rights of inheritance.[29]

There is a Chinese proverb that if a brother is of one mind, he or she can cut off gold. The Rothschilds strictly prevented wealth dilution and exodus through intermarriage within the family. In over 100 years, there have been 18 intermarriages within the family, 16 of which were between first cousins (cousins).

---

[28] Lord Rothschild, *The Shadow of a Great Man*. London: 1982.

[29] Des Griffin, *Descent into Slavery* (Emissary Publications, 1980), Chapter 5.

It is estimated that around 1850, the Rothschilds amassed the equivalent of $6 billion in total wealth, which, if calculated at a 6% rate of return, would put the family's assets at least $50 trillion more than 150 years later.

Tight family control, complete opaqueness, clockwork precision, access to information always ahead of the market, downright ruthless reasoning, a never-ending desire for gold, and, based on it all, a deep insight into money and wealth and a genius for foresight, have allowed the Rothschilds to build one of the largest financial empires in human history to date in a brutal vortex of finance, politics and warfare that has lasted more than two hundred years.

By the early 20th century, the wealth controlled by the Rothschilds was estimated to be half of the total world wealth at the time.[30]

The Rothschild family banks were spread across the major cities of Europe, and they had their own systems for intelligence gathering and rapid transmission, even to the royals and nobles of European countries when they needed to pass on various information quickly and secretly. They also pioneered the International Financial Clearing System, using their control over the world gold market, and they were the first in the family banking system to establish a system of clearing accounts without physical gold transport.

There is only one other person in this world who understands the true meaning of gold better than the Rothschilds. When the Rothschilds announced their withdrawal from the London gold pricing system in 2004, they were quietly stepping away from the center of the future world's unprecedented financial turmoil, skimming their relationship to the price of gold. The debt-ridden dollar economy and the crisis-ridden world legal tender system, as well as the world foreign exchange reserve system, are likely to face a liquidation, and the wealth accumulated over the years by Asian countries with only insignificant gold reserves will be "redistributed" to future winners. Hedge funds will strike again, only this time the target will no longer be the pound and Asian currencies, but the dollar, the backbone of the world economy.

For the bankers, the war was heavenly good news. Because expensive facilities and items that are slowly depreciated in peacetime

---

[30] Ted Flynn, *Hope of the Wicked* (MaxKol Communication, Inc., 2000), p. 38.

will be wiped out in a matter of minutes during the war, the warring parties will stop at nothing to win, and by the end of the war, the government, win or lose, will be deep in the debt trap of the banks. In the 121 years between the founding of the Bank of England and the end of the Napoleonic Wars (1694–1815), England was at war for 56 years and spent the remaining half preparing for the next war.

It is in the fundamental interest of bankers to steer and finance wars, and the Rothschilds are no exception, flashing their shadows behind almost all recent wars, from the French Revolution to the Second World War. The Rothschilds are the largest creditors in the major Western developed countries today. Mrs. (Gutle Schnaper) of Rothschild, Sr. said before her death,

> *"If my sons didn't want war, no one would love war."*

By the middle of the nineteenth century, the power to issue money in the major industrial countries of Europe, such as England, France, Germany, Austria and Italy, fell under the control of the Rothschild family,

> *"the divine monarchy was replaced by the divine gold power".*

By this time, the beautiful, prosperous and affluent American continent on the other side of the Atlantic had long since fallen into their sights.

Summary

★Nathan Rothschild was informed in advance of the Battle of Waterloo and used the British public debt to make 20 times as much money as he wanted, becoming the largest creditor of the British government and dominating the future issuance of British public debt.

★Meyer Rothschild has close ties to the royal family, building an unprecedented financial empire on Prince William's $3 million in cash and sending five sons to head up operations in five heartland regions of Europe.

★Nathan took control of the Financial City of London at the Battle of Waterloo and held the economic lifeblood of Britain. From then on, the Rothschilds held the all-important power to make decisions about currency issuance and the price of gold.

★James surreptitiously manipulates the price of French bonds, forcing Louis XVIII to turn to him for help and eventually to take complete control of French finance.

★By 1848, Solomon had become the master of Austrian finance and economy.

★Karl Rothschild gradually became the financial backbone of the Italian court, with influence across the Italian peninsula and business dealings with the Vatican See.

★By the middle of the 19th century, the major European industrial countries, such as England, France, Germany, Austria and Italy, were under the control of the Rothschild family.

CHAPTER II

The Hundred-Year War Between the International Bankers and the American President

> *"I have two main enemies: the Southern army before me, and the financial institutions behind me. Of the two, the latter is the greatest threat. I see a shuddering crisis in the future approaching us, making me tremble with fear for the safety of our country. The power of money will continue to rule and hurt the people until wealth finally accumulates in the hands of a few and our Republic is destroyed. I am now more anxious about the safety of this country than ever before, even more so than in war."*[31]
>
> —Lincoln, 16th President of the United States

If China's history revolves around the struggle for political power, and it is impossible to see the essence of Chinese history without understanding the emperor's mind, then the recent history of the West has evolved along the lines of the money struggle, and without understanding the machinations of money, one cannot grasp the pulse of Western history.

America's upbringing has been filled with interventions and conspiracies by international forces, with the penetration and subversion of the United States by international financial forces in particular being the most chilling and least known.

Democracy has been designed and built with almost total preoccupation and considerable success against the threat of feudal authoritarian forces, but it has no credible immunity to the nascent and deadly virus of money power.

---

[31] Abraham Lincoln, *Letter to William Elkins*, Nov 21, 1864 (just after the passage of the debt causing National Bank Act [June 3, 1864], right before assassination).

The emerging democracies have major loopholes in the judgement and defence of the strategic thrust of "international bankers to control the whole country by controlling the power to issue money". For more than 100 years before and after the Civil War, the "money super-special interests" and the democratically elected government of the United States fought repeatedly to the death against the financial high point of the establishment of the private central banking system in the United States, as a result of which seven United States presidents were assassinated and many members of Congress were killed. American historians point out that the casualty rate of the American president was higher than the average casualty rate of the first-line troops at the Normandy landings during the American "World War II"!

With China's full financial liberalization, international bankers are set to venture deep into China's financial hinterland in a big way, will the story that happened yesterday in the United States be repeated today in China?

Assassination of President Lincoln

On Friday night, April 14, 1865, President Abraham Lincoln, who had spent four years of brutal civil war in hardship and crisis, finally welcomed the news of the victory of the surrender of General Robert E. Lee, the Confederate general, to General Grant of the North five days earlier, and the President's highly nervous nerves immediately loosened and he went to the Ford Theater in Washington to see the show. at 10:15 a.m., the murderer infiltrated the unguarded presidential box, less than two feet behind Lincoln, and shot him in the head with a large caliber pistol, Lincoln being shot and falling forward. In the early hours of the next day, President Lincoln died.

The killer is a rather famous actor named Booth (John Wilkes Booth). He made a hasty escape after assassinating Lincoln, and the killer was reportedly killed on April 26 while on the run. In the murderer's carriage were found many letters written in code and some personal effects of Judah Benjamin, then Secretary of War and later Secretary of State in the Southern government and a powerful figure in Southern finance, because he had been in close contact with the big European bankers. He later fled to England. The Lincoln assassination is widely believed to have been a massive conspiracy. Those involved in the conspiracy may have been members of Lincoln's cabinet, bankers in New York and Philadelphia, high government officials in the South, newspaper publishers in New York, and radicals in the North.

It was a widely circulated story at the time that Booth was not killed, but let go, and that the body that was later buried was his accomplice. Secretary of War Edwin Stanton, who had heavy hands at the time, covered up the truth. At first glance, this is another ridiculous conspiracy theory claim. But when the Secretary of War's vast array of secret documents were declassified by the mid-1930s, historians were surprised to find that the truth was highly consistent with folklore.

The first to delve into this amazing history was historian Otto Eisenschiml, who published *"Why Was Lincoln Assassinated?"* shook the historiography of the time. Later, Theodore Roscoe, who published findings with broader implications, noted.

> *"The tragic portrayal of Ford's Theatre, which is the subject of much historical research on the assassination of Lincoln in the nineteenth century, is more like the presentation of a grand opera ... only a few see it as a murder: Lincoln died at the hands of a reckless criminal ... the criminal received his due legal punishment; conspiracy theories were stifled; virtue finally triumphed and Lincoln "belonged" to the past."*

However, the explanation for the assassination is neither satisfactory nor convincing. The facts show that the criminals involved in Lincoln's death have been at large.[32]

The killer's granddaughter, Izola Forrester, mentions in her memoir, This One Mad Act, that she discovered that the secret records of the Knights of the Golden Circle were carefully kept by the government in a document repository and classified by Secretary of War Edwin Stanton. After Lincoln's assassination, no one was allowed access to these documents. Because of Izola's blood ties to Booth and her status as a professional writer, she eventually became the first scholar to be granted access to these materials. She says in the book.

The mysterious old document packages were hidden in a safe in the corner of the room where the remains of the "trial of conspiracy" and the exhibition were kept. If I hadn't stumbled upon the side of the

---

[32] G. Edward Griffin, *The Creature from Jekyll Island* (American Media, Westlake Village, CA 2002) p. 393.

safe while kneeling on the floor (of that room) flipping through materials 5 years ago, I might never have found them (secret documents).

Here (the document) relates to my grandfather. I know he was a member of a secret organization, the Knights of the Golden Circle, founded by Bickley. I have a picture of him (grandfather) taken with them, all in full uniform, and this picture was found in my grandmother's Bible... I remember my grandmother saying that her husband (Booth) was "someone's tool".[33]

What exactly is the relationship between the "Knights of the Golden Circle" and the financial power of New York? How many people within the Lincoln administration were involved in the plot to assassinate Lincoln? How has the study of Lincoln's assassination systematically veered off in the right direction for so long? Lincoln's assassination and Kennedy's assassination 100 years later are quite similar in that they are also both massive organizational coordination, all-encompassing evidence suppression, systematic investigative misdirection, and the truth remains hidden in a thick historical fog.

To understand the true motives and intent of Lincoln's assassination, we must examine in greater historical context the repeated and deadly battles between elected governments and the power of money to control the right to issue money, the strategic high point of the nation, since the founding of the United States.

The Right to Issue Money and the American War of Independence

History textbooks on the analysis of the origins of the American War of Independence have more often taken the form of a comprehensive and abstract discussion of big principles and implications. Here we will take another look at the financial context of the revolution and the central role it has played.

The earliest people to make a living on the American continent were mostly very poor and destitute people who had little property or money beyond the simple luggage they carried with them. Large gold

---

[33] Izola Forrester, *This One Mad Act* (Boston: Hale, Cushman & Flint, 1937), p. 359.

and silver mines had not been found in North America at that time, so there was an extreme shortage of currency in circulation. This, coupled with a severe trade deficit with the home country, the United Kingdom, has led to a large flow of gold and silver currency to the United Kingdom, exacerbating the scarcity of currency in circulation.[34]

The large number of goods and services created by the hard work of the new immigrants in North America, which cannot be adequately and efficiently exchanged due to the shortage of currency in circulation, has severely constrained further economic development. To cope with this dilemma, people have had to use various alternative currencies to trade commodities. Acceptable items such as animal hides, shells, tobacco, rice, wheat, maize, etc., are used everywhere as cash couriers. In North Carolina alone, as many as 17 different items were used as legal tender in 1715, which were used by government and private citizens for tax payments, public and private debt repayments, and trading in goods and services. At that time, all these alternative currencies were settled in pounds sterling and shillings as accounting standards. In practice, these items vary greatly in colour, specification, acceptability and preservability, making them difficult to measure by standards, so that while the lack of money has somewhat alleviated the immediate need for it, it still constitutes an important bottleneck in the development of the commodity economy.[35]

The chronic scarcity of metallic money and the inconvenience of using it as an alternative to physical money has prompted local governments to think outside the box and start a new experiment: the printing and issuance of paper money (Colonial Script) by the government as a uniform and standardized French currency. The biggest difference between this paper currency and the popular bank notes in Europe is that it is not secured by any physical gold or silver and is a full government credit currency. Everyone in society is required to pay taxes to the government, and as long as the government accepts this paper money as proof of taxation, it has the essential elements to circulate in the market.

---

[34] Glyn Davis, *History of Money from Ancient Times to the Present Day* (University of Wales Press, 2002), p. 458.

[35] *Ibid.*, p. 459.

The new currency has indeed contributed significantly to the rapid socio-economic development and the growing prosperity of the commodity trade.

At the same time, Adam Smith of England also took note of this new fiat currency attempt by the North American colonial governments, and he was quite aware of the great stimulus to commerce that this paper currency would bring, especially to North America, which lacked metal money,

> *"credit-based buying and selling, allowing merchants to settle each other's credit balances on a regular monthly or annual basis, which would reduce the inconvenience (of transactions). A well-managed paper money system not only does not cause any inconvenience, but can even have more advantages in some cases."[36]*

But an unsecured currency was the natural enemy of the banker, for without government debt as collateral, the government did not need to borrow from the banks the most scarce metal currency at the time, and the greatest weight in the hands of the banker was lost at once.

When Benjamin Franklin visited England in 1763, the head of the Bank of England asked him why the colonies in the New World were so thriving, and Franklin replied,

> *"It's simple. In the colonies, we issued our own currency called 'colonial vouchers'. We issue equal proportions of money according to the needs of commerce and industry, so that the product can be easily passed from the producer to the consumer. By creating our own paper money in this way and guaranteeing its purchasing power, we (the government) don't have to pay interest to anyone."[37]*

This new paper currency would inevitably lead the American colonies to break away from the control of the Bank of England.

Angry British bankers acted immediately, and the British Parliament under their control passed the Currency Act in 1764, which

---

[36] Adam Smith, *Wealth of Nations*, 1776, book IV Chapter one.

[37] Congressman Charles G. Binderup, How Benjamin Franklin Made New England Prosperous, 1941. Note: Radio address given by Congressman Charles G. Binderup of Nebraska, and was reprinted in Unrobing the Ghosts of Wall Street.

severely forbade the American colonial states from issuing their own paper money and forced local governments to use gold and silver to pay all taxes paid to the British government.

Franklin painfully describes the dire economic consequences of this bill for the colonial states: "In just one year, the situation (in the colonies) was completely reversed, the boom years were over, and the economy was so badly depressed that the streets and alleys were standing full of unemployed people.[38]

> "If England did not deprive the colonies of the right to issue money, the colonial people were happy to pay tea and other goods as an additional small tax. This bill has caused unemployment and discontent. The inability of the colonies to issue their own currency and thus be permanently free from the control of King George III and the international bankers was the primary reason for the outbreak of the American War of Independence."[39]

The founding fathers of the United States had a fairly sober understanding of the Bank of England's control of British politics and the injustice it did to the people. Thomas Jefferson, author of the enduring American Declaration of Independence at the age of 33 and the third President of the United States, had a cautionary tale.

If the American people finally give private banks control of the nation's currency issuance, those banks will dispossess the people, first through inflation, then deflation, until one morning when their children wake up to the fact that they have lost their homes and the land that their fathers once pioneered.[40]

When we listen to this passage from Jefferson in 1791 again over two hundred years later, we can't help but marvel at the amazing accuracy of his foresight. Today, it is true that private banks in the United States have issued 97% of the national currency in circulation, and it is true that the American people are astronomically indebted to

---

[38] *Ibid.*

[39] *Ibid.*

[40] In 1787, when the Continental Congress met to adopt the replacement to the Articles of Confederation, which would become the Constitution, Jefferson's address regarding a central banking system.

the banks to the tune of $44 trillion, and they may indeed wake up one day and lose their homes and property, just as happened in 1929.

As America's great pioneers looked at history and the future with their wisdom and deep gaze, they wrote at the beginning of Chapter 1, Section 8 of the U.S. Constitution:

> "Congress shall have the right to make and set the value of money."[41]

The First Battle of the International Bankers: The First Bank of the United States (1791–1811)

> [I firmly believe that banking institutions are a greater threat to our freedom than enemy armies. They have created a class of moneyed aristocrats and defy government. The right to issue (money) should be taken back from the banks and it should belong to its rightful owner, the people.[42]
>
> —Thomas Jefferson, 1802

Alexander Hamilton was a heavyweight with close ties to the Rothschild family. He was born in the British West Indies and came to the United States and married the daughter of the New York Hopes after concealing his age, real name and place of birth. Payment receipts in the British Museum's collection show that Hamilton received funding from the Rothschild family.[43]

In 1789, Hamilton was appointed by President Washington as the first U.S. Secretary of the Treasury, and he remained a major promoter of the U.S. central banking system, and in 1790, faced with severe economic hardship and a debt crisis following the War of Independence, he strongly recommended that Congress establish a privately owned central bank, similar to the Bank of England, to fully carry out the duties of issuing money. His main idea was that the central bank would be privately owned, headquartered in Philadelphia, with branch banks set up everywhere, and that the government's currency

---

[41] US Constitution Article I Section 8.

[42] Letter to the Secretary of the Treasury Albert Gallatin (1802).

[43] Allan Hamilton, *The Intimate Life of Alexander Hamilton* (Charles Scribner's Sons 1910).

and taxes must be placed in this banking system, which would be responsible for issuing the national currency to meet the needs of economic development, lending money to the United States government, and collecting interest. The total capital stock of the bank is $10 million, privately owned 80 per cent, with the United States Government owning the remaining 20 per cent. 20 of the 25-member board are elected by shareholders and five are appointed by the Government.

Hamilton represented the interests of the elite class when he once noted,

> "All societies are divided into a very small minority and a majority. The former are well-born and wealthy, while the latter are commoners. The masses are volatile and changing, and they rarely make sound judgments and decisions."

Jefferson, on the other hand, represented the interests of the people at large, responding to Hamilton's view by saying,

> "We hold to be self-evident the truth that all men are created equal and that the Creator has endowed them with a number of inalienable rights, among them the right to life, liberty, and the pursuit of happiness."

The two sides are also on a tit-for-tat when it comes to the private central banking system.

Hamilton argued,

> "This society cannot succeed without pooling the interests and credits of wealthy individuals in society."[44] "The national debt, if not excessive, should be for the good of our country."[45]

Jefferson retorted,

---

[44] Quoted by Arthur Schlesinger, Jr., *The Age of Jackson* (New York: Mentor Books, 1945), p. 6–7.

[45] Written on April 30, 1781, to his mentor, Robert Morris, Quoted by John H. Makin, *The Global Debt Crisis: America's Growing Involvement* (New York: Basic Books, 1984), p. 246.

"A private central bank issuing the people's public currency is a greater threat to their freedom than an enemy army."[46] "We cannot tolerate rulers imposing permanent debts on the people."[47]

In December 1791, when Hamilton's scheme was presented to Congress for discussion, it immediately gave rise to an unprecedented amount of controversy. In the end, the Senate passed it by a slim majority, and in the House of Representatives it also passed by a vote of 39 to 20. At this point, President Washington, who was overwhelmed by the severe debt crisis, was in deep hesitation, and he consulted with then Secretaries of State Jefferson and Madison, who made it clear that the proposal was in clear conflict with the Constitution. The Constitution authorizes Congress to issue money, but in no way authorizes Congress to transfer the right to issue money to any private bank. Washington is clearly so deeply touched that he has even resolved to veto the bill.

Upon learning this news, Hamilton immediately ran to lobby Washington, and Treasury Secretary Hamilton's books seemed more convincing that the government would soon collapse if a central bank was not set up to get foreign money into its shares. Ultimately, the looming crisis overwhelmed concerns about the long-term future, and President Washington signed the authorization for the first central bank in the United States on February 25, 1791, effective for 20 years.[48]

The international bankers have finally achieved their first major victory. By 1811, foreign capital accounted for 7 million of the 10 million share capital, and the Bank of England and Nathan Rothschild became major shareholders in The First Bank of the United States, the central bank of the United States.[49]

Hamilton eventually became mega-rich. First Bank later became Wall Street's first bank with the New York Manhattan Company

---

[46] *The Writings of Thomas Jefferson* (New York: G. P. Putnam & Sons, 1899), Vol. X, p. 31.

[47] *The Basic Writings of Thomas Jefferson* (Willey Book Company, 1944), p. 749.

[48] Glyn Davies, *History of Money From Ancient Times to The Present Day* (University of Wales Press, 2002), p. 474.

[49] *Ibid.*, p. 475.

founded by Aaron Bo, which merged with Rockefeller's Chase Bank to become Chase Manhattan Bank in 1955.

The government, desperate for money, was a perfect match for the private central bank, eager for government debt, which increased the U.S. government's debt by $8.2 million in just five years, from 1791 to 1796, when the central bank was established.

Jefferson chagrined in 1798,

> *"I wish we could add even one amendment to the Constitution that would remove the power of the federal government to borrow money."*[50]

When Jefferson was elected the third president of the United States (1801–1809), he wasted no time in trying to abolish the First Bank of the United States, and by the time the bank expired in 1811, the tug-of-war had reached a white-hot pitch, with the House of Representatives defeating the bank mandate extension by only one vote, 65 to 64, and the Senate tied by 17 to 17. This time a crucial veto was cast by Vice President George Clinton to break the deadlock, and the First Bank of the United States closed for good on March 3, 1811.[51]

That's when Nathan Rothschild, sitting in London, got wind of it and threatened,

> *"Either the (America First) Bank is given a mandate extension or America will face a most disastrous war." As a result, the U.S. government was indifferent, and Nathan immediately responded, "Give these reckless Americans a lesson and beat them back to colonial times."*

As a result, a few months later, the War of 1812 between Britain and America broke out. The war lasted three years and Rothschild's purpose was clear, to fight until the US government was so heavily in debt that it finally had to bend over backwards and let the central bank in their hands continue to function. As a result, the debt of the U.S. government increased from $45 million to $127 million, and the U.S. government finally caved in 1815, when President Madison proposed a

---

[50] Thomas Jefferson, *Letter to John Taylor of Caroline*, 26 November 1798; reproduced in *The Writings of Thomas Jefferson* v. 10, edited by Lipscomb and Bergh.

[51] Glyn Davies, *History of Money from Ancient Times to the Present Day* (University of Wales Press, 2002), p. 475–476.

second central bank on December 5, 1815, resulting in the Second Bank of the United States in 1816.

International bankers make a comeback: The Second Bank of the United States (1816–1832)

> *[The domination of people's consciousness that banking institutions possess must be broken, or it will break us (the nation).*[52]
>
> —Jefferson wrote to Monroe in 1815.

The Second Bank of the United States received a 20-year operating authorization, this time raising the total equity to $35 million, still 80% in private hands and the remaining 20% belonging to the government.[53] Like the First Bank, Rothschild had a firm grip on the Second Bank's power.

In 1828, Andrew Jackson entered the presidential race, and in a speech to a banker, he falsely stated.

> *"You're a bunch of vipers. I intend to uproot you, and in the name of God, I will uproot you. If the people knew how unjust our monetary and banking system is, there would be a revolution before dawn tomorrow."*

When Andrew Jackson was elected president in 1828, he was determined to abolish the Second Bank. He noted,

> *"If the Constitution authorizes Congress to issue money, it is for Congress to exercise that power itself, not for Congress to delegate it to any individual or corporation."*

He fired more than 2,000 people associated with the bank out of a federal workforce of 11,000.

1832 was the year that President Jackson ran for re-election, and if he was re-elected, the Second Bank would have expired in 1836 (his next term). We all know the president's perception of the Second Bank, and to avoid a long night's sleep, the bank wants to take advantage of the turmoil to extend its operating franchise for another 20 years in an

---

[52] Thomas Jefferson, *Letter to James Monroe*, January 1, 1815.

[53] Glyn Davies, *History of Money from Ancient Times to the Present Day* (University of Wales Press, 2002), p. 476.

election year. Meanwhile, bankers spared no blood to fund Jackson's rival, Henry Clay, with $3 million in heavy money, and Jackson's campaign slogan was "Jackson, not the bank." In the end Jackson won in a landslide.

The proposal for the extension of banking authority passed in the Senate by a vote of 28 to 20, and also managed to pass in the House of Representatives by a vote of 167 to 85,[54] and the President of the Second Bank, Biddle, who was proud to have the powerful Rothschild financial empire of Europe as a back-up, did not have the President in mind. When there was talk that Jackson might veto the proposal, Biddle was unabashed:

"If Jackson vetoes the proposal, I will veto him."

President Jackson, of course, vetoed the Second Bank extension without question, and he also ordered the Secretary of the Treasury to take all government savings out of the Second Bank account at once and transfer them to state banks, and on January 8, 1835, President Jackson paid off the last national debt, the only time in history that the U.S. government had reduced the national debt to zero and produced a surplus of $35 million. Historians have commented on this great achievement as "the President's greatest honour and the most important contribution he has made to this country". The Boston Post compared this accomplishment to Jesus' expulsion of the moneylenders (Money Changers) from the temple.

"The bank wants to kill me, but I will kill the bank."

On January 30, 1835, Andrew Jackson, the 7th President of the United States, came to Capitol Hill to attend the funeral of a congressman. An unemployed painter from England, Richard Lawrence, quietly followed President Jackson with two loaded pistols in his pocket.

As the president entered the room where the funeral service was to be held, Lawrence was farther away, waiting patiently for a better time. After the ceremony, Lawrence stood guard between the two poles, where the president was bound to pass. Just as the president passed by,

---

[54] *Ibid.*, p. 479.

Lawrence rushed out and fired less than two meters from the president, but the pistol blew up and the bullet missed. At this point, everyone around was stunned. At this point, the 67-year-old President Jackson, who had spent his life in the military, did not panic and instinctively raised his cane in self-defense in the face of a vicious killer. By this time, the killer had pulled out a second pistol and fired, and the result was still a stink bomb. Fortunate Jackson came close to becoming the first president in U.S. history to be assassinated, and the probability of both handguns firing stink bombs is said to be only 1/125,000.

The 32-year-old assassin claimed to be the rightful heir to the King of England, whose father was killed by the US president, and refused to let him have a large sum of money. Subsequently, the court, after only five minutes of hearing, concluded that the person was mentally ill and was not held legally responsible.

Since then, mental illness has been the most appropriate excuse for murderers of all kinds.

On January 8, 1835, President Jackson paid off his last national debt, and the assassination took place on January 30. About the murderer Richard Lawrence, Griffin writes in his book,

> *"The assassin was either really mad, or feigned madness to avoid severe punishment. Later, he boasted to others that he had connections with powerful people in Europe and that he was promised protection if caught."*[55]

On June 8, 1845, President Jackson died. His epitaph contains only one line:

> *"I killed the bank."*

The US central bank was abolished again, inviting severe retaliation from the British side, which immediately stopped all kinds of loans to the US, especially the powerful trick of tightening the US gold money supply. The British financial system of the time, operated by Rothschild, had the largest circulation of gold money and had complete control over the money supply in the United States through loans and the operation of the American central bank.

---

[55] G. Edward Griffin, *The Creature from Jekyll Island* (American Media, Westlake Village, CA 2002).

The "veto" of the President by Biddle, Chairman of the Second Bank of the United States, was triggered when his request for an extension was rejected by the President. Second Bank announced an immediate recall of all loans and a halt to all new loans. The Rothschild family controlled the major European banks also tightened the U.S. silver, the U.S. fell into a serious "artificial" currency circulation of a sharp decline in the situation, finally triggered the "Panic of 1837", the economy fell into a serious recession for as long as five years, its destructive power was unprecedented, catching up with the Great Depression in 1929.

The "Panic of 1837" and later the "Panic of 1857" and the "Panic of 1907" once again confirmed Rothschild's famous quote:

> "I don't care who makes the laws as long as I can control the currency issue of a country."

New front: independent financial system

In 1837, when Martin Van Buren, President Jackson's strongly supported successor, took over the White House, his greatest challenge was to overcome the severe crisis caused by the tight money supply from international bankers. Van Buren's tit-for-tat strategy was to create the Independent Treasury System (ITS), in which all the money controlled by the Treasury was extracted from the private banking system and deposited in the Treasury's own system, which historians call "the divorce of the Treasury from the banks".

The Independent Fiscal System originated when President Jackson, while vetoing the extension of the operating authority of the Second Bank of the United States, ordered that all government money be taken out of that bank and transferred to the state banks. Who would have thought that the state banks in front had just escaped Rothschild's clutches, and that the state banks behind them were not a light to save fuel. They used government money as a reserve and then extended large amounts of credit for speculation, another reason for the "Panic of 1837". Martin Van Buren's proposal that money from the government treasury should be decoupled from the financial system is certainly an attempt to protect government money, but also takes into account the economic injustice caused by the massive speculative lending by banks with people's tax dollars.

Another feature of an independent fiscal system is that all money entering the fiscal system must be gold and silver money, so that the government has a regulatory fulcrum for the nation's supply of gold and silver money to hedge against European bankers' control of U.S. currency issuance. This idea should have been a good one in the long run, but in the short run it triggered a credit crisis in many banks, which became unmanageable with the fanning of the second US bank.

Henry Clay is a very pivotal figure in this process. He was an important heir to the idea of a private central bank in Hamilton and a favourite of bankers. He's a superbly articulate, hard-thinking and provocative man. A group of pro-banking and banker-backed MPs gathered around him, and under his organization the Pfizer Party was formed. The Whigs were firmly opposed to Jackson's banking policies and have always been committed to restoring a privately owned central banking system.

The Whigs introduced war hero William Henry Harrison in the 1840 presidential election, and Harrison was unceremoniously elected the 9th president of the United States due to the economic crisis that led to a change in public sentiment.

Henry Clay, as the leader of the Pfizer Party, has repeatedly "taught" Harrison how to run politics. In the wake of Harrison's election to the presidency, the two men's conflicts have become increasingly acute. Henry Clay "summoned" the incoming President at his home in Lexington, and Harrison came to Henry Clay's house in the interest of the greater good, with the result that the two men fell out over the National Bank, the independent financial system and other issues. Henry Clay, who thought he could call the shots as the "King Too", had asked to write the President's inaugural address without Harrison's consent and was rejected by Harrison, who also drafted the 8,000-word speech himself. In this systematic exposition of the ideas of governance, he sharply contradicts the policy ideas of private central banks and the abolition of independent finance advocated by Henry Clay, thus stinging the interests of bankers.[56]

March 4, 1841, was a cold day, and President Harrison delivered his inaugural address in a chilly wind that resulted in a chill. It was no big deal to President Harrison, who was strangely ill and died on April

---

[56] Inaugural Address of President William Henry Harrison March 4, 1841.

4. President Harrison, who had just taken office, was about to make a big splash when he suddenly "got the chill" and resigned a month earlier, which is in any case a very suspicious thing. Some historical scholars believe that the president was poisoned with arsenic, and that the possible time of poisoning was March 30, six days after President Harrison died.

The struggle around private central banks and an independent financial system has been intensified by the death of President Harrison. The Whigs, dominated by Henry Clay, twice proposed in 1841 to restore the central bank and abolish the independent fiscal system, only to be rejected twice by President Harrison's successor, former Vice President John Taylor. An exasperated Henry Clay ordered President John Taylor to be expelled from the Whig Party, with the result that President Taylor was "fortunate" to be the only "orphan" president in American history to be expelled from the party.

By 1849, with the election of another Pheughist president, Zachary Taylor, the hope of restoring the central bank seemed close at hand. The establishment of a privately owned central bank, exactly like the Bank of England, is the highest dream of all bankers, and it means that bankers ultimately decide the fate of the country and the people. With President Harrison ahead of him, Taylor maintains considerable ambiguity on major central banking issues, but he is also not willing to be a puppet of Henry Clay. Historian Michael Holt notes that President Taylor made it clear in private:

> *"The idea of a central bank is dead on arrival and it will not be considered during my term."*[57]

It was not the Central Bank's idea that turned out to be "dead", but President Taylor himself.

On July 4, 1850, President Taylor participated in a national celebration in front of the Washington Monument. The weather was so hot that Taylor drank some chilled milk and ate a few cherries, which resulted in some tummy troubles, and by July 9, the healthy president had mysteriously died again.

---

[57] Michael F. Holt; *The Rise and Fall of the American Whig Party: Jacksonian Politics and the Onset of the Civil War* (1999). P. 272.

The unexplained death of two presidents with military origins from such a trivial illness is certainly a cause for concern. In 1991, with the consent of President Taylor's descendants, his body was exhumed and his fingernails and hair tested for arsenic, but the authorities quickly concluded that a small amount of arsenic was not enough to kill him and hastily closed the case. No one knows why the President has all this arsenic in his system.

The International Bankers Strike Again: "The Panic of 1857"

The closure of the Second Bank of the United States in 1836 caused international bankers to swoop in and pump metal money in circulation in the United States, causing a severe economic crisis that lasted five years. Although two attempts were made in 1841 by agents of international bankers to restore a privately owned central banking system, both were unsuccessful, the two sides came to an impasse, and monetary austerity in the United States did not begin to ease until 1848.

The reason things started to get better was certainly not because of the international bankers' mercy, but because of the discovery of a huge gold mine, San Francisco, in California, USA, in 1848.

Beginning in 1848, and continuing for nine years, the United States saw an unprecedented increase in gold supplies, with California alone producing $500 million worth of gold coins, and the discovery of a large gold mine in Australia in 1851, which saw the world's gold supply soar from billions of shillings in 1851 to billions of shillings in 1861. And the domestic flow of metal money in the United States skyrocketed from $83 million in 1840 to billions of dollars in 1860.[58]

The big gold discoveries in the US and Australia broke the absolute control of European financiers over the supply of gold. A long sigh of relief came from the U.S. government, which was being tightened on the money supply. The availability of large amounts of quality money has greatly boosted market confidence, banks have resumed their massive credit expansion, and many of the most important foundations of the nation's wealth, such as industry, mines, transportation, and

---

[58] Glyn Davies, *History of Money from Ancient Times to the Present Day* (University of Wales Press 2002), p. 484.

machinery, were established during the golden years of the United States.

Seeing that financial containment is not working, international bankers have long had a new response. That is, financially controlled and politically divisive.

Long before the end of the crisis, they had already begun to absorb the quality assets of the United States cheaply, and by 1853, when the American economy was booming, foreign capital, especially British capital, had already owned 46% of the United States federal treasury bonds, 58% of the state bonds, and 26% of the American railroad bonds,[59] thus again caging the American economy, and once the central banking system was in place, the American economy, like the rest of Europe, was controlled by bankers.

The international bankers have once again performed their masterstroke, first by ramming out credit, blowing up the bubble and making people and other industries desperate to create wealth, and then suddenly slamming the brakes on credit, bankrupting a large number of businesses and people, and the bankers have a good harvest again. Sure enough, when the harvest season arrived, international bankers and their agents in the United States joined forces to tighten credit again, creating the "Panic of 1857", which they did not expect, when the United States was not as strong as it had been 20 years earlier, and the "Panic of 1857" did not hit the United States economy hard, recovering in just one year.

When the United States is seen to be increasingly powerful and its finances increasingly difficult to manipulate, provoking civil war and dividing the United States becomes a top priority for international bankers.

The Causes of the American Civil War:
The International Financial Power of Europe

[There is no doubt that the division of the United States into two weaker confederations, North and South, was settled by the financial powers of Europe long before the outbreak of the Civil War.

---

[59] *Ibid.*, p. 486.

—Bismarck.

America's upbringing has been fraught with interventions and intrigues by international forces, of which the penetration and subversion of the United States by international financial forces in particular has been the most chilling and yet the least known.

The largest war in American history that took place on its soil was the Civil War. This bloody war, which lasted four years and involved as many as 3 million people, or 10 per cent of the total population of both the North and the South, in which 600,000 people died, countless others were injured and a great deal of property was destroyed, has yet to fully heal the wounds inflicted on the people more than 140 years later.

Today, much of the debate about the origins of the Civil War revolves around the moral issue of the war, namely, the justification of the abolition of slavery, as Hitchens put it:

> *"If there were no slavery, there would be no war. Without the moral condemnation of slavery, there would be no war."*[60]

In fact, in mid-19th century America, the debate over slavery was one of economic interest first and moral issues second. The backbone of the Southern economy at the time was the cotton-growing industry and slavery, and if slavery was abolished and farmers had to pay their former slaves at the market price of white labor, the entire industry would be at a loss and the socioeconomic structure would inevitably collapse.

If war is a continuation of political struggle, it is the contest of economic interests that lies behind the conflict of political interests. This contest of economic interests is ostensibly the difference between the economic interests of the North and the South, but is in essence a "divide and conquer" tactic played out by international financial forces to divide the fledgling United States of America.

German Chancellor Bismarck, who had deep roots in the Rothschilds, put it plainly:

---

[60] Sydney E. Ahlstrom, *A Religious History of the American People* (Yale University Press, 1972), on p. 649.

"There can be no doubt that the division of the United States into two weaker confederations, North and South, was settled long before the outbreak of the Civil War by the financial powers of Europe."

In fact, the bankers of the "London, Paris and Frankfurt Axis" were the ones behind the American Civil War.

In order to provoke the American Civil War, international bankers engaged in a long period of meticulous and deliberate planning. After the American War of Independence, the British textile industry and the slave-owning class of the American South gradually established close commercial ties, and European financiers took advantage of this opportunity to secretly develop a network of contacts that could provoke conflict between the North and the South in the future. In the South at that time, there were all sorts of agents of the British financiers who, together with the local political forces, conspired to secede from the Union and to produce news and public opinion of all kinds. They cleverly exploited the conflicting economic interests of the North and the South on the issue of slavery to constantly reinforce, highlight and detonate what was not originally a hot topic, and ultimately succeeded in catalyzing the issue of slavery into a bitter conflict between the two sides.

The international bankers were prepared to wait for the war to start and then make a fortune out of it. In waging war, their customary way of playing is to bet on both sides, and no matter who wins or loses, the huge government debts resulting from the huge war spending are the bankers' most sumptuous meal.

In the fall of 1859, the famous French banker Solomon Rothschild (son of James Rothschild) came to the United States from Paris as a tourist, and he was the general coordinator of all plans. He traveled north and south in the United States, making extensive contacts with local political and financial dignitaries and constantly feeding the information he gathered to his cousin Nathaniel Rothschild in London, England. In talks with locals, Solomon has publicly stated his strong financial support for the South and has said he will do everything in his power to help the independent South gain recognition as a European power.[61]

The international banker's agent up north was the Jewish banker August Belmont, known as the "King of Fifth Avenue" in New York. In 1829, at the age of 15, August began his career as a banker, initially working for the Rothschild Bank of Frankfurt, where he soon developed a remarkable financial talent, and in 1832 he was promoted to a bank in Naples in order to gain experience in international finance. He is fluent in German, English, French and Italian. Sent to New York in 1837, he soon became a leading figure in New York's financial community as a result of eating into government bonds on a large scale, and was appointed financial advisor by the president. August, on behalf of Britain and the Rothschild Bank in Frankfurt, took a stand and was willing to support Lincoln in the north financially.

In 1862, the British, French and Spanish allies landed in a Mexican port to complete their buildup on the southern frontier of the United States and, if necessary, to enter the southern part of the country to fight directly with the north.

In the early days of the war, with the military offensive in the South victorious and European powers such as Britain and France surrounded by strong enemies, Lincoln was in deep trouble. The bankers had calculated that the Lincoln administration's treasury was empty at this point, and that it would be unsustainable without a huge financing war. Since the end of the war with Britain in 1812, the US treasury has been in deficit year after year, and until Lincoln's presidency, the deficit in the US government budget was sold in the form of bonds to the banks, which were then resold to the Rothschild Bank and the Bank of Bahrain in Britain, and the US government had to pay high interest rates, and the debt accumulated over the years had made it difficult.

The bankers offered President Lincoln a financing package and conditions, and when he heard that the bankers were asking for as much as 24% to 36% interest, a stunned President Lincoln immediately pointed to the door and told the bankers to leave. It was a ruthless move

---

[61] *Jewish History in Civil War*, Jewish-American History Documentation Foundation, Inc. 2006.

to bankrupt the United States government, knowing full well that the American people would never be able to pay this astronomical debt.

Lincoln's Monetary New Deal

There can be no war without money, and borrowing money from international bankers is undoubtedly putting a noose around one's neck. Lincoln pondered the solution bitterly. That's when his old friend in Chicago, Dick Taylor, gave Lincoln an idea – the government issued its own currency!

> *"Let Congress pass a bill authorizing the Treasury Department to issue currency with full legal force, pay soldiers, and then go win your war." Lincoln asked if the American people would accept this new currency, and Dick said, "All men will have no choice in the matter, so long as you give this new currency the full force of law, and the government gives them full backing, they will be as universal as real money, for the Constitution gives Congress the power to issue and set the value of money."*

Lincoln, upon hearing the suggestion, was overjoyed and immediately asked Dick to plan the matter. This stone-cold approach breaks the practice of the government having to borrow money from private banks and pay high interest. This new currency uses a green pattern to distinguish it from other bank notes, historically known as "Greenback". This new currency is unique in that it is completely free of monetary metals such as gold and silver as collateral, and offers 5% interest for 20 years.

During the Civil War, as a result of the issuance of this currency, the government overcame the severe shortage of money at the beginning of the war and greatly and efficiently mobilized the resources of the American North and laid a solid economic foundation for the eventual victory over the South. At the same time, as this low-cost currency legally became the reserve currency of the banks of the North, bank credit in the North was greatly expanded, and military industry, railway construction, agricultural production, and commercial trade received unprecedented financial support.

The great discovery of gold since 1848 gradually freed American finance from the extreme disadvantage of being completely dominated by European bankers, and it was also because of the large amount of quality money as a basis for confidence that Lincoln's new currency became widely accepted by the people and laid a reliable financial foundation for winning the Civil War. Even more surprisingly, the new currency issued by Lincoln did not cause severe inflation similar to that experienced during the War of Independence, and from the outbreak of the Civil War in 1861 to the end of the war in 1865, the price index for the entire North grew only modestly from 100 to 216, which cannot help but be considered a financial miracle considering the scale of the war and the magnitude of the destruction, and in comparison to other wars of equal size in the world. Conversely, the South also adopted paper money circulation, but the effect was truly worlds apart, with the Southern price index soaring from 100 to 2776 in the same period.[62]

Throughout the Civil War, the Lincoln administration issued a total of hundreds of millions of dollars in new currency. This new monetary mechanism worked so well that President Lincoln was very serious about making the issuance of this Debt Free Money (DFM) permanent and legalistic. And this stings deeply at the fundamental interests of the international financial oligarchy. If all governments "blatantly" issued their own money without borrowing from the banks, the bankers' monopoly on currency issuance would cease to exist, and wouldn't the banks be drinking the northwest wind?

No wonder, upon hearing the news, *The Times* of London, which represents British bankers, immediately issued a statement.

> *"If this disgusting new fiscal policy (the Lincoln Greenback), which originated in the United States, is made permanent, then the government can issue its own currency at no cost. It will be able to pay all its debts and no longer owe them, it will acquire all the currency necessary to develop commerce, it will become a prosperous nation as never before in the world, and all the world's great talents and all its wealth will pour into North America. This country must be destroyed, or it will destroy every monarchy in the world."*

The British government and the New York Associations of Banks angrily expressed their desire to retaliate, and on December 28, 1861, they announced that they would stop paying metal money to the Lincoln government. Some banks in New York have also blocked gold savers from withdrawing their gold and have announced that they are withdrawing their commitment to buy government bonds with gold.

---

[62] Glyn Davies, *History of Money from Ancient Times to the Present Day* (University of Wales Press 2002), p489.

Banks all over the United States responded by running to Washington to propose a variation to President Lincoln, suggesting the same old practice of selling high-interest bonds to European bankers; depositing U.S. government gold in private banks as a reserve for credit issuance, so that the bankers could get rich; and taxing the industrial sector and the people to support the war.

President Lincoln rightly and firmly rejected this totally unorthodox demand of the bankers. His policies were so popular that the American people bought all the bonds in droves and used them as cash under the law.

The bankers, seeing that one plan fails, have another plan. They found that the act of Congress issuing the Lincoln N. A. did not mention whether the payment of interest on the national debt was to be made in gold, and a compromise was reached with the congressmen that the national debt would be allowed to be purchased in Lincoln N. A., but the interest portion would be paid in gold coins. This was the first step in a complete plan to first peg the value of domestic Lincoln Nifty to gold in the United States, and the European bankers, who at the time owned the world's reserve currency, the sterling system, had far more gold money than the United States. The compromise by U.S. bankers and Congress has allowed international financial forces to use their control over the total volume of U.S. gold imports and exports to indirectly achieve the effect of manipulating the value of U.S. currency.

Lincoln's Russian allies

At the most dangerous moment when the kings of Europe sent large numbers of troops to the Americas before and after the outbreak of the American Civil War in 1861 in preparation for the secession of the United States, Lincoln immediately thought of the long-standing enemy of the European monarchs, Russia. Lincoln sent envoys to Tsar Alexander II for help. When the Tsar received Lincoln's letter, he did not open it immediately, but merely gave it a handful of hands, and said,

> *"Before I open this letter or know its contents, I will agree in advance to any demands it makes."*[63]

---

[63] Des Griffin, *Descent into Slavery* (Emissary Publications, 1980).

There were several reasons why the Czar was preparing for military involvement in the American Civil War. One is the concern that the international financial forces that swept through Europe during the time of Alexander II were already knocking on the Kremlin's door. The bankers strongly demanded the establishment of a privately owned central bank, modelled on the experience of the "advanced" financial countries of Europe, which the Tsar had long since seen through the secrets and firmly rejected. Seeing President Lincoln, another anti-international financial power in jeopardy, Alexander II would be next if he didn't step in to help. Another reason was that on March 3, 1861, before the outbreak of the American Civil War, Alexander II proclaimed the law for the emancipation of serfs, and the two sides were somewhat sympathetic and sympathetic in abolishing slavery. Another reason was that Russia had just lost the Crimean War, which ended in 1856, at the hands of the British and French, and that Alexander II was still ashamed of himself.

Without declaring war, the Russian fleet, led by Admiral Liviski, marched into New York Harbor on September 24, 1863. The Russian Pacific Fleet, commanded by General Popov, arrived in San Francisco on October 12. Of Russia's actions, Keating Wales commented,

> *"They came at a time when the South was at a high and the North was at a low, and their presence caused indecision in England and France, ultimately giving Lincoln time to turn things around."*

After the end of the Civil War, the U.S. government went to great lengths to pay for the Russian fleet to the tune of $7.2 million. Because the Constitution did not authorize the President to pay the war costs of foreign governments, then-President Johnson made an agreement with Russia to pay for the war by purchasing land in Russia's Alaska. The story is historically known as "Seward's Folly," and Seward was the U.S. Secretary of State at the time, who was strongly criticized for not paying $7.2 million for a wasteland that seemed worthless at the time.

For the same reason, Alexander II was assassinated unsuccessfully in 1867, and on March 1, 1881, Alexander II finally died at the hands of his assassin.

Who really killed Lincoln?

Bismarck, Germany's iron-blooded Chancellor, hit the nail on the head when he said.

> *"He (Lincoln) received authority from Congress to borrow by selling the national debt to the people, so that the government and the nation jumped out of the trap of foreign financiers. When it dawned on them (the international financiers) that America would escape their grasp, Lincoln's death was not far away."*

Immediately after emancipating the Negroes and unifying the South, Lincoln declared the entire debt that the South had incurred in the war to be written off. The international bankers, who had been providing huge financial support to the South during the war, lost a great deal. In retaliation for Lincoln, and even more so for the subversion of Lincoln's monetary New Deal, they assembled various forces unhappy with President Lincoln and planned the assassination in an elaborate manner. In the end, it turned out that assigning a few fanatics to carry out the assassination was really not a difficult task.

After Lincoln's assassination, Congress, at the mercy of international financial forces, announced the repeal of Lincoln's new currency policy, freezing the issuance of Lincoln's new currency up to a maximum of $400 million.

In 1972, the U.S. Treasury was asked how much interest Lincoln had saved on the new billions of dollars it had issued. After careful calculation, a few weeks later the Treasury Department answered: because Lincoln issued the U.S. government's own currency, it saved the U.S. government a total of $4 billion in interest.[64]

The Civil War in the United States was, at its root, a struggle between the international financial forces and their agents and the United States government's interest in fiercely competing for the issuance of the national currency and monetary policy. For more than 100 years before and after the Civil War, the two sides fought repeatedly to the death on the financial high point of the establishment of the American central banking system, as a result of which seven American presidents were assassinated and many members of Congress

---

[64] *Abraham Lincoln and John F. Kennedy* by Melvin Sickler.

were killed. It was not until 1913 that the establishment of the Federal Reserve banking system in the United States finally marked a decisive victory for the international bankers.

In the words of Bismarck:

> *Lincoln's death was a great loss to the Christian world. No one in America may be able to follow in his great footsteps, and the bankers will regain control of those who are rich. I fear that the foreign bankers with their high-handedness and cruelty will end up getting the American enrichment and then use it to systematically corrupt modern civilization.*

The Deadly Compromise: The National Bank Act of 1863

> *My role in giving birth to the National Bank Act was the most serious financial mistake of my life. The (money supply) monopoly that it (the National Bank Act) creates will affect every aspect of this country. It should be abolished, but until then the country will be divided into two sides, with the people on one side and the bankers on the other, a situation that has never occurred in the history of this country.*
> —Solomon Chase, US Secretary of the Treasury (1861–1864)

After the outbreak of the Civil War, Lincoln rejected the financial noose of Rothschild and his U.S. agents with interest rates ranging from 24 to 36 percent and instead authorized the Treasury Department to issue its own "United States Notes," also known as greenbacks, and the Legal Tender Act, passed in February 1862, authorized the Treasury Department to issue hundreds of millions of greenbacks, and then again in July 1862 and March 1863. During the Civil War, a total of hundreds of millions of greenbacks were issued.

The issuance of the Lincoln Greenback was like stabbing the hornet's nest in the international banking industry, which bankers abhorred, while ordinary people and other industrial sectors welcomed the Greenback, which remained in circulation in the US monetary system until 1994.

In 1863, when the war came to a head and Lincoln needed more greenbacks to win the war, he had to bow to the banker forces in Congress in order to obtain authorization for a third greenback issue, making an important compromise by signing the National Bank Act of 1863. The bill authorizes the government to approve the issuance of uniformly standardized bank notes (except that the issuing banks will have different names) by the National Bank, which will actually issue the national currency of the United States. Crucially, these banks are using the US Government Bond (GGB) as a reserve for issuing bank notes, effectively deadlocking US money issuance and government debt, which the government will never be able to pay off.

John Kenneth Galbraith, a leading American economist, hit the nail on the head when he said,

> *"For many years after the end of the Civil War, the federal coffers enjoyed large annual surpluses. However, it was unable to pay off its debts and pay off the government bonds that were issued, because to do so meant that there were no bonds to pledge the national currency. To pay off the debt is to destroy the currency in circulation."*

The international bankers' plot to copy the Bank of England model to the United States has finally succeeded. The interest thus paid on the permanent and ever-increasing debt of the United States Government is like a noose firmly around the neck of the American people, tightening the more they struggle. By 2006, the U.S. federal government owed an astronomical trillion dollars in debt, with an average family of four saddled with tens of thousands of dollars in national debt, and the total national debt is growing at a rate of $20,000 per second! U.S. federal spending on interest on the national debt is second only to health care and defense, and will reach a whopping $400 billion in 2006.

Beginning in 1864, bankers were able to enjoy the fine meal of national debt interest for generations. The mere seemingly insignificant difference between direct government issuance of money or government issuance of bonds and bank issuance of money creates the greatest injustice in human history. The people are forced to pay indirect taxes to the bankers for the wealth and currency that was originally created by their hard work!

To date, China is one of the few remaining countries in the world where the government issues currency directly. The huge interest costs saved by the Government and the people are an indispensable factor for China's rapid and long-term development. If it is proposed that the People's Bank of China must use government bonds as collateral to issue renminbi to learn from the "best practices" of foreign countries, the Chinese people need to beware.

Lincoln was not unaware of this permanent threat, but was compelled by the immediate crisis to make an expedient move.

Lincoln had intended to repeal the act after he was re-elected in 1865, and as a result he was assassinated just 41 days after winning the general election. On April 12, 1866, Congress passed the Austerity Act, which sought to recall all greenbacks in circulation, convert them into gold coins, and then kick them out of circulation, restoring the gold standard to which international bankers were so dominant.

In a country fresh from an unprecedented war, there is no more absurd policy than the implementation of monetary austerity. Currency circulation fell from $1.8 billion (dollars per person) in 1866 to $1.3 billion (dollars per person) in 1867, $600 million (dollars per person) in 1876, and finally to $400 million (dollars per person) in 1886, artificially creating a severe shortage of money supply at a time when America's war wounds were in desperate need of healing and the economy was in dire need of recovery and development, while the population was increasing dramatically. Most people always feel that booms and busts are the order of the day, but in fact, manipulating the money supply in the hands of international bankers when it is tight and when it is loose is the root of the problem.

In the winter of 1872, international bankers sent Ernest Seyd from England to the United States with large sums of money, and through bribery facilitated the Coinage Act of 1873, known as the "Crime of 1873," which Ernest himself drafted in its entirety, which kicked silver out of circulation and made gold the sole dominant currency. This bill has undoubtedly had an exacerbating effect on the circulation of money, which is already severely short. Afterwards, Ernest himself gushed,

> *"I made a trip to America in the winter of 1872 to secure the passage of the coinage bill to abolish the silver coin. I represent the interests of the directors of the Bank of England. By 1873, the gold coin became the only metal currency."*

In fact, the abolition of the role of the silver coin in international money circulation was intended to ensure absolute control by international bankers over the world money supply. Gold exploration and production are much rarer than the growing number of silver excavations, and having fully mastered the world's gold mining, international bankers certainly do not want the uncontrollable volume of silver in circulation to affect their hegemonic position in dominating world finance. Therefore, beginning in 1871, silver was generally abolished in Germany, England, the Netherlands, Austria, and the Scandinavian countries, leading to a significant tightening of the currency in circulation in each country, which led to a severe economic depression in Europe for 20 years (Long Depression, 1873–1896).

In the United States, the Austerity Act and the Coinage Act directly triggered the Great Depression of 1873–1879. In a three-year period, unemployment in the United States was as high as 30 percent, and there was a strong demand from the American people to return to the days when Lincoln greenbacks and silver coins together constituted currency. The American public spontaneously formed organizations such as the US Silver Commission and the Greenback Party to push for a national return to a dual system of silver and gold coins and the reissue of the popular Lincoln Greenback.

The U.S. Silver Commission report states,

> *"The dark medieval era was caused precisely by currency shortages and falling prices. Without money, civilization cannot happen, and with a reduced money supply, civilization is bound to perish. During the Christian era in Rome, the empire had the equivalent of $1.8 billion in metal money in circulation, and by the end of the 15th century, there was only $200 million in (European) metal money in circulation. History shows that no catastrophic change can compare with the fall from the Roman Empire into the darkness of the Middle Ages."*

Contrast this with the attitude of the American Bankers Association (ABA). In a letter to all members, the Association stated.

> *We recommend that you do your utmost to support the prominent daily and weekly newspapers, especially the agricultural and religious media, in their firm opposition to the issuance of greenbacks by the government, and that you stop funding candidates who do not want to express their opposition to the issuance of greenbacks by the government. Abolishing the banks from issuing the national currency or resuming the government's issuance of greenbacks will enable (the state) to provide money to the people, which will seriously hurt our profits as bankers and lenders. Immediately make an appointment with the congressman in your district and ask them to protect our interests so we can control the legislation.*[65]

---

[65] From a circular issued by authority of the Associated Bankers of New York, Philadelphia, and Boston signed by one James Buel, secretary, sent out from 247 Broadway, New York in 1877, to the bankers in all of the States.

In 1881, the 20th President of the United States, James Garfield, who came to power in the midst of an economic depression, had clearly grasped the crux of the matter when he said.

> *Whoever controls the money supply in any country is the absolute master of all industry and commerce. When you understand that the whole (monetary) system is very easily controlled by a very small number of people in one way or another, you won't have to be told the root cause of inflation and deflation.*

Only weeks after these words were uttered, President Garfield was assassinated on 2 July 1881 by another "psychopath", Charles Giteau. The president was shot twice and finally died on September 19.

Throughout the nineteenth century, international bankers succeeded in "replacing sacred kingship with sacred gold power" in Europe and "sacred gold power gradually dismantled sacred civil power" in the United States. The international bankers have had the full advantage after a century-long and bitter battle with the elected government of the United States. U.S. historians point out that the casualty rate for U.S. presidents was higher than the average casualty rate for first-line troops at the U.S. landings in Normandy.

As the bankers hesitantly held the National Banking Act of 1863 in their hands, they were only one step away from their ultimate goal – the plan to replicate exactly one Bank of England in the United States. A privately owned central bank with complete control over the issuance of American money, a banker's bank has appeared on the American horizon.

Summary

★The British Parliament, under the control of the British bankers, denied the colonies the right to issue money, causing unemployment and discontent that became the main cause of the American War of Independence.

★Hamilton, the first US Treasury Secretary, lobbied Washington to set up a central bank in order to get foreign money to buy in and receive funding from the Rothschild family.

★The closure of the First Bank of the United States made Nathan furious to teach the Americans a lesson, and a few months later, the War of 1812 between Britain and the United States broke out, hitting the U.S. government so heavily in debt that he finally had to give in in 1815 and establish a second central bank, which Rothschild had a firm grip on power.

★The second bank of the United States was vetoed by President Jackson, the Rothschild family controlled the main European banking industry at the same time tightened the United States banking, the United States fell into a serious "artificial" money circulation decreased sharply, eventually triggering the panic of 1837, the economy fell into recession for five years.

★Two presidents, Harrison and Taylor, who fought with key PFLP figure Henry Clay around a private central bank and an independent financial system, both died mysteriously.

★The gold rush discovery in the US and Australia broke the absolute control of European financiers over the supply of gold. The financially controlling, politically divisive tactics of the international bankers caused the Panic of 1857.

★The bankers of the "London, Paris and Frankfurt Axis" were behind the American Civil War. The North-South War was fundamentally a struggle between the international financial forces and their agents and the United States government's interest in fiercely competing for the right to issue the national currency and monetary policy.

★The fundamental interests of the international financial oligarchs were deeply stung by Lincoln's letting the government issue its own new currency. After the Civil War, the international bankers who had been providing huge financial support to the South during the war suffered heavy losses. In retaliation and to subvert Lincoln's monetary New Deal, the assassination of Lincoln was meticulously planned.

★The international bankers have the complete upper hand after a hundred years of intense battles with the US government.

CHAPTER III

The Federal Reserve: A Privately Owned Central Bank

"A great industrial country is firmly controlled by a credit system that is highly concentrated. The development of this country and all our (economic) activities are entirely in the hands of a few. We have fallen under the worst kind of domination, a kind of control that is the most complete and total in the world. The government no longer has a free opinion, no longer has the power of judicial conviction, no longer is the government chosen by the majority of the electorate, but is the government that (operates) under the opinion and coercion of a tiny minority of those who have the power of domination.
Many business people in this country are in awe of something. They know that this unseen power is so organized, so quietly invisible, so pervasive, so interlocked, so thorough and comprehensive, that they dare not publicly condemn it."[66]
—Woodrow Wilson, 28th President of the United States

Not to exaggerate, to this day, there are probably not many economists in China who know that the Fed is actually a privately owned central bank. The so-called "Federal Reserve Bank" is in fact neither "federal" nor "reserve", nor is it a "bank".

Most Chinese may assume that the U.S. government issues dollars, but the reality is that the U.S. government does not have the right to issue currency at all! In order for the U.S. government to get dollars, it must pledge the future taxes of the American people (treasury bonds) to the private Federal Reserve, which issues "Federal Reserve Notes", which are "dollars".

---

[66] Quoted in *National Economy and the Banking System*, Senate Documents Co. 3, No. 23, Seventy-Sixth Congress, First session, 1939.

The nature and origin of the Federal Reserve is a "no-go zone" in the US academic community and the news media. The media can debate at length on a daily basis such extraneous issues as "gay marriage" without saying a word about who really controls the currency issue, which is a "matter of interest" for everyone, every day, every penny of income, every interest payment on a loan.

Reading this, if you are surprised, indicates that this issue is important and you actually didn't know it. This chapter will tell the secret of the establishment of the Federal Reserve, deliberately "filtered out" by the US mainstream media, as we take a magnifying glass and replay in slow motion the final moments of this major event that has influenced the course of world history, with developments that will be accurate in hours.

On December 23, 1913, the elected government of the United States was finally toppled by the power of money.

The mysterious island of Jekyll: the source of the Federal Reserve

On the night of November 22, 1910, in a completely sealed train car outside New York City, all windows were tightly covered by curtains as the train slowly headed south. The carriage was filled with America's most important bankers, and no one knew where they were going. The train ends hundreds of miles away in Jekyll Island, Georgia.

Georgia's Jekyll Island is a winter resort owned by a group of super-rich Americans. The bigwigs, headed by J.P. Morgan, founded a Jekyll Island Hunting Club, where 1/6th of the wealth of the planet is gathered in the hands of the members of this club, and membership is inheritable only and not transferable. At this time, the club was notified that someone would be using the club premises for approximately two weeks and that all members would not be able to use the clubhouse during that time. All the staff of the clubhouse are transferred from the mainland, and all guests arriving at the clubhouse are addressed by first name only, and never by surname. A 50-mile radius around the clubhouse ensures that there will be no journalists.

When everything is ready, the guests appear in the clubhouse. This top secret meeting was attended by:

> ➤ Nelson Aldrich, Senator, Chairman of the National Monetary Board and grandfather of Nelson Rockefeller.

> ➤ A. Piatt Andrew, Assistant Secretary of the U.S. Treasury.

> ➤ Frank Vanderlip, President, National City Bank of New York.

> ➤ Henry P. Davison, Senior Partner, J. P. Morgan & Co.

> ➤ Charles D. Norton, President, First National Bank of New York.

> ➤ Benjamin Strong, left arm of J.P. Morgan.

> ➤ Paul Warburg, German Jewish immigrant to the United States in 1901, senior partner at Kuhn Loeb and Company, agent of the Rothschilds in England and France, chief architect of the Federal Reserve, first Fed director.

These important people came to this remote island with no interest in coming here to hunt, and their main task was to draft an important document: the Federal Reserve Act (FRA).

Paul Warburg is a master at almost all the details of banking operations. As others asked various questions, Paul not only patiently answered them, but also spoke at length about the historical origins of each detailed concept. All were impressed by his profound knowledge of banking. Paul naturally became the main drafter and interpreter of the document.

Nelson Aldrich was the only amateur of all people responsible for making the content of the document politically correct enough to be acceptable in Congress. Others, representing the interests of different banking groups, argued passionately for nine days around the details of Paul's proposed package before finally reaching a consensus.

Since the banking crisis of 1907, bankers have been so poorly portrayed in the minds of the American people that no one in Congress has dared to publicly support a bill with banker participation, so these people have traveled far from New York to hide on this secluded island to draft this document. Also, the name central bank was too much of a ploy, and since President Jefferson, the name central bank has been so heavily associated with the British international banker conspiracy that Paul suggested using the name Federal Reserve System to obscure it. But it has all the functions of a central bank, and like the Bank of England, the Fed is designed to be privately owned and will reap huge benefits from it. Unlike Bank One and Bank Two, the Federal Reserve's share composition, in which the original 20 percent of government shares were taken away, will become a "pure" privately owned central bank.

To make the Federal Reserve System even more deceptive, on the question of who controls the Fed, Paul cleverly posits,

> "Congress controls the Fed, the government has representation on the board, but the majority of the board is controlled directly or indirectly by the banking association."

Later, Paul changed the final version to read "Board members are appointed by the President of the United States", but the true function of the Board is controlled by the Federal Advisory Council, which meets regularly with the Board to "discuss" its work. That the members of the Federal Advisory Committee would be determined by the directors of the 12 Federal Reserve banks was deliberately kept from the public.

Another dilemma Paul had to deal with was how to hide the fact that the New York bankers would dominate the Federal Reserve, a region whose legislators could not possibly support a central bank dominated by New York bankers when the vast number of small and medium-sized businessmen and farmers in the Midwest, devastated by banking crises since the 19th century, resented the bankers of the East. Paul designed a genius solution for this, with 12 regional Fed banks making up the entire system. Few outside banking circles understand that the proposed establishment of regional Fed banks, under the basic premise of a high concentration of money and credit disbursement in the United States in the New York area, merely creates the illusion that central bank operations are not concentrated in New York.

One more reflection of Paul's far-sightedness is the idea of locating the Fed's headquarters in the political capital Washington, D.C., and deliberately moving away from New York, the financial capital where it actually takes orders, to further distract the public from the concerns of New York bankers.

Paul's fourth obsession was how to produce the executives of the 12 Federal Reserve regional banks, and Nelson Aldrich's congressional experience finally came in handy. He pointed out that Midwestern legislators were generally hostile to New York bankers, and that in order to avoid a runaway phenomenon, the directors of all regional banks should be appointed by the President, and not interfered with by Congress. But this creates a legal loophole, as Title I, Section 8 of the Constitution explicitly states that Congress is responsible for issuing and administering the currency, leaving Congress out of the picture, meaning that the Fed has been in violation of the Constitution from the beginning. And then it became a target for many legislators to attack the Fed.

As a result of this ingenious arrangement, the bill appears as a mockery of the separation of powers and checks and balances of the United States Constitution. Presidential appointments, congressional vetting, independents as directors, bankers as advisors, what a trickle-down design!

Wall Street 7: The Federal Reserve's Behind-the-Scenes Promoter

> *"The seven men of Wall Street now control most of America's basic industries and resources. Of these, J. P. Morgan, James Hill, and George Baker (president of the First National Bank of New York), belonged to the so-called Morgan Group; the remaining four, John Rockefeller, William Rockefeller, James Stillman (president of the National City Bank), and Jacob Schiff (Kuhn-Repo Company), belonged to the Standard Oil City Bank Group. The central hub of the capital they constitute controls the United States."*[67]
>
> —John Moody's, founder of the Moody's Investment Appraisal System, 1911

The seven big players on Wall Street were the real behind-the-scenes movers in establishing the Fed. Between them and their secret coordination with the Rothschilds of Europe, they eventually established the Bank of England in the United States as a flip-flop.

The rise of the Morgan family

JPMorgan Bank was formerly known as the lesser-known George Peabody and Company in England. George Peabody was originally a dry goods merchant in Baltimore, USA, and after making a small

---

[67] John Moody, *The Seven Men*, McClure's Magazine, August, 1911, p. 418.

fortune, came to London, England in 1835 to break into the world. Seeing that finance was a rich business, he started a business in London with some businessmen in the Merchant Bank, a very fashionable "High Finance" business at the time, whose clients were mainly governments, large corporations and the rich and powerful. They make international trade loans, issue stocks and bonds, and operate in commodities, which is what modern investment banks were.

George Peabody quickly broke into the British financial scene through the introduction of the Brown Brothers in Baltimore at the British Cent. Soon after, George Peabody was surprised to receive an invitation from Baron Nathan Rothschild to be his guest. The terrified George Peabody felt as honored to be invited by Nathan, who was famous in World Bank circles, as a Catholic would be to be received by the Pope.

Nathan gets right to the point and offers to ask George Peabody to do him a favor and be the Rothschild family's secret PR agent. The Rothschilds were hated and despised by many people for their wealth and fortune in Europe. The aristocracy of London then disdained to associate with Nathan, repeatedly rejecting his invitations, and although Rothschild was powerful in England, there was always a sense of being somewhat isolated by the aristocracy. Another reason Nathan saw George Peabody was that he was humble, well liked and an American who could come in handy later.

George Peabody, of course, was more than happy with Nathan's offer, and with all the public relations expenses paid for by Nathan, George Peabody's company soon became a famous social centre in London. In particular, the annual American Independence Day banquet, held at George Peabody's house on the 4th of July, was a major event in London's aristocratic circle. It may not have occurred to the guests that the expense of hospitality is more than an ordinary businessman could have afforded a few years ago, when his name was unknown.

Until 1854, George Peabody was a million-pound banker, but in just six years, he made a fortune of nearly £20 million and became an American heavyweight banker. It turns out that in the 1857 economic crisis in the United States, instigated by the Rothschilds, George Peabody was heavily invested in American railroad bonds and government bonds, and when the British bankers suddenly tossed all the bonds that had a stake in the United States, George Peabody was also deeply entrapped. The crisis of 1857 was completely different from the 10-year depression of 1837, and in just one year, the American economy was completely out of recession, and as a result, George Peabody quickly became a super-rich man in the hands of American bonds, which was strikingly similar to Nathan's Battle of the British Treasury in 1815. Without accurate information from the insiders, George Peabody, freshly awakened from a bankruptcy nightmare, was categorically afraid to eat into US bonds in large quantities.

George Peabody, who had no children in his life and a huge estate to inherit, took great pains to bring in the young Junius Morgan. After George Peabody retired, Junius Morgan took over the entire business and renamed the company Junius S. Morgan and Company, still based in London. Later, Junius's son J. P. Morgan took over the company, and he later renamed the American branch the J. P. Morgan Company. In 1869, J. P. Morgan and Drexel met with the Rothschilds in London, and the Morgan family fully inherited George Peabody's relationship with the Rothschilds and developed this cooperation to a new level. In 1880, J. P. Morgan began to heavily finance the commercial activities of the reorganized railroad company.

On February 5, 1891, the Rothschilds and a number of other British bankers formed the secret organization "Round Table Group", and a corresponding organization was established in the United States, led by the Morgan family. After the First World War, the "Round Table Group" in the United States was renamed the "Council on Foreign Relations" and in the United Kingdom the "Royal Institute of International Affairs". It is from these two associations that many important officials of the U.S. and British governments have been selected.

In 1899, J. P. Morgan and Drexel traveled to London, England, to attend the International Congress of Bankers. When they returned, J. P. Morgan had been appointed chief agent for the Rothschilds' interests in the United States. The result of the London meeting was that the J. P. Morgan Company of New York, the Drexel Company of Philadelphia, the Grenfell Company of London, the Morgan Harjes Cie Company of Paris, and the M. M. Warburg Company of Germany and the United States, were fully associated with the Rothschild family.[68]

---

[68] William Guy Carr, *Pawns In The Game* (Legion for the Survival of Freedom, 1978).

In 1901, J. P. Morgan bought Carnegie's steel company for a whopping $500 million and formed the world's first giant with a market value of more than $1 billion, the United States Steel Corporation, considered at the time the richest man in the world, but according to the Temporary National Economic Committee, he owned only 9 percent of his company. It seems that the infamous Morgan is still just a front man.

Rockefeller: Oil King

John Rockefeller Sr. is a controversial figure in American history and has been dubbed the "coldest and most ruthless man". His name is naturally inextricably linked to the big name Standard Oil.

Rockefeller's oil career began during the American Civil War (1861–1865), and business remained average until 1870, when he founded the American Standard Oil Company. Since getting a bunch of seed loans from National City Bank of Cleveland, he seems to have found his senses all at once, especially when it comes to displaying an uncanny imagination in vicious competition. In the petroleum refining industry, which he was very bullish on, he realized early on that petroleum refining, although extremely profitable in the short term, would eventually descend into a suicidal vicious competition due to the lack of control. There was only one way: to eliminate the competition without mercy, and to that end all means were available.

This is done by starting with an offer by an intermediary company under its control but not known to the public to buy out a competitor at a low price in cash, and if rejected, the competitor faces a fierce price war until it succumbs or goes bankrupt. If it doesn't work, Rockefeller will finally resort to the trick: violent destruction. There were few survivors after several rounds of beating rival workers, setting fire to rival factories, etc. Such a hegemonic monopoly, while arousing the public ire of its peers, also drew the keen interest of New York bankers. The bankers who love monopolies admire Rockefeller's high degree of execution in achieving them.

The Rothschilds have been desperately trying to control the increasingly powerful United States, but have repeatedly failed. It is much easier to control a European king than it is to control an elected government. After the American Civil War, the Rothschilds began to deploy plans for control of the United States. In the financial sector, there was JPMorgan and Kuhn Loeb & Co., and in the industrial sector, they hadn't been able to find the right agent to choose, and what the Rockefellers had done had caught the Rothschilds' eye. The Rockefellers would be far more powerful than the tiny Cleveland area if given a massive infusion in finance.

The Rothschilds sent their foremost financial strategist in the United States, Jacob Schiff of the Kuhn Loeb & Co. Company, to Cleveland in 1875 to direct the Rockefellers' next expansion plans. Schiff brought with him unprecedented support that Rockefeller could never have imagined, and since Rothschild had by this time controlled 95% of the railroad capacity in the United States through JPMorgan and Kuhn Loeb & Co., Schiff drew up a plan for the Shadow Company (South Improvement Company) to step in and offer Rockefeller's Standard Oil Company a very low freight rate discount under which few refining companies could survive.[69] Rockefeller soon had a complete monopoly on the U.S. oil industry and became a veritable "oil king".

Jacob Schiff: Rothschild's financial strategist

The close relationship between the Rothschilds and the Schiff family dates back to 1785, when the old Rothschild family moved to a five-story building in Frankfurt and lived with the Schiff family for many years. Also German Jewish bankers, the two had a centuries-long friendship.

In 1865, at the age of 18, Jacob Schiff came to the United States after a brief apprenticeship at the Rothschild Bank in England. After the assassination of President Lincoln, Jacob coordinated interests among European bankers' agents in the United States to promote the establishment of a private central banking system in the United States. His other purpose was to discover, train, and channel the agents of the European banks to various positions of importance in government, courts, banks, industry, the press, etc., for the time being.

On January 1, 1875, Jacob joined the Kuhn Loeb & Co. Company and has been the core of the company ever since. Backed by the powerful Rothschild family, Kuhn Loeb & Co. eventually became one

---

[69] Robert Gates Sr., *The Conspiracy That Will not Die: How the Rothschild Cabal is Driving America Into One World Government*, (Red Anvil Press, Oakland, 2011), p. 41.

of the most prominent investment banks in the United States in the late 19th and early 20th centuries.

James Hill: The Railway King

The construction of railroads was an important infrastructure that relied heavily on financial support, and the development of the vast railroad industry in the United States was made possible to a large extent by money from the capital markets of Britain and other European countries. Control over the issuance of American railroad bonds in Europe became a direct means of holding the lifeblood of the American railroad industry.

U.S. railroad bonds were not spared in 1873, when international bankers imposed a sudden financial crunch on the U.S. by wildly dumping U.S. bonds. By the time the crisis ended in 1879, the Rothschilds had become the largest creditors of the American railroads and could pinch the financial lifeblood of any American railroad at any time as long as they pleased. In these times, James Hill, who had started out in steamboat transportation and coal mining, had to fall under the banner of the financiers in order to survive and thrive in the fierce competition of the railroad industry, and Morgan was the financial backer behind him. With Morgan's strong support, and taking advantage of the massive railroad failures following the 1873 crisis, James Hill realized his plans for rapid mergers and expansion.

By 1893, James Hill's dream of having a transcontinental railroad across the United States was finally realized. In the battle for control of the Midwest Railroad (Chicago, Burlington and Quincy Railroad), James Hill met a formidable opponent, and the Union Pacific Railroad, backed by the Rockefeller consortium, made a surprise attack on him. Harriman, president of the Pacific Union Railroad, began secretly acquiring stock in the Northern Pacific, which James Hill controlled, and was 40,000 shares shy of making a splash when James Hill was alarmed that he was about to lose control. James Hill immediately sent an urgent plea for help to Morgan, the backstage boss who was on vacation in Europe, and Morgan immediately ordered his men to counter Rockefeller's challenge. All at once, the scramble for Northern Pacific Railroad stock reached white-hot proportions, with the price per share reaching a sky-high $1,000.

In the end, the international bankers had to mediate, and the final result was a new holding company, the Northern Securities Company, in which the two powers jointly controlled rail transportation in the northern United States. On the day the company was founded, President McKinley was assassinated and Vice President Roosevelt Sr. succeeded him. Over the strong opposition of Roosevelt, Sr. the Northern Securities Company was forced to dissolve by the Sherman Antitrust Act, passed by the United States in 1890. After the setback, James Hill's direction turned south, acquiring the railroad that ran straight from Colorado to Texas. By the time of his death in 1916, James Hill had accumulated an estate of $53 million.

Warburg Brothers

In 1902, brothers Paul and Felix emigrated to the United States from Frankfurt, Germany. The two brothers, who came from a banking family, were well versed in banking, and Paul, in particular, was one of the top financial minds of his time. Rothschild valued Paul's talent so much that he deliberately drew the two brothers from the M. M. Warburg and Co. of the European Strategic Alliance to the American front, where talent was desperately needed.

At this point, the Rothschild family's plan for a private central bank in the United States was nearly a century old, with its ups and downs and no final success. This time, Paul will take the lead offense. Shortly after arriving in the United States, Paul joined the Kuhn Loeb & Co. company of the vanguard Jacob Schiff and married the daughter of Schiff's sister, while Felix married Schiff's daughter.

Colonel Ely Garrison, a financial adviser to Presidents Roosevelt Sr. and Wilson, noted,

> *"It was Mr. Paul Warburg who put the Federal Reserve Act back together amidst the national resentment and opposition to the Aldrich plan. The genius intelligence behind both of these plans came from Alfred Rothschild in London."*[70]

---

[70] Eustace Mullins, *The Secrets of the Federal Reserve* (Omnia Veritas Ltd – www.omnia-veritas.com)

The Fed's Outpost: The Banking Crisis of 1907

In 1903, Paul presented a programme of action on how to introduce the European Central Bank's "best practices" to the United States to Jacob Schiff, and this document was then passed on to James Stillman, president of the National City Bank of New York (later Citibank), and to the New York banker community, all of whom found Paul's ideas truly enlightening and enlightening.

The problem is that the political and civil forces that have historically opposed private central banks in the United States are quite strong, and New York bankers have an extremely poor reputation in American circles of industry and small and medium business owners. Members of Congress have shunned like the plague any proposal from bankers for a private central bank. In such a political climate, it is harder to pass a central bank bill that favours bankers than it is to get to heaven.

In order to reverse this unfavorable situation, a huge financial crisis began to be conceived.

First, the press began to be heavily oriented with articles promoting new financial ideas, and on 6 January 1907 Paul published an article entitled "The shortcomings and needs of our banking system", from which he became the chief advocate of a central banking system in the United States. Shortly thereafter, Jacob Schiff declared at the New York Chamber of Commerce,

> *"Unless we have a central bank sufficient to control credit resources, we will experience a financial crisis of unprecedented and far-reaching proportions."*[71]

Flies don't bite without an egg, as in 1837, 1857, 1873, 1884 and 1893, the bankers had long since seen the severe bubbles in the overheated development of the economy that were the inevitable result of their constant loosening of silver roots. The whole process is figuratively said to be like a banker raising fish in a fish pond, when the banker releases water into the fish pond he is relaxing the silver roots, injecting money into the economy in large quantities, after getting a lot of money, people from all walks of life begin to work hard day and night under the lure of money, trying to create wealth, the process is

---

[71] Paul M Warburg, *Defects and needs of our banking system*, 1907.

like a fish in a pond trying to absorb all kinds of nutrients, growing fatter and fatter. When the bankers see that the time is ripe for harvest, they suddenly tighten the silver roots and start pumping water from the fish pond, at which point most of the fish in the pond are left to wait in desperation for their fate to be caught.

However, when to begin to draw fish only a few of the largest banking oligarchs know, when a country establishes a private central banking system, the banking oligarchs are more comfortable with the control of the release of water and pumping, and the more precise the harvest. Economic development and recession, wealth accumulation and evaporation have all become the inevitable result of the "scientific feeding" of bankers.

J.P. Morgan and the international bankers behind him are calculating the predicted outcome of this financial meltdown with precision. The first is to shock American society by letting the "facts" show how fragile a society without a central bank is. This is followed by the crowding out and merging of small and medium-sized competitors, especially trust investment companies, which are a source of concern for bankers. Then there's getting the important businesses that make them covet.

The fashionable FITs at the time enjoyed many businesses that banks could not operate, and government regulation was very lax, which led to FITs over-absorbing social capital and investing in risky industries and stock markets. By the time the crisis hit in October 1907, about half of New York's bank loans were being invested as collateral by trust investment companies with high interest returns in risky stock markets and bonds, and the entire financial market was in a state of extreme speculation.

JPMorgan had spent the preceding months "vacationing" between London and Paris in Europe, and after careful planning by international financiers, JPMorgan returned to the United States. Soon after, rumors of the impending bankruptcy of Knickerbocker Trust, the third largest trust company in the United States, suddenly began to spread widely in New York, and the rumors quickly spread like a virus throughout the city, with panicked depositing citizens lining up all night in front of various trust companies to withdraw their deposits. The banks demanded that the trust company repay the loan immediately, and the trust company, which had been called on by both sides, borrowed money from the stock market (Margin Loan) at an interest rate of 150%

of the sky-high price. By October 24, stock market trading was almost at a standstill.

Morgan appeared at this point as the Savior. When the chairman of the New York Stock Exchange came to Morgan's office for help, he said with a trembling voice that at least 50 dealers would go bankrupt if $25 million could not be raised by 3 p.m., and that he would have no choice but to close the stock market. At 2 p.m., Morgan called an emergency meeting of bankers, and in 16 minutes, the bankers raised the money. JPMorgan immediately sent someone to the stock exchange to announce that the interest on the loan would be available openly at 10 percent, and there was immediate cheering on the exchange. In just one day, the emergency bailout had run out of money, interest rates had gone crazy again, and eight banks and trust companies had collapsed. Morgan rushed to the Bank of Settlement in New York to request that the notes be issued as temporary currency to deal with a severe cash shortage.

On Saturday, November 2, Morgan began his long-awaited plan to "save" the still stormy Moore and Schley company. The company is $25 million in debt and on the verge of collapse. But it is a major creditor of the Tennessee Coal and Iron Company, and if Moore & Schley is forced into bankruptcy to pay it off, the New York stock market will collapse completely with untold consequences. Morgan invited all the big names in the New York financial world to his library, commercial bankers were placed in the East Room, trust company executives in the West Room, and anxious financiers waited anxiously for the fate Morgan had planned for them.

Morgan knew full well that the iron ore and coal resources in Tennessee, Alabama and Georgia owned by Tennessee Mining and Ironmaking would greatly strengthen the monopoly of U.S. Steel, the steel giant that Morgan himself founded. With the antitrust laws in place, Morgan has always been unable to get down on this big fat piece of meat, and this crisis has created a rare merger opportunity for him. Morgan's terms were that in order to save Moore & Schley and the entire trust industry, the trust would have to raise $25 million to keep the trust from collapsing, and that U.S. Steel would have to buy the Tennessee Mining and Steelmaking Company's claims from Moore & Schley. Anxious and irritable, on the verge of bankruptcy, the trust's bosses, who had been up all night and were extremely tired, finally surrendered to Morgan.

On Sunday night, November 3, Morgan sent his men to Washington, D.C., all night long to get the President's approval before the stock market opened the following Monday morning. The banking crisis brought down a large number of businesses, the loss of life savings of thousands of angry people formed a great regime crisis, and Roosevelt Sr. had to borrow the power of Morgan to stabilize the situation, and he was forced at the last moment to sign an alliance under the city. At this point there are only 5 minutes left before the stock market opens on Monday!

The New York stock market was up big on the news.

JPMorgan ate the Tennessee Mining and Ironmaking Company for an ultra-low $45 million, and the company's potential value is at least around $1 billion according to John Moody's assessment.[72]

Every financial crisis is a long-planned, precisely targeted blast, with shiny new financial buildings always built on top of the ruins of thousands of bankrupts.

From the gold standard to legal tender: the big shift in bankers' worldviews

Since the end of the 19th century, international bankers have once again made a major leap in their understanding of money.

The original Bank of England model of issuing money with the national debt as collateral, through a deadlock between the two, achieved government borrowing and the bank issuing money, ensuring that the debt became larger and larger, thus guaranteeing the bankers ever-growing huge returns. Under the gold standard system, bankers were adamantly opposed to inflation because any devaluation of the currency directly hurt the bankers' real income from interest. The main drawback is that wealth accumulation is so slow that even with fractional reserves, it is still not enough to satisfy the growing appetite of bankers. Gold and silver in particular have been slow to increase, which amounts to putting a cap on the total amount of lending banks can do.

---

[72] Ron Chernow, *The House of Morgan* (Groove Press, 1990), p. 128.

In Europe at the turn of the 19th and 20th centuries, bankers had worked out a more efficient and complex system of legal tender. Fiat Money has completely freed itself from the rigid constraints of gold and silver on the total amount of lending and has a more flexible and stealthy control over money. When bankers gradually came to understand that the gains to be made by an unrestricted increase in the money supply were far greater than the loss of interest on loans due to inflation, they then became the most enthusiastic advocates of legal tender. By rapidly increasing the issuance of money, the bankers are robbing the savers of the entire country of their enormous wealth, while inflation is much more "civilized" and encounters much less resistance from the people than the banks' forced auctions of other people's property, which are much less visible or even imperceptible.

The economics of inflation exploration, financed by bankers, was gradually steered into a purely mathematical game, and the concept of Currency Inflation, caused by the issuance of additional paper money, has been completely overwhelmed in modern times by the theory of Price Inflation, a theory of price increases.

At this point, in addition to the old fractional reserve system, the currency and the national debt deadlock, the bankers added a more powerful tool to their tool for getting rich: inflation. From there, the banker made the dramatic transition from the defender of gold to the mortal enemy of gold.

Keynes hit the nail on the head with his assessment of inflation:

> *"With this approach, governments can confiscate people's wealth in secret and undetectable ways, and it's hard for even one in a million people to detect such theft."*

To be precise, it is the private Federal Reserve that uses it in the US, not the government.

Election Beacon of 1912

> *Tuesday, the Chancellor of Princeton will be elected your (New Jersey) Governor. He will not finish his term. In November 1912, he would be elected President of the United States, and in March 1917, he would be reelected President. He will be one of the greatest presidents in American history.*
> —Rabbi Wyeth's speech in New Jersey, 1910

The reason the Wyeth, who would later become President Wilson's close think tank, was able to accurately predict the outcome of the presidential election two years ago, and even six years later, was not because he really had a magical crystal ball in his hands, but because all the results were precisely concocted in advance by the bankers.

Not surprisingly for international bankers, the banking crisis of 1907 did greatly shock American society. Anger at trust investment companies, fear of bank failures, mingled with fear of the financial oligarchy on Wall Street, a powerful current of public opinion against all financial monopolies swept the country.

Princeton University President Woodrow Wilson is a well-known activist against financial monopolies. Vanderlip, president of the National City Bank of New York, had this to say:

> *"I am writing to invite Woodrow Wilson of Princeton to a dinner and to give a speech. To let him know that this was an important opportunity, I mentioned that Senator Aldrich was also going to be there and give a speech. My friend Dr. Wilson surprised me with his answer by refusing to speak on the same stage as Senator Aldrich."*[73]

In 1908, Aldrich proposed that in an emergency, banks could issue money, secured by federal, state and local government bonds and railroad bonds. The fact that there is such a good thing in the world, with the risk borne by the government and the people and the benefits all bankers, makes one have to admire Wall Street's tactics. The bill was called the Emergency Currency Act, and this bill became the legislative basis for the Federal Reserve Act five years later. Aldrich is considered by society to be the face of Wall Street.

Woodrow Wilson graduated from Princeton University in 1879 and went on to study law at the University of Virginia, earning his doctorate at Johns Hopkins University in 1886 and becoming president of Princeton University in 1902. The pedantic Woodrow Wilson has always been a high-profile opponent of financial monopolies, and naturally refuses to get close to the spokesman for the financial oligarchy. His academic sophistication and idealism do not compensate for his extreme lack of knowledge of the financial industry, and he

---

[73] Antony C. Sutton, *The Federal Reserve Conspiracy* (Tab Books, 1995) p. 78.

knows nothing about the money-making techniques of Wall Street bankers.

The bankers saw Wilson's simple and easily exploited characteristics as well as being a well-known activist against financial monopolies, and his fresh image is a rare diamond in the rough. The bankers were ready to put a lot of money into him and "carve" him up to be of great use.

As it happens, Cleveland Dodge, a director of the National City Bank of New York, was a college classmate of Wilson's at Princeton, and Wilson's success in becoming Princeton's president in 1902 was the result of the help of the wealthy and generous Dodge. With this layer of not-so-shallow connections, Dodge, orchestrated by the bankers, began letting loose on Wall Street that Wilson was a piece of presidential material.

It is not uncommon for a principal who has only been in office for a few years to be suddenly hailed as a president. Of course, being popular always comes with a price, and Wilson began to stick it to Wall Street behind his back. Sure enough, Wilson was soon elected governor of New Jersey in 1910 with the support of the Wall Street bigwigs.

In public, Wilson remained righteously critical of Wall Street's financial monopoly, and privately understood that his position and political future depended entirely on the power of the bankers. The bankers were surprisingly tolerant and restrained in their attacks on Wilson, and there was a subtle and unspoken tacit understanding on both sides.

Just as Wilson's reputation rises, bankers rush to raise funds for his presidential campaign. Dodge set up an office at 42 Broadway Avenue in New York to raise money for Wilson and set up a bank account, with Dodge donating the first check for $1,000. Quickly, Dodge enlisted large sums of money in the bankers' circle via direct mail, 2/3 of which came from seven Wall Street bankers.[74]

In his letter to Dodge, Wilson, hard pressed for emotion after securing the presidential nomination, said, "My joy is beyond words." Since then, Wilson has fully swooped into the banker's arms. As the Democratic nominee, Wilson carries the great hopes of the Democratic

---

[74] *Ibid.*, p. 83.

Party, which has lost the presidency for years and has a hunger for power as strong as Wilson's.

Wilson challenged then-President Taft, and Taft had a big advantage over Wilson, who was not known nationally at the time. Just when the hesitantly prepared for re-election of President Taft said that he was not prepared to give the green light to the Aldrich Act, an unprecedented strange thing happened, Taft's predecessor, President Roosevelt Sr. suddenly killed, actually want to participate in the presidential campaign, this for the old Roosevelt's own chosen successor and the same Republican Taft, really bad news. Roosevelt Sr., who was famous for forcing the disintegration of the Northern securities and had a reputation for antitrust intransigence, would have seriously eroded Taft's vote with his sudden appearance.

The fact that all three candidates are backed by bankers is nothing more than the bankers secretly favoring Wilson, the most controllable of the three. Under Wall Street arrangements, Roosevelt, Sr. "accidentally" hit Taft hard, and Wilson was elected. It's a scene akin to the one in which the elder Bush was unexpectedly defeated by the rookie Clinton in 1992 after being robbed of a large number of votes by Perry.

Plan B

The banking giants' planning on Jekyll Island was highly confidential, and out of a strict professional instinct they prepared two plans. The first was the plan presided over by Senator Aldrich, responsible for feinting in order to draw the fire of the opposition, of which the Republican Party was a supporter. The other plan known as Plan B was the real main thrust, which was the later Federal Reserve Act, with the Democrats as the main driving force.

There is actually no essential difference between the two plans, just different wording. The presidential election also revolves around this core goal. Senator Aldrich's ties to Wall Street are well known, and his proposed financial reform bill was bound to fail in the prevailing strongly anti-Wall Street atmosphere in the country at the time. The crisis of 1907 was cleverly designed to achieve a bipartisan consensus that the financial system must be reformed, and in order to "respond" to public opinion, it became a logical necessity for bankers to sacrifice the Republican Party for the Democratic Party.

To further confuse the public, the bankers have resorted to the masterstroke of getting two factions that actually support different versions of the same content to attack each other. Senator Aldrich led the charge, accusing the Democratic proposal of being hostile to the banks and detrimental to the government. He declared that any legal tender policy that departed from the gold standard was a serious challenge to bankers. The *Nation* noted on October 23, 1913, that

> *"Mr. Aldrich's opposition to a government legal tender backed by no gold is exactly what his own bill of 1908 (the Emergency Money Act) would have done. He should also have known that the government had in fact nothing to do with the issuance of the currency and that it was the Federal Reserve Board that had full control over it."*

The Democrats' accusations of the Aldrich proposal are equally eye-opening, claiming that Aldrich is defending the interests of Wall Street bankers and the financial monopoly that the Democrats' Fed proposal seeks to break up and create a perfect central banking system with regional separation, presidential appointments, congressional scrutiny, and bankers providing expert advice that is mutually constraining and decentralized. Unsophisticated in financial matters, Wilson honestly believes the scheme breaks the monopoly of finance that Wall Street bankers have.

It is because of Aldrich and Vanderlip and Wall Street's relentless opposition and finger-pointing that the Democratic Federal Reserve Act has won the hearts of the people, and bankers have played the "fix it, fix it, fix it" ploy to the point of applause.

The Federal Reserve Act passes, bankers' dreams come true

At the same time that Wilson was elected president, Plan B was officially launched.

On June 26, 1913, just three months after Wilson's arrival in the White House, Plan B was formally tossed in the House by Congressman Carter Glass of Virginia, a banker who deliberately avoided overly stimulating terms such as central bank and replaced them with the Federal Reserve, which passed on September 18 by a vote of 287 to 85 without the knowledge of most members of Congress.

The proposal was forwarded to the Senate and became the Glass-Owen Bill, and Senator Robert L. Owen (R-Ohio) is also a banker. The

Senate proposal passed on Dec. 19. At this point, there are still more than 40 differences between the two proposals to be resolved, and as is customary in both houses, no important bill will pass in the week before Christmas, and according to the projection of the gap between the proposals in both houses at that time, under normal circumstances, it can only be discussed the following year, so many important opponents of the bill have left Washington to go home for the holidays.

At this time, with a temporary office on Capitol Hill, Paul Warburg, who was in direct command in the "field", saw the opportunity of a thousand years and launched a blitzkrieg. In his office, a group of lawmakers arrived every hour to discuss next steps, and on the evening of Saturday, Dec. 20, the House and Senate met in joint session to continue discussing important differences. At this time, an atmosphere prevailed in Congress to pass the Federal Reserve Act by Christmas at all costs, and the White House even announced on December 17 that it had begun to consider the list of the first Federal Reserve Board members. But until late on the night of the 20th, not a single important disagreement was resolved. It seems unlikely that it will be possible to pass the Federal Reserve Act on Monday, December 22.

At the urging of the bankers, the joint meeting decided to remain in session throughout the day on Sunday the 21st and never to adjourn without resolving the matter.

Late into the night of the 20th, the House and Senate were still not in agreement on several important issues. These disagreements include: the number of Fed regional banks, how to secure reserves, the proportion of gold reserves, currency settlement issues in domestic international trade, proposed reserve changes, whether Fed-issued money can be used as reserves for commercial banks, the proportion of government bonds used as collateral for Fed-issued money, inflation issues, etc.[75]

After a tense day on the 21st, the *New York Times* on Monday, the 22nd, carried on its front page an important story entitled "Currency Proposal May Become Law Today," which enthusiastically praised the efficiency of Congress, "with such almost unprecedented speed that the

---

[75] Eustace Mullins, *Secrets of Federal Reserve* (Omnia Veritas Limited, www.omnia-veritas.com) Chapter 3.

joint session corrected the differences between the proposals of the two houses and completed them all this morning." The time period mentioned in this article is around 1:30 a.m. to 4 a.m. on Monday. An important bill that is about to affect every American's life every day is being done in such a hurry and under such pressure that the vast majority of legislators have never had time to read the changes carefully, let alone propose amendments.

At 4:30 a.m. on the 22nd, the final document was sent for printing.

7:00 sharp, final proofreading.

At 2 p.m., the printed document was placed on the councilman's desk and a meeting was called for 4 p.m.

At 4 p.m., the meeting began.

At 6 p.m. sharp, the report of the final joint meeting was presented, by which time most of the parliamentarians had already gone to dinner and there were only a few in the room.

At 7:30 p.m., Glass began his 20-minute speech and then moved into the debate.

Voting began at 11:00 p.m. and was finally approved by the House of Representatives by a vote of 298 to 60.

On the 23rd, two days before Christmas, the Senate voted 43 to 25 (27 absent) to pass the Federal Reserve Act. In return for Wall Street's kindness, President Wilson officially signed the Federal Reserve Act just one hour after it passed the Senate.

Wall Street and the Financial City of London were in an uproar.

Rep. Lindbergh addressed the House on this day,

> This bill (the Federal Reserve Act) authorizes the largest credit on the planet. When the president signs this bill, the invisible government of money power will be legalized. The people won't know this in the short term, but they will see it all in a few years. In time, the people will need another declaration of independence to free themselves from the power of money. This monetary power will be able to ultimately control Congress. Wall Street cannot deceive us if our senators and congressmen do not deceive Congress. If we have a Congress of the people, the people will have stability (of life). Congress' biggest crime is its monetary system bill (the Federal Reserve Act). This banking bill is the worst legislative crime of our time. The

> *bipartisanship and secret meetings have once again deprived the people of the opportunity to benefit from their own government.*[76]

Bankers have been raving about the bill, with Oliver Sands, president of American National Bank, enthusiastically saying,

> *The passage of this currency bill will have a beneficial impact on the country as a whole, and its operation will be beneficial to business activities. In my opinion, this is the beginning of an era of general prosperity.*

Senator Aldrich, the originator of the Federal Reserve, revealed in an interview with him in the July 1914 issue of *The Independent.*

Prior to this bill (the Federal Reserve Act), bankers in New York could only control money in the New York area. Now they can dominate the bank reserves of an entire nation.

After more than 100 years of intense battles with the U.S. government, the international bankers finally achieved their goal of taking complete control of the national currency issuing power in the United States, and the Bank of England's model was finally replicated successfully in the United States.

Who owns the Federal Reserve?

For many years, exactly who owns the Fed has been a taboo subject, with the Fed itself always vague. Like the Bank of England, the Federal Reserve keeps the shareholder situation strictly secret. Rep. Wright Patman (R-Ky.) served as chairman of the House Banking and Currency Committee for 40 years, and for 20 of those years, he repeatedly sponsored proposals to abolish the Federal Reserve, and he has also been trying to discover exactly who owns the Fed.

The secret has finally been discovered. After nearly half a century of research, Eustace Mullins, author of *Secrets of the Federal Reserve*, finally obtained 12 of the Federal Reserve Bank's original corporate business licenses (Organization Certificates), which clearly document the share composition of each Federal Reserve Bank.

---

[76] Congressman Charles Lindberg Sr. Speech on floor of the Congress, December 23, 1913.

The Federal Reserve Bank of New York, which is the de facto controller of the Federal Reserve System, recorded on its May 19, 1914 filing with the Comptroller of the Currency a total share issue of 20,3053 shares, of which.

National City Bank of New York, which is controlled by Rockefeller and Kuhnreppo, has the largest stake with 30,000 shares.

J.P. Morgan's First National Bank owns 10,000 shares.

When the two companies merged to form Citibank in 1955, it owned nearly a quarter of the Federal Reserve's Bank of New York, which effectively decided the nominee for Fed chairman, the appointment of the U.S. president was little more than a rubber stamp, and congressional hearings were more of a walk-through show.

Paul Warburg's National Commercial Bank of New York owns 10,000 shares.

Hanover Bank, of which the Rothschild family is a director, owns 10,000 shares.

Chase National Bank owns 6,000 shares.

Chemical Bank owns 6,000 shares.

Together, the six banks owned 40 percent of the Federal Reserve's Bank of New York, and by 1983 they owned a combined 53 percent of the stock. After adjusting, their holdings are: 15% at Citi, 14% at Chase Manhattan, 9% at JPMorgan Trust, 7% at Hanover Manufacturing, and 8% at Hanover Bank.[77]

The Federal Reserve Bank of New York has a registered capital of hundreds of millions of dollars, and it remains a mystery as to whether or not these banks have paid that money. Some historians believe that they paid only half in cash, others believe that they didn't put out any cash at all, but simply paid by check, while their own accounts with the Federal Reserve, which actually operated as a "paper as collateral for the issuance of paper," had only a few numbers to change. No wonder some historians have ridiculed the Federal Reserve banking system as neither "federal" nor "reserve" nor bank.

---

[77] Eustace Mullins, *The Secrets of the Federal Reserve* (John McLaughlin 1993) p178.

On June 15, 1978, the U.S. Senate Committee on Government Affairs issued a report on the interlocking interests of major U.S. corporations, which revealed that the aforementioned banks had 470 directorships in 130 of the most major U.S. corporations, with an average of one directorship in each major corporation belonging to bankers.

Of these, Citibank controls 97 board seats, J. P. Morgan controls 99, Hanover Bank controls 96, Chase Manhattan controls 89, and Hannover Manufacturing controls 89.

On September 3, 1914, the *New York Times* published the composition of the shares of the major banks at the time of the Federal Reserve's sale.

National City Bank of New York issued 250,000 shares, James Stillman owns 47,498 shares, J.P. Morgan & Co. 14,500 shares, William Rockefeller 10,000 shares and John Rockefeller 1750 shares.

The National Bank of Commerce of New York issued 250,000 shares, George Baker owned 10,000 shares, J. P. Morgan & Co. 7,800 shares, Mary Harriman 5650 shares, Paul Warburg 3,000 shares, Jacob Schiff 1,000 shares, J. P. Morgan Jr. 1,000 shares.

Chase Bank, George Baker owns 13408 shares.

Hanover Bank, James Stillman owns 4000 shares and William Rockefeller has 1540.

Since the creation of the Federal Reserve in 1914, irrefutable facts have shown that bankers have manipulated the financial lifeblood, the industrial and commercial lifeblood, and the political lifeblood of America, as they did in the past and as they still do today. And all of these Wall Street bankers have close ties to the Rothschilds in the City of London.

Benjamin Strong, president of Bankers Trust, has been selected as the first chairman of the board of directors of the Federal Reserve Bank of New York.

> *"Under Strong's control, the Fed system has formed an interlocking (interlocking) relationship with the Bank of England and the Bank of France, Benjamin Strong died suddenly as a director of the Federal Reserve Bank of New York in 1928, while Congress was investigating the secret meetings*

between Federal Reserve directors and European Central Bank giants that led to the Great Depression of 1929. "[78]

First Board of Directors of the Federal Reserve

By his own admission later, Wilson was allowed to name only one Fed director; the rest were selected by bankers in New York. In the course of Paul Warburg's nomination and appointment to the Board, the Senate asked him to come to Congress in June 1914 to answer questions, primarily about his role in the preparation of the Federal Reserve Act, which he flatly refused. In his letter to Congress, Paul asserted that if he were asked to answer any questions, it would affect his role on the Fed's board of directors, so he would prefer to reject the nomination of a Fed director. The New York Times immediately jumped to Paul's defense, denouncing in its July 10, 1914, story that the Senate should not question Paul out of thin air.

Paul was naturally a central figure in the Fed system, except that he was only afraid that no second person at the time knew exactly how the Fed was supposed to function. In the face of his assertiveness, Congress had to bow its head and present a list of all the questions that could be provided in advance, and if Paul felt that certain questions "would affect his role," he could withhold answers. Paul finally reluctantly agreed, but asked to meet informally.

The Committee asked: I know you are a Republican, but when Mr. Roosevelt ran, you became a sympathizer of Mr. Wilson and supported him (Democrat)?

Paul W: Yes.

The committee asked: but your brother (Felix Warburg) is supporting Taft (Republican)?

Paul W: Yes.[79]

Interestingly, the three partners at Kuhn Loeb & Co. supported three different presidential candidates, with Otto Kahn supporting

---

[78] Ferdinand Lundberg, *America's 60 families* (Halcyon House, 1939).

[79] Eustace Mullins, *The Secrets of the Federal Reserve* (John McLaughlin 1993) Chapter 3.

Roosevelt Sr. Paul's explanation that the three of them did not interfere with each other's political philosophy because "finance has nothing to do with politics". Paul successfully passed a congressional hearing to become the first director of the Federal Reserve and later became vice chairman of the board.

In addition to Paul, the four other Board members appointed are.

Adolph Miller is an economist from the Rockefeller-funded University of Chicago and the Morgan-funded Harvard University.

Charles Hamlin, who was Assistant Secretary of the Treasury.

Frederick Delano, a relative of Roosevelt and railroad banker.

W. P. G Harding, President, First National Bank of Atlanta.

President Wilson's own nominee, Thomas Jones, was found by reporters to be under investigation and prosecution by the U.S. Department of Justice, and later Jones himself moved to withdraw from the board nomination.

The other two members of the Federal Reserve are the Treasury Secretary and the Monetary Auditor.

The Little Known Federal Advisory Council

The Federal Advisory Council (FAC) is a secret remote control device that Paul Warburg has crafted to manipulate the Federal Reserve Board. In more than 90 years of operation of the Federal Reserve, the Federal Advisory Committee has done an excellent job of realizing Paul's vision of the year, and little attention has been paid to the institution and its operations, and there is no extensive literature to examine.

In 1913, Congressman Glass pushed the concept of the Federal Advisory Committee hard in the House of Representatives, saying,

> "There can be no such thing as evil in this. Four times a year (the Federal Reserve Board) talks to an advisory committee of bankers, with each member representing his or her Federal Reserve district. Is there anything more protective of the public interest than this arrangement?"

Congressman Glass is a banker himself, and he has not explained or offered any evidence that bankers have ever protected the public interest in the history of the United States.

The Federal Advisory Committee, composed of one representative from each of the 12 regional banks of the Federal Reserve, meets four times a year with members of the Federal Reserve Board of Directors in Washington, D.C. The bankers make various monetary policy "recommendations" to the Federal Reserve directors, each banker represents the economic interests of the region, each has the same voting rights, in theory is simply impeccable, but in the fierce and cruel reality of the banking industry is completely different set of rules.

It is hard to imagine a small Cincinnati banker sitting at a conference table with international financial giants such as Paul Warburg and JPMorgan, making "monetary policy recommendations" to these giants, and either one of these two giants pulling a check out of his pocket and drawing two strokes on it is enough to make the small banker lose his life. In fact, the survival of each of the small and medium-sized banks in each of the 12 Federal Reserve regions depends entirely on the gifts of Wall Street's five banking giants, who have deliberately turned over large transactions with European banks to their own local "satellite banks", which have naturally become more subservient to these high-return businesses, and who also own shares in these smaller banks. When these small banks "representing the interests of their respective regions" sit down with the Big Five to discuss U.S. monetary policy, the outcome of that discussion is predictable.

Although the Federal Advisory Committee's "recommendations" are not mandatory binding on the Fed's director decisions, but the Wall Street 5 giants go to great lengths to Washington four times a year, not just to have coffee with a few Fed directors. You know, it would be strange for a super busy person like JPMorgan, who is a director of 63 companies, to have their "advice" not taken into account and still be happy to go back and forth.

Where is the truth?

The vast majority of Americans do not really understand how international lenders operate. The Fed's books have never been audited. It operates entirely outside of congressional control and it manipulates the credit (supply) of the United States.
—Senator Barry Goldwater

In order to create high prices, the Fed simply needs to lower interest rates to expand credit and create a thriving stock market. Once business has become accustomed to this interest rate environment, the Fed will in turn suspend this boom by arbitrarily raising interest rates.

It (the Fed and the bankers who own it) can either make the market's price pendulum swing gently by a slight rate hike, or it can make the market's price fluctuate dramatically by a violent rate hike, and in either case, it will have inside information about the financial situation and know in advance about the coming change.

It is the most bizarre and dangerous (market information) prophetic power that any government has ever given, and that a privileged few have.

> *The system is private, and the whole point of its operation is to use other people's money to maximize profit.*
> *They know in advance when to create panic to create the situation that is best for them. They equally know when to stop panicking. When they controlled finance, inflation and deflation were equally efficient in achieving their ends.*
> —Rep. Charles Lindbergh

> *Each dollar in circulation in Federal Reserve Notes (dollars) represents a dollar of debt owed to the Federal Reserve.*
> —Monetary Report, House of Representatives Committee on Banking and Currency

> *Federal Reserve regional banks are not government agencies, but independent, privately owned and locally controlled corporations.*
> —Case: Levis v. United States Government, Ninth Circuit, 1982

> *The Federal Reserve is one of the most corrupt institutions in the world. All of you who can hear me (the congressional speech), not one of you is unaware that our country is actually ruled by international bankers.*
> *Some people think the Federal Reserve Bank is an agency of the US government. They (the Federal Reserve Banks) are not government agencies. They are private credit monopolies, and the Fed is exploiting the American people for its own benefit and that of foreign crooks.*
> —Congressman McFadden.

When you and I write a check, we have to have enough money in our account to cover the amount of the check. However, when the Fed writes a check, there is no money in the account to back it up. When the Fed writes checks, it is creating money.
—Federal Reserve Bank of Boston

From 1913 to 1949, the Fed's assets skyrocketed from billions of dollars to $45 billion, money that went directly into the pockets of Fed bank shareholders.
—Eustace Mullins

So many presidents have repeatedly warned about the threat of money power, so many congressional records and legal cases clearly illustrate the private nature of the Federal Reserve, but how many Americans, Chinese and others know this? That's the scary part of the problem! We thought that the "free and impartial" authoritative Western news media would report the truth, but the truth is the mass of facts that they have deliberately "filtered out". What about American textbooks? The fact is that various foundations named after international bankers are picking "content health" textbooks for the next generation of Americans.

Before President Wilson died, he admitted that he had been "lied to" about the Federal Reserve, guiltily stating,

"I had inadvertently destroyed my country."

When the Federal Reserve officially began operations on October 25, 1914, World War I broke out, another perfectly timed "coincidence" and the shareholders of the Federal Reserve were destined to make a fortune!

Summary

★The 7 Wall Street bigwigs were the real behind-the-scenes movers in the creation of the Fed, and between them and their secret coordination with the European Rothschilds, they eventually established the Bank of England's version of a flippancy in America.

★J.P. Morgan is the chief agent of the Rothschilds' interests in the United States.

★The Rothschild family supported Rockefeller's expansion plans, which ultimately helped him to completely monopolize the U.S. oil industry.

★The Rothschild family supported Kuhn Loeb & Co. as one of the most prominent investment banks in the United States in the late 19th and early 20th centuries.

★Morgan strongly supports James Hill's bid for control of the Midwest Railroad.

★In the banking crisis of 1907, JPMorgan "pumped" and "released" water in the market, eating the Tennessee Mining and Iron Works at ultra-low prices.

★The simple and easily exploited Wilson was smoothly elected President of the United States, thanks to the machinations of the bankers.

★Bankers are "fixing things in the dark" and making the Federal Reserve Act win over the public.

★Bankers manipulate the financial lifeblood of the United States, the lifeblood of industry and commerce, and the lifeblood of politics through the Federal Reserve.

CHAPTER IV

"World War I" and the Great Recession: "Harvest time" for international bankers

> *"The real threat to our Republic is this invisible government, which is like a giant octopus, wrapping its countless slimy tentacles around our cities, states and nations. The head of this octopus is the Rockefeller's Standard Oil Group and a small group of financial oligarchs with great energy known as international bankers who actually manipulate the US government to satisfy their own selfish desires.*
>
> *Controlling the government by controlling the money supply makes it easier to exploit the citizens and resources of a country. That's why these big families have been doing everything they can from the very beginning of this country to keep power (they play with our "leaders") and wealth (they draw social wealth through the Federal Reserve's currency issuance) highly concentrated.*
>
> *These international bankers and the Rockefeller Standard Oil Group control most of the newspapers and magazines in this country. They use the op-eds of these newspapers to clamp down on government officials, and for those who won't budge, they use public opinion to drive those officials out of government institutions.*
>
> *They (bankers) actually control both parties (Republicans and Democrats), draft (bipartisan) political platforms, control political leaders, appoint heads of private companies, and use all means to plant candidates at the top of government who are submissive to their corrupt big business."*[80]
>
> —John Hylan, Mayor of New York City, 1927

War costs money, and the bigger the war the more money it costs, and that's a well known fact. The question is, who spends whose money? Since European and

---

[80] Former New York City Mayor John Hylan speaking in Chicago and quoted in the March 27, 1927, *New York Times*.

American governments do not have the power to issue money, governments must and can only borrow money from bankers. It is no wonder that war has always been a favorite of bankers, when it consumes materials at a burning rate, when it makes belligerents persist even when they have to work hard for money, and when it makes governments at all costs finance bankers without any conditions. They plan wars, they provoke wars, they finance wars, and the magnificent edifices of the international bankers are never built on the ruins of a pillow of death.

Another way for international bankers to make a lot of money is to create a recession. The first was to expand credit, blow up the bubble, wait for the people's wealth to go into a speculative frenzy, and then pound silver, creating a recession and a plunge in assets. When the price of quality assets plummeted to a tenth or even a hundredth of the normal price, they went on to buy them at super cheap prices, which in international bankers' terms is called "shearing". When the private central bank was established, the "shearing" operation reached an unprecedented level of intensity and scope.

The most recent "shearing" operation took place in 1997 with the Asian "Little Dragons" and "Little Tigers". Whether China, the big fat sheep, can finally avoid the doom of the "sheep shearing" depends on whether or not China will seriously study the shocking tragedy of the "sheep shearing" that happened in history.

The most fundamental difference between the full entry of foreign banks into China and the previous one is that the former state-owned banks, while having the impulse to drive asset inflation to make profits, had no malicious intention or ability to create deflation to blood wash the people's wealth. The reason why there has never been a major economic crisis in New China since its establishment is that no one has the subjective intent and objective ability to create one with malicious intent. When international bankers entered China in full force, the situation changed radically.

Without the Federal Reserve, there would be no World War I

Kissinger has an impressive comment on the outbreak of World War I in his famous book, Great Diplomacy, when he says,

> *"The surprising thing about the outbreak of World War I was not that it was merely an event that seemed insignificant compared to other previous crises, but that it (the war) dragged on for so long."*[81]

On 28 June 1914, Archduke Ferdinand, Crown Prince of the Habsburg dynasty, the orthodox European royal family, visited Bosnia, which had been annexed by Austria in 1908, and was assassinated by a young Serbian assassin. This was originally an act of revenge planned by a simple terrorist organization, and no one could have imagined at the time that it would be the trigger for a world class war involving more than 30 countries, involving 1.5 billion people and more than 30 million casualties.

Since the Franco-Prussian War, France and Germany have become world enemies, and when Britain had to emerge from the "glorious isolation" of the continental policy, it was faced with the situation of Germany being strong and France being weak. Germany is already the number one power in Europe, and if left unchecked, it is bound to become a major problem for Britain. Thus, Britain, along with Russia, which was also scornful of Germany, concluded the Triple Entente with France, and Germany allied itself with Austria, and the two rival European blocs took shape.

The two camps are constantly expanding their military readiness and maintaining large standing armies, and governments are in deep debt as a result.

> *"A detailed European public debt revenue report shows that interest payments and principal repayments on various bonds run into the hundreds of millions of dollars a year. European countries are so deeply entrenched financially that governments can't help but wonder if war, for all its terrible possibilities, might be a more worthwhile option than such an expensive and unstable peace. If Europe's military preparations do not end in war, they are bound to end in the bankruptcy of governments."*[82]

From 1887 to 1914, this unstable and costly peace stalemated, with highly armed but on the verge of bankruptcy, European governments

---

[81] Henry Kissinger, *Diplomacy* (Simon & Schuster; Reprint edition April 4, 1995) Chapter 8.

[82] *Quarterly Journal of Economics*, April 1887.

still looking on in anger. As the saying goes, when the cannon goes off, it's ten thousand taels of gold, and the European banking system, developed and established by the Rothschilds to provide credit to opposing parties, contributed fully to this military confrontation.

The war was actually fought with money and food, and by 1914 it was clear that the major European countries could no longer afford a major war. Although they have a large standing army, a universal system of military mobilization, and a modern weapons system, their economies cannot afford to support the enormous costs of war. As the Russian Privy Council Minister pointed out in his speech to the Tsar in February 1914,

> *"the cost of fighting will undoubtedly be more than Russia's limited financial resources can afford. We will inevitably have to borrow from our allies and neutral countries, but at a great cost. If the outcome of the war is unfavourable to our country, the economic consequences of defeat will be incalculable and the nation's economy will be brought to a complete standstill. Even a victory in the war would be extremely detrimental to our finances, and Germany would not be able to compensate us for our military expenditures after a defeat. The peace treaty will be subject to British interests and will not give the German economy a chance to recover sufficiently to pay our debts, even long after the war is over."*[83]

A massive war is unthinkable under the circumstances. If there was a real war, it would only be partial, short-lived, and low-level, probably more like the 1870 Franco-Prussian War, which lasted about 10 months. Such a war outcome, however, could only ease, not calm, the antagonistic situation in Europe. Thus, the time for war was only delayed in an unstable and costly peace until the Federal Reserve was established.

The United States, across the ocean, although by then the world's number one industrial power, with a large industrial production capacity and abundant resources, was until 1913 a country dependent on foreign debt, with little access to credit abroad. The reason for this is the lack of a central bank and the difficulty for New York bankers to pool the nation's financial resources (Mobilization of Credit). However,

---

[83] Henry Kissinger, *Diplomacy* (Simon & Schuster; Reprint edition April 4, 1995) Chapter 8.

the bankers' nature led them to take a keen interest in mass warfare, which could undoubtedly bring lucrative profits to the bankers. When the Federal Reserve Act was passed, the international bankers acted immediately, and on August 3, 1914, Rothschild's bank in France sent a telegram to Morgan suggesting that $100 million in credit be immediately organized for French purchases of supplies from the United States. Wilson was immediately heard to object, and Secretary of State William Jennings Bryan denounced the loan as "the worst kind of illegal transaction".

Germany had no political or economic rivalry with the United States, which at the time had about 8 million German descendants, or about 10 percent of the population, and at the beginning of the nation's existence, German was almost the official language of the United States, and German-Americans had a great deal of political influence. In addition, the Irish immigrants in the United States did not like Britain, and the United States government had been at war with Britain several times, so at the beginning of the war, the United States government took a wait-and-see attitude towards the war between Britain and France and Germany. The U.S. government appears much more calm and normal compared to bankers who are in a hurry like ants on a hot pot. It is surprising that the bankers are actively advocating a declaration of war against Germany, while the government is firmly anti-war and strictly neutral.

At this point, the bankers came up with the expedient of distinguishing between lending for the purpose of offering bonds to the Allies and providing credit to the Allies for the purchase of American goods. Under the coercion of the bankers, Wilson could only agree to the latter. As the time for re-election gradually approached, Wilson gradually tilted toward the bankers on the issue of entering the war.

On December 23, 1913, the Federal Reserve Act was passed and the conditions were finally ripe for a world-level war to break out. The long-delayed war machine of which Dr. Kissinger speaks can finally be activated.

On November 16, 1914, the Federal Reserve officially began operations, and on December 16, Davidson, Morgan's right-hand man, came to England to negotiate with Herbert H. Asquith, then Prime Minister of England, for credit from the United States, and on January 15, 1915, JPMorgan entered into a credit agreement with England in the amount of £10 million, which at the time was a pretty big deal for the

United States, and no one at the time could have predicted that the final loan would amount to an astounding $3 billion! JPMorgan took a 1% fee, $30 million went into its pockets, and JPMorgan ate its fill in the war. In the spring of the same year, JPMorgan signed another credit agreement with the French government.

In September 1915, the time had come to test Wall Street's ability to become the world's financial center, and the $500 million Anglo-French Loan operation officially kicked off. President Wilson, who was originally adamantly opposed, could not stand to be pinned down by bankers and cabinet members on both sides, and his new Secretary of State, Robert Lansing, warned,

> *"Without loans, the result will be constrained production, industrial decline, idle capital and labor, massive bankruptcy, fiscal crisis, and boiling public discontent and breeding discontent."*[84]

Wilson could hear a cold sweat and had to give in again. For this unprecedented bond sale, Wall Street bankers were also at their mercy, with 61 bond underwriters and 1570 financial institutions joining the offering.[85] This is an extremely difficult task, especially when it comes to marketing these bonds to the American Midwest. The American people generally do not see the war in Europe as having anything directly to do with them and are reluctant to throw money at the war in Europe. To dispel such doubts, the bankers vigorously claimed that the money would stay in the United States. Despite all the methods used, only one Chicago bank in the Midwest was willing to join the Wall Street camp, an act that immediately angered local German depositors, who launched a boycott of the banks. By the end of 1915, there were still hundreds of millions of dollars of bonds unsold.

When the war came to a critical point, in order to get more money, the British government announced that it would tax the interest income on American bonds held by British nationals, which the British immediately sold at cheap prices. The Bank of England quickly piled up American bonds, the British government immediately had their American agent JPMorgan sell these American bonds in full on Wall Street, American investors were naturally receptive to their own bonds,

---

[84] Ron Chernow, *The House of Morgan* (New York: Grove Press 1990) p. 198.

[85] *Ibid.*, p. 200.

and soon $3 billion in bonds turned into cash, and Britain got another huge sum to shore up the war. But the 100-plus years of creditor status Britain had accumulated against the United States went up in smoke. Since then, the Anglo-American debt relationship has undergone a fundamental change.

The credit of the United States was as if on fire, and the war began to spread rapidly, and the intensity of the war rose sharply. At the Battle of the Marne alone, the Allied Powers consumed 200,000 rounds of artillery in one day, and mankind finally saw what a terrible and protracted war could be under a modern system of industrial production and logistics, if modern financial means were added.

It is no wonder that war has always been a favorite of bankers, when it consumes materials at a burning rate, when it makes belligerents persist even when they have to sell everything, and when it makes governments lend money to banks at all costs and without conditions.

Strang's manipulation of the wartime Federal Reserve

Benjamin Strong began to attract public attention in 1904 when he became chairman of the Bankers Trust. At the time, Davidson, a JPMorgan crony, was increasingly concerned about the rising trust companies that were able to attract capital at higher interest rates because they had a broader reach than commercial banks and were subject to less government regulation. In order to cope with this new competition, Davidson, with Morgan's approval, also took up the trust business in 1903, and Strang became Davidson's specific executor. In the ensuing storm of 1907, Bankers Trust also joined in the rescue of other financial institutions, for which Strang rose to fame.

After the establishment of the Federal Reserve in 1913, Davidson and Paul Warburg found Strang for a deep conversation, wanting Strang to take the key position of chairman of the Federal Reserve Bank of New York, Strang readily agreed. From then on, Strang became the head of the Fed system in essence, JPMorgan, Paul, Schiff and other Wall Street giants of the intentions of the Fed has been unfailingly followed through.

Strang quickly adapted to his new role by setting up the informal Fed Directors Forum organization, which met regularly to discuss the wartime Fed's guidelines for action. He manipulated the Fed's monetary policy in a very clever way and centralized the power that was spread across the 12 regional Fed banks into the hands of the Fed's Bank of New York. The Fed system ostensibly allows each of the 12 local Fed banks to set their own discount rate and commercial paper collateral policies based on the actual needs of the region, in other words, the local Fed board of directors has the authority to determine which commercial paper can be used as collateral for which discount rate. By 1917, at least 13 different types of commercial paper mortgage guidelines were established.[86]

However, because of the war, the Fed's Bank of New York actually only used the rapidly increasing Treasury debt as collateralized notes. Because Treasuries were much larger than other commercial paper combined and growing rapidly, they quickly marginalized the note collateralization policies of banks elsewhere in the Fed. The "open market operation" under Strang's control soon established Treasuries as the primary and only collateralized instrument, thus taking full control of the entire Federal Reserve system.

The power of the central bank began to emerge as a result of the massive bond issue that financed the war in Europe, which reduced the circulation of U.S. currency dramatically. The U.S. government began to increase the national debt by a large amount, and the Federal Reserve also ate into it with astonishing appetite, the huge amount of Federal Reserve notes like a river to swoop into circulation, compensating for the monetary tightening caused by the European war bonds. The price was the plummeting U.S. national debt, with the result that in just four years (1916–1920) when the Federal Reserve began operating at full speed, the U.S. national debt skyrocketed 25 times from $1 billion to $25 billion, all of which was secured by the future taxes of the American people, with the result that in the war, the bankers made their money big while the people paid, worked and bled.

---

[86] Glyn Davies, *History of Money from Ancient Times to the Present Day* (University of Wales Press 2002), Chapter 9.

"For the sake of democracy and moral principles", Wilson went to war

When the German ambassador to Turkey asked his American counterpart, in disbelief, why the United States was at war with Germany, the American ambassador replied, "We Americans are in this war for moral principles." Such an answer puzzled the world. Dr. Kissinger explained it this way:

> "The United States, which since its founding has always prided itself on being different, has developed two conflicting attitudes in its diplomacy: one is that the United States has perfected democracy at home, and the other is that American values have made Americans feel obligated to promote those values to the world."[87]

It is true that the American experience was unique and that American democratic values were well known, but to suggest that the United States entered the First World War only for moral and ideological reasons is probably an understatement on the part of Dr. Kissinger.

In a confidential letter to President Wilson on March 5, 1917, Walter Hines Page, the U.S. ambassador to Great Britain, said,

> "I think the pressure of the coming crisis has exceeded the capacity of JPMorgan to provide loans to Britain and France. The greatest help we can offer to our allies is credit. Unless we go to war with Germany, our government will not be able to provide direct credit (to the Allies)."[88]

By this time, the U.S. heavy industrial system had been preparing for war for a year, and the U.S. Army and Navy departments had been purchasing military equipment in large quantities since 1916. To further increase the wealth, bankers and the politicians in their hands began to consider more measures,

> "The current conflict (World War I) has forced us to consider further developing the concept of an income tax on income, an

---

[87] *Ibid.*, p. 506.

[88] Henry Kissinger, *Diplomacy* (Simon & Schuster; Reprint edition April 4, 1995) Chapter 9.

important untapped resource. The income tax bill has been established to meet the needs of the war. "[89]

Note that the income tax here is on corporate income, not on personal income. Bankers tried twice in 1916 to pass a bill requiring personal income to be taxed, but both times it was rejected by the Supreme Court. There has never been a legal basis for the requirement that personal income be taxed in the U.S. In the film America: Freedom To Fascism, which opened across the U.S. on July 28, 2006, famed American director Aaron Russo, a six-time Oscar nominee, demonstrates this ironclad truth with a stunning shot. The film caused a strong shock to the audience when it was screened at the 2006 Cannes Film Festival, and everyone's first feeling after being confronted with a real-life American government and the financial forces behind it that are completely different from the American media propaganda is disbelief. Only five of the more than 3,000 movie theaters in the U.S. dared to show the film publicly. Still, when the blockbuster was put on the Internet, it made a huge impact in the United States, with 940,000 people downloading the film and the 8,100 people involved in rating it almost unanimously giving it the highest rating.[90]

On October 13, 1917, President Wilson made an important speech in which he said,

> *"The imminent task is the necessity of thoroughly mobilizing the banking resources of the United States. The pressure and power (to lend to allies) must be carried by every banking institution in this country. I believe such banking cooperation is a patriotic duty at this time, and the Fed's member banks are a testament to such unique and important patriotism. "[91]*

It is not surprising that Wilson, a university professor with a strong tinge of idealism, is slightly pedantic but not stupid, and knows who put him in the White House and how to return the favor. President Wilson himself did not believe in the jihad of so-called "democracy to save the world" and later admitted that "world wars are economic competition".

---

[89] Eustace Mullins, The Secrets of the Federal Reserve – The London Connection (Omnia Veritas Ltd, www.omnia-veritas.com) Chapter 8.

[90] Cordell Hull, *Memoirs* (Macmillan, New York, 1948) v1 p. 76.

[91] Ron Chernow, *The House of Morgan* (New York: Grove Press 1990) Chapter 10.

The fact is that the United States has provided $3 billion in loans to associate countries and $6 billion in exports of goods, a huge amount that has not been repaid. If Germany wins, the Allied bonds in the hands of the bankers will be worthless, and Morgan, Rockefeller, Paul Warburg, and Schiff will do everything they can to push America into war to protect their loans.

Bankers of war money

When the United States became involved in the war on April 6, 1917, Wilson gave the main power of the country to the three sets of men who made the most of his campaign: Paul Warburg took control of the U.S. banking system, Bernard Baruch became chairman of the War Industries Board, and Eugene Meyer controlled the War Finance Corporation.

Warburg Brothers again!

Paul's older brother, Max Warburg, was then head of German intelligence, while Paul was America's top financial decision-maker and vice chairman of the Federal Reserve; his third brother, Felix, was a senior partner at Repo Kuhn and his fourth brother, Fritz, was chairman of the Hamburg Metal Exchange and had made secret peace with Russia on behalf of Germany. All four of the brothers were at the top of the Jewish banking family.

Information about the Paul brothers, a secret U.S. Navy report dated December 12, 1918, states:

> *"Paul Warburg: New York, of German descent, naturalized as an American citizen in 1911, honored by the German Kaiser in 1912. Served as Vice Chairman of the Federal Reserve. There was a brother who served as head of the German intelligence service."*[92]

Another report mentions,

---

[92] Eustace Mullins, *The Secrets of the Federal Reserve – The London Connection* (Omnia Veritas Ltd, www.omnia-veritas.com) Chapter 8.

"The German Kaiser (Wilhelm II) once tapped the table and growled at Max, 'Are you always right?' But then still listen carefully to Max's views on finance."[93]

Curiously, Paul had resigned from his position at the Federal Reserve in May 1918 and is not mentioned in this report. In June 1918, after resigning from the Federal Reserve, Paul wrote a note to Wilson:

"I have two brothers who are bankers in Germany. They are naturally helping their country as much as they can now, just as I am helping mine."[94]

Bernard Baruch: the czar of American industry during the war

Starting out as a speculator, Baruch merged six major American tobacco companies to form the Consolidated Tobacco Company in 1896, and he later helped the Guggenheim family merge the American copper mining industry. He also took control of New York's transportation system in conjunction with Harriman under Schiff.

In 1901, with his brother, he founded the Baruch Brothers Company.

When President Wilson appointed Baruch chairman of the American Industrial Commission of Wartime in 1917, he immediately had the power of life and death over all American industrial companies. His purchases amounted to $10 billion a year and almost single-handedly determined the price of the U.S. government's war materiel purchases. Later, at a 1935 congressional hearing, Baruch said,

"President Wilson handed me a letter authorizing me to take over any factory or industrial enterprise. I had some bad blood with Judge Gary, the president of U.S. Steel, and when I showed him the letter, he said 'it looks like we need to work out our beefs,' and he did."[95]

Some members of Congress questioned Baruch's qualifications to exercise the power of American industry to kill, arguing that he was

---

[93] Max Warburg, *Memoirs of Max Warburg*, Berlin, 1936.

[94] David Farrar, *The Warburgs* (Michael Joseph, Ltd., London, 1974).

[95] Baruch's Testimony before the Nye Committee, Sep 13, 1937.

neither an industrialist nor had spent a day in a factory, and that he himself had described his profession as a "speculator" during congressional hearings. The *New Yorker* reported that Baruch once made $750,000 in one day after learning about the false news of peace circulating in Washington.

Eugene Meyer's Wartime Finance Corporation

Eugene Meyer's father was a partner in the prestigious international bank Lazard Freres, and Eugene had an extraordinary passion for public office. He had co-founded an Alaskan gold mining company with Baruch and had conspired together on some other financial matters, and was an old acquaintance of sorts.

One of the important missions of the Wartime Finance Corporation was to issue U.S. Treasury bonds to provide financial support for the war.

There is no more jaw-dropping act of Eugene's wartime finance company than making false accounts. When the company was later investigated by Congress, the company made ad hoc revisions to its accounts almost every night and gave them to congressional investigators the next day. Two investigations against the firm in 1925 and 1930, led by Congressman McFadden, uncovered a large number of problem accounts:

> *"duplicate bonds numbered 2,314 and duplicate discount coupons numbered 4,698, with denominations ranging from $50 to $10,000, with redemption dates ending in July 1924. Some of these duplications are the result of mistakes, others are the result of falsification."*[96]

It is no wonder that after World War I, Eugene was able to buy the Allied Chemical and Dye Corporation and later the *Washington Post*.

It is estimated that Eugene's false accounts contributed to at least hundreds of millions of dollars in the difference in the national debt.[97]

---

[96] Eustace Mullins, *The Secrets of the Federal Reserve – The London Connection* (Omnia Veritas Ltd, www.omnia-veritas.com) Chapter 8.

[97] *Ibid.*

Edward Stettinius: the founding father of the American military-industrial complex

Edward Stettinius, a meticulous man with a penchant for detail, made a fortune in Chicago in his early years as a grain speculator. He was seen by Morgan during the war and headed the Export Department, which was primarily responsible for arms procurement.

Stettinius became the world's largest consumer during the war, purchasing up to $10 million a day in military supplies, which were then loaded onto ships, insured and shipped to Europe. He spared no effort to increase productivity and transportation efficiency, and at the word of his headquarters at 23 Wall Street, countless agents and manufacturers of military parts poured into his office building, and he set up guards at nearly every door. His monthly purchases are equivalent to the world's gross national product 20 years ago. The Germans never imagined that the United States could move into military industrial production in such a short period of time.

Davidson: Morgan's close friend

Davidson, a senior partner at J.P. Morgan, who had done the work of the JPMorgan Empire, was given the fat piece of meat by the American Red Cross and thus controlled the vast sums of money donated by the American people, which amounted to billions of dollars.

The Peace of Versailles: A 20-year truce

On November 11, 1918, the bloody and brutal First World War finally came to a close. Germany, as a defeated country, would lose 13 per cent of its territory, pay $32 billion in war reparations, plus $500 million in interest per year; export products would be subject to an additional 26 per cent levy and all overseas colonies would be lost; the army would be limited to 100,000 troops, the navy would be limited to six main warships and no offensive weapons such as submarines, aircraft, tanks or heavy artillery would be allowed.

British Prime Minister David Lloyd George has declared that "the Germans' pockets will be searched to find the money," but privately, he admits:

> *"The document (the peace treaty) we have drafted will set the stage for war 20 years from now. When you impose such conditions on the German people, it can only lead to the Germans either not complying with the treaty or waging war."* British Foreign Secretary Lord Curzon shared that view, saying, *"This will not bring peace, this is just a 20-year truce."*

Seeing the agreement, U.S. President Wilson also frowned and said,

> *"If I were German, I don't think I would have signed this agreement."*

The question is not whether politicians are aware of the problem, but whether the "masters" behind them are the real decision makers. Among the bankers who accompanied Wilson to Paris were Paul Warburg, chief financial advisor; J.P. Morgan and his lawyer Frank; Thomas Lemon, senior partner at J.P. Morgan; Baruch, chairman of the wartime Industrial Commission; and the Dulles brothers (one was the head of the later CIA and one was Eisenhower's secretary of state). The British Prime Minister was followed by Sir Philip Sassoon, a direct descendant of the Rothschilds. French Prime Minister Clemenceau's high counsellor was Georges Mandel, whose real name was Jeroboam Rothschild. The chief representative of the German delegation was Max Warburg, Paul's big brother. As the international bankers gathered in Paris, Baron Edmund Rothschild, later the "Father of Israel", provided a warm reception as host, placing the head of the American delegation in his own luxurious estate in Paris.

The Paris Peace Conference was in fact a carnival of international bankers who, after a war bonanza, sowed the seeds of the next war – the Second World War.

"Shearing" and the 1921 agricultural decline in the United States

> *On September 1, 1894, we will stop all loan extensions. On that day, we will claim our money back. We will own and auction off the outstanding property. We will get 2/3 of the farmland west of the Mississippi River and thousands of dollars east of it at a price we set ourselves. Farmers will (lose their land) become hired people, just like in England.*
> 1891 American Bankers Association (recorded in the Congressional Record on April 29, 1913)

"Shearing" is a term used exclusively in banker circles to mean taking advantage of the opportunities created by the boom and bust process to own someone else's property at a fraction of its normal price. When the bankers took control of the money issuing power in the United States and the boom and bust became a process that could be precisely controlled, the act of "shearing" was like an evolution for the bankers from the nomadic stage of hunting for a living to the stable and productive stage of scientific feeding.

World War I brought widespread prosperity to the United States, and large-scale purchases of war materiel greatly boosted American production and services in all industries. The Federal Reserve pumped a lot of money into the economy from 1914 to 1920, and the New York Fed rate fell from 6 percent in 1914 to 3 percent in 1916, and remained there until 1920.

In order to provide loans to the European Allies, bankers conducted four large bond collections, called Liberty Bonds, in the two years 1917 and 1918, with interest rates ranging from an important purpose of these bond issues is to absorb the money and credit that the Fed has severely over-issued.

In the war, the workers were paid high wages, the peasants' food was sold at a high price, and the economic situation of the working class improved considerably. When the war ended, the farmers were left with large amounts of cash in their hands due to frugality in living and spending, and this vast wealth was out of the control of Wall Street bankers. It turns out that Midwestern farmers generally kept their money in conservative local banks, and these small and medium-sized bankers were generally resistant and confrontational to international bankers in New York, neither participating in the Federal Reserve banking system nor supporting war loans to Europe. Wall Street bigwigs have long wanted to find an opportunity to fix these hillbillies, plus the peasants this group of "fat sheep" and fat body, has long looked at the hot Wall Street bankers are ready to do "shearing".

Wall Street bankers first resorted to a "catch-all" ploy by creating an institution called the Federal Farm Loan Board to "encourage" farmers to invest their hard-earned money in the purchase of new land, an organization that would provide long-term loans, which farmers, of course, wanted. As a result, a large number of farmers, coordinated by the organization, applied for long-term loans from international bankers and paid a high percentage of their down payments.

Farmers may never know they have fallen into an elaborate trap.

During the four months from April to July 1920, the industrial and commercial trading sectors received large credit increases to help them through the coming credit crunch. Only the farmers' credit applications were rejected in their entirety. It was an elaborate financial directional blast from Wall Street! Small and medium-sized banks that aim to plunder the wealth of farmers and destroy agricultural areas that refuse to obey the Federal Reserve.

Senate Banking and Currency Committee Chairman Owen (who cosponsored the Federal Reserve Act of 1913) said at the 1939 Senate Silver Hearing, "In the early 1920's, the farmers were very wealthy. They accelerated their mortgage payments and borrowed heavily to buy new land, and in the second half of 1920, a sudden credit and monetary crunch caused them to go bankrupt en masse, and what happened in 1920 (farmer bankruptcy) was the exact opposite of what should have happened."[98]

The over-issuance of credit due to the war was supposed to be resolved gradually over a number of years, but the Board of Directors of the Federal Reserve got together for a secret meeting on May 8, 1920, without the public's knowledge at all. They conspired together for a full day, with as many as 60 pages of minutes, which finally appeared in the Senate papers on February 19, 1923. (Federal Reserve) Class A directors, members of the Federal Reserve Advisory Committee, attended the meeting, but Class B directors, representing business, trade and agriculture, were not invited, and Class C directors, representing the American people, were similarly not invited.

Only the big bankers attended this secret meeting, and their meeting that day led directly to the credit crunch and ultimately to a $15 billion drop in national income the following year, millions of people losing their jobs, and a $20 billion plunge in land and farm values.

Wilson's Secretary of State Brian hit the nail on the head:

> "*The Federal Reserve Bank, which is supposed to be the farmer's most important protector, has become the farmer's*

---

[98] *Ibid.*, Chapter 9.

greatest enemy. The credit crunch on agriculture is a calculated crime. "[99]

After the "shearing" operation on agriculture, after a good harvest, the Midwest's resilient small and medium-sized banks were also destroyed, and the Federal Reserve began to relax the bank.

The International Bankers' 1927 Plot

Benjamin Strong, who took the chairmanship of the Federal Reserve's Bank of New York with the joint support of JPMorgan & Co. and Repo Kuhn, conspired with Norman, the chairman of the Bank of England, on many important events in Anglo-Saxon finance, including the world-wide Great Depression of 1929.

Norman's grandfather and maternal grandfather both served as chairman of the Bank of England, and such an illustrious lineage is unprecedented in British history.

In *The Politics of Money*, author Johnson writes:

> *"As close friends, Strong and Norman often vacationed together in the South of France, and from 1925 to 1928 Strong's monetary easing in New York was a private agreement between him and Norman to keep interest rates in New York lower than in London. For the sake of this international cooperation, Strang deliberately depressed New York's interest rates until irreversible consequences occurred. New York's monetary easing encouraged the U.S. boom of the 1920s and sparked a speculative frenzy.* "[100]

Regarding this secret agreement, the House Stabilization Hearing, led by Congressman McFadden in 1928, conducted an in-depth investigation and concluded that international bankers were creating a collapse in American stocks by manipulating the flow of gold.

Rep. McFadden: Could you briefly state what influenced the final decision of the Federal Reserve Board of Governors (referring to the interest rate cut policy in the summer of 1927)?

---

[99] *Hearst Magazine*, Nov 1923.

[100] Brian Johnson, *The Politics of Money* (New York: McGraw Hill 1970) p. 63.

Fed Director Miller: You asked a question that I can't answer.

McFadden: Perhaps I can be a little clearer about where the advice that led to the decision to change interest last summer came from?

Miller: The three largest European central banks send their representatives to this country. They are the directors of the Bank of England (Norman), Dr. Yalma Shachter (president of the German Central Bank) and Professor Lister of the Bank of France. These gentlemen were meeting with the Fed's Bank of New York. About a week or two later, they showed up in Washington and stayed for most of the day. One night they came to Washington, D.C., and the next day they were received by the directors of the Federal Reserve, who returned to New York that afternoon.

McFadden: Were the Fed's directors present at the luncheon?

Miller: Oh, yes. The Federal Reserve Board of Directors intentionally arranged for everyone to get together.

McFadden: Was that a social event, or was it a serious discussion?

Miller: I think it's mostly a social event. Personally, before the luncheon, I had a long talk with Dr. Yalma Shachter, and also with Professor Lister for half the day, and after the meal, Mr. Norman and I also talked for a while with Strang (Chairman of the Federal Reserve Bank of New York).

McFadden: Was that a formal (Federal Reserve) board meeting of sorts?

Miller: No.

McFadden: Was that just an informal discussion of the outcome of the New York talks?

Miller: I think so. It was just a social event. What I'm saying is in generalities, and so are they (the directors of the European Central Bank).

McFadden: What do they want?

Miller: They are very sincere about various issues. I wanted to talk to Mr. Norman, and we all stayed after dinner, and the others joined in. These gentlemen are so worried about the way the gold standard works that they are eager to see New York's monetary easing and low interest rates, which will stop the flow of gold from Europe to the United States.

Mr. BIDDY: Have these foreign bankers reached an understanding with the board of the Federal Reserve Bank of New York?

Miller: Yes.

Mr. Bidi: These understandings are not officially recorded?

Miller: No. Then the Open Market Policy Committee had a meeting and some of the measures were settled. As I recall, under this plan, about $80 million in notes were bought (issuing base currency) by (the Federal Reserve Bank of New York) in August alone.

McFadden: Such a policy change directly contributed to the most serious financial system anomaly ever seen in this country (the stock market speculation boom of 1927–1929). It seems to me that such a major decision should have an official record in Washington.

Miller: I agree with you.

Rep. Strang: The fact is they came here, they had secret meetings, they gorged themselves, they talked high and mighty, they got the Fed to lower the discount rate, and then they took (our) gold.

Mr. Sturger: Is this policy that has stabilized European currencies but subverted our dollar, is that right?

Miller: Yes, this policy is designed to do just that.[101]

The Federal Reserve Bank of New York is in de facto complete control of the entire Fed, and the Fed's seven-person board in Washington is nothing more than pendulum. European bankers held a week-long substantive secret meeting with the Federal Reserve Bank of New York, and after less than a day in Washington and just socializing, the decisions of the New York secret meeting led to the flow of $500 million worth of gold to Europe, a decision so important that there is no written record of it at all in Washington, and thus the actual status of the seven-member board.

The bubble burst in 1929: another "shearing" operation.

> *"The Federal Reserve tightened money in circulation by one-third from 1929 to 1933, destined for the Great Recession."*

---

[101] The House Stabilization Hearings of 1928.

—Milton Friedman.

Immediately after the secret meeting, the Federal Reserve Bank of New York acted, reducing interest rates from 4 percent to, in 1928 alone, $60 billion in currency to its favored member banks, which pledged their 15-day bank drafts. If all this money were converted into gold, it would be six times the total amount of gold in circulation in the world at the time! The amount of dollars issued in this way is 33 times more than the amount of currency issued by the Federal Reserve Bank of New York by buying notes on the open market! To add to the consternation, in 1929 the Federal Reserve Bank of New York issued another $58 billion in currency to its member banks![102]

The New York stock market at the time allowed dealers to buy stocks for 1% of the money, with the rest of the money being lent by the dealer's bank. When a bank with a huge credit fever meets a greedy, hungry securities dealer, the two really hit it off.

Banks from the Federal Reserve Bank of New York can lend money at about 5% interest, and then lend to securities dealers at 12% interest, eat a full 7% spread, the world has such a beautiful thing!

At this point, it's impossible for New York's stock market to think about not skyrocketing.

In the United States at this time, from North to South, East to West, people were encouraged to take all their savings and "invest" in stocks. Even the politicians in Washington have been mobilized by the bigwigs on Wall Street, with Treasury Secretary Mellon assuring the people in a formal speech that the stock market in New York is not high, and President Coolidge addressing the nation with a speech drafted for him by the bankers and saying it is still safe to buy stocks.

In March 1928, in response to a Senate question, the director of the Federal Reserve replied to a question from the Senate as to whether the securities dealers' loans were excessive:

> *"I'm not in a position to say whether the securities dealers' loans are excessive, but I'm sure they (the securities dealers) tend to be safe and conservative."*

---

[102] Congressional Record, 1932.

On February 6, 1929, Norman of the Bank of England mysteriously came to the United States again, immediately after the Federal Reserve began to abandon the accommodative monetary policy it had been pursuing since 1927. The British bankers seemed to be ready for something big, and the time had come for the American side to step in.

In March 1929, Paul Warburg, the godfather of American finance, warned at the annual meeting of the shareholders of the International Promissory Bank:

> *"If this unbridled greed continues to expand, the eventual collapse will strike not only the speculators themselves, but the entire nation into decline."*[103]

Paul, who had remained silent for three full years of "unbridled greed", suddenly jumped in with a stern warning and, because of his influence and stature, his remarks, as reported by the *New York Times*, instantly caused the markets to panic.

The final death sentence for the stock market came on April 20, 1929, when the *New York Times* of that day published an important message.

The Federal Advisory Committee has formed a resolution and submitted it to the Federal Reserve Board, but their intentions remain strictly confidential. The next move by the Fed's advisory commissioners and the Fed's board of directors remains shrouded in an air of intense mystery. The confidentiality of this unusual meeting was very tight. The journalist could only get some vague answers.[104]

On August 9, 1929, the Federal Reserve raised interest rates to 6 percent, immediately followed by the Federal Reserve Bank of New York raising interest rates for securities dealers from 5 percent to 20 percent, and speculators were instantly caught in the money trap, with no way out but to desperately escape the stock market. The stock market took a sharp turn for the worse, as selling orders swept through the stock market in October and November, and the $160 billion in wealth went

---

[103] Eustace Mullins, *The Secrets of the Federal Reserve – The London Connection* (Omnia Veritas Ltd, www.omnia-veritas.com) Chapter 12.

[104] *New York Times*, April 20, 1929.

up in smoke at once. Close to the sum of all the vast quantities of materials produced by the United States in World War II.

Here's how one Wall Street stockbroker described it that year:

> "The 1929 crisis, caused by a precisely planned, sudden and precipitous reduction in the supply of loans to invest in stocks on the New York money market, was actually a calculated 'shearing' operation against the public by the international money barons."[105]

Faced with a devastated American economy, the *New York Times* of July 4, 1930, could not help but lament that,

> "the prices of raw material commodities have fallen to the level of 1913. A total of 4 million people have lost their jobs due to a surplus of labour and reduced wages. JPMorgan controls the entire Federal Reserve system by controlling the Federal Reserve Bank of New York and the mediocre and weak Federal Reserve Board in Washington."

From 1930 to 1933, a total of 8,812 banks failed, and the vast majority of banks that dared to fight the five major banking families in New York, and did not buy into the Federal Reserve system, went bankrupt.

The Real Plot for the Great Recession

There is no doubt that the stock crash of 1929 was something that was hammered out in a secret meeting in 1927, as interest rates in New York were artificially depressed, London rates were deliberately plucked up, and the spread between the two places led to the flow of gold from the United States to Britain to help Britain and other European countries restore the gold standard.

In fact, European financiers have long known that the plundering of wealth by inflationary means is far more efficient than the interest income derived from lending. The use of gold as the cornerstone of currency issuance and the free conversion of paper money into gold will undoubtedly greatly limit the effectiveness of the bankers' liberalization of inflation as a highly effective weapon. What is puzzling

---

[105] Col. Curtis Dall, *My Exploited Father-in-Law*, Liberty Lobby, 1970.

is why the European financial community, represented by British bankers at the time, wanted to restore the gold standard.

It turns out that the international bankers are playing a big game.

The First World War ended with the defeat of Germany, and the huge war reparations could not, of course, be borne by the German Rothschilds and the Warburg family banks, which not only had to pay a fortune in national disaster. So, the first step was for the German bankers to start the inflationary wealth grinder to quickly plunder the savings of the German people, and mankind saw for the first time the power of hyperinflation.

From 1913 to 1918, during the war, German currency issuance multiplied, with the German mark depreciating only 50 percent relative to the dollar, and from 1921 onwards, the German Central Bank's currency issuance was in a volcanic eruption, increasing fivefold in 1921 over 1918, tenfold in 1922 over 1921, and 72.53 million times in 1923 over 1922. From August 1923 onwards, prices reached astronomical levels, with a loaf of bread or a postage stamp costing up to 100 billion marks. German workers have to pay their wages twice a day and spend it within an hour after they get it.[106]

The German bankers bloodwashed the savings of the middle class and reduced a large number of the mainstream of society to abject poverty overnight, thus laying the mass base for the Nazis to come to power later and deeply planting the seeds of German hatred for Jewish bankers. The suffering of the German people was much deeper than in France after the defeat of the Franco-Prussian War in 1870, and all the incentives for the next, more tragic world war were already in place by 1923.

When the wealth of the Germans had been more or less raided, it was time for the German mark to be stabilized. Under the dispatch of the international bankers, the gold of the American people became a lifeblood to stabilize the German currency.

It was the British banker's turn to make a big move on the second move. Due to frequent German submarine raids in the Atlantic Ocean following the outbreak of World War I in 1914, British ships carrying

---

[106] Glyn Davies, *History of Money from Ancient Times to the Present Day* (University of Wales Press 2002) p. 575.

gold were unable to leave port, resulting in the Bank of England having to declare a temporary halt to gold exchange and the gold standard of the pound being extinct in name only.

In 1924, Churchill, who later became famous in England, became Chancellor of the Exchequer. Churchill, who had no sense of financial matters at all, was prepared to restore the gold standard at the behest of the London bankers on the grounds that it was necessary to defend the pound's absolute authority in world finance, and on 13 May 1925 the Gold Standard Act was passed in Britain. At that time, Britain's national power after the violent consumption of the war has been seriously damaged, its economic strength has been far inferior to the emerging United States, and even in Europe is not a dominant situation, the forced restoration of the gold standard is bound to lead to a strong pound, a serious blow to Britain's export trade has been increasingly uncompetitive, but also caused the decline in domestic prices, shrinking wages, unemployment rate has risen sharply and other economic consequences.

At this time, a generation of Patriarch Keynes came out of nowhere. Keynes, who had served as a delegate to the British Treasury at the 1919 Paris Peace Conference, was adamantly opposed to the draconian terms imposed on Germany and went out of his way to protest by resigning. He advocated the abolition of the gold standard, creating an incompatible situation with the banker power in London. At the British Government's Macmillan Commission to investigate the feasibility of a gold standard, Keynes was impassioned and argued the evils of the gold standard, which in his view was a "relic of barbarity" and a constraint on economic development. Nor did the Bank of England's Norman weaken, insisting that the gold standard is essential for honest bankers, no matter how heavy the burden on the UK, no matter how many sectors are badly damaged, or else the super credibility of London's Financial City bankers. The British people are confused. As in the United States, the London bankers have a bad reputation among the people, and since it is the bankers who support them, it must be bad, and a fierce attack on the views of the bankers should be directed at the people.

And that's the good part of the play.

With Keynes playing the role of a pleader for the people, and the bankers appearing as golden guardians, the duet is so well played that public opinion and the hearts of the people are easily manipulated.

Without Keynes' "prophecy" and the bankers' plan, the British economy plummeted after the restoration of the gold standard, unemployment soared from 3 percent in 1920 to 18 percent in 1926, various strikes followed, the political situation plunged into chaos and the British government faced a serious crisis.

And what the bankers want is a crisis! Only by creating a crisis could "financial reform" be pushed forward, and amidst strong calls for a change in the law, the Currency and Bank Notes Act 1928 was passed, which broke the tightrope that had been placed on the Bank of England's head for 84 years, capping the Bank of England's issuance of sterling backed by treasury bonds at £1,975,000, with the remainder of the sterling notes to be backed by gold. Issuing "debt" money backed by treasury bonds and bypassing the pesky gold constraint, like the up-and-coming Federal Reserve, is a realm that haunts London bankers. Just a few weeks after the new bill was passed, the Bank of England issued hundreds of millions of pounds of "debt". The new bill also gives the Bank of England the power to issue unlimited "debt" pounds sterling in emergency situations, provided that the Treasury and Parliament give their approval after the fact.[107] The Federal Reserve's near-unrestricted power to issue money has finally been taken over by the Bank of England.

The third move was that it was time for the sheep to burst into shearing again, and after a secret meeting in 1927, the Federal Reserve's low interest rate policy caused a huge outflow of gold worth $500 million from the United States, and after the Federal Reserve raised interest rates violently in 1929, causing banks to lack gold reserves and unable to effectively extend credit, the sturdy sheep of the United States went into shock due to extreme blood loss. International bankers then swarmed the market, eating into blue chips and other quality assets at ultra-low prices at fractions or even tens of a percent of normal prices. Rep. McFadden described it this way:

> *"60,000 properties and farms were recently auctioned in one day in one state alone. In Oakland County, Michigan, 10,000 homeowners and ranchers have been swept out of their homes. Something similar is happening in every county in the United States."*

---

[107] *Ibid.*, p. 377.

In the midst of this unprecedented American economic havoc, only a few people in the innermost circles knew in advance that the biggest speculative fiasco in American history was coming to an end, and these people were able to dump all their stocks in time to hold large amounts of government bonds, all of them with close ties to the Rothschilds in London. Those outside this circle, some even the super-rich, have not been spared. This circle includes J. P. Morgan and Coon Rapo, as well as their selected "priority clients" such as partner banks and prominent industrialists, important politicians and rulers of friendly countries with whom they maintain goodwill.

When banker Murrison resigned from the Federal Reserve, this is what Newsweek of May 30, 1936 had to say about him:

> *"The consensus was that the Federal Reserve had lost an able man. In 1929 (before the stock crash), he called a meeting and ordered several banks under him to end all lending to securities dealers by September 1. So they were able to ride out the subsequent decline."*[108]

Joe Kennedy's wealth increased from $4 million in 1929 to $100 million in 1935, a 25-fold increase. Bernard Barrows sold all of his stocks before the Great Crash and switched to holding Treasuries. Henry Morgenthau rushed to the Bankers Trust Company a few days before "Black Tuesday" (October 29, 1929) and ordered his company to sell all of its stock worth a total of $60 million within three days. Confused, his men advised him to gradually liquidate his position over the course of a few weeks, so that he could make at least $5 million more. Henry Morgenthau burst into a rage and snarled at his men,

> *"I didn't come here to discuss it with you! Do as I say!"*

Looking back at this history after almost 80 years, we still have to marvel at the intelligence of these international bankers, who are without a doubt the most intelligent group of people in the human race. Such tactics, such power, such a close design, such boldness in playing with the world in the palm of the shares, is really breathtaking. Even to this day, most people are completely unconvinced that their fate is actually being manipulated in the hands of a very small number of people.

---

[108] *Newsweek*, May 30, 1936.

After the "woolly" harvest of the international bankers, Keynesian "cheap money ideas" became the latest wealth reaper for the bankers, and the "Roosevelt New Deal" under their leadership opened a new harvest season for the bankers.

Summary

★The bankers supported the United States in the war against Germany in World War I and spared no effort in lending money to the government and making a fortune in the war.

★Strang became the head figure of the Fed system in essence, JPMorgan, Paul, Schiff and other Wall Street giants' intentions in the Fed were followed through uncompromisingly.

★If Germany wins, the Allied bonds in the hands of the bankers will be worthless, and Morgan, Rockefeller, Paul Warburg, and Schiff will do everything they can to push the United States into war to protect their loans.

★The Paris Peace Conference was just a carnival for the international bankers who, after making a fortune from the war, sowed the seeds of the next war – the Second World War.

★Wall Street orchestrated a targeted demolition of farmers with "shearing" operations designed to plunder their wealth and destroy small and medium-sized banks in agricultural areas that refused to comply with the Federal Reserve.

★The Federal Reserve Bank of New York is in fact in complete control of the entire Fed, and the Fed's 7-person board in Washington is just a pose.

★The most of them dared to fight with the five major banking families in New York, the Federal Reserve system does not buy the banks have bankruptcy.

★After the international bankers plundered the wealth of Germany, Britain and the United States through "shearing", Keynes's "cheap money idea" became the latest wealth reaping machine at the bankers' door.

CHAPTER V

The "New Deal" of cheap money

"Lenin once said that the best way to subvert the capitalist system is to devalue its currency. Through a continuous process of inflation, the government can confiscate a portion of a citizen's wealth in secret and out of sight. In this way, people can be arbitrarily deprived of their wealth and, in impoverishing the majority, the minority can be enriched. There is no means of subverting the current regime as stealthily and reliably as it (inflation) does. This process potentially accumulates disruptive elements in various economic laws, and not even one person in a million can see the root of the problem."[109]

—Keynes, 1919

Keynes called gold a "barbaric relic" and this "popular" comment is well known in China. What was Keynes' motivation for demonizing gold? How did Keynes, once staunchly anti-inflation, become a mortal enemy of gold?

Greenspan, at 40, was still a staunch defender of the gold standard, and when he became chairman of the Federal Reserve, he began to dwell on the gold issue. Although by 2002 he still acknowledged that "gold is the ultimate means of payment for all currencies", he was "on the sidelines" of a conspiracy by Western central bankers to suppress the price of gold in the 1990s.

Why do international bankers and their "royal" theorists loathe gold so much? Why is Keynes's "cheap money" theory so popular?

In the 5,000 years of human social practice, in whatever era, in whatever country, in whatever religion, in whatever race, gold has been recognized by the world as the ultimate form of wealth. This deep-

---

[109] John Maynard Keynes, *The Economic Consequences of the Peace*, 1919.

rooted awareness can never be dissolved by a few words of "gold is a barbaric relic" from Keynes and others.

The inevitable connection of people to gold and wealth has long been a natural logic in life. When people are not bullish about government policies and the economic situation, they have the option to exchange the paper money in their hands for gold coins to wait for the bad situation to improve. The free exchange of paper money for gold actually became the cornerstone of the people's most basic economic freedom, and it is only on this basis that any democracy and other forms of freedom can have practical meaning. When the government forcibly deprives the people of their innate right to exchange paper money for gold, it also fundamentally deprives the people of their most basic freedoms.

International bankers know very well that gold is by no means an ordinary precious metal, in essence, gold is the only, highly sensitive and deeply historical "political metal", if not handled properly, it will cause a financial storm in the world. Under normal social conditions, the abolition of the gold standard would inevitably lead to serious social unrest and even violent revolutions, and only under extremely exceptional circumstances would people be forced to temporarily relinquish their innate power, which is why bankers need a serious crisis and recession. Under the threat of crisis and recession, people are most easily compromised, unity is most easily broken, public opinion is most easily misled, social attention is most easily distracted and bankers' schemes are most easily realized. So crises and recessions have been used repeatedly throughout history by bankers as the most effective weapon against governments and people.

The severe economic crisis since 1929 has been paved the financial way to the Second World War by the international bankers' "opportunistic" efforts to achieve the "abolition of the gold standard", which is extremely difficult to achieve under normal conditions.

Keynesian "cheap money"

It is clear that Keynes had already recognized the enormous potential harm that inflation could do to people and society when he attended the Paris Peace Conference in 1919, and in that pamphlet, The Economic Consequences of Peace, which made him an overnight success, he pointed out the essence of inflation profoundly and poignantly, while Germany's 1923 super-inflation had fully validated the enormous killing power of inflation.

This is true of Greenspan, who published Gold and Economic Freedom at the age of 40, in which Gertrude's views on inflation are in line with Keynes', stating,

> *"In the absence of a gold standard, there will be no way to protect (the people's) savings from inflation and there will be no safe habitat for wealth. That's the secret to the fierce opposition to gold by those welfare statisticians. Deficit finance is simply a conspiracy to confiscate wealth, and gold stands in the way of this insidious process, acting as a protector of property rights. If one grasps that core point, it's not hard to understand the vitriol being directed at the gold standard."[110]*

As Greenspan notes, the gold standard has firmly contained the flood of inflation. In this sense, both Keynes and Greenspan should have been staunch advocates of the gold standard, so how is it that one later reduced gold to a "barbaric relic" and the other simply kept quiet about its monetary status after it had risen to prominence?

For Greenspan, it's not up to him in the world. When Greenspan threw himself into J.P. Morgan's arms and became a director of J.P. Morgan and other Wall Street banks, he began to understand that there are rules in the financial world.

While the world's spotlight is on Greenspan's unpredictable wrinkles, I'm afraid he alone understands that the real decision maker is the Federal Reserve Bank of New York, which was hounded by Texas Congressman Ron Paul in a congressional hearing in 2002, before Greenspan said he never betrayed the views of 1966, and that he still considers gold the "means of final payment" of all currencies, and that the Fed is "mimic" the gold standard.

Keynes' situation is different from Greenspan's.

An insightful account of Keynes's personality traits is given by the eminent American scholar Murray Rothbard, who argues that Keynes's extreme egocentrism, self-righteousness to the British ruling elite, and

---

[110] Alan Greenspan, "Gold and Economic Freedom", 1966, quoted in *Capitalism: The Unknown Ideal* (Signet, 1967).

contempt for social mores had a direct influence on his system of thought.

In particular, the Apostle, a secret society at the University of Cambridge in England, had a strong influence on Keynes. These secret societies in European and American universities are by no means loosely based on what is commonly understood to be university fraternities or literary societies; they are more like the core of an elite with a deep religious mission, some with a hundred-year history and lifelong ties, constituting the most indestructible interest group of the ruling class in Western society.

The "Apostolic Society" at Cambridge consisted of twelve of the finest members of Trinity College and King's College, men not only of the highest intelligence, but also of distinguished birth, each destined to become a member of the English ruling class. They meet every Saturday in a secret meeting place where discussions range from philosophy and aesthetics to politics and business. They have their own strict cleanliness of rules and precepts, and at the same time contempt for the common morals of society; they think they have the wisest minds of mankind; they think they are born rulers of the world, and they inculcate this belief repeatedly among themselves. In a letter to a friend, Keynes put it this way:

> *"Isn't this sense of moral superiority of ours a bit arrogant? I have a feeling that the vast majority of people in this world never see anything (for what it is) (because) they are too stupid, or too evil."*[111]

In this circle, in addition to scholarly elites like Kearns and the famous philosopher Russell, there are financial giants like Baron Rothschild. After leaving Cambridge, the adult apostles who continued to attend the secret meetings of the "Apostolic Council" every Saturday were called "angels" and were actively involved in the selection of new apostles and other activities.

Victor Rothschild, a few years younger than Keynes, was the first grandson of Nathan Rothschild, who held the right to issue currency throughout the British Empire and was the third generation heir to the baronet title. Victor and Kearns with the United States "Foreign Affairs

---

[111] Murray N. Rothbard, *Keynes, the Man* (Ludwig von Mises Institute, 2010), p. 15.

Association" (Council of Foreign Relationship) and the British Royal Institute of International Affairs (Royal Institute of International Affairs) active advocates, these two organizations can be described as the "central party school" of European and American politics, over the past hundred years for the European and American ruling groups to convey a large number of "cadres".

Victor was familiar with Wall Street, as is customary with European and American family banks, having spent time at J.P. Morgan Bank. He is also a director of the Dutch oil company Shell. Victor was a senior official in the British Intelligence Service (MI5) and later served as security adviser to the British Prime Minister, Margaret Thatcher, and his uncle, Baron Edmund Rothschild, was known as the "Father of Israel". With Victor's advice and guidance, the enlightened Keynes quickly sniffed out cheap debt money and inflation theory, which was the main thrust of the international bankers of the time.

Keynes was rarely troubled by his own political lies, because he was not at all bound by the moral code of the common man. He habitually falsifies data to fit his economic philosophy. As Rothbard points out,

> "he believed that principle would only hinder his chances of attaining power at the right moment. Therefore, he is willing to change his previous beliefs at any time, even for a coin, in a given situation."[112]

Keynes understood that for an economist to make his doctrine "explicit", he had to have the big names in finance and politics behind the scenes and in front of the stage, to be "popular" as the term is now used. When Keynes identified "the right way forward in history", he immediately displayed his true gifts: eloquence and an amazing ability to sell.

Under the aura of Adam Smith, Li Ka Tu and Marshall, it seemed only natural that Cambridge would become the birthplace of world economic theory. In 1936, after the publication of his major book *The General Theory of Money, Interest and Employment*, the international bankers, of course, loved the economic theory that was so sensitive to their minds, and the politicians showed a willingness to push back on

---

[112] *Ibid.*, p. 25.

the cheap monetary policy of "borrow, print and spend", and the controversy and applause immediately swept the academic world.

Keynes had long been convinced that his idea of cheap money would be strongly supported by international bankers and politicians, and that the ordinary people who suffered the most were "too stupid, or too evil", and that the rest was to take care of academia.

Keynes first declared the dichotomy between the two camps represented by him, modern economic theory and old traditional economic theory, and then went on to claim that his tough new economic "Bible" could only be understood by "young economists under 30". This claim was immediately cheered by young economists, and Paul Samuelson, in a letter to a friend, rejoiced that he was not yet 30 years old, saying, "It is good to be young". But it is this same Samuelson who admits that the General Commentary is a "badly written, disorganized, confusing book."[113]

American scholars believe that if the book had been written by a professor at a remote college in the American Midwest, it might have been difficult to even publish, let alone become famous.

1932 Presidential Election

The 1932 presidential election kicked off in the midst of an economic depression, with 13 million unemployed and a 25 percent unemployment rate, putting the current President Hoover under pressure. In the face of Democratic presidential candidate Roosevelt's fierce attacks on economic policy since 1928 and his scathing rebuke of President Hoover's close ties to Wall Street banker power, President Hoover kept a tolerable silence, but he recorded his true thoughts in his own memo this way.

> *"In response to Roosevelt's statement that I should be held responsible for the (1929) speculative frenzy, I pondered whether I should bring to light the responsibility of the Federal Reserve for its deliberate inflationary policy under the influence*

---

[113] *Ibid.*, p. 38.

of European forces from 1925 to 1928, which I was then against."[114]

It is true that President Hoover was somewhat wronged, and although he was the President of the United States, he did not have much influence over economic and monetary policy. Since the government does not have the power to issue money, any policy will be empty talk if the privately owned Federal Reserve Bank of New York does not cooperate.

President Hoover's fall from grace on Wall Street began with a deviation from the bankers' established course on the issue of German payouts. In May 1931, not long after the plan was implemented, it caught up with the financial crisis in Germany and Austria, and the bailout of the Rothschild Family Bank and the Bank of England failed to contain the spread of the crisis. Ramon also warned that if the European financial system were to collapse, the US recession would also intensify.

President Hoover had already promised the French government that he would consult it first on any matter involving German war reparations, and Hoover, as a politician, could not go back on his word.

> ' *"You can't stay in New York to understand the sentiment about the debt between these governments as a nation as a whole."[115]*

Lamont also nonchalantly put down the word:

> *"You must have heard a lot of rumors these days that someone was ready to step aside your class at the (Republican) convention in 1932. If you follow our plan, these rumors will go up in smoke overnight."*

Finally, Ramon handed over a carrot, and if it was successful, all the credit went to the President. The president thought about it for a month and finally just bowed his head.

By July 1932, Ramon again sent someone to the White House to tell the President that Germany's war reparations should be

---

[114] Eustace Mullins, *The World Order – A Study in the Hegemony of Parasitism* (Omnia Veritas Ltd, www.omnia-veritas.com)

[115] Ron Chernow, *op. cit.,* p. 328.

reconsidered, and this time Hoover couldn't stand it, shouting with resentment and frustration:

> *"Ramon got the whole thing wrong. If there is one thing that the American people hate and oppose, it is that this collusion (waiving or postponing German, English and French debts to the United States) offends their interests. Ramon doesn't understand the anger (at the bankers) that is sweeping the country. They (the bankers) want us (the politicians) to be complicit in the 'mob' too. Perhaps they (the bankers) had reached an agreement with the Germans on the payout, but it was done in the worst possible way."* [116]

As a result, Hoover rejected Wall Street's demands, and France emerged to pay its arrears.

What made the Wall Street bankers even more furious was that the series of financial scandals that resulted from President Hoover's relentless pursuit of stock market shorting, coupled with unprecedented unemployment, a depleted economy and a population that had been swept under the rug by the stock market, had all converged into one forceful rage against the Wall Street bankers. President Hoover, confident that public opinion was available, ripped into the bankers and was bent on making the problem bigger. Hoover bluntly denounced the New York stock market as a big casino run by bankers, with market-shorting speculators hindering the recovery of market confidence. He warned New York Stock Exchange President Whitney that he would initiate congressional investigative action and regulate the stock market if stock market shorting is not restricted. Wall Street's answer to the President's request was simple and dry:

> *"Ridiculous!"*

President Hoover, ready to put a fish out of water, ordered the Senate Banking and Currency Committee to begin investigating stock market shorting. An exasperated Wall Street immediately sent Ramon to the White House to have lunch with the President and Secretary of State in an attempt to interrupt the investigation, and the President was unfazed. [117]

---

[116] *Ibid.*, p. 351.

[117] *Ibid.*, p. 352.

When the investigation expanded into the stock-trading scandals of the late 1920s, major cases were brought to light, and many stock market scandals, such as Goldman Sachs and JPMorgan, were revealed to the world.

When the logical relationship between the stock market crash and the Great Depression was made clear to the public, the anger of the people finally focused on the bankers.

And President Hoover and his career were also cut short by the double fury of the bankers and the people. In his stead was what is known as the greatest American president of the 20th century – Franklin Delano Roosevelt.

Who was Franklin Delano Roosevelt?

> *As you and I both know, what is true is that the financial forces in the vast (power) core have controlled government since the days of President Andrew Jackson, and this country is about to repeat the Jacksonian struggle with the banks, only on a larger and broader basis.*[118]

—Roosevelt, November 21, 1933

This "true confession" of Roosevelt is more or less like the Wilson of that year, and if it is true that Wilson was a scholar and not familiar with the methods of bankers, then it is a bit of a stretch to say that Roosevelt's experience was used to make such a statement. In his campaign speech in Ohio on August 20, 1932, Roosevelt said eloquently.

> *"We found that 2/3 of U.S. industry is concentrated in the hands of a few hundred companies that are actually controlled by no more than five people, We found that the securities dealers of about 30 banks and commercial banks determine the flow of capital in the United States. In other words, we find a highly centralized economic power being manipulated in the hands of a concentrated minority, all of which is the opposite of what Mr. President (Hoover) calls individualism."*[119]

---

[118] *F.D.R.: His Personal Letters* (Duell, Sloan and Pearce, New York, 1950), p. 373.

[119] Antony C. Sutton, *Wall Street and FDR* (Arlington House Publishers, 1975).

While Roosevelt made himself feel as much as possible like the banker-aligned President Jackson who was heartily loved by the American people, a brave president who was willing to challenge the financial moguls for the little guy, Roosevelt's experience unfortunately showed that he had only a small amount more to do with international bankers than President Hoover.

Roosevelt's great-grandfather, James Roosevelt, founded the Bank of New York in 1784, arguably one of America's oldest banking families, and it was the bank that was accused of manipulating the price of U.S. Treasuries in the 2006 Treasury bond auction market. The bank was in business until Roosevelt's presidential campaign when it was run by his cousin George. Roosevelt's father, also named James, was an American industrial tycoon who graduated from Harvard Law School and owned a number of huge industries such as coal mines and railroads, and was the founder of the Southern Railway Security Company, which was the first securities holding company in the United States to merge mainly with the railroad industry. Roosevelt himself was a Harvard graduate and a lawyer, and his main clients included JPMorgan. Backed by a strong banking background, Roosevelt became Assistant Secretary of the U.S. Department of the Navy in 1916 at the age of 34, and it was Morgan's senior partner who often hammered President Hoover's Lamont into giving Roosevelt the new home he had arranged in Washington.

Roosevelt also had an uncle who was president, Leonardo Roosevelt. Their other cousin, George Emmanuel Roosevelt, was also a prominent figure on Wall Street, having reorganized at least 14 railroad companies in the era of the great railroad mergers, and as a director of the Guaranty Trust Company under J.P. Morgan, the Chemical Bank, and the New York Savings Bank, the list of other companies on which he was a director could be typed up in a pamphlet.

Roosevelt's mother, the Delano family, was also a family of hairpins, and nine presidents were related to their family. No president in recent American history has had greater political and banking resources than Roosevelt.

In 1921, Roosevelt moved from government to Wall Street to become a director or vice president of a number of financial institutions, using his extensive contacts in politics and banking to make huge profits for his companies. In the course of pulling government bond business for a financial firm, Roosevelt was blunt in his letter to old friend Congressman Meher:

> *"I hope I can use our long friendship to ask for your help, and we hope to get some bond contracts from the big boys in Brooklyn. A large number of bonds are related to municipal projects, and I hope my friends will remember me. I cannot bother them at this time, but since my friend is also your friend, it would be a great help to me if you could have a disposition. I'll keep your help in mind."[120]*

In a letter to a friend who got a big deal in the Navy Department, Roosevelt mentioned,

> *"My friend in the Navy Department and I were chatting in passing about a contract given to your company for an 8-inch gun, which reminded me of the pleasant cooperation we had when I was Assistant Secretary of the Navy. I was wondering if you could get my company in to underwrite some of your bonds. I would very much like to have one of my sales reps give you a call."[121]*

In some business matters of great interest, Roosevelt once blatantly stated that "purely private friendship is not enough". A more vivid Roosevelt jumped off the page when reading the correspondence from within these companies.

In 1922, Roosevelt participated in the formation of United European Investors (LTD) and became its president. Among the company's directors and advisors are former German Prime Minister Wilhelm Cuno, who single-handedly created the German super-inflation of 1923, and Max Warburg, whose brother Paul was the Fed's chief architect and vice chairman. Of the 60,000 preferred shares issued by the company, Roosevelt is the largest individual stockholder. The company was mainly engaged in various speculative businesses in Germany, and while the German people were being swept away by super-inflation, Roosevelt's United European Investment Company was reaping the national disaster fortune in a feverish fashion.[122]

---

[120] *Ibid.*

[121] *Ibid.*

[122] *Ibid.*

Hyperinflation has always been a "super-wealth reaper", with a massive wealth transfer occurring in the course of the country's dramatic currency devaluation.

> *"The worst moral collapse of inflation occurred in Germany in 1923. Anyone with some dollars or pounds in hand can live like a king in Germany. A few dollars can make a person live like a millionaire. Foreigners flocked around, snapping up (German) family wealth, real estate, jewelry and artwork at incredibly cheap prices."[123]*

As happened in the hyperinflation of the former Soviet Union in the early 1990s, vast social wealth was looted in a frenzy, the middle class was poured out, the purchasing power of the dollar or pound was magnified by thousands, and wealth quietly changed hands in the course of the wild plunge and surge between these currencies. As Keynes said,

> *"In this way (hyperinflation) people can be arbitrarily deprived of their wealth, and in the process of impoverishing the majority, the minority can be enriched... The process potentially accumulates the destructive elements of various economic laws, and not one person in a million can see the root of the problem."*

When Roosevelt righteously criticized Hoover's Wall Street background, he branded himself as the savior of the common people, clean and honest, only his experience and background could not be further from the truth.

Abolishing the gold standard: the historical mission given to Roosevelt by the bankers

Under the constraints of the gold standard, World War I had already left European countries so heavily indebted that the scale of the war could only have been localized if the Federal Reserve had not been established, thus pooling the financial resources of the United States. The First World War left the international bankers gorging themselves, longing for their next meal. However, even after the United States has the Federal Reserve, under the strict constraints of the gold standard, financial resources have been stretched to support another world class

---

[123] Marjorie Palmer, *1918-1923: German Hyperinflation* (Traders Press, New York, 1967).

war, the abolition of the gold standard has become a top priority for European and American bankers.

Gold has gradually become the final form of currency universally recognized by all countries in the world during the 5,000 years of evolution of human society, and the inevitable link between gold and wealth has long since become the natural logic of life. When people are not bullish about government policies and the economic situation, they have the option to exchange the paper money in their hands for gold coins to wait for the bad situation to improve. The free exchange of paper money for gold actually became the cornerstone of the people's most basic economic freedom, and it is only on this basis that any democracy and other forms of freedom can have practical meaning. When governments forcibly deprive people of the power to freely exchange gold and paper money, they also fundamentally deprive people of their most basic freedoms.

Under normal social conditions, the abolition of the gold standard would inevitably lead to serious social unrest and even violent revolutions, and only under extremely exceptional circumstances would people be forced to temporarily relinquish their innate power, which is why bankers need a serious crisis and recession. Under the threat of crisis and recession, people are most easily compromised, unity is most easily broken, public opinion is most easily misled, social attention is most easily distracted and bankers' schemes are most easily realized. So crises and recessions have been used repeatedly throughout history by bankers as the most effective weapon against governments and people.

In 1812, the abolition of the First Bank of the United States invited Rothschild's retaliation, the outbreak of the Anglo-American War of 1812, which ended with the U.S. government yielding and establishing the Second Bank of the United States.

In 1837, President Jackson abolished the Second Bank of the United States, bankers immediately went on a rampage in London tossing U.S. bonds and calling back all kinds of loans, and the U.S. economy fell into a severe recession until 1848.

In 1857, 1870, and 1907 to force the U.S. government to re-establish a privately owned central bank, international bankers again set out to create a recession. Finally, a privately owned central bank, the Federal Reserve, was established, thus taking full control of the issuance of money in the United States.

The ultimate goal of the Great Recession of 1929 was to abolish the gold standard and implement a cheap money policy, thus paving the financial way for World War II.

On March 4, 1933, Roosevelt was inaugurated as the 32nd President of the United States. At the beginning of his tenure, Roosevelt raised the banner of incompatibility with Wall Street, and on the same day he took office, he announced that the nation's banks would cease operations as of March 6 (Bank Holiday) and would not reopen until an investigation into the settlement of accounts was completed, which was the first time in U.S. history that the nation's financial arteries had been closed. The world's largest economy, in an unprecedented state of almost complete banklessness, lasted at least 10 days.[124]

Then, Roosevelt tightened his grip on the Wall Street investigation that had been underway since the Hoover era, pointing the finger directly at the Morgan family. In a series of hearings, Jack Morgan and his associates were made to look grim before the entire American people.

Roosevelt's heavy-handed move against Wall Street bankers came with a vengeance when he signed another Glass-Steagall Act on June 16, 1933, which eventually led to the spinoff of JPMorgan into JPMorgan Bank and Morgan Stanley, with the former restricted to the traditional business of commercial banking and the latter to investment banking.

Roosevelt was also unfazed by the New York Stock Exchange, passing the Securities Act of 1933 and the Securities Exchange Act of 1934, establishing the Securities and Exchange Commission (SEC) to regulate the stock market.

Roosevelt's New Deal began with a thunderous start that won the general public's approval and brought out the long-standing anger against Wall Street bankers that had been building up in people's minds.

Even the Morgan family admits,

> *"The whole country is filled with admiration for President Roosevelt. What he has accomplished in just one week of being*

---

[124] Glyn Davies, *op. cit.*, p. 512.

president is unbelievable, and we have never been through a similar process."[125]

The New York stock market opened big in 1933, recording a staggering 54% return.

The heroic Roosevelt impassionedly proclaimed,

"The Money Changers (Money Changers) have escaped from the throne of the Temple of Civilization, and we can now at last restore the ancient truth of this sacred temple."[126]

The problem is that there is often a huge gap between the historical truth and the public feeling deliberately shaped by the media, and there is inevitably a misperception that the scenes are carefully choreographed.

Let's look at the truth beneath the surface of Roosevelt's thunderbolt.

After the long bank holiday, many Midwestern banks that adamantly refused to join the Fed never opened again, and large swaths of the market gave way to being reshuffled by Wall Street bankers. Roosevelt's choice for Treasury Secretary was the son of Henry Morgenthau Sr. and Wall Street insider, Morgenthau Jr. who, as mentioned earlier, had gotten reliable information before the 1929 stock market crash and was going to pull out of the stock market entirely within three days at the expense of $5 million.

Roosevelt's choice for SEC chairman was even more tearful, as the first SEC chairman was Joseph Kennedy, the famous speculator who was desperately shorting the stock market before the 1929 stock market crash. His assets went from $4 million in 1929, after a major stock market crash, to soaring 25-fold to over $100 million in just four years in 1933. Joseph Kennedy was also in the circle of Jack Morgan, whose son was President Kennedy of great fame.

The sponsors of the Glass-Steagall Act, which gained its reputation by spinning off J.P. Morgan, were Senator Glass, who orchestrated the Federal Reserve Act of that year, and it did not hit J.P. Morgan hard, but the fact is that J.P. Morgan's business soared and prospered, and 25

---

[125] Ron Chernow, *op. cit.*, p. 357.

[126] *Ibid.*

of J.P. Morgan's 425 employees were set aside to form Morgan Stanley, in which Jack Morgan and Lamont maintained a 90 percent controlling interest. In fact, the two spun-off companies remained entirely under the control of Jack Morgan, who in 1935, in his first year of operation, Morgan Stanley secured a staggering $1 billion in bond underwriting business, sweeping up 25 percent of the total market share.[127] In fact, the major corporate bond issues are still aimed at JPMorgan, which holds the superb stick of the Federal Reserve Bank of New York, and any major U.S. company has to be afraid of JPMorgan.

And the most dramatic congressional hearings on JPMorgan were also the hot news that caught the public's attention. In the midst of all the hullabaloo, Roosevelt quietly passed several important decrees abolishing the gold standard.

Just one week after he took office, on March 11, he issued an executive order halting the banks' gold exchange in the name of stabilizing the economy. This was followed on April 5 by an order that U.S. citizens must turn in all their gold, which the government bought for $20.67 an ounce. In addition to rare gold coins and gold jewelry, anyone who privately collects gold will receive a heavy 10-year prison sentence and a $250,000 fine. Although Roosevelt argued that it was only a temporary measure in a state of emergency, the act was not repealed until 1974, when the Gold Reserve Act was passed again in January 1934, positioning the price of gold at $35 an ounce, but the American people had no right to exchange it. The people have just surrendered their gold, and their savings over the years have been drastically reduced by half! The "preferred clients" of the international bankers, who had received insider information before the stock market crash of 1929, were able to withdraw large sums of money from the stock market and convert it into gold, which was shipped to London, where it was sold at $35 an ounce, making an instant profit of 69.33%.

When Roosevelt asked Thomas Gore, the most learned and blind of the U.S. Congressmen, what he thought of his abolition of the gold standard, Gore coldly replied, "It's obvious theft, isn't it? Mr. President?" Roosevelt has been sorely disappointed in Senator Gore's candor. The senator was the grandfather of later US Vice President Al Gore.

---

[127] *Ibid.*, pp. 386–390.

Another Congressman, Howard Buffett, who spent his life pursuing a return to the gold standard, stated in 1948,

> *"I warn you that politicians of both parties will oppose a return to the gold standard, and those here and abroad who have made their fortunes on the continued devaluation of the United States currency will oppose a return to an honest money system. You must be prepared to face their objections intelligently and with resourcefulness."[128]*

Buffett Sr., who had a lifelong belief in gold as the ultimate currency, did not see the restoration of the gold standard, but that belief is deeply imprinted in the mind of his son, today's great stock god Warren Buffett. When Buffett saw through the historical inevitability of the eventual collapse of the French currency system, he decisively ate up 1/3 of the world's physical silver stock in 1997 when the price of silver hit a near historical low.

It is not a simple and easy task to completely remove gold from the currency and the process is divided into three stages to implement it. The first step was to abolish the circulation and exchange of gold coins within the United States, and the second step was to abolish the monetary function of gold throughout the world, with the second step being achieved by the Dollar Exchange Standard established by the Breton system in 1944 in place of the Gold Exchange Standard, and the third step finally completed by Nixon in 1971.

Keynes waved the flag, the bankers pushed for more fuel, Roosevelt finally pulled the cap off the gold standard this demon bottle, the twin monsters of deficit finance and cheap debt money finally struggled out of the prison.

Keynes, who valued only the power in front of him, famously said, "In the long run we are all dead.", but people's actions and their consequences will go down in history forever.

Venture Capital picked Hitler

The *New York Times* of November 24, 1933, reported on a pamphlet titled Sidney Warburg. The book was first published in the

---

[128] *The Commercial and Financial Chronicle*, 6 mai 1948.

Netherlands in 1933 and was outlawed after only a few days on the shelf. Several surviving copies of the book were translated into English, and the English version of the book was exhibited at the British Museum and was later banned from the public and researchers. The author of the book, "Sidney Warburg", is believed to be a member of the Warburg family, one of the largest banking families in the United States, and the contents of the book were later firmly denied by the Warburg family.

This mysterious pamphlet exposes the secret history of the American and British banking families that financed and supported Hitler's rise to power. According to the book, around 1929, Wall Street helped Germany repay war reparations through the Dawes Plan and the Young Plan. From 1924 to 1931, Wall Street gave Germany a total of DM 138 billion in loans through these two schemes, while Germany paid a total of only DM 86 billion in war reparations during this period, and Germany actually received huge financial support from the United States to regroup. The loans to Germany actually raised public money through the sale of German bonds on Wall Street, in which the Morgan and Warburg families were lucrative.

One issue that has arisen in this process is the high-handed policy of the French government on the issue of German reparations. This policy resulted in a significant portion of U.S. loans being frozen in Germany and Austria, and France receiving a major portion of the German compensation, the ultimate source of that money being Wall Street. Watching France's increasingly unhappy Wall Street bankers hold a meeting in June 1929, JPMorgan, Rockefeller and Federal Reserve heads got together to discuss how to "liberate" Germany from France's oppression. It was agreed that the "revolution" must be used to free France from its clutches. One possible candidate for leader is Hitler. Armed with a U.S. diplomatic passport and carrying personal letters from President Hoover and Rockefeller, Sidney Warburg was instructed to make personal contact with Hitler.

Sidney's contacts with the Nazis did not go well, the American consulate in Munich was ineffective, and it was with the help of the mayor of Munich that Hitler was later met. At the initial meeting, the Wall Street bankers offered "an offensive foreign policy and incitement to retaliation against France", and Hitler's offer was not low, offering 100 million marks for anything. Sidney sent Hitler's offer back to New York, and the bankers felt that the Hitler lion's mouth was wide open and that $24 million was outrageously high, and they made a counter-offer of $10 million. Hitler promised to come down in one fell swoop, before it was time.

At Hitler's request, the money was called to a Dutch bank (Mendelsohn & Co. Bank) and sent in several batches of checks to 10 cities in Germany. When Sidney returned to New York to report to the bankers, Rockefeller was deeply fascinated by Hitler's Nazi claims. Immediately afterwards, the New York Times, which had always been unconcerned with Hitler, suddenly began a regular introduction to Nazi doctrine and Hitler's speeches, and in December 1929, Harvard University began to study the National Socialist movement in Germany.

When President Hoover promised the French government in 1931 that it would be the first to be consulted on any solution to the debt, he immediately fell out of favor on Wall Street, and many historians believe that President Hoover's subsequent election defeat had a direct bearing on the matter.

In October 1931, Hitler sent a letter to Sidney. So the bankers of Wall Street convened another meeting, this time with Norman, the chairman of the Bank of England. Two schools of thought formed at the meeting, with those led by Rockefeller leaning toward Hitler and others less certain. Norman thought the $10 million spent on Hitler was more than enough, and he doubted Hitler would ever act. It was finally decided to further support Hitler.

Once again, Sidney came to Germany and at a meeting of Hitler's supporters, it was brought to his attention that the Nazi Charge and SS were in great shortage of machine guns, carbines and pistols. By this time, a large quantity of weapons and equipment had been cantoned in the Belgian, Dutch and Austrian cities on the German border and could be picked up as soon as the Nazis paid cash. Hitler told Sidney that he had two plans, a violent seizure of power and a legal reign. Hitler asked,

> "It takes 500 million marks to take power by violence, 200 million marks to come to power legally, what will you bankers decide?"

Five days later, a call back from Wall Street stated, "Such an amount is completely unacceptable. We don't want to and can't accept that. To this person it was explained that the mobilization of funds on this scale to Europe would shake the entire financial market."

Sidney made a further report, and three days later, a call back from Wall Street said:

"Report received. Prepare to pay $10 million, up to $15 million. It is necessary to suggest that this man take an offensive approach to foreign policy."

The path to a legitimate $15 million reign was finalized by Wall Street bankers. Payments had to be made with the source of the funds concealed, with $5 million going to Mendelsohn & Co. Bank in Amsterdam in the Netherlands, $5 million to Rotterdamsehe Bankvereinigung and $5 million to Banca Italiana.

On February 27, 1933, the night of the German Reichstag arson, Sidney and Hitler had their third meeting, and Hitler offered that at least another 100 million marks were needed to complete the final power grab, with Wall Street only promising up to $7 million. Hitler offered $5 million to the Italian Bank in Rome and another $2 million to the Renania Joint Stock Company in Düsseldorf.

After finally completing his mission, Sidney couldn't help but lament,

"I carried out my mission strictly to the last detail. Hitler was the biggest dictator in Europe. The world had been watching him for months. His actions will ultimately prove him good or bad, and I think he is the latter. As far as the German people are concerned, I sincerely hope I am wrong. The world is still going to succumb to Hitler, poor world, poor mankind."

Nazi Germany funded by Wall Street

On January 30, 1933, Hitler was appointed Chancellor of Germany, and Germany not only emerged completely from the economic disaster of super-inflation in 1923, but also quickly recovered from the severe recession that swept the globe, and under the enormous economic pressure of bearing the huge war payoffs, equipped Europe's most powerful armed forces with amazing speed and started World War II on September 1, 1939, in only six years!

And the United States, then the world's number one power, was still struggling in the quagmire of the Great Recession of 1929, and it wasn't until 1941, when the United States went directly to war, that America's economic situation was radically reversed.

Germany's rapid economic recovery and preparations for a massive war in a mere six years would have been completely unthinkable without strong financial support from outside. A logical explanation for such a huge infusion of foreign funds would be difficult to come by if it were not for the preparation of a war.

In fact, Wall Street was the biggest source of funding for Nazi Germany.

As early as 1924, when German hyperinflation had just subsided, Wall Street bankers were planning how to help Germany prepare for war, and both the Dawes Plan, which began in 1924, and the Young Plan in 1929 were designed for that purpose.

> *"The Dawes Plan of 1924 fits perfectly with the plans of the military economists of the German Staff Headquarters."*[129]

Owen Young, president of J.P. Morgan's U.S. General Electric, is also the foremost financial backer of the United European Investment Corporation, which Roosevelt founded. It was also this Owen Young who founded the Bank of International Settlement (BIS), which coordinates international banker partnerships. As noted historian Carroll Quigley, Clinton's benefactor at Georgetown University, noted,

> *"It (the Bank for International Settlements) was creating a financial system to control the world, a (mechanism) that was controlled by a few and could dominate the political system and the world economy."*[130]

From 1924 to 1931, Wall Street provided Germany with a total of DM 138 billion in loans through these two schemes, while Germany paid a total of only DM 86 billion in war reparations during this period, and Germany actually received a huge financial contribution of DM 52 billion from the United States, which allowed the entire German military industry to grow rapidly. As far back as 1919, British Prime Minister Lloyd George foresaw the huge payouts that Germany could not afford in the Versailles Peace Treaty, which would inevitably lead to the Germans either defaulting or going to war, both of which unfortunately ended up happening.

Faced with rows and rows of brand new modern military factories in Nazi Germany, and looking at the rusty production plants of the United States during the Great Depression, it is no wonder that

---

[129] Testimony before Unites States Senate, Committee on Military Affair, 1946.

[130] Carroll Quigley, *Tragedy & Hope* (MacMillan, 1966), p. 308.

Congressman McFadden denounced Wall Street bankers and the Federal Reserve for taking American taxpayer money to fund the German war machine.

> *"Mr. Chairman, if Germany's Noble Explosives sells explosives to the Japanese military for use in Manchuria (northeast China) or elsewhere, it can settle the bill of sale in U.S. dollars and send it to the open discount market in New York, where the Federal Reserve Bank will discount the bill and issue new U.S. dollar notes as collateral, the Federal Reserve is actually helping the German explosives company stuff its inventory into the American banking system. If that is the case, why are we sending representatives to Geneva to participate in the (German) Conference on Disarmament? Aren't the Federal Reserve Board and the Federal Reserve Bank making our government pay off the debt of German arms companies for the Japanese military?"[131]*

In addition to providing low-interest short-term financing to the German and Japanese military industries in the New York commercial paper discount market, the Fed also shipped U.S. gold reserves directly to Germany.

> *"A huge amount of money that would have belonged to American bank depositors was given to Germany without any collateral. The Federal Reserve Board and the Federal Reserve Bank issued U.S. currency solely on German commercial paper. Billions of dollars were pumped into the German economy, a process that continues to this day. Cheap German commercial paper was priced and deferred here (New York), pledged to the credit of the U.S. government, and paid for by the American people, and on April 27, 1932, the Federal Reserve shipped $750,000 worth of gold that would have belonged to the American people to Germany. A week later, another $300,000 of gold was shipped to Germany in the same way. As much as $12 million in gold was shipped to Germany by the Federal Reserve Board and the Federal Reserve Bank in mid-May alone. Almost every week there are gold carriers sailing to Germany.*

---

[131] Speech by Louis T. McFadden to the House of Representatives, June 10, 1932, Congressional Record.

*Mr. Chairman, I believe Bank of America savers have a right to
know what the Federal Reserve is doing with their money.* "[132]

In addition to Wall Street's massive funding, Hitler's reforms of
the financial system played a considerable role, the most crucial of
which was the withdrawal of the right to issue money from the private
German central bank. After escaping from the inefficient and costly
process of issuing currency secured by the national debt, the German
economy rocketed, with unemployment in Germany reaching 30 per
cent in 1933 and a labour shortage by 1938.

It has long been no secret that American companies gave Germany
enormous technical and financial support, which has been interpreted
by later historians as an "accident or short-sighted act". It was these
"unexpected short-sightedness" that greatly increased the production
capacity of the German military industry.

In 1934, Germany's oil production capacity was 300,000 tons of
natural oil and 800,000 tons of synthetic gasoline (coal to oil), with the
remainder entirely dependent on imports. After Standard Oil's patent
for hydrogenated oil was transferred to Germany, Germany was able to
produce 5.5 million tons of synthetic gasoline and 1 million tons of
natural oil by 1944.

> *"Although the German military planning department required
> industrial companies to install modern production equipment
> for mass production, German military economists and industrial
> companies did not fully understand the meaning of mass
> production until the two major American automobile
> manufacturing plants opened their eyes to the new type of plant
> in Germany to enter the European market. German experts were
> sent to Detroit to learn the expertise of module production and
> assembly line operations. German engineers were not only given
> tours of aircraft manufacturing plants, but were also allowed to
> view other important military installations from which they
> learned a great deal of technology, which they eventually used
> against the United States.* "[133]

Other American companies that maintain close relations with the
German military-industrial production system are General Motors, Ford

---

[132] *Ibid.*

[133] Antony C. Sutton, *Wall Street and FDR*, op. cit.

Motor, General Electric, DuPont, etc., all of which belong to JPMorgan, Rockefeller Chase or Warburg's Manhattan Bank.

Expensive War and Cheap Money

Churchill famously said, "It is far more difficult to wage war than to end it". At first glance, this may sound unrealistic, but a careful taste will reveal that it is indeed a wise saying. Ending a war often requires only secret representatives of the governments of the two belligerents to sit down and bargain, nothing more than the terms of an end to the conflict, or a loss or a gain, no deal is off the table.

But waging war is much more difficult, and forging social consensus in a democratic society is an extremely taxing task, which indeed saddens the international bankers.

As Morton notes,

> *"In their (international bankers') eyes there is no war or peace, no slogans or declarations, no sacrifice or honor, and they ignore those things that confuse the eyes of the world."*

Napoleon, who saw the essence of international bankers, also hit the nail on the head when he said:

> *"Money has no fatherland; financiers do not know what is patriotic and noble; their only purpose is to make profit."*

The American people, who had been robbed by Wall Street bankers, were not so easily fooled after the First World War and the Great Depression of 1929, and no one wanted to serve as cannon fodder for the bankers before sending their children to Europe to fight in the war.

In 1935, a special committee headed by Senator Gerald Nye issued a 1,400-plus page report detailing America's involvement in World War I, the conspiracies and misdeeds of bankers and arms companies in the war effort, and the recent JPMorgan hearings revealing the scandals of Wall Street's 29-year stock market crash, making anti-war sentiment extremely strong. At this time, Milis's best-selling book, "The Road to War," provoked a heated debate about participation in the war. In response to this public opinion, the United States passed three neutrality bills between 1935 and 1937 that strictly forbade the United States from being lured into war again.

On the domestic economic front, more than five years after the Roosevelt New Deal began, the U.S. economy never picked up, unemployment remained as high as 17 percent, and by 1938 the U.S. was once again in a severe recession.

Both the bankers and Roosevelt believed that only the super-deficit fiscal, Keynesian-inspired binge-firing of cheap money could save the economy, and that only a massive war could do so.

After the abolition of the gold standard in 1933, all obstacles on the road to war had been removed, and all that was left was an excuse for war.

Charles C. Tansill, a history professor at Georgetown University, argued that the war against Japan had been planned long before Roosevelt came to power in 1933, and by 1932 the U.S. Navy had proven that an attack 60 miles from Pearl Harbor could hit the Pacific fleet hard. U.S. intelligence broke the Japanese military's code in August 1940 and was able to decode all earlier intercepts of Japanese telegram records. American-made code-breaking machines were sent around the world, leaving out Pearl Harbor, the largest American naval base in the Pacific. Many historians believe that Roosevelt knew in advance that the Japanese Navy would sneak up on Pearl Harbor.

On January 13, 1943, Roosevelt and Churchill made a declaration in Casablanca that Germany must surrender unconditionally, a declaration that surprised the forces within Germany that opposed Hitler and advocated peace with the Allies. Germany had originally offered the terms of peace with the Allies as early as August 1942, when Germany returned to the borders prior to September 1, 1939, to end a war that Germany was bound to lose.[134]

Internal German forces advocating the overthrow of Hitler and the Nazi regime were already working on planning a military coup, and Roosevelt's statement dealt a serious blow to the influence of anti-war forces within Germany. Here is how Kissinger explained the motivation for the Roosevelt Casablanca Declaration,

"Roosevelt made this statement for several reasons (Germany must surrender unconditionally). He feared that discussion of the terms of peace with Germany might divide opinion within the

---

[134] Walter Schellenberg, *The Schellenberg Memoirs* (André Deutsch, London, 1956).

Allies, who he wanted to concentrate first on winning the war, and he was anxious to assure Stalin, who was stuck in a stalemate at Stalingrad, that he would never make peace with Germany alone. But the most fundamental reason was Roosevelt's attempt to prevent later German revisionists from rising up and claiming that Germany had been screwed by empty promises to armistice that year. [135]

Kissinger certainly has a point, but the truth is that the brutal and costly war was prolonged for more than two years and countless lives and wealth were reduced to ashes. This included the six million Jews who died at the hands of the Nazis, a significant number of whom would very likely have survived if the war had ended in 1943, after all, the Allies could have had a big say in the agreement on Germany's conditional surrender.

However, the international bankers who have just warmed up are not going to be able to easily end the opportunity to get rich. When the war was finally extinguished in August 1945, and the US national debt skyrocketed from a mere $16 billion in 1930 to $269 billion in 1946, Keynes's claims of deficit finance and cheap money were finally "tested" in the smoke of World War II. The international bankers had another stroke of fortune in the Second World War.

Summary

★Keynesian ideas of cheap money are strongly supported by international bankers and politicians.

★President Hoover fell out of favor on Wall Street by deviating from the bankers' established policy on German payouts, and his pursuit of shorting the New York stock market tore his face off with the bankers and ultimately cut his career short.

★Roosevelt, who ostensibly branded himself as the savior of the clean and honest common people, actually had close ties to international bankers.

---

[135] Henry Kissinger, *op. cit.* p. 346.

★With the support of Keynes and the bankers, Roosevelt abolished the gold standard system.

★Hitler's rise to power and the funding and support of bankers in the United States and Britain had a lot to do with it.

★ Wall Street was the largest source of funding for Nazi Germany, helping Hitler to quickly complete economic recovery and prepare for mass war in six years.

CHAPTER VI

The elite club that rules the world

The financial capital forces have an extremely long-term plan to create a financial system to control the world, a (mechanism) that is controlled by a few and can dominate the political system and the world economy.

The system was controlled by central bankers in the mode of feudal despotism, which was coordinated by secret agreements reached in frequent meetings.

At the heart of the system is the Bank for International Settlements in Basel, Switzerland, a privately owned bank, and the central banks that control it are themselves equally private companies.

Each central bank is committed to controlling its respective government by controlling fiscal lending, manipulating foreign exchange transactions, influencing the level of economic activity in the country, and providing rewards to politicians who remain cooperative in the business arena.[136]

—Caroll Quigley, Georgetown University's renowned historian, 1966

In our lives, terms such as "world government" and "world currency" appear more and more frequently. Without the relevant historical context, you would be very likely to dismiss such a reference as ordinary news hype when, in fact, a huge project is being launched. It is worrying that China still knows very little about this.

In July 1944, when the entire Eurasian continent was still covered with beacons, just over a month after Britain and the United States opened the Second Battlefield on the European continent, representatives of 44 countries from around the world came to Bretton Woods, a famous resort in New Hampshire, to discuss the blueprint for

---

[136] Carroll Quigley, *Tragedy & Hope* (MacMillan, 1966), p. 308.

a new post-war world economic order. The international bankers embarked on their long-plotted plan: to control currency issuance around the world!

By this time international bankers had established a core set of organizations: The Royal Institute of International Affairs and the Council on Foreign Relations. Subsequently, two new branches were created from these two core institutions: the Bilderberg Group in the economic field and the Trilateral Committee in charge of politics.

The ultimate goal of these organizations is to establish a world government ruled by a very small number of Anglo-American elites and an eventual unified system of world currency issuance, followed by a "world tax" on all Earth's citizens, which is called the "New World Order"!

Under such a system, all sovereign States must be deprived of their right to make decisions on monetary policy and economic domestic affairs, and the economic and political freedoms of all sovereign States and their peoples must be manipulated. The shackles that are placed on modern people are no longer chains but debts. In order to maximize the benefits of every modern "slave", the sloppy management must transition to an efficient scientific "breeding" phase, where cashless society, electronic money, internationally unified RFID (RFID Identifier), ID cards implanted in the human body, and other technologies will become the symbols that will eventually turn modern people into "slaves". Relying on RFID technology, international bankers will eventually be able to monitor every Earthling at any location at any time. When cash disappears from society, with just a few taps on a computer keyboard, everyone can be deprived of the power to acquire their wealth at any time. It's a super scary picture for anyone who values the power of freedom. But for international bankers, this is the height of the "New World Order".

The elite believe that their plan is not a "conspiracy" but an "open conspiracy". Unlike traditional conspiracies, they do not have a clear leadership structure, but rather a "loose" "social circle of like-minded people". However, what is disturbing to ordinary people is that these "like-minded" heavyweights always seem to "enrich" their "ideals" at the expense of ordinary people.

Colonel House, founder of the American Foreign Service Association and the first proponent of the League of Nations after the end of World War I, was an important manipulator of this scheme in the United States.

Colonel House, the "spiritual godfather"

> *In Washington, the real rulers are invisible, and they come from behind the scenes to exercise power.*[137]
> —Felix F. Frankfurter, Justice of the United States Supreme Court

Colonel House's name was Edward House, and the Colonel's title was a recognition by the Governor of Texas for his contributions to local elections in Texas. Born to a wealthy banker's family in Texas, Haus's father, Thomas, was an agent of the European Rothschilds during the American Civil War. House spent his early years in England, and like many American bankers of the early 20th century, House preferred to see England as his homeland and maintained a close relationship with the British banking community.

In 1912, House published an anonymous novel, *Philip Dru: The Administrator*, which later became of intense interest to historians, in which he conceived of a benevolent dictator seizing power in both parties in the United States, establishing a central bank, implementing a federal progressive income tax, abolishing protective tariffs, establishing a social security system, forming a League of Nations, and so on. The future world he "predicted" in his book was so strikingly similar to what would later happen in America that its "foresight" went straight after Keynes.

In fact, what Colonel House and Keynes wrote is more accurate than a prophetic book of the future, a plan for future policy implementation.

Colonel House' book attracted the attention of the American elite as soon as it was published, and its predictions for the future of the United States were highly in line with those expected by international bankers. Colonel House quickly became the "spiritual godfather" of elite circles. For the Democratic nomination for the 1912 presidential election, the Democratic bigwigs arranged for Colonel House to "interview" Wilson, one of the candidates. When Wilson arrived at

---

[137] Ted Flynn, *op. cit.*, p. 88.

House's hotel in Yonhue, the two men talked for an hour, deeply resentful of each other and, in Wilson's own words,

> *"Mr. House is my second nature. He is another separate being of my own. It's hard to separate his thoughts from mine. If I were in his place, I would do everything he suggested."*[138]

House played a communicative and coordinating role between politicians and bankers, and before Wilson was elected, at a banquet held by Wall Street bankers, House assured the financial bigwigs that "the Democratic donkey, ridden by Wilson, will never kick back in the road..." and Schiff, Warburg, Rockefeller, Morgan and others pinned their hopes on House.[139] Schiff compares House to Moses, while himself and the other bankers are Aaron.

After the November 1912 presidential election, President-elect Wilson went to Bermuda for a holiday, during which time he carefully read House's *Philip Dru: Administrator*. From 1913 to 1914, Wilson's policies and legislation were almost a rehash of House' novel.

When the Federal Reserve Act was passed on December 23, 1913, Schiff, a Wall Street banker, wrote to House,

> *"I would like to say a word of thanks for your quiet and fruitful contribution in the passage of this monetary bill."*[140]

When the heavy lifting of establishing a privately owned U.S. central bank was completed, House began to turn his attention to international affairs. With extensive contacts in Europe and America, House quickly became a heavyweight on the world stage.

> *"He (Haas) has a very deep connection to international bankers in New York. His influence extended to many financial institutions and bankers, including brothers Paul and Felix Warburg, Otto Can, Louis Marburg, Henry McKinza, brothers Jacob and Mortimer Schiff, and Herbert Lieman. House has an equally strong circle of bankers and politicians in Europe."*[141]

---

[138] Charles Seymour, *Intimate Papers of Colonel House* (Houghton Mifflin, 1926), Vol. I, p. 114.

[139] George Sylvester Viereck, *The Strangest Friendship in History*, 1932.

[140] Charles Seymour, *op. cit.*, p. 175.

[141] Dan Smoot, *The Invisible Government* (Dan Smoot Report, 1962).

On May 30, 1919, Baron Edmund Rothschild convened a meeting at a hotel in Paris, France, with members of the Inquiry and the British Round Table, centered on the integration of the British and American elites, which met again on June 5 and decided that it would be better to separate the organization and coordinate its actions.

When Roosevelt was Assistant Secretary of the Navy under Wilson, he read House's *Philip Dru: Administrator* and was inspired. The "moderate dictator" described in the book was a true reflection of what Roosevelt later became. When Roosevelt was elected president, House immediately became an indispensable high counsellor in the White House.

Roosevelt's son-in-law wrote in his memoir.

> *"For a long time, I have thought that it was Roosevelt himself who came up with all the claims and ways to benefit the United States. This is not the case in practice. Most of his ideas, his political 'ammunition', were carefully concocted for him in advance by diplomatic associations and organizations advocating a world single currency."*[142]

Paul Warburg's son, banker James Warburg, who was a financial advisor to Roosevelt and a member of the Foreign Affairs Association, said to the Senate Foreign Relations Committee on February 17, 1950,

> *"We should have a world government, whether people like it or not. The only question is whether this world government will come about by (peaceful) consensus or (forceful) conquest."*[143]

A December 9, 1950, editorial in the *Chicago Tribune* noted,

> *"Members of the (diplomatic) association have a far greater influence on society than ordinary people. They used the superiority established by wealth, social status, and educational background to steer this country down the path of economic bankruptcy and military collapse. They should look at their hands, which are stained with the blood that has dried up from the last war and is still bright red from the latest one."*[144]

---

[142] Col. Curtis Dall, *op. cit.*

[143] David Allen Rivera, *Final Warning: A History of the New World Order* (2004).

[144] *Chicago Tribune*, 9th december 1950.

In 1971, Congressman John Rarick of Louisiana put it this way:

> *"The Foreign Affairs Association, dedicated to the creation of a world government, financially supported by several of the largest tax-exempt foundations, wields the baton of power and influence and wields great influence in the financial, business, labor, military, educational and mass media communities. Every citizen who cares about good government committed to protecting and defending the U.S. Constitution and the spirit of free commerce deserves to know it (Foreign Affairs Association). Our country's press, which defends the right to know, has always been very aggressive in exposing scandals, but has always been suspiciously silent when it comes to the activities of diplomatic associations and their members. The Diplomatic Association is an elite organization. Not only does it wield power and influence at the highest decision-making levels of government to maintain top-down pressure, it also supports the transformation of a sovereign constitutional republic into a servant of a dictatorial world government by funding individuals and institutions to exert pressure from below and from above."*[145]

The Foreign Affairs Association has absolute influence on American politics. Since World War II, almost all but three of the presidential candidates have been members of the Association. For decades, the two parties have taken turns in power, and the government's policies have remained consistent because members of the Foreign Affairs Association have held almost every important position in government. In addition to the overwhelming majority of Treasury Secretaries since 1921, and the National Security Adviser under Eisenhower, who was essentially appointed by the Association, the Foreign Affairs Association has produced 14 Secretaries of State (all of whom have been appointed since 1949), 11 Secretaries of Defense, and 9 Directors of Central Intelligence.

From this perspective, the Diplomatic Association is the "central party school" of the American elite.

> *"Once the core members of the Foreign Affairs Association have decided on a particular policy of the U.S. government, the Foreign Affairs Association's large research organization goes into full swing, and they launch a variety of rational and*

---

[145] David Allen Rivera, *op. cit.*

> *emotional arguments to strengthen the persuasiveness of the*
> *new policy. Politically and ideologically, to confuse and demean*
> *any opposing views.* [146]

Whenever there is a vacancy (an important position) in Washington, the first thing the White House plays is a call from the New York Foreign Affairs Association, and the Christian Science Gag claims that almost half of the members of the Foreign Affairs Association have been invited into the government or have served as advisors to the government.

The Diplomatic Association's 3,600 members must be U.S. citizens, including influential bankers, leaders of major corporations, senior government officials, media elites, prominent university professors, think tanks at top think tanks, senior generals in the military, etc. These people form the "hard core" of the American political elite.

With regard to the "opinion orientation" of the mainstream media in the United States, the 1987 Foreign Affairs Association report noted that as many as 262 journalists and media experts were members, not only "interpreting" the Government's foreign policy, but "formulating" it. Members of the Foreign Affairs Association control television networks such as CBS, ABC, NBC, and PBS.

In terms of newspapers: members of the Foreign Affairs Association control: the *New York Times*, the *Washington Post*, the *Wall Street Journal*, the *Boston Globe*, the *Baltimore Sun*, the *Los Angeles Times* and other major newspapers.

In the magazine field, Foreign Affairs Association members control: *Time, Fortune, Life, Money, People, Entertainment Weekly, Newsweek, Business Week, U.S. News & World Report, Reader's Digest, Forbes, The Atlantic*, and other mainstream magazines. In the publishing field, members of the Diplomatic Association control: the largest publishing companies, such as McMillan, Rand, Simon & Schuster, Harper Brothers, and McGraw-Hill. [147]

U.S. Senator William Jenner once said,

---

[146] Phyllis Ward, Chester Schlafly, *Kissinger on the Couch* (Arlington House, 1975).

[147] Ted Flynn, *op. cit.*, p. 89.

> *"The road to dictatorship in America today can be fully legitimized in a way that Congress, the President and the people can neither hear nor see. On the surface, we have a government under the Constitution, but there is also a power within our government and political system that represents the view of the 'elites' who believe our Constitution is outdated and time is on their side."*

The power to decide America's internal and external affairs is no longer in the hands of the Democratic and Republican parties, but in the small circle of the super-elite club.

Bank for International Settlements: a bank for central bankers

The famous monetary expert Franz Pick once said,

> *"The fate of money will eventually become the fate of the nation as well."*

Likewise, the fate of the world's currency, ultimately, determines the fate of the world.

Although the Bank for International Settlements is actually the world's first international banking organization, it has deliberately kept a low profile and virtually invisible to the public, and as a result has received very little academic research.

Except for August and October, 10 times a year a group of well-dressed mystics from London, Washington and Tokyo come to Basel, Switzerland, and then quietly check into the Euler Hotel. They come to the world's most secretive, low-key, but high-impact regular meetings. The dozen or so people each have their own offices and secret dedicated phone lines to their respective countries, and a regular team of over 300 people provides them with a full range of services from drivers, cooks, security guards, messengers, translators, stenographers, secretaries, and research work, along with supercomputers, fully enclosed country clubs, tennis courts, swimming pools, and other facilities for them.

There are strict restrictions on who can join this superclub, and only those central bankers who set the daily rates of interest, the size of credit, and the money supply in each country are eligible. They include the directors of the Federal Reserve, the Bank of England, the Bank of Japan, the Swiss National Bank and the German Central Bank. This institution has $40 billion in cash, government bonds, and gold equivalent to 10 percent of the world's total foreign exchange reserves, and its gold holdings are second only to those of the United States Treasury. The profits from the lending of gold alone would fully cover the bank's expenses. The purpose of the monthly private meetings is to coordinate and control monetary activities in all industrial countries.

The headquarters building of the Bank for International Settlements has an underground building that can withstand a nuclear attack, complete hospital facilities, three redundant fire protection systems and no need for external firefighters even in the event of a major fire. The top floor of the building is a luxurious restaurant for the exclusive use of the dozen or so super VIPs who attend the "Basel Weekend". The view from the restaurant's huge glass terrace is breathtaking, with beautiful views of Germany, France and Switzerland.

In the building's computer centre, all computers are connected directly to the network of national central banks by a dedicated line, and data from international financial markets are displayed in real time on screens in the lobby, where 18 dealers process short-term loan transactions on the European money market without interruption. The other tier of gold dealers are almost perpetually trading gold positions between central banks on the phone.

The Bank for International Settlements (BIS) has virtually no risk in the various transactions, as all loans and gold transactions are secured by deposits from various central banks, and BIS charges high fees in the transactions. The question is, why are these central banks willing to hand over these uncomplicated operations to the Bank for International Settlements and let it earn extremely high fees? There is only one answer: a secret deal.

The Bank for International Settlements was founded in 1930, the Great Depression that swept the world was at its worst, and international bankers had begun to conceive of an amplified version of the Federal Reserve, creating a bank with a central banker. Under the Hague Agreement of 1930, it operates entirely independently of Governments and is completely exempt from taxation to Governments, whether in war or in peace. It accepts deposits only from national central banks and charges a substantial fee for each transaction. During the 1930s and 1940s, when the world economy was in severe recession and turmoil, European central banks deposited their gold reserves with the Bank for International Settlements (BIS) and, accordingly, various international payments and war reparations were settled through BIS.

The mastermind of the whole scheme was Germany's Hjalmar Schacht, the same Schacht who had conspired in 1927 with Strang of the New York Fed and Norman of the Bank of England to plan the stock market crash of 1929. He began following the Nazi faith in 1930. He designed the Bank for International Settlements to provide a platform on which central bankers could provide untraceable funds for clandestine transfers. In fact, it was through this platform that international bankers in Britain and the United States provided substantial financial support to Nazi Germany during World War II to help Germany drag out the war as long as possible.

After Germany declared war on the United States, large quantities of U.S. strategic supplies were shipped under the banner of a neutral state, first to fascist Spain and then to Germany. Many of these financial operations are settled through the Bank for International Settlements.

The Board of Directors of the Bank for International Settlements was surprisingly made up of bankers from both sides of the war, with Thomas McKittrick of the United States serving on the board along with Hermann Schmitz, the figurehead of the Nazi German industrial trust, I. G. Farben, the German banker Baron von Kurt Schroeder, and Walther Funk and Emil Pauhl of the Reichsbank, the latter two even being nominated by Hitler himself.

In March 1938, when the Germans occupied Austria, they ransacked Vienna's gold, which was deposited in the vaults of the Bank for International Settlements, along with gold later looted in the Czech Republic and other European countries occupied by Germany. Nazi Germany's directors prohibited discussion of the topic on the board of a clearing bank. Among other things, the Czech gold had been transferred to the Bank of England before the German occupation, and the Nazi occupation forces forced the Czech bank to claim it from the Bank of England, which Norman of the Bank of England immediately did, and the gold was used by Germany to buy large quantities of strategic goods.

When the news was revealed by a British journalist, it immediately raised eyebrows. U.S. Treasury Secretary Henry McKinsey personally called British Treasury Secretary John Simon to verify the situation, and Simon made a lot of excuses. Later when Prime Minister David Chamberlain was asked about it, Chamberlain's response was that there is no such thing. It turns out that Chamberlain was the majority shareholder in the Imperial Chemical Industries, which was a close business partner with I. G. Farben of Nazi Germany.

Cochran, assigned by the United States Department of the Treasury to the Bank for International Settlements (BIS) to verify the situation, described the relationship between the directors of BIS hostile countries in this way.

> "The atmosphere in Basel is completely friendly. Most central bankers have known each other for years, and the reunion of everyone is a pleasant and highly profitable affair. Some of them have suggested that they should abandon mutual cross-examination and that perhaps everyone should go fishing with President Roosevelt and get over everyone's pride and complications and get into a good place, so that the current complex political relationship can be made simple."

The Bank of England was later forced to acknowledge the fact that Czech gold had been transferred to Germany, their explanation being that it was only a technical operation and that the physical gold had never left the UK. Of course, thanks to the Bank for International Settlements, transporting gold to Nazi Germany required only a few changes in the accounts of the Bank for Settlements. One has to admire Yalma Shachter for devising such a clever financial platform in 1930 to support Germany's future wars.

In 1940, American Thomas H. McKittrick was appointed president of the Bank for International Settlements, a graduate of Harvard University, a former president of the British-American Chamber of Commerce, fluent in German, French and Italian, with close ties to Wall Street, and a history of extensive lending to Germany. Shortly after taking office, he traveled to Berlin for a secret meeting with the German Central Bank and the Gestapo to discuss how banking should continue once the United States entered a state of war with Germany.

On 27 May 1941, United States Secretary of State Hull, at the request of Secretary of the Treasury Morgenthau, sent a telegram to the United States Ambassador to the United Kingdom to investigate in detail the relationship between the British Government and the Bank for International Settlements, which was under Nazi control. The results of the investigation caught Morgenthau off guard and Norman of the Bank of England has been a director of the Bank for International Settlements. In fact, the American, British, and French banking institutions were indeed friendly and cordial with their mortal enemy on the battlefield, the Germans, on the boards of the liquidating banks, and this quaint relationship continued until the end of the war.

On February 5, 1942, two months after the Japanese sneak attack on Pearl Harbor, the United States had entered full-scale war with Germany, and strangely enough the German Central Bank and the Italian government agreed that McKittrick, an American, would remain president of the Bank for International Settlements until the end of the war, while the Federal Reserve remained in business with the Bank.

The UK Labour Party has been skeptical of the Bank of England's unclear relationship with the Bank for International Settlements, repeatedly urging the Treasury to have a say, explaining that

> *"this country has multiple rights and interests in the Bank for International Settlements and these arrangements are based on agreements between governments. It is not in our best interest to cut ties with this bank."*

In an era of war, even the non-aggression treaties between countries can be abandoned at any time, but the British Treasury is strictly adhering to the agreement between the bankers of various countries, so that people can not help but "admire" the British people's "serious attitude" to the law. The problem was that in 1944 it was finally discovered that Germany had received the vast majority of the dividends of the liquidating banks, and the generosity of Britain could not help but make one wonder.

In the spring of 1943, McKittrick traveled between the belligerents "at the risk of personal safety". Although he was neither an Italian citizen nor a U.S. diplomat, the Italian government granted him a diplomatic visa and was escorted by Himmler's secret police throughout his journey to Rome, the capital of the belligerents, and then back to the United States via Lisbon aboard a Swedish ship; in April, he traveled to New York for consultations with Federal Reserve officials, and then, armed with a U.S. passport, he traveled to Berlin, the German capital, to convey confidential financial information and the attitude of the U.S. top brass to officials at the German Central Bank.

On March 26, 1943, Congressman Jerry Voorhis of California introduced a proposal in the House of Representatives to investigate the Bank for International Settlements in an attempt to figure out "why an American citizen should be president of a bank designed and operated by the Axis powers", and neither the United States Congress nor the Treasury Department was interested in investigating.

By January 1944, another "good" deputy, John Kaufer, angrily stated:

> *"The Nazi government had 85 million Swiss francs in the Bank for International Settlements. Most of the directors are Nazi officials, and our American money is flowing all the way there."*

One never understood how Switzerland could remain "neutral" in the face of war on all sides, while the equally weak Belgium, Luxembourg, Norway and Denmark could not escape the Nazis even if they wanted to remain neutral. The problem was that the Bank for International Settlements was located in Switzerland, and its actual function was to finance the war for Germany by American and British bankers in order to make the war last longer.

On 20 July 1944, at the Bretton Woods Conference, the topic of the abolition of the Bank for International Settlements finally came to the table. Both chief architects, Keynes and Harry Dexter White, had initially supported the abolition of the Bank for International Settlements in view of its dubious conduct in the war, but their attitudes soon changed. When Keynes knocked on the door of U.S. Treasury Secretary Morgenthau's room, Morgenthau looked in amazement at the emotionally-charged Keynes, whose attitude and demeanor were impeccable, and whose face was flushed with red, and said in as calm a tone as possible that he thought the Bank for International Settlements should remain in operation until the new International Monetary Fund and World Bank were established, while Mrs. Keynes lobbied Morgenthau. Upon sensing the tremendous political pressure on Morgenthau to dissolve the Bank for International Settlements, Keynes took a step back and acknowledged that the bank should be closed, but the timing of the closure was also important. For his part, Morgenthau insisted that "the sooner the better".

Frustrated, Keynes returned to his room and immediately called an emergency meeting of the British delegation, which was held until 2 a.m., when Keynes personally drafted a letter to Morgenthau asking the Bank for International Settlements to continue its operations.

At the next day's meeting, Morgenthau's delegation surprisingly adopted a resolution to dissolve the Bank for International Settlements. Upon learning of this decision, McKittrick immediately wrote to

Morgenthau and the British Chancellor of the Exchequer, stressing that the Bank for International Settlements would still have a large role to play after the war, but at the same time stating that the accounts of the Bank for International Settlements could not be made public. In fact its accounts have never been made public to any government in the 76 years from 1930 to the present.

Despite McKittrick's dubious conduct during the war, he was admired by international bankers, and he was later appointed by Rockefeller as vice president of Chase Manhattan Bank. And the Bank for International Settlements was not ultimately dissolved.

After the war, the activities of the Bank for International Settlements became more secretive. It is made up of six or seven central bankers in what is called a "core club", with the directors of the Federal Reserve, Swiss National Bank, Deutsche Bundesbank, Bank of Italy, Bank of Japan, Bank of England, the Bank of France and other national central banks excluded from the core.

The most important idea of the "core club" is to firmly exclude Governments from the international monetary decision-making process. The Swiss National Bank was originally a private bank, completely free from government control. The Deutsche Bundesbank is almost as unconventional as the Swiss banks and does not greet the government at all on decisions as important as interest rate changes, and its president, Poole, would not even take a government-arranged flight to Basel for a meeting, preferring to travel to Switzerland in his limousine. Although the Fed is subject to certain government procedures, the White House and Congress are completely indifferent to monetary decisions. The Bank of Italy in theory had to come under government control, but its president never bit the chord with the government, and in 1979 the government even threatened to arrest Bank of Italy president Paolo Baffi, under pressure from international bankers, but the government did nothing. The case of the Bank of Japan is more unique, but after the collapse of the Japanese real estate bubble in the 1980s, the Ministry of Finance's intervention in the Central Bank of Japan was described as the culprit, and the Bank of Japan took the opportunity to break free from the government's grip. The Bank of England is looked at very closely by the government, but his presidents are all hand-eyed big shots, so they count as core members. Not so lucky for the Bank of France, which is seen as a puppet of the government and firmly excluded from the inner circle.

International Monetary Fund and World Bank

> *"They would say that the IMF is very arrogant. They will say that the IMF has never really listened to the developing countries that it is trying to help. They will say that the IMF's decisions are secret and undemocratic. They will say that the IMF's economic 'therapy' has often exacerbated the problem – making (economic development) slowly deteriorate into a slump and from slump to recession. They're right. I was Chief Economist of the World Bank from 1996 until September (2000), when I experienced the worst world economic crisis in half a century (Asian financial crisis, Latin American and Russian financial crisis). I witnessed first hand the measures taken by the IMF and the U.S. Treasury Department in response to this crisis and I was stunned."*
> —Stiglitz, former World Bank Chief Economist

Joseph Stiglitz, as the World Bank's chief economist, delivered this powerful attack on the two largest international financial institutions a week before the World Bank and IMF's annual meeting in 2000, and he was immediately "forced to retire" by World Bank President Wolfensohn. In fact, it was not Wolfensohn who fired Stiglitz, but US Treasury Secretary Lawrence Summers, who owns 17% of the World Bank, has the power to appoint and remove the President of the World Bank and a veto, and in effect controls the operations of the Bank. Samos was so fed up with Stiglitz that he could not bear to force Stiglitz to retire in silence, but was bound to humiliate him by the extreme form of "removal" (Removal).

Stiglitz was awarded the Nobel Prize in Economics in 2001, and Stiglitz also served as President Clinton's chief economic advisor.

The problem is not that Stiglitz's economics are inadequate, but that his "political stance" is problematic, mainly his negative attitude towards "globalization", to which international bankers are particularly keen. His assessment and insights about the two international financial institutions were, of course, based on a great deal of first-hand information, but what he did not expect at all was that "creating and exploiting these problems" was the mission of the two institutions.

Stiglitz does not believe in "conspiracy theories" at all, and likewise most economists and staff working at the World Bank and IMF, including those from the Chinese side, do not agree that there is any "conspiracy" in their work. In fact, from the operational level, all the work is completely scientific and rigorous, every data has a source, every algorithm has a scientific analysis, every scheme has a success story, if there is a "conspiracy" in their daily work, it is really wrong to say, anyone else with the same mathematical model and method will come to the same conclusion.

That's where the master designer comes in handy! The details and operations are completely transparent, scientific and almost impeccable, while the real "conspiracy" is at the Policy Level. The classic war case is that Poland and the former Soviet Union had very different effects of economic transformation.

Harvard professor Jeffrey Sachs, Soros, along with former Federal Reserve Chairman Paul Volcker and Citibank Vice President Anno Ruding, concocted the "oscillation therapy". Soros himself summed up the therapy this way.

> *"I took into account the need to show that changes in the political system will lead to economic improvement. Poland is one place to try. I have prepared a number of broad economic reform measures, which consist of three components: monetary tightening, structural adjustment and debt restructuring. I think it's better to have all three objectives accomplished simultaneously than separately. I advocate a kind of macroeconomic debt-share swap."*

As a result, the Polish "oscillation therapy" was implemented with substantial monetary support from the United States Treasury and international bankers, and with the "blood transfusion" of large sums of money, the Polish "oscillation therapy" was very effective.

Waiting for the "polar bear" by the economic "doctor" put on the operating table, a burst of open, the United States aid and international bankers originally promised good financial "blood transfusion", but stopped, the patient's fate can be imagined. No wonder Professor Sachs exclaimed "wrongly accused", obviously the successful "surgery" was verified by the Polish case but the accident, "polar bear" patient surprisingly killed.

In fact, the success of "oscillatory therapy" in Poland was originally a set, a conspiracy at the "policy level" that Professors Sachs and Stiglitz could not understand at the "operational level".

At the beginning of the design of the Breton system, these two financial institutions were established to establish the hegemony of the dollar as the world currency. The international bankers' ideal of abolishing the gold standard was achieved in three major steps, and Roosevelt completed the first step in abolishing gold when he abolished the traditional gold standard system in 1933 and the direct exchange relationship between gold and the dollar (Gold Standard) was replaced by an indirect exchange of gold (Gold Exchange Standard). In the internationally circulated market, foreign dollar holders can still convert dollars into gold. And the Bretton system is a step further, with the dollar exchange (Dollar Exchange Standard) replaced the gold was gold indirect exchange, that is, the national currency and the dollar peg, the dollar and gold peg, only foreign central banks can take the dollar for gold, gold was further squeezed out of the currency circulation field, since then, the abolition of gold completed the second step.

In order to prevent the situation from spiraling out of control, the US Treasury Department has designed provisions on many major issues that must be implemented with more than 85% of the votes in favor, thus giving the US Treasury Department (17% of the votes) a veto. In the case of the World Bank, where the United States Treasury selects the President, the threshold of 85 per cent of votes in favour is only rarely set in order to increase "efficiency", since it is the United States Treasury that selects the President and has full authority over personnel. This is the gap between playing "policy design" and limiting it to "operational processes".

Keynes, the chief architect of the Bretton system, also came up with an even more "brilliant" concept: "Special Drawing Rights" (SDRs) to construct the future world monetary framework, the so-called "paper gold" to make up for the physical shortage of gold in the United States, caused by a chronic shortage of money. This is an unprecedented "invention" in the history of mankind, which artificially stipulates that a certain "paper currency" will never be "devalued", equivalent to gold, but can never be converted into gold. The concept was "grandly introduced" in 1969 during the severe gold payment crisis in the United States, but it still failed to save the collapse of the international commitment to the dollar-gold exchange relationship. Following the collapse of the Bretton system, "special drawing rights" were redefined to be pegged to the exchange rate of a "basket" of currencies. To date, this "world currency", conceived by Keynes in the 1940s, has not been of much use.

The historic mission of the IMF and the World Bank was virtually over when Nixon announced the suspension of the relationship between gold and the dollar in 1971, but international bankers soon found a new niche for them: "helping" developing countries to "globalize".

Before Stiglitz was fired, he had access to a large number of confidential World Bank and IMF documents. These documents show that the IMF requires countries receiving emergency aid to sign up to 111 secret clauses, including the sale of core assets of the recipient country: water, electricity, gas, railways, telecommunications, oil, banks, etc.; the need for the recipient country to take extremely destructive economic measures; and the opening of bank accounts in Swiss banks for politicians in the recipient country, with billions of dollars secretly paid in return. If the politicians of these recipient countries reject these conditions, they will not be able to take out emergency loans in the international financial markets.

That's why international bankers have been unusually angry lately about China's no-strings-attached lending to Third World countries, where China has offered new options for desperate countries. Stiglitz revealed that all countries have the same kind of prescription waiting for them.

First by-product: privatization. More precisely, "bribery". The leaders of the recipient countries would receive a 10 per cent commission, paid in full to a secret account in a Swiss bank, whenever they agreed to cede state assets at bargain prices. In Stiglitz's words, "You'll see their eyes wide open", and that will be billions of dollars! When the biggest bribe in history occurred in 1995 during the privatization of Russia,

> "the U.S. Treasury thought it was great because we needed Yeltsin to be elected, We don't care if this is a corrupt election. We want the money to rush to Yeltsin."

Stiglitz is not a conspiracy theorist, he is simply an upstanding academic who, as an economist, conscience and sense of justice made him very uncomfortable with the despicable shenanigans of the World Bank and the U.S. Treasury when he saw the country plunge into a severe recession due to unprecedented corruption that caused Russian economic output to almost halve.

The second by-pill: capital market liberalization. In theory, capital liberalization means that capital flows in and out freely. But the reality of the Asian financial turmoil and the Brazilian financial crisis is that the free flow of capital to speculate in the real estate, stock and exchange markets. The IMF's conditions for reaching out to the rescue include tightening the monetary base and raising interest rates to the absurd level of 30%, 50%, 80%, such high interest rates will only ruthlessly destroy real estate values, destroy industrial production capacity and drain the wealth accumulated by society over the years.

Third by-product: market pricing. In 1998, when the IMF cut food and fuel subsidies in Indonesia, a massive riot broke out. Bolivia's citizens are rioting due to rising water prices. Ecuador has caused social unrest due to soaring gas prices. And this has long been figured out by the international bankers, in their terminology, called "Social Unrest". And this "social unrest" has a very good effect, and that is that money is scattered like frightened birds, leaving an extremely cheap asset waiting for the mouths of international bankers who are already salivating over it.

When Ethiopia's first democratically elected president received aid from the World Bank and IMF during the crisis, she was forced to deposit it into her account with the United States Treasury at a meager interest rate of 4 per cent, while at the same time having to borrow from international bankers at a high rate of 12 per cent for the relief of the hungry people. When the new president begged Stiglitz to use World Bank and IMF aid money for disaster relief, Stiglitz could only refuse his request. It was a cruel test of the human conscience, and Stiglitz clearly could not bear such torture.

Fourth by-product: poverty reduction strategies: free trade. In this context, Stiglitz likened the free trade provisions of the WTO to the "Opium War". Stiglitz was particularly outraged by the "intellectual property" clause, which, at such a high level of "intellectual property" "tariffs" to pay for brand-name drugs produced by pharmaceutical companies in Western countries, was tantamount to "cursing the local people to death, who (Western pharmaceutical companies) do not give a damn about their lives".

In Stiglitz's view, the IMF, the World Bank and the WTO are different brands outside of the same institution, and the IMF's market opening is even more onerous than the official WTO.

And *Confessions of an Economic HitMan,* published in 2004, adds a wonderful footnote to Stiglitz's perspective from the practitioner's perspective.

The book's author, John Perkins, uses his own personal experience to graphically and meticulously portray the beginnings of a secret, undeclared financial war waged by international bankers against developing countries. As a client, the author was recruited by the NSA (National Security Agency), the largest spy agency in the United States, in the late 1960s, and after a number of tests, the author was considered a very suitable candidate for the "economic assassin". In order to prevent his identity from being revealed, the author was sent by an internationally renowned engineering firm as "chief economist" to work as an "economic assassin" in various countries of the world, and if the author's plan was not revealed, the country concerned could only blame the greed of private companies because of the total lack of official background. It is the author's job to persuade developing countries to borrow heavily from the World Bank, far more than is actually needed, in order to determine that the debt is bound to become unpayable. Hundreds of millions of dollars in monetary bribes are paid in cash at any time in order to give those in power a taste of the sweet spot. When the debt cannot be paid, the World Bank and the IMF, on behalf of the international bankers, claim "the pound of flesh and blood that is owed" in exchange for the cession of important national assets, such as water systems, gas, electricity, transportation, communications and other industries.

If the work of the "economic assassins" fails, the CIA "jackals" are sent to assassinate the country's leaders, and if the "jackals" also fail, the military machine is finally used to wage war.

In 1971, the author was sent to Indonesia, where he successfully completed his mission as an "economic assassin", resulting in the country going into serious debt. Later, the author went to Saudi Arabia and personally manipulated the "recycling of Petrodollar back to the United States" (Cycling of Petrodollar) program, which contributed to Kissinger's later success in lobbying Saudi Arabia to disassociate himself from the OPEC organization. Later, the author travelled to Iran, Panama, Ecuador, Venezuela and other countries, where he did many outstanding things. When the events of 9/11 in 2001 left the author with the painful feeling that the United States was hated by the world because of the good work of "economic assassins" such as himself, the author finally resolved to tell the truth. The reason no major New York publisher has dared to publish his autobiography is that the book is so explosive. He wrote the book quickly in the "circle" spread, an international famous company with a high salary to hire him to "sit on the bench", the condition is not to publish the book, which is a "legal" bribe. When the author took the risk and pressure to publish the book in 2004, it became the best-selling novel in America almost overnight. The choice of fictional form was also made out of necessity, and the publisher was concerned that if it appeared in documentary form, it would inevitably lead to unintended consequences.

The elite group that rules the world

> *"It is better that we build the "edifice of world order" from the bottom up, rather than the other way around. Ending national sovereignty (the work) can be done with a bit by bit approach of encroachment, which will get us there faster than the old approach."*
> - Richard Gardner, *Foreign Affairs Magazine,* April 1974

On July 16, 1992, when Clinton accepted her bid for the presidential nomination at the Democratic convention, she made a number of high profile statements about unity, ideals, people and country that were nothing new. But at the end of his speech, Clinton suddenly mentioned the influence of his mentor from his Georgetown University days, the famous American historian Carroll Quigley, and compared this influence to that of President Kennedy.[148] Clinton repeatedly mentioned Carlo Quigley's name throughout his subsequent presidency, so what exactly is it about Carlo Quigley's claims that is so engrained in Clinton's bones?

It turns out that Professor Quigley is an authority on the Anglo-American secret elite, which he believes decisively affects almost all major events in the world, in other words, Professor Quigley is a master of "conspiracy theory".

A graduate of Harvard University, Professor Quigley has served at Brookings Think Tank, the U.S. Department of Defense, the Department of the Navy, and has worked closely with numerous senior CIA officials. Another reason was that, since he had been exposed to a large number of top secret documents during his 20 years of research,

---

[148] Bill Clinton, Acceptance speech to the Democratic National Convention by Governor Bill Clinton of Arkansas", New York - NY, 16 July 1992.

there was no second person in American history who had the opportunity to repeat his research, so there were few challengers to his work.

In Professor Quigley's view, the Royal Society of International Affairs, the American Foreign Service Association (CFR), the Bilderberg Group, and the Trilateral Commission are clearly the central organizations of the world political elite manipulating the world situation. Membership in the 3,600-member Diplomatic Association, which is the equivalent of a "central party school" in the United States, is the gateway to American politics and the future of world policy-making. The Bilderberg Club added elites from Europe, while the Trilateral Commission, with 325 members, added elites from Japan and other Asian countries. Weighty members of the American Foreign Service Association are often members of other organizations as well. The elite of these organizations include heavyweights who have taken the world by storm: former U.S. Secretary of State Henry Kissinger, David Rockefeller of the J. P. Morgan International Committee, Nelson Rockefeller, Prince Philip of England, McNamara, who served as U.S. Secretary of Defense in President John F. Kennedy's administration and later as President of the World Bank, former British Prime Minister Margaret Thatcher, former French President (and the main architect of the European Constitution) Bernie de Stein, U.S. Secretary of Defense Rumsfeld, former U.S. National Security Adviser Brzezinski and Federal Reserve Chairman Alan Greenspan, and the great master of the generation Keynes. The international bankers are the big bosses behind these organizations, and the Rothschild family has chaired many Bilderberg meetings, the 1962 and 1973 meetings in the Swedish holiday sanctuary of Sarthebaden were hosted by the Warburg family.

Clinton, who is in college, immediately realized that in order to make a mark in politics, personal struggle is doomed to failure, and must enter the circle of power to reach the realm of "good wind with power, let me rise to the top".

As it turned out, Clinton joined the Trilateral Commission and the Diplomatic Association, as well as the Rhodes Scholars, a training course designed to train important "cadres" of future "world governments". Clinton joined the Diplomatic Association in 1989, and in 1991, Clinton, then governor of Arkansas, appeared at the annual meeting of the Bilderberg Club in Germany that year,[149] knowing that many governors of large states in the United States wanted to attend this "super elite gathering".

The Bilderberg Club

> *"If we had opened our doors to the public in those years, we would not have been able to develop a development plan for the world. However, the world is increasingly complex and ready to move towards world government. A supranational sovereign entity composed of intellectual elites and world bankers is certainly better than national self-determination as practiced in past centuries."*[150]
>
> —David Rockefeller, 1991

The Bilderberg Club, named after a Dutch hotel, was founded in 1954 by Prince Bernhard of the Netherlands. The Bilderberg Club is the "international version" of the American Foreign Service Association and is composed of bankers, politicians, business leaders, media moguls and leading academics from the United States and Europe. Each of them was picked up one by one by Rothschild and Rockefeller, many of whom were also members of the American Foreign Service Association, Pilgrims Society, Round Table, and Trilateral Commission. The Bilderberg Club is the curatorial home of almost all the joint European institutions, including the EU, whose ultimate aim is to establish a world government.[151]

The greatest characteristic of the organization is its "mystique".

The Bilderberg Club is based in Leiden in the western Netherlands and even has a phone number. But there is no website. A few independent detectives, such as Tony Gosling in England or James Tucker in the United States, had to go to great lengths to get information about the location and agenda of the Bilderberg meeting, and Tucker followed the Bilderberg Club for 30 years. Tucker has published a book

---

[149] "Marc Fisher", *Washington Post*, Tuesday, January 27, 1998.

[150] Pepe Escobar, "Bilderberg Strikes Again", *Asia Times*, May 10, 2005.

[151] Ibid.

about the Bilderberg Club. Historian Pierre de Villemarest and journalist William Wolf have jointly published Facts and Chronicles Denied to the Public, volumes 1 and 2 of which tell the secret history of the development of the Bilderberg Club. A book by the Belgian sociologist Geoffrey Geuens also has a chapter devoted to the Bilderberg Club.

Etienne Davignon, former vice-president of the European Commission and a member of the Bilderberg Club, insists that "this is not a conspiracy of capitalists to manipulate the world". Thierry de Montbrial, director of the French Institute of International Relations and a member of the Bilderberg Club for nearly 30 years, said it was just a "club". For example, the official press release from Bilderberg's 2002 meeting said, "The Club's only activity is to hold its annual meeting. There will be no resolutions, no votes, no policy statements." The Bilderberg Club is a "flexible, informal, small international forum. In the forum, participants can express a variety of views and improve their understanding of each other".

British economist Will Hutton says that the agreement reached at each Bilderberg meeting is "a prelude to world policy making", a statement that is fairly close to the truth. The decisions taken at the Bilderberg meeting will later become the established policy of the G8 Summit, the IMF and the World Bank.

The media have always been meek as silent lambs in front of the Bilderberg Club, and in 2005 the *Financial Times* stole the show in typical fashion, downplaying the boisterous conspiracy theories.

In fact, anyone who questions this most powerful club in the world is ridiculed as a conspiracy theorist. Members of the Bilderberg Club, such as British parliamentarians or United States policymakers, describe it as "nothing more than a place to discuss issues", a forum where everyone can "express their views freely".

In his book *A Century of War: Anglo Americanoil politics and the New World War*, William Engdahl details a little-known mystery that took place at the 1973 Bilderberg Conference in Sweden. In the first few years after the collapse of the Bretton system, the dollar's position was in an unprecedented crisis around the world. Having been decoupled from gold, the credibility and value of the dollar has been lost in the world's financial turmoil like a kite with a broken string. The international bankers at that time were still far from being ready for the world currency, and their ideas and concepts were extremely confused, and the "grand" introduction of the world currency "special drawing rights" in 1969 was simply unappreciated in the international financial markets. Seeing that the situation was about to spiral out of control, international bankers consulted urgently at the 1973 Bilderberg Conference in an attempt to contain the world financial crisis of the time and regain confidence in the dollar. US financial strategist Walter Levy has come up with a bold and stunning plan to let go of the 400% world oil price spike and plan how to make a killing from it.

The meeting was attended by 84 members of major oil companies and consortia. Engdahl concluded that,

> "The purpose of these powerful people gathering at Bilderberg is to reorient the balance of power in the direction of U.S. financial interests and the dollar. To that end, they decided to use their most prized weapon – control of the global oil supply. The policy of the Bilderberg Club is to trigger a global oil embargo, forcing a surge in global oil prices. From 1945 onwards, world oil was priced in US dollars, in accordance with international practice, because US oil companies controlled the post-war oil market. Thus, the sudden rise in global oil prices implies a corresponding surge in world demand for the dollar (to buy the necessary oil), thereby stabilizing the value of the dollar currency."[152]

Kissinger used the phrase "a steady flow of petrodollars" to describe the result of soaring oil prices.

Trilateral Commission

> Our country can have great democracies, and we can create great wealth and accumulate it in the hands of a very few, but we cannot have both.
> —Louis Brandeis, Justice of the United States Supreme Court.

Zbigniew Brzezinski is clearly a central figure in the Trilateral Commission and a think tank for David Rockefeller. At his suggestion, Rockefeller was determined to "bring together the world's best brains" to solve the problems of the future. The idea was first proposed at the

---

[152] William Engdahl, *A Century of War: Anglo American Oil Politics an the New World War*, Pluto Press, 2004, Chapter 9.

beginning of 1972 and was widely discussed and accepted by the "collective" at the 1972 Bilderberg Annual Conference.

Brzezinski published his famous *Between Two Ages* in 1970, calling for a new international monetary system and world government, which is considered the "Bible" of the Trilateral Commission. The Rockefeller Foundation and the Ford Foundation are rightfully "generous" in their financial support of the Trilateral Commission's operations.

The main members of the Commission are major bankers, entrepreneurs and prominent politicians from North America, Western Europe and Japan, with three headquarters in New York, Paris and Tokyo, each chaired by a member from each of these three regions. The chairman of the New York headquarters is rightfully Mr. David Rockefeller. Brzezinski then became the Executive Director who presided over the day-to-day work at this headquarters.

Brzezinski had pressed David Rockefeller for Carter, then governor of Georgia, to join the Trilateral Commission, and Carter was unceremoniously absorbed into the Trilateral Commission upon David Rockefeller's personal nomination. It was a crucial step for him to make it to the steps of the White House five years later, and it was the foundation and beginning of what would become his and Brzezinski's crossroads.

As a young man, Clinton, under the tutelage of his mentor, Quigley, struggled to actively lean into organizations such as the Trilateral Commission and the Diplomatic Association, eventually realizing his presidential dream.

The Trilateral Commission is as much a peripheral body of the American Foreign Service Association as the Bilderberg Club, and the most confidential and important decisions are only hammered out in the circles of a very few people in London and Wall Street. The role of the Trilateral Commission and the Bilderberg Club is one of "unity of mind" and "coordination of pace".

The Trilateral Commission's most important mission was to spare no effort in preaching the grand ideals of "world government" and "world currency", ultimately paving the way for a "new world order" under the control of the London-Wall Street axis, and in a report entitled "An Outline for Remaking World Trade and Finance", held in Tokyo, Japan, in 1975, the Trilateral Commission stated that "close trilateral

(US, European, and Japanese) cooperation to maintain peace, manage the world economy, foster economic development, and reduce world poverty will increase the chances of a peaceful transition to a world system."

The Trilateral Commission differed from the Bilderberg Club in that it expanded the base of the "world's elite" by incorporating a number of prominent entrepreneurs and bankers from Japan, then a rising economic power. International bankers are well aware of the importance of the constant "fresh blood" for the future "great cause" of "world government", "world currency" and "world taxation". Later, as other countries and regions in Asia developed, the "elites" of those regions also became favoured by international bankers.

The question is not whether a "world government" is good or not, but who is in charge of it and whether it can truly achieve universal wealth and social progress worldwide. In the light of more than 200 years of social practice, the general public does not seem to expect the promises of the "elite".

After many wars and recessions, the common people have finally understood that without economic freedom, political freedom is just a ploy; without economic equality, democracy loses its roots and becomes a prop for money to play with.

If the essence of freedom is that people have the right to choose, there is only one path to the future "world government", and the "world elite" has already chosen it for the people of the world. In the words of Paul Warburg's son, banker James Warburg:

> *"We should have a world government, whether people like it or not. The only question is whether this world government will come about by (peaceful) consensus or (forceful) conquest."*

Summary

★After the publication of the novel *Philip Dru Administrator*, Colonel House became the "spiritual godfather" of elite circles and played a role of communication and coordination among politicians and bankers.

★The members of the Foreign Affairs Association form the "hard core" of the American political elite and have absolute influence on American politics, where the decision on internal and external affairs is no longer in the hands of the Democrats and Republicans, but in the small circle of the super elite club.

★The Bank for International Settlements, which deliberately keeps a low profile, is a central bank that accepts deposits only from national central banks and charges a substantial fee for each transaction.

★The International Monetary Fund and the World Bank are both effectively controlled by the United States.

★Clinton took the teachings of her benefactor and joined the Trilateral Commission and the Diplomatic Association of the Caucus of Power, eventually defeating the notorious George W. Bush Sr. in the general election to be elected president.

★In order to stabilize the value of the dollar currency, the Bilderberg Club manipulates the international oil price and profits from it.

CHAPTER VII

The Last Stand for Honest Money

"History shows that lenders use all means, including abuse of power, subterfuge, deception and violence, to secure their control over money and currency issuance in order to achieve control of government."
—James Madison, 4th President of the United States.

I n the entire modern history of the world, no event has trampled on democratic politics so blatantly, so unabashedly, so recklessly, as the assassination of President Kennedy. In the three short years since Kennedy's assassination, 18 key witnesses have died, six of them by gunshot, three in car accidents, two by suicide, one by throat slitting, one by neck breaking and five "natural" deaths. A British mathematician claimed in the *London Sunday Times* in February 1967 that the probability of this coincidence was 1 in 10 trillion. From 1963 to 1993, 115 of the witnesses involved committed suicide or were murdered in various bizarre incidents.[153]

The coordination and organization on such a large scale, the blocking of evidence and witnesses on such an obvious scale, suggest that the Kennedy assassination was in fact no longer a secret murder, but more of a public execution, intended to warn future U.S. Presidents to figure out who is really in charge of this country!

Generally speaking, if a United States President dies while in office, "public opinion" is bound to be unanimous that it is a "death of natural causes". If the President had been shot in full view, "public opinion" would have reported that "the killer was a lone nutcase". If there were several killers involved, "public opinion" would conclude that "the killers were isolated lunatics who did not know each other". Whoever is in doubt will be ridiculed as a "conspiracy theorist". It's

---

[153] Craig Roberts, *JFK: The Dead Witnesses* (Consolidated Press International, 1994), p. 3.

just that the Kennedy assassination plot was so obvious that no one with the slightest bit of normal thinking would believe the official conclusions. Under such circumstances, deliberate misdirection of conspiracy theories became a remedy and, for more than 40 years, conspiracy narratives proliferated and the real conspiracy was "hidden".

Criminalistics is all about evidence, without which no conclusion can be drawn. The various evidence and witnesses to the Kennedy assassination have long since gone up in smoke over the course of more than 40 years, and people will never be able to get conclusive evidence to determine who the real killer really is. But criminal psychology may open the door to the truth by examining the motives for murder from a different perspective.

This chapter will begin with an analysis of the motives behind the Kennedy assassination case and unravel a series of dramatic historical events triggered by international bankers in the 1960s and 1970s to abolish gold and silver, the "honest currencies" of the world.

Presidential Decree 11110: JFK's Death Certificate

For Americans, November 22, 1963 was an unusual day when President John F. Kennedy was assassinated and killed in Dallas, Texas. The whole of America was in shock and grief when the bad news came. Decades later, when people speak of this moment, many can clearly remember what they were doing at the time. There is still a lot of disagreement about who and why Kennedy was assassinated. The official U.S. Warren Commission ultimately concluded that a murderer named Oswald worked alone, but the case was so much in doubt that various conspiracy theories have been circulating in society for decades.

The most obvious suspicion is that the murderer was shot at close range by another Jewish assassin less than 48 hours after he was caught by the police, in full view of the millions of people who watched the murder on television, and that his motive was

"to show the world the courage of the Jewish people".

Another huge mystery is exactly how many people were involved in Kennedy's murder, and the Warren Commission concluded that Oswald fired three shots in a row in a span of 5.6 seconds, one of which went off, one hitting Kennedy in the neck and the other fatally in the head. Almost no one believed that Oswald could accurately shoot three times in such a short period of time, and it was even stranger that the bullet that hit Kennedy in the neck was the one that hit the Texas governor sitting in front of Kennedy before hitting him, and the chances of that being the case were almost zero, so people called it a "magic bullet". More experts believe that more than one person shot at Kennedy from a different direction, and more than three rounds.

A patrolman who later escorted Kennedy's car recalled,

> "While Kennedy was busy shaking hands with the welcoming crowd at the airport, Johnson's (Vice President) Secret Service came up to us to give us instructions on security work. What surprised me the most was when they said that the President's route of travel in Dealey Plaza (the site of the assassination) was temporarily modified. If the original route is maintained, the killer may not have a chance to get down at all. They also gave us an unheard of order that normally, the four of us motorcycle guards should stay close to the perimeter of the President's car, but this time they told us to all back up and under no circumstances go beyond the rear wheels of the President's car. They said it was to give everyone an 'unobstructed view'... Another friend of mine saw him (Johnson, Vice President of Protection) start bending over in his car 30 or 40 seconds before he heard the first shot, even before the convoy turned onto Houston Street. Maybe he was looking for something on the carpet in the car, but he looked as if he had a premonition that a bullet would come flying."[154]

When First Lady Jacqueline arrived at Washington airport with her husband's body on Air Force One, still wearing a coat splattered with Kennedy's blood, she insisted on doing so so that "they would see the crime committed", while the killer, Oswald, was still in police custody, and who was this "they" Jacqueline was talking about? Jacqueline said in her own will that on the 50th anniversary of her death (May 19, 2044), if her youngest child had died, she authorized the Kennedy Library to release a 500-page document on Kennedy. What didn't occur to her was that her youngest son was killed in a plane crash in 1999.

---

[154] Jean Hill, *JFK: The Last Dissenting Witness* (Pelican Publishing Company, 1992), pp. 113–116.

Kennedy's brother Robert, a prominent promoter of the civil rights movement, would almost certainly end up as president after his election as the Democratic presidential candidate in 1968, but just as he was celebrating his victory, he was again mobbed to death in a large public setting.

In the three short years since Kennedy's assassination, 18 key witnesses have died, six of them by gunshot, three in car accidents, two by suicide, one by throat slitting, one by neck breaking and five "natural" deaths. A British mathematician claimed in the *London Sunday Times* in February 1967 that the probability of this coincidence was 1 in 10 trillion. From 1963 to 1993, 115 of the witnesses involved committed suicide or were murdered in various bizarre incidents.[155]

The Warren Commission also raised questions about the sealing of all documents, files and evidence for 75 years until 2039, involving the CIA, FBI, the President's Secret Service, NSA (National Security Agency), State Department, Marine Corps and other agencies. In addition, the FBI and other government agencies are suspected of destroying evidence.

On the 40th anniversary of JFK's assassination in 2003, ABC Radio conducted a poll in which 70 percent of Americans believed that the assassination of JFK was a larger conspiracy.

The coordination and organization on such a large scale, the obvious evidence and the suppression of witnesses suggest that the Kennedy assassination was no longer really a secret murder but more of a public execution, intended to warn future U.S. presidents to figure out who is really in charge of this country.

The problem is that the Kennedys were also "in the loop" of the international bankers' group. Their father, Joseph, made a fortune during the stock market crash of 1929, and was later appointed by President Roosevelt as the first chairman of the U.S. Securities and Exchange Commission (SEC), and was among the billionaires as early as the 1940s. So how did Kennedy offend the entire ruling elite to the point of murder?

There is no doubt that Kennedy was an ambitious and talented figure who, when he took the presidency at a young age, encountered

---

[155] Craig Roberts, *JFK: The Dead Witnesses* (Consolidated Press International, 1994)

such a major challenge as the Cuban Missile Crisis, with a steadfast and remarkable performance, uncompromising in the face of the great danger of a possible nuclear war with the Soviet Union, which eventually forced Khrushchev back. JFK also heroically promoted the U.S. space program that eventually brought mankind's footsteps to the moon for the first time, and although he did not see this great moment in person, his magical inspiration accompanied the entire program. The Kennedys were even more credited with advancing the civil rights movement, and when the first black college student attempted to enroll at the University of Mississippi in 1962, sparking fierce opposition from local whites, the eyes of the entire United States were focused on this focus of the civil rights movement. Kennedy's resolute order to send 400 federal law enforcement officers and 3,000 National Guardsmen to escort the black student to school shocked American society and Kennedy was instantly loved by the people. At his call, American youths have joined the Peace Corps in droves, volunteering in Third World countries to help develop education, health and agriculture there.

In the short three years of Kennedy's presidency, it is indeed a generational feat to have such a dazzling record. With such ambition and determination, coupled with the love of the American people and the admiration of all countries in the world, was JFK a figure willing to be a "puppet"?

As Kennedy became increasingly intent on running this country according to his own good intentions, he was bound to come into sharp conflict with the powerful and invisible ruling elite group behind him. When the focus of the conflict involved the most central and sensitive issue of the ruling elite dominated by international bankers – the right to issue money – Kennedy may not have known his big time had come.

On June 4, 1963, Kennedy signed a little-known Executive Order 11110, which ordered the U.S. Treasury Department to "issue 'Silver Certificates' backed by any form of silver owned by the Treasury, including silver ingots, silver coins, and standard silver dollars," and immediately put it into circulation. Kennedy's intent was clear, to take back the power to issue money from the private central bank, the Federal Reserve! If the plan is finally implemented, the U.S. government will gradually move away from the absurdity of having to "borrow" money from the Federal Reserve and pay high interest rates, and the silver-backed currency is not a debt currency to "overdraft the future", but an "honest money" based on the fruits of people's work already. "The circulation of "silver notes" will gradually reduce the liquidity of the Federal Reserve Notes issued by the Federal Reserve, which will likely eventually force the Federal Reserve banks into bankruptcy.

The loss of control over the issuance of money would deprive international bankers of most of their influence over the United States, the largest wealth-creating nation, a fundamental question of life and death. To figure out the origins and significance of Presidential Decree 11110, we must start with the few ups and downs of silver in the United States.

The historical status of the silver dollar

Silver becoming legal tender in the United States began with the Coinage Act of 1792, which established the legal status of the dollar. A dollar contains 24.1 grams of pure silver and a 1:15 gold to silver ratio. The dollar's metric as the most benchmark of U.S. currency is based on silver. Since then, the United States has long maintained a dual-track system of gold and silver currencies.

By February 1873, the Minting Act of 1873, under pressure from the Rothschilds of Europe, abolished the monetary status of silver and introduced a single gold standard, and since the Rothschilds held most of the world's gold minerals and gold supplies, they effectively controlled the entire European money supply. The origin of silver is more fragmented than gold, and the production and supply is much larger and more difficult to control, so around 1873, the Rothschild family coerced most European countries to abolish the monetary status of silver and implement a full gold standard. The United States is also a step in this overall step. The bill sparked strong opposition in the silver-producing western states of the United States, and was dubbed the "Crime of 1873", which led to a rousing grassroots movement in support of silver.

The U.S. Congress, in an effort to balance the influence of bankers with European backgrounds in the New York area, passed the Bland-Allison Act of 1878, which required the U.S. Treasury to purchase between $2 million and $4 million worth of silver per month, with the gold-silver ratio reset to 1 to 16. Silver coins had the same legal effect as gold coins and could be used to pay all public and private debts. Like the "gold certificate", the Treasury also issues "silver certificates", one dollar of which corresponds directly to one dollar of silver for ease of circulation. (One dollar "silver voucher", directly convertible into one dollar silver equivalent)

Later the Brand-Ellerson Act of 1878 was replaced by the Sherman Silver Purchase Act of 1890, and the new act increased the amount of silver the Treasury had to purchase, adding 4.5 million ounces per month to the previous basis.

Since the establishment of the Federal Reserve in 1913, the Federal Reserve Note was issued, and by the time of the Great Recession in 1929, the Federal Reserve Note had gradually taken a major share of money in circulation. By 1933, "Federal Reserve Notes" could still be exchanged for gold equivalents. (1914 dollar "Federal Reserve Note", indirectly convertible into gold equivalent)

In 1933, there were also "Gold Certificates" and "U.S. Government Certificates" in the money market. (1913 $50 gold note, directly convertible into $50 gold equivalent, illegal to hold after 1933) "The United States Note is the first currency issued by Abraham Lincoln during the Civil War, the "Lincoln Greenbacks". Its total circulation was limited to 6,681,016. in 1960, it accounted for only 1% of the total currency in circulation in the United States. ("U.S. Government Vouchers", or "Lincoln Greenbacks")

In addition to the four major currencies mentioned above, a small number of other forms of currency coexist.

After Roosevelt abolished the gold standard in 1933 and made it illegal to own gold, gold certificates were withdrawn from circulation. The only remaining money in circulation in the United States is "Federal Reserve Notes", "Silver Notes" and "United States Government Notes", which are not considered a major threat by international bankers because of their congenital deficiencies and their issuance limits. "Silver vouchers" are a lot more problematic.

Since the U.S. Treasury was required by law to buy silver all year round, by the 1930s, the U.S. Treasury already had over 6 billion ounces of silver (Troy Once), a huge reserve of about 200,000 tons, plus silver minerals all over the world and a considerable amount of production, if all of them were to be monetized and issued "silver bonds", it would become the biggest nightmare for international bankers.

After Roosevelt helped international bankers abolish the gold standard in 1933, U.S. money circulation was effectively under a "silver standard".

Without the abolition of the monetary status of silver, the "great business" of "cheap money" and "deficit finance" will be severely hampered and the plans of international bankers to unwittingly plunder the wealth of citizens through a more efficient financial instrument, inflation, will be hampered.

The demand for silver from the electronics and aerospace industries, which began to flourish in the 1950s, increased sharply, and by the time Kennedy took over the White House in the early 1960s, the Treasury's silver reserves had dwindled to 1.9 billion ounces. At the same time, the market price of silver has soared and has gradually approached the monetary value of silver coins at $1.29. When the "silver coupons" were exchanged for real silver, the "silver coupons" naturally withdrew from circulation, and the effect of the "Gresham's Law" of "bad coin to drive out good coin" appeared. All of this is the big background to Kennedy's signing of Presidential Order 11110. Defending silver and abolishing its monetary status became the focus of Kennedy's and the international bankers' struggle.

The End of the Silver Standard

For international bankers, the complete abolition of gold's monetary status is in the full scheme of things, but solving the silver problem holds a higher priority. Because the potential mineral resources of silver are so vast, once the world's countries begin to explore and exploit on a larger scale, guided by market prices, not only will the goal of abolishing the gold standard be difficult to achieve, but they will also be caught in a two-front battle between gold and silver. Once the supply of silver rises sharply, "silver bonds" is likely to be resurrected to compete with "Federal Reserve bonds", because the U.S. government holds the power to issue "silver bonds", by then it is not yet certain who will die. The survival of the Federal Reserve is at great risk if "silver bullion" prevails.

The most urgent task for international bankers is therefore to depress the price of silver to the maximum extent possible, on the one hand by leaving the world silver mining industry at a loss or marginally profitable, thus slowing down the exploration and development of silver and reducing the supply, and on the other hand by driving up the volume of industrial silver, making research and application of alternative silver materials unnecessary and thus depleting the only remaining silver reserves in the United States Treasury at the fastest possible rate. When the Treasury could not get the silver, the "silver note" naturally fell without a fight, and the abolition of silver's monetary status was a natural consequence. The key is to buy time.

Kennedy, of course, knew this well and, while indicating to the international bankers that the appropriate time would come to consider abolishing the monetary status of silver, he made other arrangements. Unfortunately, his Treasury Secretary, Douglas Dillon, was not at his heart; Dillon came from a large Wall Street banking family, and as a Republican was forced into Kennedy's Democratic cabinet by international bankers, to whom Dillon was primarily responsible for fiscal power. After Tyrone took office, his first priority was to deplete the Treasury's silver reserves as fast as he could. The Silver Users Association, founded in 1947, echoed Dillon's call to "sell [the Treasury's] remaining deposits to satisfy the needs of the silver users"

The New York Times, 19 March 1961, reported the following,

> "Senator complains about low US (Treasury) sell-off (silver) Senator Alan Bible (R-Ky.) today asked the Treasury Department to revisit its policy of selling large amounts of silver at prices below the international market. The Nevada Democrat said in a letter to Treasury Secretary Douglas Dillon that domestic silver development in the U.S. has lagged behind consumer demand, and that the Treasury's dumping is controlling an unrealistic price ceiling. The world's silver shortage can only be solved by the massive development of new capacity in North and South America. He said: "This will only be possible when the Treasury eases the harsh price pressures on the domestic market and neighbouring countries."

The New York Times of 19 August 1961 also carried the following message,

> Thirteen Western Democratic senators, mainly from silver-producing states, today submitted a joint letter to President Kennedy demanding that the Treasury Department immediately stop selling silver. Dumping by the Treasury has depressed silver prices in both international and domestic markets.

On 16 October 1961, The New York Times,

> *The Treasury's sell-off of silver reserves has put a tight cap on silver market prices. Industrial users know they can get 91 to 92 cents per ounce of silver from the Treasury, so they refuse to pay more to new silver producers.*

On 29 November 1961, The *New York Times*,

> *Silver producers were delighted to hear yesterday that President Kennedy had ordered the Treasury Department to stop selling the currency, silver, to industry. The industrial users of silver were shocked.*

On 30 November 1961, The *New York Times*,

> *The price of silver hit its highest level in the New York market in 41 years, with President John F. Kennedy's announcement on Tuesday of a complete change in the U.S. government's silver policy and the decision to let the market determine the price of silver. The first step was to immediately stop the Treasury from selling silver that didn't have to back up paper money ("silver bills").*

President Kennedy finally struck, though it was a little late, as the Treasury had less than 1.7 billion ounces of silver left at this point. But his decisive measures have sent a clear signal to market silver prices to silver producers around the world that a rise in silver production and a stabilization of Treasury stocks are to be expected. Silver's stock skyrocketed.

This act by Kennedy subversively undermined the international bankers' agenda. In April 1963, Federal Reserve Chairman William Martin said at a congressional hearing,

> *"The Federal Reserve Board is convinced that there is no need for silver in the U.S. monetary system. While some people feel that taking silver out of the monetary system that underpins part of us could cause a devaluation, I can't subscribe to that view."*[156]

As a general rule, when the silver market gets a clear signal of rising prices, it will take about five years for new resource exploration to begin again, new equipment to expand the scale of production, and finally increase the total supply, so the key moment will be 1966 if

---

[156] Federal Reserve Bulletin, April 1963, p. 469.

silver's monetary status can finally be preserved, thus preserving the hope that the U.S. government will issue money directly.

The high point of Kennedy's battle with the international bankers was the monetary status of silver, and the whole battle was about whether the elected government of the United States would finally retain the right to issue money. Once the supply of silver resumes in large quantities, Kennedy can join forces with the western silver-producing states to further promote legislation to revalue the silver content of the dollar currency and increase the issuance of "silver vouchers," which are bound to rise again.

At that point, Presidential Decree 1,110, signed by Kennedy on June 4, 1963, would immediately become a stalemate against "Federal Reserve Notes".

Unfortunately, the international bankers saw Kennedy's deployment just as well. The president, beloved by voters, will almost certainly be re-elected in the late 1964 election, and if Kennedy is president for another four years, the situation will become untenable. Getting rid of JFK became the only option.

When the Vice-President whom the international bankers favoured succeeded the 36th President of the United States of America on the plane on the day of Kennedy's assassination, he knew exactly what the international bankers expected of him, and he could not and dared not live up to that "expectation".

In March 1964, shortly after Johnson took office, he ordered the Treasury Department to cease the exchange of "silver certificates" with physical silver, thereby effectively abolishing the issuance of "silver certificates". The Treasury again began selling large amounts of silver reserves to industry with $1.29 as support to continue to squeeze silver prices, depressing the production momentum of silver producers and preventing a rise in silver supply.

Immediately following this, Johnson ordered the dilution of the purity of silver coins in June 1965, further reducing the status of silver in coin circulation, saying,

> *"I want to state absolutely categorically that these changes (the dilution of the purity of silver coins) will not affect the purchasing power of our coins. Within the United States, the new*

silver coins will be interchangeable with notes of equal denomination."[157]

A story in the *Wall Street Journal* on June 7, 1966, responded sarcastically,

> *"Indeed! But the purchasing power of that famous paper currency has been gradually eroded away under the same government's inflationary policies for over 30 years. Because of this, it's no wonder our currency has completely parted ways with gold and silver."*

By its own admission, the Fed has systematically and "scientifically" reduced the purchasing power of the dollar by 3 to 4 per cent each year so that the working class can "see" that wages are rising. By the summer of 1967, the Treasury had virtually no more "idle" silver to sell. The great business of ending silver money was finally in Johnson's hands.

Gold Mutual Fund

In the process of abolishing the monetary status of gold and silver, international bankers have adopted a strategic approach of "silver before gold". The main reason for taking silver first was that by the early 1960s, only a few countries in the world were still using silver as currency, and "removing silver" from the U.S. monetary system was only a partial operation with limited resistance and reach.

The problem with gold is much more complex and difficult. In the 5,000 years of human social practice, in whatever era, in whatever country, in whatever religion, in whatever race, gold has been recognized by the world as the ultimate form of wealth. This deep-rooted awareness can never be dissolved by a few words of "gold is a barbaric relic" from Keynes and others. International bankers know very well that gold is by no means an ordinary precious metal, in essence, gold is the only, highly sensitive and deeply historical "political metal", if not handled properly, it will cause a financial storm in the world. Before the battle for silver is over, the gold side of the battle must be stabilized.

---

[157] Remarks by President Lyndon B. Johnson at the signing of the Coinage Act on July 23, 1965.

As a result of the Fed's massive inflationary policies since the 1930s, the Fed's monetary issuance has been severely oversold, and the excess paper money has inevitably pushed up the price of gold and silver in the pursuit of limited gold and silver money. At home in the United States, the Treasury Department is responsible for stepping in to suppress the price of silver, and internationally, there must be a corresponding organization to act as the Treasury Department's function, responsible for selling gold to the market and suppressing the raging gold offensive in beachhead positions.

The advent of the jet age allowed international bankers to meet frequently and discuss countermeasures in secret. The Bank for International Settlements in Basel, Switzerland, then became the site of their famous "Basel Weekend" conference.

In November 1961, after intensive consultations, international bankers agreed on a "brilliant" plan to establish a "gold mutual fund" by the United States and seven major European countries, the main thrust of which was to suppress the price of gold in the London market. The fund is contributed by the central bank of the participating countries, the total amount of 270 million U.S. dollars of gold equivalent, of which the United States is the largest financial atmosphere, exclusive half, Germany's post-war economy took off, the purse is also increasingly bulging up, plus the defeated countries feel dwarfed, so the amount of pledges second only to the United States, reaching 30 million U.S. dollars. 25 million for England, France and Italy, and 10 million for Switzerland, Belgium and the Netherlands. The Bank of England was actually in charge of the operation, first advancing gold from its own vault, and then settling at the end of the month on a pro rata basis with the other incoming central banks.

The primary objective of the "Gold Mutual Fund" is to meet the gold price if it exceeds $35.20, which includes the cost of transporting the gold from New York. All central banks participating in the fund pledged not to buy gold from the London market, nor from third countries such as South Africa, the Soviet Union, etc., and the United States pledged to lobby central banks in other countries to adopt the same policy, whenever possible.

The contents of all "gold mutual funds" were at that time top financial secrets and, like the traditional secret meetings of the Basel Bank for International Settlements, no written record was allowed, not even a single piece of paper. Any agreement is made verbally, and just as old JPMorgan closed huge deals with handshakes and verbal agreements, the verbal promises of international bankers have an equal or even higher binding force.[158]

In its first years of operation, the "Golden Mutual Fund" was a great success, even better than one could have imagined. Gold-producing countries in the Soviet Union in the autumn of 1963, a serious agricultural failure, had to sell a lot of gold to import food, the Soviet Union in the last quarter of 1963 sold an astonishing total of 470 million U.S. dollars of gold equivalent, significantly more than the "gold mutual fund" of the entire gold family, in 21 months, the "gold mutual fund" of the gold ammunition depot soared to 1.3 billion U.S. dollars, international bankers can hardly believe their good luck.[159]

However, the escalation of the Vietnam War led the Federal Reserve to increase the supply of dollars, and the flooded dollars soon swallowed up the surplus and most of the money in the "gold mutual fund". France, seeing that the momentum has gone, the first to withdraw from the "gold mutual fund", not only that, the French government stepped up the hands of a large amount of the growing loss of purchasing power of the United States dollar into gold, from 1962 to 1966, France from the hands of the Federal Reserve to exchange nearly 3 billion dollars of gold and transported back to Paris for storage.

By the end of November 1967, the "gold mutual fund" had lost a total of $1 billion in gold, nearly 900 tons. The dollar is in the midst of a worldwide crisis of confidence.

President Johnson finally sank down, he wanted to do something about it. President Johnson was surrounded by a group of national bankers who acted as his senior advisers, and they repeatedly instilled in the President the idea that the long pain was better than the short pain, and that instead of being drained of gold reserves by other countries little by little, it would be better to throw a wager, take out all the gold, flood the London metal trading market, solve the problem of gold's appreciation against the dollar once and for all, and restore world confidence in the dollar. Johnson took the near-crazy advice and the

---

[158] Ferdinand Lips, *Gold Wars, The Battle Against Sound Money as Seen From a Swiss Perspective* (The Foundation for the Advancement of Monetary Education, New York, 2002), p. 52.

[159] *Ibid.*, p. 53.

Fed's entire gold reserves were bet on the table on an unprecedented scale. Tens of thousands of tons of gold bricks were shipped to the Bank of England and the Federal Reserve Bank of New York, ready to teach the world's bullish gold speculators a bitter lesson. If the plan goes well, the Bank of England and the Federal Reserve Bank of New York join forces to sell gold in large quantities, causing a sudden oversupply of gold, knocking the price below $35, speculators are bound to go into a full-blown panic and eventually hit their stop-loss line, causing a larger gold sell-off. After completely destroying the popularity of gold buyers, then gradually buying back the gold at a low price, people unknowingly return the gold to the vault. It really is a pie-in-the-sky plan. Within a few weeks in early 1968, the plan was implemented. To the extreme horror of President Johnson and everyone else, the market has all but absorbed the selling of gold. In total, the Fed lost 9,300 tons of gold during that campaign. President Johnson, who loved power but lost miserably, soon announced he would not run for re-election as president.[160] In March 1968, the "Golden Mutual Fund" was on the verge of collapse.

On March 9, Special Assistant to the President Rostow wrote this in a memo to Johnson.

> *"The conclusion of all (presidential economic advisers) is that there is unanimous opposition to allowing gold prices to rise in response to the current crisis. Most preferred to keep the "gold mutual fund" running, but they found it difficult to coordinate with the European side and restore calm to the market. So they thought we would eventually have to close the "gold mutual fund". There was some confusion as to how to persuade non-Golden Mutual Fund countries to cooperate with us, as they felt that the IMF (International Monetary Fund) might be of use. They think we have to have a clear idea of where to go and act within 30 days.*
> *VERDICT: You can see that these ideas are not much different from ours. After this weekend's Basel Conference (Bank for International Settlements), we will be able to get a more accurate picture of what the Europeans think.*

On March 12, in another memo, Rostow wrote.

> *Mr. President.*

---

[160] *Freemarket Gold & Money Report,* « Thinking The Unthinkable », 25 avril 1994.

My understanding of Bill Martin (Bill Martin, Fed Chairman, who just attended the late Basel meeting) is the following.

1. The British and Dutch are likely to favour this option (keeping the "gold mutual fund") in relation to changes in the price of gold. The Germans were hesitant. The Italians, Belgians and Swiss were strongly opposed.

2. He reached an agreement to add $500 million in gold and to guarantee the continued operation of the fund by promising another $500 million. (At the current rate of gold loss in the London market, this gold will only support a few days)

3, Europeans realize that we will soon be faced with very unpleasant choices. They were prepared to close the London gold market and let the gold go with them.

4. Under these circumstances, the Treasury Department, the State Department, the Federal Reserve, and the President's economic advisers have been busy all day thinking about how countries will coordinate once we announce the closure of the "golden mutual fund".

5, We don't yet know the personal views of Fowler (Treasury Secretary) and Bill. We'll exchange ideas with them tonight or tomorrow morning.

My personal feeling is that we are getting closer to the moment when the truth comes.

On 14 March, on the issue of gold, Rostow further reported.

Your senior advisor agrees that.

1. The current situation can't go on any longer and hopefully things will get better.

2. We need to convene a meeting of the "Golden Mutual Fund" participating countries in Washington this weekend.

3. We will discuss: rules for gold during the transition period, measures to keep financial markets afloat, intensification of special drawing rights (SDR's)

4. During the transition period, we will exchange the official central bank dollar holders at the original price.

5. If no agreement can be reached, we will suspend the official exchange of US dollars for gold, at least temporarily. An emergency meeting was then called.

6. This will probably throw world financial markets into chaos for some time, but it is the only way to force other countries to accept a long-term solution. We agree that letting the price of gold rise is the worst consequence.

You must now resolve whether or not to close the London gold market immediately.[161]

On 17 March 1968, the "Golden Mutual Fund" scheme was finally closed. The London gold market was closed for a full two weeks at the request of the US.

At the same time as the fiasco of the Federal Reserve's Gold War, the situation in the Vietnam War took a dramatic turn when the Vietnamese guerrillas launched a simultaneous massive offensive against the provincial capitals of 30 provinces in South Vietnam on January 30, 1968, even capturing some important targets in Saigon and the capture of the ancient capital of Hue. According to Kissinger, the offensive, although a political victory for North Vietnam, was its greatest defeat from a military point of view, with the guerrillas abandoning the erratic style of play that they were good at and concentrating their efforts in a position battle with the U.S. Army, which suffered heavy casualties under superior U.S. firepower. The prospects for the Vietnam battlefield might have radically improved if the U.S. had launched a major offensive against the main North Vietnamese force, which had already lost its guerrilla cover, and, to Kissinger's chagrin, Johnson had given up such an opportunity.[162] By this time Johnson's dismal defeat on the financial battlefield had stripped him of the courage to hold on to the Vietnam War.

The fiasco in London's gold market sent America's policymaking elite into a full-blown panic, with conservatives who cling to the gold standard having a heated debate with the mainstream who call for its abolition. But both sides agreed that with such a messy financial situation, it was time for the Vietnam War to end.

Thus, a fundamental shift in the direction of American press opinion began, and on 27 February 1968 Walter Cronkite "predicted" that America would fail. The *Wall Street Journal* asks,

> *"Has the state of affairs messed with our original goal of being able to navigate? If not ready, the American people should be prepared to accept the bleak prospect of events in Vietnam."*

---

[161] U.S. Department of State, Foreign Relations of the United States, 1964–1968, Vol. VIII (Government Printing Office, Washington, 1998), Documents 187, 188, 189.

[162] Henry Kissinger, *op. cit.*, pp. 607–608.

The *Times* said on March 15,

> *"1968 has made Americans realize that winning in Vietnam, or even just getting a favorable situation, is no longer within the reach of (the United States) as a world power."*

At this point, the long-sleeping senators also awoke, and Senator Fulbright began to question,

> *"Does the government have the right to expand the war without the consent of Congress?" Mansfield, for his part, declared, "We are in the wrong place, engaged in the wrong war."*

On 31 March 1968, Johnson announced the suspension of bombing operations in areas north of the 20-degree line, and stated that he would not send large numbers of additional troops to Vietnam, declaring that "our goal in Vietnam was never to destroy the enemy". He also announced that he was abandoning his bid for re-election to the presidency.[163]

The end of the Vietnam War was essentially due to the loss of the financial "bottom line" of the ruling elite as a result of the fiasco in London's golden battlefield.

Special Drawing Rights

Monetarists throughout the recurring dollar crises have insisted that it is the shortage of gold that has caused the monetary crisis, and from the history of the gold standard, it is clear that this is the reverse cause, that the shortage of gold is not the cause of the problem, and that unbridled dollar over-issuance is the root cause of the crisis. As with the prolonged suppression of silver prices, one of the main purposes of the long-term distortion of gold prices is to create the dilemma of insufficient gold production. When a crisis comes, it is strange that people usually resort to the tactic of covering their ears rather than being honest about the nature of the problem. After the "gold mutual fund" shot all the "bullets", international bankers again remembered Keynes' first idea of "paper gold" in the 1940s, repackaged it, and finally came up with the "great invention" of "special drawing rights" (SDR).

---

[163] Henry Kissinger, *op. cit.*, pp. 606–607.

As the famous French economist Jacques Rueff points out,

> *"At the same time, monetarists have invented a new gadget to cover up the fact that the US currency is in a state of bankruptcy. The central bank of each country is assigned a special international reserve currency. But in order not to cause inflation, SDRs must be strictly limited. That way, even with the support of SDRs, the U.S. is still unable to repay a fraction of its dollar debt."[164]*

But Wall Street was on the other side of the happy-go-lucky spectrum, hailing it as a modern financial historical creation: a victory for America over paper gold.

Treasury Undersecretary Paul Volcker told the news media with a smile on his face, "We've finally implemented it (the SDR plan)." *The Wall Street Journal* hailed this as a major victory for the American school of economics because it was a direct blow to the age-old idea that gold must be the sole baton and economic panacea for monetary value.

But the Wall Street Journal forgot to say that even SDRs are defined in terms of their gold content, so gold is still the baton of the currency, and SDRs cannot be "devalued".

Hopper has a brilliant account of the SDR: one day it (the SDR) will be ranked by historians alongside the great human 'invention' of the 'South Sea Bubble' created by John Law's Mississippi Conspiracy. Defining it as the equivalent of gold but not convertible into gold is simply absurd patentable. Any banknote or credit unit can only be considered 'equivalent' to gold if it is unrestrictedly convertible into gold at a fixed rate.

The German economist Palyi was also sharply critical of the concept of 'paper gold':

> *"this new SDR reserve currency can only stimulate more reckless financial expansion and inflation around the world. Adopting SDR is a victory for the inflation molecule. It removes*

---

[164] Jacques Rueff, *The Inflationary Impact the Gold Exchange Standard Superimposed on the Bretton Woods System* (Committee for Monetary Research and Education, Greenwich, CT, 1975).

the last stone that stands in the way of a fully controlled 'world currency' that will never be 'in short supply' in the world. "[165]

On March 18, 1969, the U.S. Congress lifted the mandatory requirement that Fed-issued dollars have a 25 percent gold backing, an act that severed the final legally mandatory relationship between gold and dollar issuance.

The world is not far from the final truth.

Of course, the plans of the international bankers did not always come to fruition, and Keynes's 1940s vision of a future "world currency" with SDRs was indeed a bit too "avant-garde". However, the optimism of the international bankers back then was not entirely unwarranted. The "prototype" of the United Nations as a "world government" had been realized on schedule just after the end of World War II, and the International Monetary Fund and the World Bank, the "world's unified monetary issuer", were in place at the same time, so if the SDRs were to become the world currency again on schedule, it would be a done deal. It is a pity that the plan cannot catch up with the changes. The British Keynesian version of the "beautiful blueprint" of the future world is quite different from White's American version, the Americans are in a good position to take advantage of the time and the people, and they are also rich. It also fails to anticipate the ferocious wave of national independence in the Third World countries, the rise of Asia, which has shaken the basic contrast in world power, and the SDRs, which have never been repaired.

The general attack on the abolition of the gold currency

Nixon did not understand, or did not want to understand, how gold could run away like a river on a dike, no matter how much the U.S. government tried to stop it. The essence of the problem is that the U.S. is running an explosive deficit on its balance sheet and the U.S. is effectively powerless to maintain a fixed exchange rate on gold. It's not that there's too little gold, it's that the US banking system creates too many dollars.

---

[165] Melchior Palyi, « A Point of View », in *The Chicago Commercial And Financial Chronicle*, 24 juillet 1969.

John Exter of the Federal Reserve tells the final story of this golden showdown:

> *"On August 10, 1971, a group of bankers, economists, and monetary experts held an informal discussion on the currency crisis at the New Jersey waterfront. At about 3:00 p.m., Paul Volcker's car arrived. He was then Undersecretary of the Treasury, responsible for monetary issues.*
>
> *We get together to discuss various possible solutions. As you know, I've always supported conservative monetary policy, so my suggestion of a significant increase in interest rates was rejected by the majority. Others don't think the Fed will slow credit expansion, fearing a recession or worse. I again suggested raising the price of gold, which Paul Volcker thought made sense, but he thought it would be difficult for Congress to pass. World leaders like the United States are unwilling to acknowledge to their people the reality of a devalued currency, no matter how serious the problem. It's just too embarrassing for them that up to this point, the people are mostly clueless about the (monetary) crisis we're having. It's not like in 1933 the country was in a state of emergency and Roosevelt could do whatever he wanted.*
>
> *At this point, Paul Volcker turned to me and asked me what I should do if I came to the decision. I told him that because he didn't want to raise interest rates and didn't want gold to go up, it would be pointless to just close the gold exchange window and continue to sell Treasury gold at $35 an ounce, and five days later, Nixon closed the gold window."*[166]

On August 15, 1971, the final truth finally came. The U.S. is no longer able to meet its international commitments with the dollar tied to gold, which is the second time the U.S. has gone rogue on the international community since Roosevelt went rogue on the American people at home in 1963. In his speech that evening, Nixon sharply attacked speculators in the international financial markets for creating chaos in the financial markets and for having to "temporarily" abandon the dollar for gold in order to defend the dollar. The question is, who are the "opportunists" that Nixon was referring to? Be aware that back then the Soros were young and the foreign exchange market was almost negligible due to the constraints of the Bretton system. Not every investor can look to the U.S. for gold, only the central banks of each

---

[166] Ferdinand Lips, *op. cit.*, pp. 76–77.

country can do so. And it was the French Government that started the "fiasco".

When the last link between gold and the dollar was severed by President Nixon on August 15, 1971, the moment that made international bankers nervous finally came, and for the first time in the history of mankind, the whole world came together into the era of French money, it was too early to say whether this would be a blessing or a curse for human society and civilization.

Having broken free of the gold spell, the Western industrialized countries, led by the Federal Reserve, have embarked on an era of unprecedented credit expansion, with monetary issuance reaching unrestrained and arbitrary levels, and as of 2006, the total debt owed by the United States government, corporations and private individuals reached $44 trillion, or $2.2 trillion per year in interest payments alone, if estimated at a minimum interest rate of 5 per cent.

The problem is that such a debt has reached the point where it cannot be repaid, and the debt has to be repaid, either by those who owe it, or by those who borrow it, or worse, it will end up being repaid by the hard-working taxpayers of the world.

"Economic killers" and the return of petrodollars

On 6 October 1973, the Fourth Middle East War broke out. Egypt and Syria launched simultaneous attacks on Israel. As expected by international bankers, on 16 October, Iran, the Saudis and four Arab countries in the Middle East unleashed their "oil weapons" and announced a 70 per cent increase in oil prices as a result of the United States policy of favouritism towards Israel. This has had an extremely profound impact on the world landscape after the 1970s.

At the meeting of Arab ministers in Kuwait, the Iraqi representative strongly called for the targeting of the United States as the main target, and he suggested that other countries join in confiscating and nationalizing United States commercial property in Arab countries, imposing an oil embargo on the United States and withdrawing all funds from the United States banking system, which he believed would cause the United States to fall into the biggest economic crisis in 29 years. Although these overbearing proposals were not adopted, on October 17 they agreed to cut oil production by 5 percent and continue to cut production by 5 percent per month until their political goals are met.

On October 19, President Nixon asked Congress to provide $2.2 billion in immediate emergency aid to Israel, and on October 20, the Saudis and other Arab countries announced a complete halt to oil exports to the United States. International oil prices soared, from $1.39 a barrel in 1970 to $8.32 in 1974. Although the oil embargo lasted only five months until it ended in March 1974, the event shook Western society greatly.

International bankers, for their part, are scheming in every way so that petrodollars flowing into countries such as Saudi Arabia must flow back to the United States.

After careful analysis, the United States decided to adopt the strategy of "divide and rule" to divide and dismantle the Middle East oil-producing countries from within. And the main direction of the assault was chosen for the Saudis. Saudi Arabia is a sparsely populated country, rich in oil, located in the hinterland of the Middle East, surrounded by Iran, Syria, Iraq, Israel and other strong neighbors, the military defense force is extremely thin, the Saudi royal family has a deep sense of insecurity. Having inspected this weakness, the United States offered the Saudis attractive terms of solicitation, full political support, military protection if necessary, and technical support, military training to ensure the perpetuation of the Saudi royal family. The conditions are that oil transactions must be settled in United States dollars, that the Saudis must use the petrodollars earned to purchase United States Treasury bills to ensure United States oil supplies, that oil price fluctuations must be sanctioned by the United States, that the Saudis are obliged to make up the resulting shortfall in oil supplies in the event of an Iranian, Iraqi, Indonesian or Venezuelan oil embargo against the United States, and that the Saudis need to "dissuade" other countries from imposing oil embargoes against the United States.

Mr. "Economic Assassin" Perkins was sent to Saudi Arabia to be the specific operator of the scheme. As "chief economist" of a world-renowned engineering firm, Mr. Perkins's task was

> "to use his imagination to the best of his ability to make a substantial investment in the Saudi economy seem very promising, provided that American engineering and construction firms were awarded the bid".

After much contemplation, Perkins had a sudden inspiration that the sheeple on the streets of Riyadh, the Saudi capital, were so far removed from the breath of modernity that large-scale urban construction could earn back many petrodollars. Perkins, on the other hand, is well aware that economists in OPEC member states are crying out for deep processing of oil and owning their own petroleum refining industry in order to make a higher profit than selling crude oil. Perkins came up with a solution that would satisfy "everyone," starting with the sheep, where petrodollar revenues could be used to pay for the most expensive modern garbage disposal facility in the U.S., and where the beautification of Riyadh's municipal construction would require a large number of highly sophisticated American products. On the industrial side, the petrodollar will be used for the transportation of crude oil, the infrastructure for processing crude oil, the huge oil-processing industrial zones that will rise up in the desert, surrounded by large industrial parks, large power plants, power transmission systems, highways, oil pipelines, communication systems, airports, seaports, and the huge services system that goes with them.

Perkins's plan is divided into two main categories: contracts for the construction of basic hardware facilities, and long-term service and management contracts, which will be used by various U.S. companies for decades to come.

Perkins also has in mind the farther outlook of protecting the huge industrial chain that the Arabian Peninsula has generated. U.S. military base construction, defense industry contracts and all other related activities, as well as more extensive management and service contracts. All of this, in turn, will result in a new wave of construction contracts, such as military airfields, missile bases, personnel training centres and all the other projects associated with them.

Perkins's goal is not only to get the vast majority of petrodollars flowing back to the United States, but also to have all of the interest income generated by this huge sum spent on American companies.

The Saudis will be proud of such "modern" industrial infrastructure and urban amenities, and other OPEC countries will be envious of how quickly Saudi Arabia has become a "modern country", and then this set of plans will be used in other countries.

Much to the satisfaction of the big bosses behind the scenes, Parkin's brilliant planning and lobbying ability led Dr. Kissinger to Saudi Arabia in 1974 to finalize the petrodollar's grand scheme. The dollar has finally found refuge in oil, having escaped the stormy waters of the gold standard.

The Reagan Assassination: Crushing the Last Hope of the Gold Standard

Although the gold standard has been completely abolished worldwide, with the exception of a few countries such as the Swiss gold franc, where gold and paper money are completely unconnected, it is the continued rise in the price of gold throughout the 1970s that has given international bankers the most trouble, and preventing the restoration of the gold standard is a top priority for international bankers.

On January 1, 1975, in order to show the world that gold is just a common metal and increase confidence in the pure paper dollar, the United States government decided to lift the 40-year gold holding ban imposed on the American people. Other countries have adopted a heavy taxation approach to gold to reduce people's demand for gold, in some cases even levying up to 50% VAT on gold. Americans have become very rusty with gold after 40 years of its disappearance, and coupled with the cumbersome and inconvenient nature of the purchase, the unbundling of gold has not created the anticipated tension, and international bankers are finally breathing a long sigh of relief. When later Fed Chairman Paul Volcker saw the gold coins being played with in the hands of former central banker John Exeter, he couldn't help but ask curiously, "John, where did you buy your gold coins from?"

Ernest Wilke, in Why Gold? points out the essence of the international bankers' suppression of gold:

> *"Beginning in 1975, the United States, with the cooperation of the major members of the IMF, began its journey to 'suppress' the world gold market. The purpose of suppressing gold prices is to convince people in major countries that paper money is better than gold. A successful (controlled gold price) operation will ensure that the process of over-issuing paper money can go on indefinitely."*[167]

---

[167] Ernest P. Welker, WHY GOLD?, Economic Education Bulletin (American Institute for Economic Research, Great Barrington, MA, 1981), p. 33.

Economists are unanimous in their belief that gold will prove to be something of little value after the loss of official government buying demand. Some even consider $25 an ounce to be the "intrinsic value" of gold.

In August 1975, in order to further eliminate the influence of gold, the United States and Western industrial countries decided that the amount of gold reserves in each country would no longer increase, and the IMF gold needs to sell 50 million ounces to depress the gold price. But the price of gold remained firm, and in September 1979, it surged to $430 an ounce, more than a dozen times higher than it had been at the time of the collapse of the Breton system in 1971.

The U.S. Treasury began its first auction of gold in January 1975 and has since grown from 300,000 ounces to 750,000 ounces, still struggling to resist gold buying. It was only when the Treasury announced an unprecedented 1.5 million ounces in November 1978 that market prices fell back a little. By 16 October 1979, the United States Department of the Treasury was finally unable to hold out and announced that the regular auctions had been changed to "surprise" auctions.

The $400 gold price is generally considered to be a reasonable reflection of the fact that the dollar has been severely over-issued since 1933 and should be stable and sustainable.

But the outbreak of the "Iranian hostage crisis" in November 1979 changed the course of the long-term price of gold. The Fed quickly announced the freezing of Iran's gold reserves in the United States after the outbreak of the crisis, a move that made the world's central banks from the heart of a chill, if Iran's gold can be frozen, everyone's gold in the United States is also not safe. As a result, countries are buying gold and shipping it directly back to their own stockpiles. Iran, in particular, was on a buying spree in the international market, and Iraq, not to be outdone, joined the super-buyers, with gold jumping up to $850 an ounce in a matter of weeks.

In January 1981, Reagan asked Congress to establish a "Gold Commission" to study the feasibility of restoring the gold standard. In a direct violation of the no-go zone for international bankers, on 30 March 1981, Reagan, who had been in the White House for only 69 days, was shot in the heart just 1 millimetre from the heart by a star-crossed man named Hinkley. The man is said to have done so in order to attract the attention of famous movie star Judy Foster. Of course, like the vast majority of those who assassinate the President of the United States, this man is considered to have a nervous problem.

On March 30, 1981, Reagan survived assassination attempt. In March 1982, the 17-member "Golden Council" rejected the idea of a return to the gold standard by a margin of 15-2, and President Reagan hastened to "heed good advice".

Since then, no American president has dared to touch the idea of the gold standard.

Summary

★Kennedy's intent to take back the power to issue money from the Federal Reserve and strip international bankers of most of their influence over the United States ultimately led to his assassination.

★The defense of silver and the abolition of its monetary status became the focus of the fight between Kennedy and the international bankers.

★Johnson came to power and abolished the issuance of silver certificates, while selling off large amounts of silver reserves, eventually ending the silver currency.

★The essence of the end of the Vietnam War is the London gold market fiasco, leading to the ruling elite's financial "bottom line" depleted.

★International bankers have come up with the great invention of "special drawing rights" to cover up the fact that the US currency is bankrupt.

★Nixon closed the gold exchange window and the Western industrial nations, led by the Federal Reserve, began an era of unprecedented credit expansion after breaking free of the gold as a shackle.

★Perkins, the "economic killer", has proposed an oil-processing infrastructure plan for Saudi Arabia to help transform the country into a modern state, with the aim of getting most of the petrodollar back to the United States and finding an oil haven for the dollar.

★Convinced that only a return to the gold standard could save the American economy, Reagan directly violated the no-go zone for international bankers, and in the end Reagan was stabbed, dashing the last hope of a return to the gold standard.

CHAPTER VIII

The undeclared currency war

> *We are like a pack of wolves standing on a high ridge overlooking a herd of elk. Thailand's economy looks more like a wounded prey than a small Asian tiger. We choose the sick and weak (for hunting) to keep the deer herd healthier overall.*[168]
> —*The American Times, 1997*

It is well known that whoever can monopolize the supply of a certain commodity can make super profits. And money is a commodity that everyone needs, and whoever has a monopoly on the issuance of a country's currency has the means to make an unlimited amount of super profits. That is why, for centuries, international bankers have sought to monopolize a country's currency issuance by all means, by all means, by all means. Their highest calling is to have a monopoly on the issuance of money around the world.

In order to ensure control of the world currency issue as the high point of financial strategy, international bankers, beginning in the 1970s, launched a series of currency wars aimed at consolidating confidence in the dollar, "dismembering" the economies of developing countries and defeating potential rivals, with the ultimate strategic goal of "controlled disintegration" of the world economy and laying a solid foundation for the completion of a "world government", "world currency" and "world taxation" under the London-Wall Street axis.

Note that the international bankers are a "super special interest group" that is not loyal to any one country or government, but rather controls them. They used the dollar and the power of the United States for a certain period of history, but when their preparations were ready, they could attack the dollar at any time, thus creating a worldwide economic crisis of the class of 1929, a serious crisis that would prompt

---

[168] Eugene Linden, "How to Kill a Tiger", *Time Asia*, November 3, 1997, Vol. 150. No. 18.

and coerce Governments to give up more sovereignty and impose regional currencies and regional governments.

Cracking down on China's financial system is undoubtedly a top priority for them. It is never a question of if, but when, and how, to strike at China. At this point, any fluke of an idea can have disastrous consequences. Their likely strategic tactics are very similar to those used against Japan, starting with the creation of a Chinese super-asset bubble, and with their "help" the Chinese economy will have several years of extreme prosperity, similar to that of Japan from 1985 to 1990. They will then kill them and carry out a "long-range non-contact" financial nuclear strike, destroying world confidence in the Chinese economy and scattering international and domestic funds in fear. Finally, China's core assets will be acquired at a jump price and the Chinese economy will be "completely dismantled", completing the most difficult step in the process of world unification.

1973 Middle East War: The Dollar Fight Back

In fact, the outbreak of the Fourth Middle East War on October 6, 1973 was no accident. At the annual meeting of the Bilderberg Club in May of that year, 84 international bankers, multinational giants and selected politicians met to discuss how to cope with the headache of a dollar that had lost its gold support. David Rockefeller brought in heartthrob Brzezinski, and the result of the discussion was the need to revive confidence in the dollar and take back the reins of the financial battlefield that had gotten out of hand.

International bankers have come up with an amazing plan to get international oil prices up 400%! This bold plan would serve several purposes: on the one hand, the fourfold surge in oil prices due to the widespread use of the United States dollar for world oil transactions would lead to a surge in world demand for the dollar, offsetting the side effects of the sell-off of the dollar by countries as it loses its gold support. On the other hand, thanks to the excellent work of the "economic assassins" of the previous years, many countries in Latin America and South-East Asia have already fallen prey to excessive lending, and these economically backward and resource-rich countries will become a herd of fat lambs to be slaughtered once oil prices soar and the United States raises interest rates sharply in tandem.

The most brilliant thing about this plan is that it "shames people". The provocation of Egypt and Syria to attack Israel, the open support of the United States for Israel to anger the Arabs, and finally the imposition of an oil embargo on the West by the Arab States in a fit of rage, with the price of oil bound to soar and all the anger of the world being directed at the Arab States. The international bankers, while sitting on the mountain watching the tiger fight, while counting the petrodollar banknotes flowing back, not only regained the dollar in one fell swoop, regained the initiative in the financial battlefield, but also took advantage of the sheep shearing the wool of Latin American countries such as Indonesia. It's a brilliant plan.

Throughout history, international bankers have always followed an "optimal algorithm" and have achieved more than three main objectives in every major strategic move. International bankers have always been the masters of the "combination punch".

The two international bankers, Brzezinski and Kissinger, were in full synch, and the whole thing went completely unpredictably. Brzezinski conceived the plan and Kissinger was directly involved in its implementation as the intelligence "czar" of the Nixon administration. William Engdahl, in *A Century of War*, pointed out that,

> *"Kissinger consistently suppressed the flow of (Middle Eastern) intelligence to the United States, including confirmation of war preparations by Arab officials intercepted by U.S. intelligence services. Washington's famous 'shuttle diplomacy' during and after the war, Kissinger executed the course of the May meeting at Bilderberg with precision. Arab oil-producing countries become scapegoats for the world's anger, while Anglo-American interests quietly hide behind the scenes."* [169]

At Kissinger's temptation and coercion, the Saudis were the first OPEC country to enter into cooperation with the United States, using petrodollars to buy U.S. bonds and thus "petrodollars back". Then Kissinger crossed the line, and by 1975, OPEC ministers agreed to settle oil only in dollars. The world currency has thus entered the era of the "oil standard".

---

[169] William Engdahl, *A Century of War: Anglo-American Oil Politics And The New World Order* (Pluto Press, London, 2004), p. 130.

The surge in oil prices has led to a surge in demand for the dollar from oil trade settlements, finally regaining strong international support for the dollar.

World oil prices remained stable at $1.90 a barrel from 1949 to 1970. From 1970 to 1973, oil prices gradually rose to $3 a barrel, and shortly after the outbreak of war on 16 October 1973, OPEC raised oil prices by 70 per cent to $5.11 a barrel, and on 1 January 1974, they doubled again to $11.65. From the price of oil prior to the 1973 Bilderberg meeting to January 1974, oil prices had risen by almost 400%.

In 1974, unidentified President Nixon also tried to get the U.S. Treasury to pressure OPEC to bring oil prices back down, a government official with inside knowledge wrote in a memo:

> *"The bankers ignored this suggestion and instead emphasized the fatal decision to use the 'petrodollar return' strategy against high oil prices."*

In the era of high oil prices that followed, causing double-digit inflation in Western countries, people's savings were siphoned off. Even more unfortunate are the defenseless developing countries, as Engdahl explains:

> *"The 400 per cent surge in oil prices has had a major impact on economies where oil is the main energy source. Most economies lacking petroleum resources have suddenly encountered an unexpected and difficult to pay 400% of the cost of imported energy, not to mention the rising cost of fertilizers, etc. from oil used in agriculture.*
>
> *In 1973, India's trade was surplus and in a healthy state of economic development. By 1974, India, with $629 million in foreign reserves, was paying twice as much for imported oil, or $1,241 million. Also by 1974, Sudan, Pakistan, the Philippines, Thailand, Africa and Latin America, one country after another, were facing trade deficits. According to the IMF, the trade deficit of developing countries reached $35 billion in 1974, an astronomical figure at the time. Not surprisingly, the total deficit is exactly four times the 1973 level, that is, proportional to the rise in oil prices.*
>
> *The strong industrial production and trade of the early 1970s was replaced by a worldwide contraction of industry and trade*

from 1974 to 1975, the most severe since the end of World War II."[170]

In the mid-1970s, many developing countries undergoing industrialization had become heavily dependent on low-interest loans from the World Bank, and soaring oil prices had swallowed up much of their capital in high oil prices. Developing countries are faced with either stopping the industrialization process and thus being unable to repay the World Bank's excessive loans, or having to borrow more money from the Bank to buy oil and repay the principal and interest on the huge debt.

The international bankers who have joined hands with the IMF have long been waiting for it, and the IMF has offered some harsh aid conditions, and then forced these developing countries, which are in a mess, to drink the famous "four remedies of the IMF", namely, the privatization of the country's core assets, the liberalization of the capital market, the marketization of the basic elements of life and the internationalization of free trade, most countries drink these remedies are either dead or wounded, and individual countries with strong resistance also suffer a lot of damage, and the people are poor and weak. Just as developing countries struggle to borrow dollars everywhere to import expensive oil, another bolt from the blue awaits them.

Paul Volcker: The "controlled disintegration" of the world economy

> *"Volcker was elected because he was Wall Street's choice. That's their opening price. What is known is that he is smart and conservative, what is not known is that he is about to make a big change."*
>
> —Charles Geisst, historian.

In 1973, David Rockefeller, Chairman of the Chase Manhattan Bank of the United States, formed a group called the Trilateral Commission between the United States, Europe and Japan, at the initiative and with the assistance of Brzezinski, in order to strengthen relations between the financial communities of North America, Western Europe and Japan. The main members of the Commission are

---

[170] *Ibid.*

major bankers, entrepreneurs and prominent politicians from North America, Western Europe and Japan, with three headquarters in New York, Paris and Tokyo, each chaired by a member from each of these three regions. The chairman of the New York headquarters was, of course, David Rockefeller, and Brzezinski, who was a close advisor to David Rockefeller, became the executive director who presided over the day-to-day work of this headquarters. Brzezinski had a close friend who was a professor at Columbia University, named Dean Rask, a Georgia native who served as Secretary of State when Kennedy Johnson was in charge of the White House. He suggested to Brzezinski that Georgia Governor Jimmy Carter be invited to the Trilateral Commission, and repeatedly praised Carter's entrepreneurial drive and political vision.

Brzezinski and Carter met in person under the warmth of Rask. Brzezinski had a crush on Carter at first glance, and he was sure that he would become a great man in the future, so he was naturally eager to recruit him. So, Brzezinski made a recommendation to Mr. David Rockefeller and gave Carter a great deal of credit. The Chair of the Trilateral Executive Committee took his advice and personally nominated him. And just like that, little Georgia Governor Jimmy Carter's name was added to the list of US members of the Trilateral Commission. It was a crucial step for him to be able to step onto the White House steps five years later.

After Carter's arrival in the White House in 1977, Brzezinski, his "party introducer", logically became President Carter's national security aide, in effect "regenting" on behalf of the international bankers in a role similar to that of Kissinger during the Nixon era.

In 1978, the vacancy of the Federal Reserve chairmanship, which is a key corner of the international bankers very much valued, David Rockefeller to Carter to recommend his staff Paul Volcker to play this post, President Carter could not refuse this request.

The bearish New York stock market also rose a rare 9.73 points as the dollar strengthened on international markets, with the *New York Times* saying

> *"Volcker's appointment was endorsed by European banks in Bonn, Frankfurt and Switzerland".*

Since Eugene Meyer's resignation from the Federal Reserve in 1933, members of the international banking family have all withdrawn from the front lines of financial markets to the backroom, where they control the Fed's operations primarily through the strict selection of the Fed's Bank of New York governor. Walker fits the bill very well for their selection. He studied at Princeton and Harvard in his early years, then went to the London School of Economics for further study, and in the 1950s worked as an economist at the Federal Reserve Bank of New York, then at Chase Manhattan as an economist, and in the 1960s worked at the Treasury Department, where he was one of the main operators of the abolition of the gold standard during the Nixon era.

On November 9, 1978, a spirited Volcker revealed in a speech at Warwick University in England that

> *"some degree of 'controlled disintegration' of the world economy was a reasonable goal for the 1980s."*

The question is, whose body? How does it unravel? Naturally, the most heavily indebted third world countries bear the brunt, followed by the Soviet Union and Eastern Europe.

Volcker began his tenure by raising the bright banner of fighting "world-wide inflation" and making dollar borrowing prohibitively expensive, along with close allies Britain. The average interest rate on dollar borrowings rose steadily from 11.2 per cent in 1979 to 20 per cent in 1981, with the base rate reaching 21.5 per cent and the national debt surging to 17.3 per cent.

When British Prime Minister Margaret Thatcher was elected in May 1979, she vowed to "drive inflation out of the economy", raising the benchmark interest rate from 12 per cent to 17 per cent in 12 weeks in just one month in office, and soaring borrowing costs in all sectors by 42 per cent in such a short period of time, unprecedented in peacetime industrialized countries. She also earned the title of "Iron Lady".

Under the banner of "anti-inflation", the economy is in deep recession and people and businesses are suffering the costs, while American and British bankers are making a fortune.

The slogans of government spending cuts, tax cuts, industry liberalization and the breaking up of trade unions are resounding, and the developing countries, which are burdened by a heavy debt burden, are in a state of great sadness and death. By this time, the debt of developing countries had soared fivefold from $130 billion at the time of Bilderberg's May 1973 meeting to a staggering $612 billion by 1982.

When the United States and Britain suddenly raised interest rates to around 20 per cent under the slogan of "anti-inflation", the huge debts of the developing countries were being squeezed by such alarming "usury" that they were destined to become fish on the knife of the international bankers. Asian, African and Latin American countries with no sense of financial warfare preparedness will pay dearly for their negligence.

U.S. Secretary of State Schultz pointed out at the United Nations meeting on September 30, 1982, the IMF should closely monitor the debt service of developing countries, he urged developing countries to make their exports "more attractive to the West", only "free trade" can save them, and increased efforts to sell their raw materials can speed up the process of debt repayment.

For his part, Mexican President Portillo pointed out tit-for-tat that the strategy of Anglo-American international bankers was to make high interest rates and the accompanying low prices of raw materials "the two edges of the scissors that kill the construction gains already made by some developing countries and the possibility of progress for the rest". He further threatened to lead developing countries to stop debt payments. He noted that

> *"Mexico and other third-world countries cannot pay their debts on time on terms that are vastly different from reality. We, the developing countries, do not want to be subordinate (to the West). We cannot afford to cripple our economy or put our people in a more miserable position to pay these debts, which have tripled in cost without our participation, for which we are not responsible. Our efforts to eradicate hunger, disease, ignorance and dependence have not created an international crisis."[171]*

Unfortunately, Portillo was replaced only two months after his address to the United Nations by a candidate favoured by international bankers, and the IMF intervened in the settlement of Mexico's debt as the "policeman of lending order", a history described by Engdahl as follows:

> *"The largest organized robbery in modern history began on a scale far greater than that of similar activities in the 1920s.*

---

[171] William Engdahl, *op. cit.*, p. 189.

> *Contrary to the elaborate cover-up by the Western European or American media, the debtor countries have paid their debts several times, and it is with blood and 'a pound of flesh' that they have paid the modern-day Shylocks of New York and London, and it is not true that the developing countries stopped paying their debts after August 1982. They had a gun to their heads and, under the IMF's bullying, signed what the bankers falsely called a 'debt settlement' involving the famous Citibank or Chase Bank of New York."[172]*

IMF loans are only available if the debtor country signs a series of "special clauses", including cuts in government spending, higher taxes and currency devaluation. The debt is then rolled over and developing countries are required to pay an additional "service charge" to international bankers, which is credited to the principal of the debt.

Mexico was forced to cut government subsidies for medicine, food, fuel and other necessities, while the peso was devalued to disastrous levels; in early 1982, under President Portillo's series of economic reforms, the peso was valued at 12 to 1 against the dollar, while by 1989 it had depreciated to 2,300 to 1, and the Mexican economy had in effect been "dismantled in a controlled manner" by international bankers.

According to the World Bank, from 1980 to 1986, more than 100 debtor countries in the world paid $326 billion in interest alone to international bankers, another $332 billion in principal payments and a total of $658 billion to developing countries for a debt of $430 billion (1980). Despite this, by 1987, 109 debtor countries owed $1.3 trillion to international bankers. The only fear is that developing countries will never have time to pay off their debts if they roll over on such an alarming basis. As a result, international bankers and the IMF began to implement bankruptcy settlements against debtor countries. Countries that accepted the bankers' "debt solution" were forced to sell off a large number of core assets, such as water, electricity, gas, railways, telephones, oil, banks, etc., at jump prices.

One can finally see how lethal the "controlled disintegration" of the world economy, orchestrated by international bankers, can be!

---

[172] William Engdahl, *op. cit.*, p. 190.

The World Conservation Bank: To circle 30% of the Earth's land

At a time when the developing countries of Asia, Africa and Latin America are deep in debt, the international bankers have begun to plan a larger operation in a way that goes beyond the limits of the imagination of ordinary people, and people of normal intelligence would never have thought that "environmental protection" was an entry point for a larger scheme.

It is impossible to understand the enormous power of the dazzling "combinations" of international bankers without looking at the issue from a historical perspective!

In early August 1963, a sociology professor at a prestigious university in the Midwest, under the pseudonym "John Do", received a call from Washington inviting him to participate in a secret research project in which 15 experts were among the top scholars at prestigious American universities. Professor "John Do" reported with curiosity to a place called "Iron Mountain". "Iron Mountain" is close to Hudson City, New York State, where the huge underground facilities built during the Cold War to defend against Soviet nuclear strikes and where hundreds of the largest American companies have temporary headquarters. These companies include Standard Oil of New Jersey, Shell Oil Company and Hanover Manufacturing Trust, among others. If a nuclear war were to break out, it would become the most important center of U.S. business operations to ensure that the U.S. business system would remain viable after a nuclear war. During normal times, this is where these companies store their confidential document files.

This enigmatic research group will examine the challenges the United States would face if the world were to enter a phase of "permanent peace" and the U.S. response strategy. This research effort lasted for 2 1/2 years.[173]

In 1967, the 15-member group completed a top-secret report, the authors of which were asked by the government to keep it strictly confidential. However, one of them, Professor "John Do", felt that the report was too important to be hidden from the public. He then found

---

[173] Larry Abraham, *The Greening* (Second Opinion Pub., Inc., 1993).

the famous author Leo Levin, and with Leo Levin's help, the book, called The Report from Iron Mountain, was officially published by Dell Publishing in 1967. Upon its release, the book immediately shocked all sectors of American society. Everybody's guessing who the hell is "John Doe". The report is believed to have been orchestrated by then Defense Secretary McNamara, a member of the Foreign Affairs Association and later President of the World Bank. The research institute that operates is thought to be the Hudson Institute, whose founder, Herman Cain, is also a member of the Diplomatic Association.

In response to the leak, John Xun's Special Assistant for National Security Rostow immediately came forward to urgently "sanitize" the report, which he noted was purely untrue. Time, also controlled by Henry Ruth, a member of the Foreign Affairs Association, also called the report a "clever lie". Whether the report is true or false is still a matter of debate in American society to this day.

However, the *Washington Post* had featured the book in its Book Review section on November 26, 1967. Introducing the book was Galbraith, a distinguished professor at Harvard University who is also a member of the Diplomatic Association, in which he states that he has first-hand information that proves the report to be true, as he himself was among those invited. Later, although he was not able to participate in the work of the project, the project has been consulting with him on various issues and he has been told to keep it confidential.

> *"I am willing to vouch for the authenticity of this document ('Iron Mountain Report') with my personal reputation, and I am willing to confirm the validity of its conclusions. All I have reservations about is the wisdom of publishing it to an unprepared public."*[174]

The authenticity of the report was later reiterated twice by Galbraith in other media. What, then, were the report's shocking conclusions that made the "elite" so nervous?

It turns out that the report reveals in detail the plans of the "world's elite" for the future of the world. The basic tenet of the report is that it is a "purely objective" report that does not discuss the question of right and wrong, does not consider such empty concepts as freedom and

---

[174] *News of War and Peace You're Not Ready For*, de Herschel McLandress (alias of Galbraith), (Book World, Washington Post, 26 novembre 1967, p. 5).

human rights, and does not occupy any place in all positions such as ideology, patriotism and religion.

The report begins by stating:

> *"Sustained peace, while not theoretically impossible, is not sustainable. Even if (the goal of peace) is attainable, it is certainly not the best option for a stable society … war is a special function of our social stability. Unless other alternatives can be developed, the war system should be maintained and strengthened."*[175]

The report argues that only in times of war, or under the threat of war, are people most likely to obey the government without complaint. The hatred of the enemy and the fear of subjugation and plunder make the people more able to bear the excessive taxes and sacrifices, and war is again the catalyst for the strong emotions of the people, and in the spirit of patriotism, loyalty and victory, the people can obey unconditionally, and any dissent will be considered an act of treachery. Conversely, in a peaceful situation, people will instinctively oppose high tax policies and hate excessive government interference in private life.

> *"The system of war is not only necessary for the existence of a State as an independent political system, but is also essential for political stability. Without war, the 'legitimacy' of the government to rule the people would be in question. The possibility of war provides the basis on which a government can have power. History is replete with examples of regimes that have lost the credibility of the threat of war and have ultimately led to the disintegration of power, a destructive effect that stems from inflated individual interests, resentment of social injustice, and other disintegrating factors. The possibility of war becomes a factor of political stability in maintaining the structure of social organization. It keeps the society stratified and guarantees the people's obedience to the government."*

The report argues, however, that the traditional approach to war also has its historical limitations, in which the great cause of world government will be difficult to achieve, especially in the era of nuclear war, where the outbreak of war becomes an unpredictable and risky

---

[175] Léonard C. Lewin, *Report from Iron Mountain – On the Possibility and Desirability of Peace* (Dial Press, 1967).

problem. Considering that the study began precisely shortly after the Cuban missile crisis, the shadow of the nuclear war with the Soviet Union must have influenced the authors to some extent.

The question is, if there is a "permanent peace" in the world, what is the way out for American society? That's exactly the answer this secret research team is after.

In other words, they need to find a new alternative to "war" for the United States. After careful study, the experts suggest that new alternatives to war must be accompanied by three conditions: (1) they must be economically "wasteful", consuming at least 10 per cent of annual GDP; (2) they must be a major, large-scale, credible threat similar to the danger of war; and (3) they must provide a logical justification for the compulsion of people to serve their Governments.

A piece of easy work. The experts first thought of a "war on poverty". The problem of poverty, though large enough, was not fearful enough to be quickly abandoned. The alternative was an alien invasion, which, while scary enough, lacked credibility in the 1960s, and was dropped again. Finally, one thinks of "environmental pollution", which is, to a considerable extent, a fact and has the credibility to work under the propaganda of environmental pollution to the extent of post-nuclear war apocalyptic horror; it is indeed economically very "wasteful" to keep polluting the environment; it is very logical for people to endure high taxes and lower quality of life and accept government intervention in private life in order to "save Mother Earth".

This is a fantastic choice!

It is scientifically estimated that the time frame for environmental pollution to reach the point of causing a strong worldwide crisis is about a generation and a half, or 20 to 30 years. The report was published in 1967. Twenty years later...

In September 1987, the fourth General Assembly of the World Wildlife Conservation Commission was held in Denver, Colorado, United States, with the participation of 2,000 delegates from over 60 countries. The 1,500 delegates who attended the conference were surprised to find that a document called the Denver Declaration was ready for them. The Denver Declaration states:

> "Because new funds must be mobilized to expand the scope of environmental protection activities, we should create a new banking model to integrate international assistance for

environmental management with the resource management needs of recipient countries."[176]

This new banking model is the "World Bank for Environment" programme. In stark contrast to previous similar meetings, a large number of international bankers were present, led by Baron Edmund Rothschild, David Rockefeller and US Treasury Secretary Jamie Baker. These super-busy people spent six full days at an environmental conference to present and market the "World Environment Bank" financial programme to the General Assembly.

In his address to the General Assembly, Edmund Rothschild referred to this "world environmental bank" as the "Second Marshall Plan", the establishment of which would "rescue" developing countries from the debt quagmire, while protecting the ecological environment. Note that as of 1987, the total debt of developing countries amounted to $1.3 trillion.

The core concept of the World Bank for Environment is "replacing natural resources with debt". The "ecological land" of the developing countries that the international bankers have circled is spread across Latin America, Africa and Asia, covering a total area of 50 million square kilometres, equivalent to the area of five countries, or 30 per cent of the Earth's land area, as the international bankers plan to refinance the $1 trillion debt of the developing countries, transfer the debt to the World Bank for the Environment, collateralize the land on the brink of ecological crisis, and receive debt extensions and new soft loans from the World Bank for the Environment!

In the 1970s, loans from developing countries to the IMF and international bankers were overwhelmingly unsecured and based solely on national credit, and when debt crises erupted, international bankers were less likely to go bankrupt. When these debts were transferred to the World Bank for the Environment, it was hard to watch the dodgy accounts of international bankers turn into quality assets. Since the WEF owns the land as collateral, the large tracts of mortgaged land legally belong to the WEF once the developing countries are unable to pay their debts, and the international bankers who control the WEF are naturally the actual owners of the large tracts of fertile land. Given the

---

[176] Fourth World Wilderness Congress conference, interview with George Hunt: "Beware of bankers bringing gifts."

scale of the human enclave movement, the World Bank for the Environment is unprecedented.

It is no wonder that people like Rothschild and Rockefeller have to "care" about the six-day-long environmental conference for such huge benefits.

Dr. Cuesta, a senior official in Brazil's finance ministry, stayed up overnight after hearing about Rothschild's World Environmental Bank proposal. He argues that soft loans from environmental banks may help Brazil's economy in the short term, and at least the economic engine can start up again, but in the long run, Brazil will not be able to repay these loans anyway, and the end result will be that the feng shui treasures of the Amazon, which serve as collateral for the loans, will no longer be owned by Brazil.

The resources being mortgaged are not limited to the land, but water sources and other natural resources above and below ground are also being mortgaged.

The World Bank for the Environment, with a more prominent name, was eventually established in 1991 as the Global Environment Facility, managed by the World Bank, of which the U.S. Treasury is the largest shareholder. The long-term plans of the international bankers are now being gradually implemented.

Financial nuclear bomb: targeting Tokyo

> *Japan has accumulated enormous wealth internationally, while the United States is in unprecedented debt. The military superiority that President Reagan sought was an illusion that came at the cost of losing our lender status in the world economy. Despite Japan's attempts to continue to hide in the shadows of the United States and grow quietly, Japan has in fact become a world-class banker. Japan's rise to world dominance as a financial power is a very disturbing thing.*
> —George Soros, 1987.[177]

When Britain ceded its status as an international lender to the United States in World War I, what was lost at the same time was the global hegemony of the British Empire. This event is certainly fresh in

---

[177] George Soros, *The Alchemy of Finance*. Wiley.

the minds of international bankers, and the rapid economic rise of East Asian countries after World War II was a wake-up call to London's Wall Street bankers that everything that could thwart and undermine any potential rival to the world government and world unified currency dominated by them must be vigilantly guarded.

Japan, as the first Asian economy to take off, has rapidly reached a level that has alarmed international bankers, both in terms of the quality of its economic growth, the competitiveness of its exports of industrial products, and the speed and scale of its wealth accumulation. In the words of Clinton-era U.S. Treasury Secretary Samos,

> *"an Asian economic zone topped by Japan created fear among most Americans who saw Japan as a threat to the United States even more than the Soviet Union".*

Japan started out after the war by imitating Western product design, then quickly reduced production costs, and in turn, eventually captured the European and American markets. The oil crisis of the 1970s saw the U.S.-built eight-cylinder fuel-consuming sedan quickly lost to Japan's cheap and fuel-efficient cars. The U.S. has gradually lost its ability to resist the Japanese car attack in the low-tech auto industry. Since the 1980s, Japan's electronics industry has made rapid progress, Sony, Hitachi, Toshiba and a large number of other electronic enterprises from imitation to innovation, in addition to the central processing unit, almost all the integrated circuits and computer chip manufacturing technology, in industrial robots and cheap labor under the advantage of the U.S. electronics and computer hardware industry, Japan has even reached the extent of U.S.-made missiles must use Japanese chips. At one time almost everyone in the United States believed that it was only a matter of time before Toshiba and Hitachi bought IBM and Intel in the United States, while American industrial workers feared that Japanese robots would eventually steal their jobs.

While the high interest rate policy implemented by the United States and Britain in the early 1980s saved the confidence of the dollar and killed many developing countries in Africa and Latin America, the high interest rate also severely damaged the industrial strength of the United States, resulting in a situation in which Japanese products entered the United States market in the 1980s.

While the nation of Japan was in the throes of a "Japan can say no" euphoria, a war of attrition against Japanese finance was already being deployed by the international bankers.

In September 1985, the international bankers finally began to strike. The "Plaza Agreement" was signed at the Plaza Hotel in New York by the finance ministers of the United States, England, Japan, Germany and France to allow a "controlled" depreciation of the dollar against other major currencies, and the Bank of Japan was forced to agree to appreciate under the pressure of U.S. Finance Minister Baker. Within a few months of the signing of the Square Agreement, the yen appreciated from 250 yen to one dollar to 149 yen to one dollar.

In October 1987, the New York stock market crashed. U.S. Treasury Secretary Baker put pressure on Japanese Prime Minister Nakasone to keep the Bank of Japan lowering interest rates, making the U.S. stock market look a little more attractive than the Japanese stock market to attract capital flows to the United States from the Tokyo market. Baker threatened to get tough on Japan over the US-Japan trade deficit if the Democrats came to power, then Baker pulled out the hulloop again, promising that the Republicans would stay in power, Bush Sr. would surely give a big boost to US-Japan goodwill, Nakasone bowed his head, soon yen interest rates fell to a mere 2.5%, the Japanese banking system began to flood with liquidity, massive amounts of cheap capital poured into the stock market and real estate, Tokyo's stocks grew by as much as 40% a year, real estate even exceeded 90%, and a huge financial bubble began to form.

In such a short period of time, this dramatic change in currency exchange, Japan's export producers beat the bleeding heart, in order to make up for the loss of export decline caused by the appreciation of the yen, companies have been from the bank low interest rate borrowing speculation in stocks, the Bank of Japan's overnight lending market quickly became the world's largest center. By 1988, the top 10 largest banks in the world were being swept up by Japan. By this time, the Tokyo stock market had risen 300% in 3 years, and real estate had reached eye-popping proportions, with the total real estate market in one Tokyo area exceeding the total value of real estate in the United States at the time, in dollar terms. Japan's financial system has reached a precarious point.

What Japan did not expect was an undeclared financial strangulation by international bankers, which might have been a soft landing with moderate austerity but for the devastating external shocks. Given Japan's financial strength, there is no certainty of victory in the traditional conventional financial battlefield.

In 1982, the Chicago Mercantile Exchange of the United States was the first to "develop" successful stock index futures, an unprecedented financial weapon. It was supposed to be used as a tool to steal business from the New York Stock Exchange, and when people traded in Chicago with confidence in the New York Stock Index, they no longer had to pay commissions to New York stock traders. A stock index is nothing more than a list of listed companies, weighted to produce data, and stock index futures are bets on the future stock price movements of the companies on this list, which neither buyers nor sellers own, nor intend to own, themselves.

The stock market plays on the word confidence, and massive shorting of stock index futures inevitably leads to a stock market crash, as was effectively demonstrated in the New York stock market crash of October 1987.

Japan's economic take-off in the 1980s gave the Japanese a sense of superiority over the world. At a time when Japanese stock prices are so high that no sane Western commentator can comprehend them, the Japanese still have plenty of reasons to believe they are unique. An American investment expert who was in Japan at the time put it this way:

> *"There is a belief here that the Japanese stock market cannot go down, and it was still the case in '87, '88, and even '89. They felt that there was something very special that existed in their (stock) markets, in the entire Japanese nation, something special that could make Japan defy all the laws that existed around the world."*

The insurance company is a very important investor in the stock market in Tokyo. When the international bankers sent a group of investment banks, such as Morgan Stanley and Solomon Brothers, to Japan as a major surprise force, they looked around for potential targets with large amounts of cash in hand and their briefcases full of "stock index put options," a new financial product unheard of in Japan at the time. The Japanese insurance companies are the ones who are interested in this, and in the eyes of the Japanese, these Americans must have gotten into their heads and used a lot of cash to buy the possibility of an unlikely Japanese stock market crash, and as a result the Japanese insurance industry is quick to commit. Both sides are betting on the direction of the Nikkei, if the index goes down, the Americans make money and the Japanese lose money, if the index goes up, the situation is exactly the opposite.

Perhaps even the Japanese province of Okura cannot count how many such derivative contracts were traded before the stock market plummeted, and this undetected "financial virus" flourished in a booming illusion of an almost unregulated, secret, over-the-counter underground market.

On December 29, 1989, Japan's stock market reached an all-time high, with the Nikkei Index rushing to 38915, and the massive short-selling options on the stock index finally began to take hold. On 12 January 1990, the Americans struck a killer blow when a new financial product, the Nikkei Put Warrant, suddenly appeared on American exchanges and stock options bought by Goldman Sachs from the Japanese insurance industry were resold to the Kingdom of Denmark, which sold them to the purchasers of the warrants and promised to pay the owners of the Nikkei Put Warrants the proceeds in the event of a Nikkei downturn. The Kingdom of Denmark is just here to let Goldman Sachs lend her credibility to the Nikkei options sales in Goldman Sachs' hands, supercharged. The warrants immediately sold in the United States, a large number of U.S. investment banks have followed suit, the Japanese stock market can no longer eat, "Nikkei put warrants" listed in less than a month to sell hot collapse of the total collapse.

The stock market collapse spread first to Japan's banking and insurance industries, and eventually to manufacturing. Japan's manufacturing sector used to be able to raise money on the stock market at least half the cost of its American competitors, all of which is yesterday's yellow flower as the stock market slumped.[178]

Since 1990, Japan's economy has been in a decade-long recession, with the Japanese stock market plunging 70 percent and real estate falling for 14 consecutive years. In Financial Defeat, author Motobu Yoshikawa argues that in terms of the proportion of wealth lost, the consequences of Japan's financial defeat in 1990 were almost equal to those of its defeat in World War II.

William Engdahl put it this way when he commented on Japan's financial debacle:

---

[178] Gregory Millman, *Vigilante Economics: How Wall Street Shattered Tokyo and London gave Frankfurt Woe* (The Alicia Patterson Foundation, 1992).

"No country in the world has more faithfully and actively supported the Reagan-era policies of fiscal deficits and massive spending than the United States' former enemy, Japan. Not even Germany has ever met Washington's demands unconditionally like that. And in the eyes of the Japanese, Tokyo's loyal and generous purchase of U.S. Treasuries, real estate and other assets in return for the most devastating financial disaster in world history."[179]

In the summer of 2006, the new U.S. Secretary of the Treasury Paulson visited China, when he heard him enthusiastically "wish China success", people could not help but feel a chill behind. I wonder if his predecessor, Baker, said the same thing when he held the hand of Japanese Prime Minister Nakasone.

Soros: The International Banker's Financial Hacker

For a long time, the media around the world have portrayed Soros as a "maverick" or a "maverick" financial genius, and the legends about him have added to his mystique, as Grumman once joked that this surname, which reads both positive and negative, is different.

Soros is really a maverick, with his "financial hacking genius" alone against the Bank of England, to shake the German mark, sweeping the Asian financial market? I'm afraid only simple-minded people would believe such a legend.

Soros' Quantum Fund that swept the world's financial markets was registered in Curaçao, a tax haven in the Dutch Antilles, a Dutch dependency in the Caribbean, allowing it to conceal the fund's main investors and the movement of funds, which is also the most important international centre for drug laundering.

Given that U.S. securities laws require that no more than 99 U.S. citizens be "sophisticated" investors in hedge funds, Soros went to great lengths to ensure that none of the 99 super-rich were American. In such an offshore hedge fund, Soros is not even on the board of directors, but is involved in the fund's operations as an "investment adviser". Not only that, but he also chose to take on this advisory role in the name of Soros Fund Management, which he established in New York. If the U.S.

---

[179] William Engdahl, *op. cit.*, pp. 225–226.

government asked him to provide details of the fund's operations, he could claim that he was merely an investment adviser to shirk responsibility.

Soros' Quantum Fund is not easy to investigate. His Board of Directors includes:

—Director, Richard Cates, Cates is a director of the Rothschild Bank in London and president of the Rothschild Family Bank of Milan in Italy.

—Director, Nice Tob is a partner in the London syndicate, which is also largely run by the Rothschild family.

—The director, William Rees-Mogg, a columnist critic for The *Times* of London, is also a partner under the control of the Rothschild family.

—Director, Edgar Pisito is the most controversial figure in Swiss private banking and has been called "the smartest banker in Geneva". Pisito's close friends include Safra, owner of the Republican Bank of New York, who has been identified by U.S. law enforcement as being linked to the Moscow banking cartel and officially identified by Switzerland as being involved in drug money laundering in Turkey and Colombia.

Also in Soros's "circle" are prominent Swiss speculators Mark Rich and Terry Ivey, and Israeli intelligence arms dealer Shal Eisenberg.

Soros' secret relationship with the Rothschild circle makes him the front man for the most powerful and secretive financial group in the world. Not only were the Rothschilds once the rulers of the financial city of London, the founders of Israel, the grand masters of the international intelligence network, the backstage of the five largest banks on Wall Street, the setters of the world's gold price, but they still run the Wall Street axis in London. No one knows how much wealth they really have, and while Rothschild and other international bankers are shining the spotlight on the world's richest man, Bill Gates and the stock god Warren Buffett, their own wealth several orders of magnitude higher than the "richest man" is hiding out in offshore accounts in Switzerland or the Caribbean.

Soros also has extraordinary ties to America's elite circles, having invested $100 million of his own personal money in the prestigious US arms contractor, the Carlyle Investment Group, which includes such heavyweights as Bush Sr. and former US Treasury Secretary Jamie Baker. As early as the 1980s, Soros co-founded the National Endowment for Democracy, an organization that was actually a joint venture between the CIA and private capital, with a number of American political figures, such as former Secretaries of State Brzezinski and Madeleine Albright.

Tuned in by international bankers, Soros has taken the world financial markets by storm since the 1990s. At the heart of each of Soros's major actions is the major strategic intent of the international bankers to bring about the "controlled disintegration" of the world's economies in order to finally complete the preparations for a "world government" and a "world currency" under the control of the London-Wall Street axis.

In the early 1980s, international bankers largely achieved the "controlled disintegration" of the economies of developing countries in Latin America and Africa, and in the mid-to-late 1980s, they succeeded in containing the expansion of Japanese financial power. After taking control of Asia, Europe returned to the focus of international bankers, and the collapse of Eastern Europe and the Soviet Union was their next major attack.

Soros, who undertook this important mission, became a famous "philanthropist", setting up numerous foundations in Eastern Europe and the former Soviet Union, modelled on the "Open Society Institute" he founded in New York, which promoted the idea of extremely irrational individual freedom, such as the Central European University, which he funded, promoting the concept of a sovereign state as evil and "anti-individualistic" in the face of young people living under a socialist system, economic liberalism as a panacea and "authoritarianism" in the rational analysis of social phenomena. The school's keynote speeches were often on topics such as "The Individual and Government", and these educational ideas were naturally highly praised by the American Foreign Service Association.

The famous American commentator Gilles Emery accurately described the true intentions of the Soros and the international organizations they "generously" funded:

> *"Behind the veil of legitimacy and humanitarianism, one can always find the same group of billionaire 'philanthropists' and the various organizations they funded, such as the Soros 'Open*

> *Society Institute', the Ford Foundation, the American Peace Association, the National Endowment for Democracy, Human Rights Watch, Amnesty International, World Crisis Group, etc. Among them, Soros is the most conspicuous, reaching out like a giant octopus to the entire Eastern and South-Eastern Europe, the Caucasus region and the former Soviet republics. With the cooperation of these organizations, (Soros) can not only shape but create news, public agendas, and public opinion to control the world and its resources to advance the American-made ideal of perfect world unity."[180]*

Soros played an immeasurable role in the disintegration of the socialist states of Eastern Europe. In Poland, the Soros Fund is credited with the seizure of power in the country by Solidarity and has direct influence over the first three presidents of the new Poland.

Soros, together with Paul Volcker, former Chairman of the Federal Reserve, Arnold Rudin, Vice President of Citibank, and Geoffrey Sachs, Professor at Harvard, concocted the "oscillation therapy" that gave Eastern Europe and the former Soviet Union a shot in the arm. Soros himself summed up the therapy this way:

> *"I took into account the need to show that changes in the political system would lead to economic improvement. Poland is one place to try. I have prepared a number of broad economic reform measures, which consist of three components: monetary tightening, structural adjustment and debt restructuring. I think it's better to have all three objectives accomplished simultaneously than separately. I advocate a kind of macroeconomic debt-share swap."*

Restructuring the industrial structure is tantamount to a complete operation on the macroeconomic order, while at the same time tightening the money supply, which is tantamount to a major operation but refusing to give blood transfusions to patients.

At this time, international bankers are easily acquiring the core assets of these countries in a bloodbath of "debt-to-equity" sales. Poland, Hungary, Russia, Ukraine, one by one, have been sacked, and their economies have not recovered for 20 years. In complete contrast to the weak and defenceless African and Latin American countries, the

---

[180] Gilles d'Aymery, "The Circle of Deception: Mapping the Human Rights Crowd in the Balkans", 23rd July 2001.

former Soviet Union and Eastern European countries, with military forces so powerful that the United States could not sleep, were subjected, for the first time in the history of mankind, to an organized madness of looting while still in a state of military power.

It's Soros's mastery of not having to shed blood that makes him so powerful. It seems that destroying a country before destroying its mind is indeed a proven solution.

Sniping the "crisis arc" of the European currency

When the strategic goal of "controlled disintegration" of Eastern Europe and the Soviet Union was largely achieved, the core of old Europe, Germany and France, which had never been excluded from the core of power, became uneasy. Immediately after losing the huge external threat of the Soviet Union, there was a desire to start a new business, the euro, to differentiate itself from the Anglo-American financial forces. Once established, the euro is bound to have a serious destabilizing effect on the hegemony of the dollar system. The currency conflict between the London-Wall Street axis and the German-French alliance is growing more intense.

The root of the problem lies in the disintegration of the Bretton system in 1971, which caused a serious disorder in the world monetary system. Under the indirect gold-based Brettonian system, the currency exchange rates of the world's major countries are almost highly stable, and there are no serious imbalances in the trade and finances of countries, since countries in deficit are bound to lose real national wealth, thereby reducing the credit capacity of their banking systems, automatically leading to austerity and recession, shrinking consumption, inevitably falling imports and disappearing trade deficits. When people begin to save, bank capital begins to increase, the scale of production expands, trade runs a surplus, and total social wealth increases. This beautiful system of natural cycles and control has been repeatedly validated by all human social practices prior to 1971, where severe deficits have nowhere to hide, currency risk hedging is almost unnecessary, and financial derivatives are not a condition for survival. Under the constraints of gold, all nations must work honestly and hard to accumulate wealth, which is the root cause of the international bankers' aversion to gold.

After the loss of gold, the international monetary system is naturally in chaos, after the artificially created "oil crisis" caused by the strong demand for the dollar, and by the high interest rates since 79 years, the dollar gradually gained a firm footing. The dollar, the world's reserve currency, is so up and down in price, and its manipulation is entirely in the hands of the London-Wall Street axis, that European countries are forced to follow the currency roller coaster, which is naturally full of misery. So, in the late 1970s, German Finance Minister Schmidt approached French President Der Stein about establishing a European monetary system to eliminate the headache of exchange rate instability in trade between European countries.

In 1979, the European monetary system became operational and worked well, and European countries that had not yet joined expressed interest in doing so. Concerns about the system's possible future evolution into a unified European currency began to strongly haunt London-Wall Street's elite circles.

Even more disturbing is the fact that Germany and France have been meddling in OPEC affairs since 1977, when they planned to supply specific oil-exporting countries with high-tech products and help them industrialize, in exchange for Arab countries guaranteeing a long-term stable supply of oil to Western Europe and depositing the oil revenues into the European banking system. The London side was adamantly opposed from the outset to the German-French plan to start a different one, refusing to join the European Monetary System after all efforts had failed.

Germany had a bigger agenda at the time, and that was to finally complete its unification, and a unified and powerful Germany would eventually dominate the European continent. To this end, Germany began to approach the Soviet Union, ready to maintain moderate and mutually beneficial relations and cooperation with it.

In order to deal with the German and French attempts, London-Wall Street schemers put forward the theory of "crisis arc belt", the core of which is the release of Islamic radical forces, so that the Middle East oil-producing regions in turmoil, the rest of the waves can even spread to the Muslim region in the south of the Soviet Union, this scheme has not only struck the prospects of cooperation between Europe and the Middle East, hindering the pace of European unified currency, but also restrained the Soviet Union, and for the United States to prepare for future military intervention in the Gulf region, it is really a three-birds effect of one stone.

National Security Adviser Brzezinski and Secretary of State Vance did a great job, and the situation in the Middle East was in serious turmoil, with the 1979 revolution in Iran and the second oil crisis in the world. In fact, there has never been a real oil supply shortage in the world, and the shortfall of 3 million barrels of oil per day interrupted by Iran is perfectly capable of being made up by Saudi and Kuwaiti production under tight US control. The oil and financial oligarchs on Wall Street in London let oil prices soar, of course, also to further stimulate the demand for the dollar.

Brzezinski's other trick was to play the "China card". In December 1978, the United States officially established diplomatic relations with China, and China soon returned to the United Nations. The Soviet Union immediately felt that it had enemies on all sides, with NATO to the east, China to the west and the "crisis arc" to the south. The Soviet Union, which had fought a cold war, immediately broke off its already fragile partnership with Germany.

When the Berlin Wall came down in November 1989 and the Germans celebrated reunification, Wall Street had something else on its mind:[181]

> "Indeed, when the financial history of the 1990s was being written, analysts might have likened the fall of the Berlin Wall to the financial shocks of the long-feared Japanese earthquake," said an American economist. The fall of this wall means hundreds of billions of dollars of capital will flow to a region that has been insignificant in world financial markets for over 60 years.
> While Germany has not been a major foreign investor in the U.S. in recent years, and Britain has been the largest since 1987, Americans should not take lightly the fact that Britain could not have invested in the U.S. on such a large scale without receiving significant savings from Germany."[182]

---

[181] William Engdahl, *op. cit.*, p. 211.

[182] David D. Hale. *The Weekly Money Report. Chicago*, Kemper Financial Services, 29 janvier 1990, in William Engdhal, op. cit., p. 252.

The feeling was stronger in London, where Thatcher's strategists even exclaimed that the "Fourth Reich" had appeared. The editor of the London *Sunday Telegraph* commented this way on 22 July 1990:

> *"Let us assume that a united Germany will be a giant of goodness, and what about that? What if we further assume that a unified Germany taught Russia to be a giant of goodness as well? In fact, such a threat can only get bigger. Even if a united Germany were determined to compete according to our rules, who in this world could effectively prevent Germany from taking our power?"*[183]

In the summer of 1990, a new intelligence service was formed on the London side, significantly increasing intelligence activities against Germany. British intelligence experts strongly suggested that American counterparts should recruit members from the old East German intelligence staff to build up American intelligence "assets" in Germany.

The German side is grateful for Russia's eventual support for German unity and is determined to help Russia rebuild its crippled economy. The German finance minister envisioned a bright future for the new Europe, a modern railway linking Paris, Hannover and Berlin, and eventually to Warsaw and Moscow, a unified currency, a mixed economy, a Europe where there would be no more war and smoke, only a dreamy future.

But this is by no means the dream of the international bankers, who are considering how to defeat the mark and the yet-to-be-formed idea of the euro, and who must not let the reconstruction of the new Germany succeed.

This is the big backdrop to the Soros blocking of the pound and the lira in the early 1990s under a London-Wall Street plot.

In 1990, the British government actually disregarded the opposition of the London Financial City, blatantly joined the European currency exchange system, watching the euro system gradually take shape, will inevitably become a major hidden danger of the London-Wall Street axis, international bankers then planned to break the various methods of fighting, want to hang the euro system in the cradle.

---

[183] Peregrine Worsthorne, « The Good German », *Daily Telegraph*, 22nd July 1990.

In 1990 the Berlin Wall was brought down and Germany reunified. The ensuing huge spending was unexpected in Germany, where the Bundesbank had to raise interest rates to combat inflationary pressures. The UK, which joined the European currency exchange system in the same year, also fared less well, with inflation three times that of Germany, interest rates as high as 15 per cent and the bubble economy of the 1980s on the verge of bursting. By 1992, the currencies of the United Kingdom and Italy had become significantly overvalued due to the pressure of double deficits, speculators led by Soros saw this opportunity to launch a general attack on September 16, 1992, shorting the total value of the pound as much as $10 billion, by 7:00 p.m., the United Kingdom announced surrender, this battle Soros captured as much as $1.1 billion, in one fell swoop to kick the pound and the lira out of the European currency exchange system. Immediately afterwards, Soros took advantage of the victory to take down the franc and the mark with a bang, not taking advantage of the $40 billion bet. Soros was able to borrow such a large amount of money with 25 times the leverage, and the powerful secret financial empire behind it played a decisive role.

Asian Currency Stranglehold

In the early 1990s, the London-Wall Street axis, on the eastern front, thwarted the aggressive momentum of the Japanese economy, on the western front, crushed the economy of Eastern Europe and the Soviet Union, Germany and France's dream of a unified European currency also temporarily stranded with the Soros's stirring up, Latin America and Africa has long been in the bag, with the ambition, look around the world, only to see the flourishing Southeast Asia "Asian economic model" increasingly unpleasant. This broad policy of government-led economic development, with the State focusing its resources on breaking through critical areas, export-oriented development and high savings of the people as the main features, has been rapidly gaining popularity in South-East Asia since the 1970s, and the effect of its operation has been unprecedented economic prosperity, a substantial increase in the living standards of the people, a steady rise in the average level of education and a rapid decline in absolute poverty. This alternative model, which is a complete departure from the "free market economy" so strongly promoted by the Washington Consensus, is increasingly attracting the interest of other developing countries and seriously undermining the basic strategic approach of "controlled disintegration" developed by the international bankers.

The main strategic objective of launching an Asian currency war of attrition is to shatter the "Asian development model" signboard and allow Asian currencies to depreciate severely against the United States dollar, both to depress United States import prices for inflationary purposes and to sell the core assets of Asian countries at par value to European and American companies to accelerate the implementation of "controlled disintegration". There is also a very important purpose, which is to stimulate demand for the dollar in Asian countries. For Asian countries that have experienced the financial turmoil, how "precious" the dollar reserves were at the critical moment, and the bitter lesson will make them never dare to think of abandoning them.

In December 1994, Grumman's masterpiece "The Myth of the Asian Miracle", published in Foreign Affairs, predicted that the Asian economy was bound to hit a high wall. There is certainly merit in the article's observation that there is a general underinvestment in productivity improvement in Asian countries and that scale up alone will have its limits. However, the problem is that the starting point of Asian countries is generally very low, and the key to development lies in adapting to the local context, adapting to the time, taking advantage of the situation and building on strengths and avoiding weaknesses. These problems are themselves natural phenomena in the rapid upward momentum of these countries, and it is entirely possible to resolve them in a benign manner in the course of development. Judging by the effect of Grumman's article, the effect is the equivalent of a flare for an Asian currency strangulation war.

The international bankers are targeting Thailand first.

The *Times* once interviewed a financial hacker who had directly contributed to the wild devaluation of the Thai baht, and his description was brutally honest:

> "We were like wolves standing on a high ridge looking down on a herd of elk. Thailand's economy looks more like a wounded prey than a small Asian tiger. We choose the sick and weak (for the hunt) to keep the deer herd healthier overall."

Since 1994, the crisis has taken shape as Thai exports have weakened under the upward and downward pressure of the depreciation of the renminbi and the yen, while the Thai baht, which is pegged to the dollar, has been dragged to the point of extreme emptiness by the strong dollar. While exports have declined, a steady influx of hot money from outside has continued to push up real estate and stock market prices. At the same time, Thailand's foreign exchange reserves, although as much as $38 billion, but its total external debt is as high as $106 billion, since 1996, Thailand's net outflow of funds equivalent to 8% of its GDP. The situation of a deeply indebted Thailand has been exacerbated by the fact that the Bank of Thailand has had to raise interest rates to combat inflation.

There is only one way out for Thailand, and that is to actively and quickly devalue the baht. International bankers estimate that the loss will be mainly in the form of dollar-denominated debt becoming more expensive and foreign exchange reserves shrinking by about $10 billion, but that this loss will be quickly recovered as international financial markets affirm their decisive response. But the financial hackers have concluded that the Thai government will fight to the death to protect the baht and will not stop at nothing.

Subsequent developments have proved to be very accurate judgments of financial hackers. Unlike the situation against Japan at that time, Japan has extremely strong financial strength and foreign exchange reserves, a direct attack on the Japanese currency is tantamount to striking a stone with an egg, so the international bankers used new financial derivatives weapons, took the time "long-range" and "ultra-visual range" strike, the effect is just like the new aircraft carrier tactics against battleships during the Second World War, so that the Japanese giant battleships powerful cannon power can not be used to bury the sea. With Thailand's deadlocked position warfare, complete exposure of strategic intent, lack of tactical flexibility and abruptness, and the overwhelming disparity of power between the enemy and us, ultimate failure is inevitable. In their battle against Thailand and other Southeast Asian countries, financial hackers have struck mainly at their currencies themselves, forming a pincer offensive through local currency forward contracts and stock index futures to sweep across Southeast Asia and Thailand over a six-month period.

After a complete defeat in the head-on battlefield against financial hackers, Thailand has mistakenly taken the initiative to fall into the IMF's trap. The blind trust in "international organizations" and the ease with which the safety and security of States are left to outsiders to adjudicate is once again an irreparable mistake.

The huge external debt is the main cause of the crisis in developing countries. It is really the same thing with states and states, high indebtedness leads to a fragile state of economic health, and survival can only be achieved by chance when the external financial environment is completely uncontrollable. In the real world, international bankers, manipulating international geopolitical trends, can easily reverse what had appeared to be a reliable financial environment, thereby substantially increasing the debt burden of developing countries, and financial hackers can then take advantage of the situation to launch an onslaught with a high probability of success.

There is a complete lack of risk awareness, and especially a lack of preparedness for the possibility of an undeclared war by the huge and invisible forces of London-Wall Street. This is the second major reason for Thailand's financial defeat.

A complete misjudgement of the enemy's main direction of attack led to the first defeat of the financial hackers and then to the IMF's slaughter, equivalent to two defeats. The South-East Asian countries have generally repeated the process of financial defeat in Thailand.

Wolves have their own wolf logic, and wolves have even more wolf division. When the Soros began their hunt, conspired by a large group of prestigious banks such as Citibank and Goldman Sachs, the wounded and fallen prey was handed over to the IMF for slaughter and auction, and the auction table was packed with salivating European and American companies.

If investment bankers who acquire a company for spin-off packaging can make hundreds of millions of dollars selling it to other companies, spinning off and auctioning off the core assets of a sovereign nation can make at least ten, if not a hundred times as much money.

When Asian countries attempted to establish their own "Asia Fund" to provide emergency relief to countries in distress in the region, it was rightly met with widespread opposition from Western countries. U.S. Under Secretary of State Talbot said,

> *"We believe that the appropriate body to address these types of issues is one that is trans-regional and international, not one that is handed over to a newly created regional organization, because the issue itself is far-reaching and transcends the boundaries of the Asia-Pacific region."*

Addressing the Japan Association in New York, U.S. Treasury Secretary Summers insisted that "this notion of financial regionalization that relies on regional aid in times of crisis ... carries real risks." He noted that such an approach would reduce the resources available to deal with future storms and the ability to deal with "transcontinental crises". "This is an important reason why we believe the IMF must play a central role,"

First Deputy Chairman of the International Monetary Fund (IMF) Fisher warned that regional funds could not be as strict as the IMF in requiring countries to make overall economic reforms in exchange for aid. "We don't think it would be helpful to have a huge fund or a long-term institution with different terms," said Fisher.

Japan was supposed to be an active advocate of the "Asia Fund", but was forced to succumb to pressure from London-Wall Street, and Japan's Finance Minister, Hiroshi Mitsuka, said that

> *"the International Monetary Fund has always played a central role in the international financial institutions in maintaining global financial stability. This fund, which the Asian countries have proposed to organize, will serve as a subsidiary body of the International Monetary Fund".*

The new concept, designed by Tokyo, will be an unfunded fund. According to Tokyo's new concept, that would be a rescue agency, able to mobilize funds in advance with a plan and at a rapid pace, to aid currencies that are under international speculator sniping. When the proposal to establish an Asian fund was presented at the annual meetings of the World Bank and the International Monetary Fund in Hong Kong, it immediately raised alarm in the United States and the West, who feared it would undermine the work of the IMF.

In the end, Japanese Prime Minister Ryutaro Hashimoto could only say that

> *"we are not so arrogant as to think that we are capable of acting as a locomotive for the (economic) recovery of the Asia-Pacific region";*

he said that while Japan had contributed and would continue to do so in assisting some traumatized Asian countries, pulling Asia out of the economic quagmire was not its role to play.

Singapore's Deputy Prime Minister Lee Hsien Loong, referring to the Asia Fund, argued that there would be "moral hazard" in setting up an Asia Fund to replace the role of the International Monetary Fund.

The establishment by Asian countries of their own funds to support each other in times of distress, which was a natural thing to do, was resolutely and unjustifiably opposed by the London-Wall Street axis, while Japan, as the largest economy in the region, was completely at the mercy of others and lacked the minimum courage and guts to lead the Asian economies out of their predicament, which could not but chill the desperate countries of South-East Asia. Most puzzling is Singapore's view of how "moral hazard" can arise from giving oneself and one's neighbours the minimum power to help one another in the event of a pillage. Whose "morality" is such a "morality at risk"?

Malaysian Prime Minister Mahathir, an Asian leader who has seen the essence of the crisis better, said:

> *"We don't know where their money is coming from, or who is really doing the deal, let alone who is behind them. We don't know if they pay taxes after they earn money? Meanwhile, to whom do these taxes pay? We equally don't know who's behind them?"*

He argued that under the current system of monetary transactions, no one knows if the money is coming from legitimate channels or if someone is laundering it, "because no one can ask and there is no way to find out". As soon as these people launch an offensive against any country, untold amounts of money will pour into that country or conduct a selling campaign that no one can resist. Whether it is a market for goods, futures or securities, it must be conducted under a proper regime, "so we must regulate currency transactions and make them transparent". Mahathir was then subjected to a full-scale siege by Western opinion circles. Mahathir's scathing questions may not be appropriate for a diplomatic setting, but he does ask the questions that are on the minds of all Asians.

South Korea, another staunch Cold War partner of the United States, reached out to the United States for help after being swept away by the financial crisis, not expecting the U.S. rejection to come so quickly and so firmly. In the eyes of international bankers, the close relationship with Korea has become a wreck of the Cold War. The United States Government has debated the matter vigorously, with Secretary of State Albright and the National Security Adviser arguing that the little brother should be reached out and the Treasury Department, representing Wall Street, vehemently opposed, even accusing Albright of not knowing economics. In the end, Clinton deferred to the Treasury Department.

The crisis is the perfect time to kick down the door of the South Korean economy, in the view of Finance Minister Rubin, who has pressured the IMF to impose harsher than traditional conditionalities on South Korea to deal with the begging ally, who has been under pressure from the U.S. Treasury Department to increase the conditions for "aid" to South Korea, including the need for South Korea to immediately settle all trade disputes with the U.S. on terms favorable to the U.S. The South Koreans angrily accuse the IMF of always offering unreasonable conditions to the U.S.

Stiglitz, the World Bank's chief economist, argues that South Korea's descent into financial crisis stemmed from the U.S. Treasury Department's desperate efforts to force the country into a full and rapid financial capital market opening. Stiglitz, who is Clinton's chief economic adviser, is adamantly opposed to such recklessness, arguing that such openness does not serve America's security interests in favor of Wall Street's bankers.

The Korean government was forced to accept many harsh conditions from the United States, allowing the establishment of bank branches in the United States, increasing the share of foreign companies in listed companies from 26% to 50%, and the share of foreign individuals in companies from 7% to 50%, Korean companies must use international accounting principles, financial institutions must be audited by international accounting firms, the Central Bank of Korea must operate independently, free currency exchange under full capitalization, transparency in import licensing procedures, supervision of corporate structures, labor market reforms, etc. U.S. bankers have long salivated over South Korean companies and are ready to swarm in and tear their prey to shreds just as South Korea signs the deal.

But international bankers underestimate the strong national consciousness of Koreans, and countries that have that consciousness to back them up can hardly be ruled by outside forces. The isolated Koreans have been donating their gold and silver to the country, and with all their foreign exchange reserves depleted, gold and silver, which are the ultimate means of payment, have become a form of debt repayment that foreign creditors are very happy to accept without any hindrance. Even more surprising to international bankers is the fact that South Korea has not seen the massive wave of corporate and bank failures they had envisioned, with Western companies barely acquiring any large Korean companies. When South Korea finally survived the most difficult spring of 1998, South Korea's export surplus quickly rebounded, the South Korean government, which had thoroughly seen the tricks of Wall Street, resolutely abandoned the IMF poison. All cases of large corporations preparing to file for bankruptcy were frozen, and the government decisively stepped in to write off $70 to $150 billion of bad loans from the banking system, and when the government took over these bad loans, control of the banks was restored to the government, thus excluding the IMF from the reconstruction of the banking system.

The international bankers and the U.S. Treasury Department have not only made an empty glee, but have also made Korea more aware of the absolute necessity of government-led economy. Microsoft's attempt to annex South Korea's largest software company fell through, with eight local South Korean software companies finally winning. Ford's plan to buy South Korea's KIA Motors aborted, and the local company shattered Ford's good dreams. The takeover of two large local banks by foreign banks was suspended and the Korean government temporarily put the two banks under management.

South Korea's economy has rebounded strongly under the government's full leadership. The funny thing is that Korea is being touted by the IMF as a classic example of a successful rescue.

When, in 2003, Thailand finally redeemed itself from the IMF by paying off $12 billion in debt in advance, Prime Minister Thaksin stood in front of the huge flag and vowed that Thailand would "never again be a wounded prey (of international capital)" and would never again beg for "assistance" from the IMF. The Thai government even privately encouraged Thai businesses to refuse to repay the debts of international bankers in retaliation for the frenzied looting of foreign banks in 1997, and in September 2006, Thailand staged a military coup and Thaksin stepped down.

The Fable of China's Future

Resident Mahathir locates the neighborhood film police officer Greenspan and reports that something has been stolen from the home and that the thief may be repeat offender Soros.

The police officer Greenspan laughed and said,

> *"We can't blame all the thieves, we should find the reason from ourselves. Who made your house a good lock to pick?"*

Resident Mahathir said disgruntledly,

> *"Then why don't the thieves go and steal from China and India?"*

Police Officer Greenspan sighed and said,

> *"The Chinese and Indian yard walls are too high, Soros is inconvenient to climb in and out, if you fall down again and someone dies, isn't it still my business?"*

Thief Soros listened from the sidelines and sneered,

> *"Wouldn't a few holes in their yard walls solve the problem?"*

Police Officer Greenspan hurriedly looked around and whispered,

> *"Paulson has been sent to China, and I've heard that a few big holes can be dug by the end of 2006."*

Thief Soros listened with glee, took out his cell phone and started texting his companions,

> *"People are stupid, lots of money, go to China quickly."*

Summary

★International bankers, in an effort to revive confidence in the dollar, regained control of the financial battlefield, which had gone out of control, and made international oil prices rise by 400% to regain the dollar's fortunes in one fell swoop, while at the same time exacerbating conflicts in Arab countries and the world and further embarrassing the economies of developing countries.

★ Federal Reserve Chairman Paul Volcker used the "fight against world-wide inflation", forcing the world economy "planned disintegration".

★In an effort to find a new way for peacetime America, international bankers have proposed an environmental plan to replace natural resources with debt, making international bankers the de facto owners of large tracts of fertile land.

★At the time of Japan's rapid economic growth, international bankers forced the yen to appreciate, leading to Japan's financial bubble, and "stock put options" to strangle Japan's financial markets, sending Japan into a decades-long recession.

★The world's financial markets have been stormed by Soros since the 1990s under the tutelage of international bankers, and each of his major actions has reflected the major strategic intent of the international bankers, the core of which is the "controlled disintegration" of national economies and the eventual completion of preparations for the "world government" and "world currency" under the control of the London-Wall Street axis.

★International bankers plotted Soros's sniping of the pound and the lira in the early 1990s in order to defeat the mark and the as yet unformed idea of the euro and prevent the new Germany from being rebuilt.

★In an effort to get Asian currencies to depreciate severely against the dollar while stimulating Asian demand for the dollar, international bankers launched an Asian currency stranglehold that led to Thailand's financial defeat, but the South Korean government resisted the pressure and the economy rebounded strongly.

CHAPTER IX

The Dollar's Dead Spot and the Gold One Yang Index

> *"If all bank loans were repaid, bank deposits would cease to exist and the entire money circulation would be depleted. It was a startling thought. We (the Federal Reserve) are totally dependent on commercial banks. Every dollar in our currency circulation, whether in cash or credit, must be borrowed by someone to produce it. If commercial banks (by granting credit) make enough money, our economy will prosper; otherwise, we will be in a recession. We definitely don't have a permanent monetary system. The pathetic absurdity of our (monetary system) and the incredible helplessness of (the Fed) becomes so obvious when one grasps the crux of the whole issue. Money is the most important issue that people should investigate and think about, and its importance is that unless people understand this (monetary) system broadly and take immediate steps to fix it, our present civilization will collapse."[184]*
>
> —Robert Hamphill, Federal Reserve Bank of Atlanta

Money, by its very nature, can be divided into two categories, debt money and non-debt money. Debt money is the system of armament that is in place in the major developed countries today, and its main component is made up of "monetized" debts of Governments, corporations and private individuals.

The dollar is a prime example of this. Dollars are created as the debt is created and destroyed as the debt is repaid. Every dollar in circulation is a note of debt owed, and every note owed generates interest on the debt in every day, and adds up profitably, to whom does the astronomical interest income go? to the banking system that created

---

[184] Irving Fisher, *100% Money* (Pickering & Chatto Ltd., Set Only edition, Forward, 1996).

the dollar. The interest on the debt dollar is additional to the original monetary total and necessarily requires the creation of new debt dollars in addition to the existing monetary total, in other words, the more money people borrow, the more money they must borrow. The logical corollary of the deadlock between debt and currency is that debt grows forever until its debt currency is completely abandoned or its interest burden crushes its own economic development, leading to the eventual collapse of the entire system. The monetization of debt is one of the most serious potential destabilizing factors of the modern economy, which is to meet the needs of the present by overdrafting the future. There is an old Chinese saying, "Yin eat dao grain" means exactly that.

The other type of currency is non-debt currency, represented by gold and silver money. This currency is not dependent on the promises of anyone, is not a debt to anyone, it represents the fruits of human labor that has been accomplished and has evolved naturally through thousands of years of human social practice. It does not require any coercion by governmental force, it can transcend times and borders, and it is the ultimate means of payment in money.

Of all currencies, gold and silver money means "actual possession", while free money means "note + promise". There is an essential difference in the "gold content" of the two values.

China's yuan is somewhere in between. Although there is also an element of "debtorized money" in the RMB, it is still, in its subject matter, a measure of the products and services that have been completed in the past. The issuance of the renminbi is not collateralized by national debt, as in the case of the US dollar, but by a private central bank, thus avoiding the huge interest payments that fall into the private pockets. At the same time, since the renminbi is not backed by gold and silver, it has the basic properties of a French currency and must rely on the coercive power of the government to guarantee its value.

A true understanding of the intrinsic nature of the Western French currency system, especially the dollar system, is a necessary prerequisite for the future reform of the RMB.

The fractional reserve system: a source of inflation

> "The (modern) bank was originally unjust, and it was born with sin. The bankers own the earth. Stripping them of everything, but leaving them with the power to create savings, they only need to

move the pen to create enough savings to redeem everything they have lost. But if they are deprived of the power to create savings, all good fortune in wealth will disappear, including my own, and they (the power to create savings) should disappear because it will lead to a happier and better world. But if you are willing to continue to be slaves to the bankers and pay for your enslavement, then let them continue to create savings. "[185]

—Sir Josiah Stamp, Governor of the Bank of England, (1928– 1941) second richest man in England.

The earliest goldsmith bankers offered a purely "gold coin deposit business" in which depositors handed over gold coins to the bankers, who provided standard-form receipts, which were called "bank notes", and these "derivatives" of gold coins gradually became the medium of social transactions, called money.

At this time, the bank was under a complete reserve system and could exchange "bank notes" for gold coins at any time. Its main income is the "fiduciary fees" paid by depositors.

Over time, the "clever" goldsmith banker found that usually only a small number of depositors come to request the "bank notes" into gold coins, looking at the gold in the gold cellar lying there to sleep, the banker could not help but begin to itch, how can "revitalize" these sleeping assets?

There are always people in society who are in desperate need of money, so bankers tell them that they can come to the bank and borrow money, as long as they repay the principal within the stipulated period and pay some interest. When the borrower comes to the bank, the banker issues more "receipts" and more "bank notes" to make loans and collect interest. As long as it does not increase the number of issues too much, it will generally not arouse suspicion among depositors. Long-term experience shows that it is safe to issue, for example, 10 times more "bank notes". Since the interest income from the loans was a windfall that was created out of nothing, of course, the more the better, the bankers started pulling depositors around, and in order to attract

---

[185] Sir Josiah Stamp, informal discussion before 150 professors of history, economics and social sciences at the University of Texas, 1920s. Source: *The Legalized Crime of Banking*, by Silas W. Adams (Meador Publishing Company, Boston, 1958, Omnia Veritas Ltd., www.omnia-veritas.com), chapter VII.

people, they started paying interest on the depository escrow business that was originally charged.

When the goldsmith banker, who was in the business of storing gold coins, started the lending business, he actually offered two very different service products to the original depositors, the first being pure "gold coin storage" and the second being "investment savings". The essential difference between the two is "ownership of the gold coins". In the first case, the depositor has absolute ownership of the gold coins deposited with the banker, who must promise that the depositor can take receipts for the gold coins at any time. In the second case, the depositor loses ownership of the gold coin over a period of time, and the banker makes a risky investment so that when the investment is recovered, the depositor regains ownership.

The first "gold coin deposit" corresponds to a "de facto existence" of bank notes, which are full reserves, while the second "investment savings" corresponds to a "note of indebtedness + promise", where the number of bank notes issued is greater than the actual amount of gold coins held by the bank and is a partial reserve. This kind of "note + promise" bank notes are inherently risk-factor and inflationary in nature, which destines them to be very unsuitable for the medium of exchange of social goods and services.

The fractional reserve system has an innate urge to blur the lines between the two banking service products. Bankers have "standardized" the design of banknotes, making it difficult for ordinary people to distinguish the essential differences between the two types of banknotes, and the Anglo-Saxon countries have been litigious for centuries as a result. When angry depositors sued the bankers for lending what the depositors considered to be "fiduciary gold coins" to others without their permission, the bankers claimed that they had the right to dispose of the depositors' gold coins. The most famous of these is the case of Frey v. Hill and others of 1848.

> *"When (the depositor's) money is deposited in the bank, it ceases to belong to the depositor at all; it then belongs to the banker, who is obliged to return the corresponding amount if the depositor so requests. Money deposited in a bank and managed by a banker is, in all senses and connotations, the money of the banker, who has the right to dispose of it as he pleases. He is not obliged to answer whether the depositor of this money is in danger, whether he is engaged in harmful speculation, and he is not obliged to keep and treat it as he would treat the property of*

another; but he is certainly obliged to the amount (of the money deposited by the depositor), because he is bound by the contract."[186]

Under the common law system, this decision by the English judge undoubtedly became an important turning point in financial history when depositors' own hard-earned money deposited in banks suddenly lost the protection of the law, in a serious violation of citizens' property rights. After that, the banks of the Anglo-Saxon countries completely refused to recognize the legality of "savings escrow", the full reserves lost their legal status and all savings became "venture capital". The monopoly of the fractional reserve system was legally established.

At the Battle of Waterloo in 1815, the Rothschild family bank learned the end of the war with a time difference of 24 hours earlier than the British official, thus mastering the British bond market, controlling the currency issuance of the British Empire, and soon afterwards, controlled the currency issuance of France, Austria, Prussia, Italy and other countries, holding the world gold market pricing power for nearly 200 years. The banking networks set up in various countries by the Rothschild, Schiff, Warburg and other Jewish banking families, which in fact formed the earliest international financial system and world clearing house, allowed the checks of other banks to circulate across borders only by joining their clearing networks, and they gradually formed a cartel of bankers. These family banking norms have become the "international practice" of the world financial industry today.

The banking cartel is the most important driver of the fractional reserve system and the biggest beneficiary. When the energy of such "financial special interests" reaches a considerable scale, they are bound to foster or even directly establish the rules of the political and judicial game in their best interest.

In 1913, when the international banking cartel finally succeeded in establishing the Federal Reserve, the "model" of the fractional reserve system in the United States, the currency of the full reserve system was gradually expelled from the competition as "bad currency". The then U.S. government issued "silver notes" and "gold notes" can be called the survivors of the full reserve system, both notes are backed by 100%

---

[186] Murray N. Rothbard, *op. cit.*, p. 92.

of the U.S. government's real gold and silver, one ounce of gold and silver corresponds to the equivalent paper money, even if all the debts of the banking system are paid at the same time, the market still has full reserves of "gold and silver dollars" in circulation, the economy can still develop, just like before the existence of the Federal Reserve in 1913.

Since 1913, the fractional reserve Fed "bad dollar" began to gradually expel the full reserve of real gold and silver "good dollar" from the market, and the international bankers, in order to create a fait accompli of the fractional reserve system monopoly of the modern financial world, and to kick governments out of the field of currency issuance, so they used every means to demonize gold and silver, and finally succeeded in abolishing the silver dollar in the 1960s, and in 1971 cut off the final link between gold and the dollar, and since then the fractional reserve system finally completed the monopoly.

How the Debt Dollar Is Made

Here's how the Fed's Bank of New York describes the dollar,

> "The dollar cannot be exchanged for Treasury gold or any other asset. The question about the assets backing the 'Fed notes' has no practical significance, it is only the bookkeeping aspect of the need … the bank generates the currency when the borrower promises to pay it back. Banks are creating money by 'monetizing' these private and commercial debts."

The Fed's Bank of Chicago explains,

> "In the United States, neither paper money nor bank deposits have the same intrinsic value as commodities; the dollar is just a piece of paper. Bank deposits are also just a number of numbers in the books. Coins, while possessing some intrinsic value, are usually well below their face value.
> So what is it that makes these instruments such as checks, notes, coins, etc., acceptable to people at their face value in the payment of debts and other monetary purposes? The main thing is the confidence of people that they can exchange these currencies for other financial assets and real products and services whenever they want. Part of this is because the

government uses the law to say that these 'fiat' coins must be accepted."[187]

That is, the "monetization" of debt creates the dollar, and the face value of the dollar must be forced by external forces. So how exactly does debt become dollars? To understand the details of "debt to money", we must take a closer look at the mechanism of monetary operations in the United States with a magnifying glass.

As a non-financial professional reader, you may need to read the following repeatedly to fully understand the "money-making process" of the Federal Reserve and banking institutions. This is the core "trade secret" of the Western financial industry.

Since the U.S. government does not have the right to issue money, but only to issue bonds and then pledge them to the Fed, a privately owned central bank, in order to issue money through the Fed and the commercial banking system, the source of the dollar is in the treasury bonds.

The first step is for Congress to approve the size of the issuance of Treasuries, and the Treasury Department to design the Treasuries into different types of bonds, of which those with a term of less than one year are called T-bills, those with a term of 2 to 10 years are called T-notes, and those with a term of 30 years are called T-bonds. these bonds are auctioned on the open market at different times and at different frequencies. The Treasury finally sends all the bonds not sold in the auction transaction to the Federal Reserve, which collects them in full, at which point these bonds are recorded on the Federal Reserve's books under "securities assets".

National debt is considered the "most reliable asset" in the world because it is secured by the U.S. government against future taxes. When the Fed acquires this "asset", it can use it to create a liability, which is the "Fed check" printed by the Fed. This is a key step in "creating something out of nothing". Behind this first check from the Fed, there is no money to support this "short check".

It is a carefully designed and disguised step that exists to make it easier for the government to control "supply and demand" when auctioning bonds, the Fed gets "interest" on the money it lends to the

---

[187] *Modern Money Mechanics*, Federal Reserve Bank of Chicago.

government, and the government gets money conveniently without showing signs of printing a lot of money. Clearly an empty-glove white wolf of the Federal Reserve, in the accounting accounts is completely balanced, the "assets" of the national debt and the "liabilities" of the currency is exactly equal. The entire banking system is subtly wrapped under this shell.

It is this simple but crucial step that has created the greatest injustice in the world. The future tax revenue of the people is pledged by the Government to the private central bank to "lend" dollars, and since the money is "borrowed" from private banks, the Government owes a huge amount of interest. This injustice is reflected in:

—The people's future taxes should not be mortgaged because the money has not been earned, and mortgaging the future will inevitably lead to a devaluation of the purchasing power of the currency, thus hurting the savings of the people.

—The future taxation of the people should not be pledged to a private central bank, and bankers suddenly have the promise of the future taxation of the people with almost no money, which is a typical "white wolf with empty gloves".

—The Government owes huge amounts of interest for no good reason, and these interest payments eventually become a burden on the people. The people have not only inexplicably mortgaged their future, but are now paying immediate taxes to pay back the interest the government owes the private central bank. The larger the issue of dollars, the heavier the interest burden on the people, and the more it will never be paid back for generations!

Step two, when the federal government receives and endorses a "Fed check" from the Federal Reserve, this magical check is deposited back into the Federal Reserve Bank and transformed into "government savings" and deposited in the government's account with the Federal Reserve.

In the third step, when the federal government starts spending money, federal checks, large and small, form the "first wave" of money coming into the economy. The companies and individuals who received the cheques deposited them into their commercial bank accounts, which in turn became "commercial bank savings". At this point they present a "dual personality", on the one hand they are liabilities of the bank, since the money belongs to the depositors and will have to be paid back sooner or later. But on the other hand, they constitute "assets" of the bank and can be used to lend money. From the accounting accounts everything is still in balance and the same assets make up the same liabilities. Here, however, commercial banks are beginning to prepare to "create" money with the aid of the "fractional reserve" amplifier.

As a fourth step, commercial bank savings were reclassified as "bank reserves" in the bank accounts. At this point, these savings have gone from being ordinary "assets" of the bank to "reserves" for seed money. Under the "fractional reserve" system, the Federal Reserve allows commercial banks to keep only 10 per cent of their savings as "reserves" (generally, United States banks keep only 1 to 2 per cent of total savings in cash and 8 to 9 per cent of notes in their "vaults" as "reserves") and lend out 90 per cent of their savings. Thus, 90 percent of this money will be used by the banks to extend credit.

There's a problem here, after 90% of the savings are lent to someone else, what if the original saver writes a check or uses the money? In fact, when the loans were made, they were not original savings, but "new money" created out of nothing. This "new money" immediately increased the total amount of money held by banks by 90 per cent over the "old money". Unlike "old money", "new money" can generate interest income for the bank. This is the "second wave" of currencies coming into the economy. When the "second wave" of money returned to commercial banks, more waves of "new money" creation were generated, with a decreasing trend.

By the end of the "twentieth wave", one dollar of Treasuries, in close coordination with the Federal Reserve and commercial banks, had created an incremental $10 of money in circulation. If the volume of national debt issuance and its money-creating residuals produce an increase in money circulation that is greater than needed for economic growth, the purchasing power of all "old money" declines, which is the fundamental cause of inflation. When the United States added $3 trillion in new national debt between 2001 and 2006, a significant portion of that went directly into currency circulation, which, combined with the redemption of national debt and interest payments made years earlier, resulted in a dramatic depreciation of the dollar and a significant increase in the price of commodities, real estate, oil, education, health care and insurance.

However, most of the increased issuance of Treasuries does not go directly into the banking system, but is purchased by foreign central banks, non-financial institutions in the United States, and individuals. In this case, these purchasers are spending dollars that already exist, so they are not "creating" new dollars. Only when the Federal Reserve and America's banking institutions buy U.S. Treasuries will new dollars be created, which is why the U.S. has been able to keep inflation under control for a while. However, Treasuries in the hands of non-U.S. banks, sooner or later, will mature and the additional interest will have to be paid semi-annually (30-year Treasuries), at which point the Fed will inevitably make new dollars.

In essence, the fractional reserve system coupled with the debt monetary system is the culprit of long-term inflation. Under the gold standard, the inevitable result is that the volume of bank notes issued gradually exceeds the volume of gold reserves by a large margin, leading to the inevitable disintegration of the gold standard. Under the Bretton-Woods system, it is the inevitable collapse of the gold exchange system. And under a purely legal tender system, it would inevitably end up with hyperinflation, which would eventually lead to a severe worldwide recession.

Under a debt currency, the United States will never be able to pay its national, corporate and private debts, because the day the debt is paid is the day the dollar disappears. The total debt of the United States is not only unlikely to decrease, but will continue to rise at an ever-increasing rate as the snowball effect of interest rolling in on debt and the economy's natural growth in monetary demand.

The "river of debt" of the United States and the "white slips" of the Asian people

The unprecedented size of the U.S. treasury bonds issued in the 1980s, with their high interest rates, greatly attracted investors from private and non-banking institutions and foreign central banks, and less new dollars were created in the process of repurposing the existing dollars. By the 1990s, the United States had witnessed a golden age of high growth and low inflation, as the world's major competing currencies were defeated, dollar-denominated Treasuries remained in demand, and the price of imported daily commodities became exceptionally cheap in the face of widespread devaluation of Third World currencies, forcing the United States to issue more Treasuries to replace the old ones as a result of the massive spending on the war on terror and the maturity of the various maturities of Treasuries issued in large numbers since the 1980s, as well as increasing interest payments. From 1913 to 2001, the United States accumulated a total of $6 trillion in national debt in 87 years, but from 2001 to 2006, in just over five years, the United States increased its national debt by nearly $3 trillion, and the total U.S. federal national debt has reached $8 trillion and is increasing at a rate of $2.55 billion per day. The U.S. federal government already has the third-highest interest payments in government spending, after health care and defense, at nearly $400 billion a year, or 17 percent of its total fiscal revenue.

United States treasury debt: From 1982 to 1992, the United States monetary increase was a "modest increase" of 8 per cent per year. However, from 1992 to 2002, United States monetary growth entered a "fast-track", reaching 12 per cent. Beginning in 2002, as a result of the war on terror and the need to stimulate a recession-ridden economy, U.S. currency issuance grew at a staggering 15 per cent with post-war interest rates near their lowest point. In fact, judging by the steepness of the increase in U.S. Treasury debt, everything is already a given. It is no coincidence that the Federal Reserve announced in March 2006 that it was discontinuing the M3 broad money statistics report.

(No country in human history has ever so severely overdrawn its future, and the United States has overdrawn not only the wealth of its own people, but the future wealth of the people of other countries just as severely, and anyone familiar with stock investing can clearly foresee what this steep curve will ultimately mean.)

Since 9/11 2001, when Greenspan recklessly lowered interest rates from 6 percent to 1 percent to save the stock and bond markets, causing the dollar to flood the world with credit, people finally understood that the dollar was actually a piece of paper with a green pattern on it. The world's major dollar holders pounced almost simultaneously on real estate, oil, gold, silver, commodities and other things that the Fed can't make out. One French investor said, "New Yorkers can issue dollar bills, but only God can issue oil and gold." As a result, the price of crude oil rose from $22 to $60 a barrel and the prices of gold, silver, platinum, nickel, copper, zinc, lead, soybeans, sugar, coffee and cocoa were 120 to 300 per cent of 2002 prices, respectively. But economists still swear by the fact that inflation is only 1 or 2 percent, and one can't help but recall Mark Twain's famous quote that there are three kinds of lies in the world: lies, damned lies and statistics.

Even more troubling is the fact that the total debt of the United States has reached $44 trillion, which includes the sum of federal national debt, state and local government debt, international debt, and private debt. These debts are spread evenly over every American to the tune of nearly $150,000, with a family of four carrying nearly $600,000 in debt. Most notable among the private debts are the large number of home mortgages and credit card debt. At a conservative interest rate of 5 percent, $44 trillion would require an annual interest payment of up to $2.2 trillion, which is almost equal to the total fiscal revenue of the U.S. federal government for the entire year. Nearly 70 per cent of the total debt was "created" after 1990. It is no longer possible for the current US to lasso third world countries by waging the high interest rate wars of the early 80's because the US itself is so heavily indebted that any high interest rate policy is tantamount to economic suicide.

The "monetization" of debt, coupled with the super-amplifier that is fractional reserves, has severely drained the future wealth of the American people. By 2006, the total amount of personal income tax paid by Americans, after only a short stay with the federal government, was immediately transferred to the banking system to pay interest on debt dollars. None of the income taxes paid by individuals go to the government, the education spending in each region is largely dependent on local property tax revenues, the construction and maintenance of highways throughout the U.S. uses a gasoline tax, and the cost of warfare for foreign troops coincides with the corporate tax paid by U.S. corporations. In other words, 300 million Americans have been "indirectly taxed" by bankers for decades, and continue to be exploited year after year. The savings of the American people are then scraped off by bankers' "potential taxes" through long-term inflation.

Regardless of whether the U.S. debtors can still pay off this lucrative debt, the problem is that the U.S. government has no intention of paying off the national debt at all. The U.S. government just keeps replacing the old bonds and the interest accrued on the old debt with new ones that add up forever, and the cycle goes on and on forever. As the Federal Reserve Bank of Philadelphia points out,

"On the other hand, a growing number of analysts now consider Treasuries to be very useful, even (economic) gospel. They don't think the national debt needs to be reduced at all."[188]

Yes, if one can live a lavish life by constantly borrowing more and more debt, and can never have to pay it back, one can only fear that such good things will never be found again under heaven. This "good thing", which sounds like an "economic perpetual motion", is now taking hold in the United States. The idea that these economists can enjoy the "good life" forever by increasing debt is not fundamentally different from the idea that a country can get rich by printing more money.

These scholars have gone on to accuse Asia and other countries of excessive savings as the root cause of the structural dysfunction of the world economy, an argument that has proved the alarming degradation of their academic morality. Excessive savings in Asian countries? Where do they have excess savings? These decades of hard-earned savings are being sucked by the United States into the "great experiment" of "economic perpetual motion" on a scale unprecedented in human history, through the purchase of United States treasury bonds.

The demand for U.S. national debt from the "export-oriented" economies of Asian countries is like an addiction to drugs, which will not be able to be absorbed into the bloodstream for a moment. And the United States is also happy to take this essentially "never-ending" national debt to the people of Asia. Eventually, however, Asian countries will realize that the real risk of irreversible and dramatic devaluation of dollar assets for a nominal return of only 5 per cent on United States Treasuries is not a sound investment in any case.

Former U.S. Secretary of the Treasury Summers pointed out that if China stops buying an average of billions of dollars a week of national debt, the U.S. economy will be in big trouble, but the Chinese economy will also be in big trouble because of shrinking exports to the United States, in fact, the two sides have fallen into a state of "financial terror balance".

---

[188] *The National Debt, Series for economic education*, Federal Reserve Bank of Philadelphia.

The "hegemony business" of the financial derivatives market

If at least $2 trillion of the annual interest payments that are added at a rolling rate are sooner or later "created" into the monetary system, although some of this can be piled into the future at the cost of higher debt, and some of the additional interest dollars are enough to cause significant inflation, it is strange that inflation in the United States does not seem to be obvious. How does the international banker's magic work?

The trick is that there has to be a place to go to absorb the massive currency additions that have been monstrously inflated in the derivatives market over the last decade or so.

Twenty years ago, the total nominal value of financial derivatives worldwide was almost zero, and by 2006, the total size of this market had reached $37 trillion! It is more than eight times the world's combined GDP. Its growth is fast and large enough to hold up any normal human imagination.

What is the nature of financial derivatives? Like the dollar, it's also debt! They are packaged debts, they are collections of debts, they are containers of debts, they are warehouses of debts, they are Himalayas of debts.

These are the same liabilities that flood the portfolios of hedge funds as assets, and the same liabilities that are held in accounts by insurance companies and pension funds as assets. These debts were traded, deferred, squeezed, stretched, rolled, filled, plucked out, and it was a feast of debts, and a feast of gambling. Behind the cumbersome mathematical formulas, with only empty and two more options, every contract is a gamble, and every gamble is bound to see win or lose.

Since it's a multi-billion dollar bet, there must be a dealer in this casino. Who is the bookmaker? The five largest banks in the United States, which are not only heavyweight players, but are also in the business of "domination".

The U.S. Department of the Treasury released the second quarter of 2006 commercial banks financial derivatives market report pointed out that the five largest U.S. banks, JPMorgan Chase, Citigroup, etc., accounted for 97% of all 902 banks financial derivatives combined, with 94% of the income. Of all bank financial derivatives categories, the largest is the "interest rate products category", which accounts for 83 per cent of the entire plate, with a nominal value of $98.7 trillion.[189]

In the interest rate product category, "interest rate swaps" predominate. The main form of an "interest rate swap" is a "floating interest cash flow" in exchange for a "fixed interest cash flow" for a certain period of time, and the transaction generally does not involve principal. Its main use is to "simulate" the operation of long-term fixed-rate bonds at a "lower cost". The two companies that use this tool the most are Freddie Mac and Fannie Mae in the United States. The two mega-financiers issue short-term bonds to finance 30-year fixed-interest real estate loans, supplemented by "interest rate swaps" to hedge against the risk of future interest rate changes.

JPMorgan Chase is alone with a share of $74 trillion of the $98.7 trillion in interest rate derivatives. In the financial field, 10:1 capital leverage ratio to invest is already very "adventurous", 100:1 is "crazy type" investment, in the 1990s the famous super hedge fund "Long-Term Capital Management Fund" under the guidance of two Nobel Prize winners, built the world's most complex risk hedging mathematical model at that time, with the world's most advanced computer hardware facilities, in this leverage ratio to invest, inadvertently lost all the money, and nearly brought down the entire world's financial system. JPMorgan Chase's potential leverage ratio for interest rate derivatives is 626:1, the highest in the world.[190]

J.P. Morgan is actually in the "hegemonic" business of the interest rate derivatives market, which is the home of almost all hedged interest rate risky companies. In other words, the vast majority of people need to invest against a sudden spike in future interest rates, and JPMorgan Chase, which assures everyone that interest rates won't skyrocket, sells just such an insurance policy.

What mysterious crystal ball would allow JPMorgan Chase to dare to take such an astounding risk to predict interest rate changes that only Greenspan and the Fed will know by then? There is only one reasonable answer, JPMorgan Chase itself is one of the largest shareholders of the

---

[189] U.S. Treasury Report, OCC's Quarterly Report on Bank Derivatives Activities, second quarter 2006.

[190] Adam Hamilton, *The JPM Derivatives Monster*, Zeal Research, 2001.

Federal Reserve Bank of New York, and the Federal Reserve Bank of New York is an uncompromising private company, JPMorgan Chase can not only know the news of interest rate changes earlier than others, but also the real maker of interest rate change policy, while the Federal Reserve "Committee" in Washington is just an executive body, the change in interest rate policy is not as the world imagined in the Fed regular meeting before voting on the temporary decision. Sure, the voting process was realistic, but the voters were planted by the international bankers from the beginning.

So JPMorgan Chase is doing a sure-fire no-lose deal. It's like JPMorgan Chase is a company that can artificially control rainfall and it sells flood insurance, it certainly knows when it's going to flood and it even knows which areas it's going to flood. Einstein once said that God does not roll the dice. JPMorgan dared to play the "hegemonic" business of the derivatives market, but also did not roll the dice.

With the explosive growth in the size of the financial derivatives market, government regulation has long since lagged far behind. A large number of derivatives contracts are carried out outside the formal trading market, also known as "over-the-counter transactions", and it is difficult in the accounting system to analogize derivatives transactions with regular commercial transactions, let alone tax calculations and asset-liability accounting. Due to its size, high financial leverage, difficult to control domestic risk and lax government regulation, it is a time bomb for the financial markets.

It is this unprecedented boom in the speculative market that has absorbed the astronomical liquidity "created" by the interest payments on US debt. As long as huge amounts of new dollars being issued and dollars returning from overseas are swept into this fast spinning market without leaking into other markets in droves, the core inflation index will be miraculously contained. Similarly, once the financial derivative markets collapse, we will witness the worst financial turmoil and economic crisis the world has ever seen.

Government Sponsored Enterprise: "Second Federal Reserve"

"Many financial institutions do not seem to understand the risky nature of these (short-term) bonds issued by the GSE. Investors mistakenly believed that their investments were completely immune to the credit risk of the GSEs because, in the event of a

crisis, they believed that there was enough warning time to wait for these short-term bonds to mature in a few months' time to cash in comfortably. The problem is that when a financial crisis strikes, the GSE's short-term bonds can become completely illiquid in a matter of hours, days at most. While any one investor can opt out, when all investors flee at the same time, no one can run. As is the case with bank runs, attempts to sell off the GSEs as a whole will not be successful because the real estate assets underlying these short-term bonds cannot be liquidated quickly."[191]

—William Poole, President,
Federal Reserve Bank of St. Louis, 2005

Government Sponsored Enterprise here refer to Fannie Mae and Freddie Mac, the two largest companies licensed by the U.S. government for real estate loans. The two companies are responsible for building a secondary market for U.S. real estate lending, with a total of $4 trillion in real estate-backed bonds (MBS) issued. In fact, most of the $7 trillion in real estate loans issued by the U.S. banking system were resold to these two companies. They packaged these long-term real estate mortgages into MBS bonds, which were then sold on Wall Street to financial institutions in the US and central banks in Asia. There was a spread between the MBS bonds they issued and the real estate mortgages they acquired from the banks, which constituted a source of profit for both companies. Statistically, 60 percent of U.S. banks hold more than 50 percent of the bank's capital in the bonds of these two companies.[192]

As publicly traded companies, Fannie Mae and Freddie Mac are both profit-driven and it is more profitable for them to hold real estate mortgages directly, where interest rate fluctuations, early mortgage repayments and credit risk are taken on themselves. While the Fed began the long process of raising interest rates from 2002, Fannie Mae and Freddie Mac began eating into and directly holding real estate mortgages in large quantities, which totaled $1.5 trillion by the end of 2003.

---

[191] GSE Risks, Federal Reserve Bank of St. Louis, Review, March/April 2005 (vol. 87, n° 2, Part 1), p. 85.

[192] *Fannie Mae, Freddie Mac and the need for GSE reform, now,* Office of Federal Housing Enterprise Oversight (OFHEO).

As a financial institution with such large debts, it should have been careful to hedge its risks, and one of the most important strategies is to match the maturities of the assets and debts, otherwise the risk of interest rate fluctuations will be difficult to control. Second, short-term financing to support long-term debt should be avoided. The traditional conservative approach is to issue long-term recoverable bonds that synchronize the asset and debt timeframes, while locking in spreads, so that the two risks of interest rate fluctuations and early mortgage repayment can be completely avoided. In reality, however, the two companies are financing themselves primarily with long-term fixed and short-term bonds, with short-term financing as large as $30 billion in short-term bonds that must be rolled weekly, thus exposing themselves to high levels of risk.

In order to hedge against the risk of interest rate fluctuations, they must adopt sophisticated hedging strategies, such as using debt and "interest rate swaps" to generate a combination of short-term debt + future fixed interest cash flows to "simulate" the effects of long-term bonds. A "swap option" is used to hedge the risk of early mortgage repayment. In addition to this, they use "imperfect dynamic hedging" strategies, which are "focused on defending" against potential short-term interest rate volatility and "unprotected" against long-term, unlikely interest rate shocks. With these measures, everything looks solid and fairly inexpensive, which seems like a perfect way to go.

Beneath a strong desire for profit, in the portfolios of Fannie Mae and Freddie Mac, they also ate heavily into the MBS bonds they issued themselves. At first glance it may seem counterintuitive, where does it make sense to issue one's own short-term bonds and buy one's own long-term bonds?

There's a truth to weird things. Fannie Mae and Freddie Mac are monopoly operators in the secondary market for real estate loans authorized by the U.S. government, which provides indirect guarantees to both companies. Indirectly, it means that the U.S. government provides a certain amount of credit to the two companies that can be used in an emergency. Also, the Fed can discount Fannie Mae and Freddie Mac's bonds, meaning central banks can monetize their bonds directly, something no corporate bond has had in nearly half a century, except for U.S. Treasuries. When the market learned that the bonds issued by Fannie Mae and Freddie Mac were almost equal to cash in U.S. dollars, their creditworthiness was second only to that of U.S. Treasuries. So the short-term bonds they issue pay only slightly higher interest than Treasuries, and with such a cheap source of financing, there's certainly still room to arbitrage by buying your own long-term bonds.

It is not an exaggeration to say that the bonds of these two companies play to some extent the role of United States Treasury bonds, and that they have effectively become the "second Federal Reserve", providing a great deal of liquidity to the United States banking system, especially when it is not convenient for the Government. This is why, after the Fed has carried out 17 consecutive rate hikes, the financial market still shows a flood of liquidity, the liquidity that was originally sucked back by the Fed, and the GSEs eat into bank real estate loans and flow back to the financial market. This situation is similar to the movie "Tunnel War" in which the ghosts keep pumping water from the well and then into the village's tunnel, the clever guerrillas through the tunnel again to send the water poured into the tunnel back to the well, causing the ghosts to wonder how deep the tunnel really is.

The GSE's arbitrage behavior of buying long-term MBS bonds with short-term bonds, coupled with the international bankers' financing from the yen market at very low cost and buying options on U.S. Treasuries with high leverage, artificially created a "boom" in U.S. long-term bonds (Treasuries and 30-year MBS bonds), which depressed the yield rates of long-term bonds, after whitewashing, it looks like the market's worries about long-term inflation are unfounded. So, foreign investors hesitated to return to the U.S. long-term bond market, so that savings from other countries could continue to fund the U.S. "economic perpetual motion experiment", and so the feast of desire continued to revel.

It's just that any illusion that is more wonderful is an illusion after all. While the GSEs continue to supply alcohol to the carnival, unwittingly, their own capital funds have fallen to an extremely dangerous 3.5%. With trillions of dollars of crippling debt on its back, its capitalization is so low in the midst of a fiercely volatile international interest rate market that it is enough to make Greenspan lose sleep. The Russian debt crisis has caused the perfect hedge fund, which was admired internationally, to disappear in a flash, under the guidance of the world's "most economically savvy" guru and with the most complete and complex risk hedging model. Can a GSE hedging strategy that relies heavily on financial derivatives withstand the unexpected and unexpected?

The weakness of the GSE is that it is seriously flawed in its protection against short-term interest rate mutations. Federal Reserve Bank of St. Louis President William Poole, worried about the GSE's resilience to interest rate shocks, concluded after analyzing the magnitude of daily interest rate fluctuations in U.S. Treasuries over the past 25 years:

> *"In more than 1 percent of all Treasury price fluctuations, about 3/4 of them exceed the 3.5 standard deviation of their absolute value, which is 16 times higher than the usual normal distribution model estimates. Assuming 250 trading days in a year, the probability of interest rate fluctuations of this intensity occurring is twice a year, rather than the one in eight years that one would estimate. The normal distribution model completely misjudges the risk of dramatic interest rate fluctuations. Super-intense swings above a standard deviation of 4.5 or greater, not seven parts per million as one would expect, but 11 times in 6,573 trading days, would be enough to shake up a company that is highly dependent on financial leverage. There is also the point that drastic fluctuations tend to be concentrated bursts. This characteristic is important, and it means that a company will be shaken violently several times in a very short period of time. Incomplete hedging in the face of dramatic interest rate fluctuations could lead to the complete failure of this company."[193]*

If financial hackers suddenly attack the dollar, terrorists carry out a nuclear or biological attack on the United States, gold prices continue to soar and other unexpected events, the U.S. Treasury market is bound to shake violently, GSE if there is a problem, trillions of dollars of bonds may lose liquidity within a few hours, the Federal Reserve is even too late to rescue, and such a scale of collapse even the Federal Reserve can only be willing but unable to rescue. Eventually 60 percent of U.S. banks could be dragged down, the highly vulnerable $3.7 trillion financial derivatives market would avalanche, and the world financial markets would see a frantic flight of terror.

The huge risks in the financial derivatives market reflected in the GSE are just the tip of the iceberg.

---

[193] William Poole, GSE Risks, Federal Reserve Bank of St. Louis, Review, March/April 2005, 87 (2, Part 1), p. 88.

Kiyosaki, author of "Poor Dad Rich Dad", describes the "debt boom" in the world today in his article "The Extravagant Desire for Debt" as follows.

> "The problem, in my opinion, is that these companies that were (sky-high) acquired were not bought by money and capital, they were bought by debt. My common sense tells me that someone will have to pay these debts in the future. The eventual collapse of the Spanish Empire was due to excessive greed for war and conquest, and I fear that the world today will end up repeating the same mistakes due to the expensive extravagance of debt. So what's my advice? For the moment, revel in the (feast of desire) party, but don't drink too much and stand near the exit."[194]

In the midst of a huge, colourful and lively casino, where people were intently betting on the dollar, which Kiyosaki called "funny money", those who were not yet drunk and sober enough to see the smoke starting in the corners of the casino quietly walked as calmly as possible towards the narrow exit. By this time the flames were visible and people were still unaware of them, but more people smelled the smoke, and they looked around, and someone started to whisper. Fearing that everyone would notice the fires that had appeared, the casino owner shouted and played more thrilling games, and most people were drawn back to the tables. The fire finally faded into flames and more people started to stir, some started to run, most were at a loss for words. The casino owners started shouting that it was normal to have some fire and smoke that would stimulate casino business and that the fire (inflation) was completely manageable, as it has been since 1971. The shouting had a stabilizing effect on hearts and minds, so people continued to bet money. Only, more and more people were crowding towards the exit. At this moment, what I am most afraid of is a scream...

When disaster strikes, everyone looks for their own exit. For Kiyosaki, the casino's export is gold and silver. In his article "Bet on Gold, Don't Bet on Funny Money," he states,

> "I think gold is cheap and will go up when the price of oil goes up and Russia, Venezuela, Arab countries and Africa become increasingly reluctant to accept our dollar. For now, we can still pay for other countries' products and services with our 'funny

---

[194] Robert Kiyosaki, « A Taste for Debt », in Yahoo Finance Experts Column, 27th October 2006.

currency', but the world is getting tired of the dollar. My strategy for years has been: invest real money, they are gold and silver. I likewise continue to lend funny money to buy real estate. Whenever the price of gold and silver plummeted, I bought more of the physical stuff. What kind of smart investor would be reluctant to borrow funny money to buy cheap real money?"[195]

The King of Money under House arrest

"Gold has many destabilizing factors, of which several large governments have been trying to shake the price of gold. If you pay attention to the government's policy towards gold over the past 20 years, you'll see that at a time when gold prices were as high as $800 an ounce (in 1980), no government sold gold. It should be a good deal to sell at that time, and it will stabilize the gold price. But the government sold (1999) gold at the lowest price, which is exactly what the UK government did. This government practice of selling gold at the lowest price is one of the factors that contribute to the instability of the gold price."
—Robert Mundell, 1999

What Mundell calls gold's instability is an important part of the overall strategy of international bankers to demonize gold since 1980. But the manipulation of the price of gold was the first time in the history of mankind that a well-planned, masterful, undetectable plan of genius succeeded in suppressing the price of gold over a period of more than 20 years.

The most incomprehensible is the Bank of England's bold announcement on 7 May 1999 to sell half of its gold reserves (415 tonnes). It was the largest gold sell-off in Britain since the Napoleonic Wars. The shocking news sent the already weak international gold price tumbling to $280 an ounce.[196] One wonders what the Bank of England is up to. Investment? Unlike. Had the investment been made it would have sold for $850 an ounce in 1980 and bought the 30-year U.S. Treasury bond, which at that time had a 13 percent return, would have made a lot of money. As a result, the Bank of England insisted on selling gold at a near-record low of $280 in 1999 and then investing in US

---

[195] Robert Kiyosaki, « Bet on Gold, Not on Funny Money », in Yahoo Finance Experts Column, 24th July 2006.

[196] Ferdinand Lips, *op. cit.*, p. 215.

Treasuries, which at the time returned less than 5%, so no wonder Mondale couldn't read it.

Is it the Bank of England that doesn't know how to do business? Of course not. The Bank of England was established in 1694, from the beginning, and dominated the international financial market for nearly 300 years, can be called the ancestor of the modern financial industry, what kind of turmoil has never seen, the Federal Reserve in front of it is just a schoolboy, to say that it does not understand the reasoning of low buying and high selling, is simply a nightmare.

The Bank of England is acting against the basic laws of business for one thing, and that is fear! What it fears, on the contrary, is not a continued fall in the price of gold that will lead to a devaluation of gold reserves, but rather, what it fears is a continued rise in gold! Because the gold recorded on the accounts of the Bank of England has long since disappeared, the gold that was marked as gold under the accounts receivable may never be recovered.

The Swiss banker Ferdinand Phillips once made the intriguing remark that if the people of England were to learn how their central bank had been madly and recklessly disposing of the real wealth that the people had accumulated over the centuries – gold – there would be a rolling of heads at the guillotine. In fact, it would be more accurate to say that if the people of the world finally learned how central bankers manipulate the price of gold, the greatest financial crime in human history would come to light.

Where did the Bank of England's gold go? As it turns out, it has already been "leased" to "gold ingot bankers".

Here's how it happened, when the London-Wall Street axis succeeded in crushing the Japanese economy in the early 1990s and halting the process of European monetary unification, the true enemy, gold, was nevertheless treated lightly, despite the spring and glory of the moment. You know, the euro and the yen are just scabies for the London-Wall Street axis, gold is the big problem. If gold were to flip, all the French currency systems would be subjugated. Although gold is no longer the world's currency, it has always been the biggest obstacle to international bankers looting the wealth of the world's people through inflation. Although it is silently "under house arrest" outside the monetary system, its historical status and its status as a symbol of real wealth radiates a powerful appeal all the time. The slightest breeze on the international scene and people involuntarily run to the gold and accept its solid shelter. To completely depose this "king of the currency", even the one-handed international bankers would not dare to hope, and they would only try to "put gold under house arrest forever".

In order to achieve the "house arrest of gold", the world must "see" how incompetent and weak gold, the "king of money", can neither protect people's savings, nor provide stable indicators, nor even attract the interest of speculators. So the price of gold must be tightly controlled.

Having learned the lesson of the fiasco of the "gold mutual fund" in 1968, international bankers have learned the hard lesson and will never make the foolish mistake of using physical gold against the huge market demand. After the adoption of an extreme 20 per cent interest rate in 1980 temporarily suppressed the price of gold and restored confidence in the dollar, they began to make heavy use of the new weapon of financial derivatives.

The Art of War says that attacking the heart is the top and attacking the city is the bottom. International bankers have a lot to say about this. Gold, or the dollar, or stocks, bonds, real estate, playing to the top is all playing with confidence! And financial derivatives are super confidence weapons. After successfully testing the "financial derivative bomb" during the 1987 stock market crash, this highly effective weapon was used again on the Tokyo stock market in 1990, to the delight of international bankers for its lethal power. However, the use of nuclear explosions has both short-term and strong effects, and in the case of gold, a chronic and long-term threat, multiple weapons of confidence must be used and attacked in a "cocktail" style hybrid manner.

The central banks, which are controlled by private banks, are among those "leasing" the country's gold reserves. In the early 1990s, international bankers began to promote the idea that gold was kept in the warehouses of central banks without any interest income, and that, in addition to dust, its preservation required another expense, so that it could be "leased" to reputable "gold ingots" bankers, with interest rates as low as 1 per cent, but at least a stable income, and that this method soon became popular in Europe.[197]

---

[197] *Ibid.*, p. 149.

Who are the so-called "gold-tipped bankers", the international bankers led by JPMorgan? With their own "good" reputation from the central bank with a very low interest rate of 1% "borrowed" gold, and then sell it on the gold market, get the money in hand to buy the 5% return rate of the United States Treasury bonds, eat a steady 4% spread, which is called "gold arbitrage trading". In this way, the selling of central bank gold both suppressed the price of gold, but also ate the spread of the meal, but also stimulated the demand for U.S. Treasury bonds, depressing the long-term interest rate, can really be described as one arrow carved a wonderful plan.[198]

However, there is a risk involved. Gold ingot bankers borrow gold from central banks mostly for short-term peace contracts of about six months, but invest in long-term bonds that are likely to put them in a precarious position if the central bank matures to claim the gold, or if the gold price continues to rise.

In order to "hedge" this risk, the financial geniuses of Wall Street took a shot at the gold producers. They have repeatedly instilled in gold producers the "historical certainty" that the price of gold is bound to fall in the long term and that only by locking in future selling prices now can future losses be avoided. In addition, international bankers can offer low-interest loans of about 4 per cent for gold producers to continue exploration and development, which is too much to refuse, plus the fact that the international price of gold is falling year by year, so instead of waiting for a future sale at a reduced price, it is better to sell the future gold production that is still in the ground at a good price now. This is called a "gold forward contract".

Thus, the gold ingot bankers had in their hands the future output of the gold producers as security for repaying the central bank's gold leases. This, coupled with the fact that the central banker and the gold ingot banker were originally one family, meant that the "lease contract" could be extended almost indefinitely. Thus, the gold ingot banker had double insurance.

Shortly after this initial idea took off, talented Wall Street bankers continued to introduce new derivatives such as deferred spot contracts,

---

[198] *Ibid.*, p. 150.

conditional forwards, variable forwards, delta hedges, and various option contracts.

Fuelled by the investment banks, gold producers have been caught up in this unprecedented financial speculation. Countries have "overdraft" gold producers in the future, the possible underground reserves are converted into existing production for "pre-sale". Australian gold producers are even selling out the next seven years of gold production. Ashanti, a major Ghanaian gold producer in West Africa, purchased a total of 2,500 financial derivatives contracts under the "staff" of Goldman Sachs and 16 banks, and by June 1999 had financial assets on its hedge account of $290 million. Commentators have pointed out that contemporary gold producers, rather than mining gold, are engaging in dangerous financial speculation using gold mining as a gimmick.

In the wave of "hedging revolution" set off by gold producers, Barrick Gold Company can be considered a veritable big brother. The size of Barrick's hedge has long since gone beyond what is reasonable in terms of risk control, and it is no exaggeration to say that its strategy is financial boosterism. In its massive one-way short selling of gold, Barrick has invisibly created a peer-to-peer race to the bottom, with the inevitable result of self-destructing the market. On Barrick's annual report, it systematically misled investors by boasting that its sophisticated hedging strategies always made it possible to sell gold at above-market prices. In fact, Barrick sold a considerable part of the gold in the market is through the "gold ingot bankers" to the central banks of various countries low interest "borrowed" gold, it in the market to sell these "borrowed" gold proceeds, used to buy the United States Treasury bonds, the yield of the spread, is the so-called "complex hedging instruments" produced by the real source of wonderful effects. This constitutes typical financial fraud.

It is in the interest of all participants that the price of gold continues to fall as a result of the combined efforts of several parties. As gold producers have long locked in the selling price, they short various "financial assets" of gold on their books and appreciate when the gold price falls. Thus, gold producers have strangely become complicit in the fall in the gold price. What producers gain is a short-lived sweetener and what they lose is a long-term gain.

Bill Murphy, chairman of the Gold Antitrust Action Committee, called the special interest group that is plotting to crack down on the price of gold the "gold cartel", whose core members include JP Morgan, the Bank of England, Deutsche Bank, Citibank, Goldman Sachs, the Bank for International Settlements (BIS), the US Treasury and the Federal Reserve.

When gold prices are pushed higher and higher by strong market demand, central banks rush to the front of the line and publicly sell off large amounts of gold until they scare investors off.

Greenspan declared at a House Banking Committee hearing in July 1998,

> *"Gold is another commodity with large amounts of financial derivatives traded over-the-counter, and investors have no control over the supply of gold, and central banks are ready to 'lease' gold reserves to increase supply if the price of gold rises."*[199]

In other words, Greenspan openly admitted that the price of gold was completely under the control of central bankers if necessary.

The situation changed subtly when the war in Kosovo broke out in March 1999. NATO's air strikes were slow to pay off and gold prices began to build up explosive power, supported by strong purchasing power. If the price of gold gets out of control and continues to move higher, the "bullion bankers" will have to buy gold back from the market at high prices and return it to the central bankers. If there is no such a lot of spot in the market, or the initial "underground future" gold production as collateral for the gold producer bankruptcy, and perhaps there is simply not enough gold underground, not only the international bankers have to bear huge losses, central bankers gold reserve accounts will also appear huge deficit, if the matter is revealed, the people know the truth, only afraid that someone will really be guillotined. In desperation, the Bank of England finally rushed to the front line on May 7, 1999. If you can scare off investors and the price of gold continues to fall, naturally, everyone will be happy, even if you miss and sell the gold in bad debt, then you will be dead. As the saying goes, "Gold goes bad and is sold once it is sold". That's why when central bankers sell gold, people never know who the buyer is.

---

[199] Alan Greenspan, Fed Chairman, Parliamentary Hearings, July 24, 1998.

Despite the fact that the Kosovo war ended on 10 June 1999, and that shocked central bankers felt that they had overplayed their hand, coupled with the fact that investors in the international gold market had begun to claim to sue central bankers for gold price manipulation, politicians in various countries had also begun to focus on the gold price. Things look like they're about to get big.

In this context, in September 1999, European central bankers reached the "Washington Agreement", which limits the amount of gold that countries can sell or rent out over the next five years. The news came that the gold "rental" rate had jumped from 1 per cent to 9 per cent in a matter of hours. Producers and speculators who shorted gold lost heavily on financial derivatives.

The nearly 20-year bear market in gold has finally come to an end, and it heralds the arrival of a big bull market in commodities.

The year 1999 was an important strategic turning point on the golden battlefield, the significance of which is comparable to that of the "Stalingrad" defence in the Second World War. Since then, attempts to suppress the price of gold have never been able to gain the strategic initiative of the gold battlefield. The dollar-led French currency system will continue to falter in the face of a powerful gold offensive until it eventually collapses.

In addition to the main battlefield of controlling the price of gold, the national bankers have opened a second battlefield, which is the war of opinion and the academic war. International bankers have been most successful in systematically brainwashing the economics community, channeling academic hot buttons into mathematical formula games that are grossly out of touch with the workings of the real world economy. While most modern economists puzzledly ask what gold is really good for, international bankers should take great comfort in the fact that everything is still under control.

It is natural to ask, what is wrong with the French currency system? Haven't we been living under the French currency system for over 30 years? Is the economy not growing as it is?

John Exter, former Vice President of the Federal Reserve Bank of New York and Vice President of Citigroup, replied,

> *"Under such a system, no country would have to pay another country a truly value-preserving currency. Because they have no discipline to exchange (gold coins). We can use paper money to*

buy oil, no matter how many such notes we print. They (economists) chose to ignore the people's desire for a solid currency that would store their wealth. In fact, they refuse to recognize gold as money and arbitrarily conclude that it is just a common commodity that has no place in the monetary system like lead and zinc. They even suggested that there was no need for the Treasury to continue storing gold and that it should be gradually dumped in the market. After taking out the gold, they arbitrarily define the value of the paper money. They don't tell us how this 'IOU' (I owe you) debit that is forever increasing at a magical rate can perform the function of monetary preservation. They seem to be completely oblivious to the fact that increasing paper money at this magical rate could one day cause debt problems."[200]

Keynes and Friedman are just 20th century John Law rip-offs. They have chosen to ignore the iron law of paper money for gold, and to deliberately print paper money at the speed of some economist or politician's mindset, which they believe will cheat the laws of nature and 'create' wealth out of nothing, eliminating the business cycle and ensuring full employment and perpetual prosperity. This means that certain economists make policy for a particular political leaning, risking their own money in the market without using their own, in the general wisdom of John Law back in the day, being omniscient about economic matters, arbitrarily deciding on monetary, fiscal, tax, trade, price, income, etc., and telling us it's best for us. So they 'fine-tuned' our economy.

Most of today's economists were groomed by Keynesian disciples, including those who won Nobel Prizes, such as Paul Samuelson, author of the famous textbook, *Economics*. His textbooks are filled with mathematical formulas and various color charts. But when reading his views on gold, it becomes clear that his views have hardly any historical depth and appear very superficial. He is a classic example of 20th century academia in which economists have completely ignored the study of the history of money, or have chosen to deliberately ignore it for some reason.[201]

---

[200] John Exter, "The International Means of Payment", in Inflation and Monetary Crisis (ed. G. C. Wiegand, Public Affairs Press, Washington, DC, 1975), p. 137.

[201] Ferdinand Lips, *op. cit.*, pp. 86–87.

Samuelson, in his famous commentary on the two-track system of gold prices after 1968, said that outside the IMF (International Monetary Fund), gold was eventually completely de-monetized. Its price is determined entirely by supply and demand, just like copper, wheat, silver or salt.

> "A Middle Eastern sheikh who bought gold at $55 an ounce and sold it at $68 would have made a lot of money. However, if he was a $55 buy and $38.50 or even $33 toss, he would lose the shirt on his body."[202]

Samuelson firmly believes that once gold is kicked out of the monetary system, then demand for gold will be limited to a very few industrial needs, such as the jewelry industry. So after Nixon closed the gold window on August 15, 1971 and the Bretton system collapsed, gold was no longer the currency, who needs gold anymore? By 1973, when the big professor published this grand statement, he determined that the 1972 gold price of $75 an ounce would certainly not hold and that gold might eventually fall below $35. What dislocated the professor's jaw was the fact that seven years later, the price of gold had shot up to $850 an ounce. Thankfully, Samuelson is not a hedge fund manager on Wall Street, otherwise he would have lost more than just his upper body shirt.

Level 1 alert: Rothschild withdraws from gold pricing in 2004]

The source and ultimate form of power of all hegemony is reflected in the right to set prices. The process of controlling prices is used to achieve a distribution of wealth that benefits oneself and disadvantages others. The struggle for pricing power is as fierce as the struggle for the throne, full of power and deceit, and prices rarely arise naturally in the course of the operation of an equal, free and reasonable market, and the party with the advantage always uses whatever means are available to secure its own interests, which is no different in any way from war.

Discussing the price issue must be done with the mindset of studying wars and war cases to get closer to the way things are. Setting prices, overturning them, distorting them and manipulating them are all

---

[202] Paul E. Samuelson, *Economics* (McGraw-Hill, New York, 1973), p. 722.

the result of repeated and intense fights between the parties, and it is impossible to understand the trajectory of price formation without the human factor as a reference background.

It's easier to understand why someone is calling the shots in the boss's place, while most people can only obey because everything cuts to the chase. But the boss of the boss who indirectly controls the crowd by controlling the boss is not so clear and intuitive, and the further up this chain of power the smaller the number of people. The same is true for the acquisition of pricing power, where controlling the price of a commodity is never a top-down act.

In the case of gold, whoever controls the world's largest gold trader controls the price of gold. By control, it means that traders actively or passively accept the arrangements of those in power for their own benefit or to force their way into power.

It has been nearly 200 years since the Rothschilds seized gold pricing rights in one fell swoop in the Napoleonic Wars of 1815. The modern gold pricing system was established on September 12, 1919, when five representatives of the various consortia gathered at the Rothschild Bank and the price was set at 4 pounds, 18 shillings and 9 pence, which was about $7.50. Although quoted in United States dollars in 1968, its mode of operation remains essentially unchanged. The representatives who participated in the first gold price setting were, in addition to those of the Rothschilds, Mocatta & Goldsmid, Pixley & Abell, Samuel Montagu & Co. and Sharps Wilkins. The Rothschilds then became regular chairmen and conveners. From this day on, five representatives met twice a day at the Rothschild Bank to discuss the delivery price of physical gold. The Chairman suggests an opening price, which is immediately communicated by telephone to the trading room, where the Chairman then asks who wants to buy and sell how many 400-ounce standard gold bars, and in what quantity, based on the bids and the price at which the deal is finalized, at which point the Chairman announces that the gold price has been "finalized" (The London Good Fix).

This gold pricing system was in operation until 2004. On April 14, 2004, the Rothschild family abruptly announced their withdrawal from the London gold pricing system, and the shocking news immediately shocked investors around the world. David Rothschild explained:

> *"Our revenue from trading in the London commodities market (including gold) has fallen to less than 1% of our total business*

revenue over the last five years and from a strategic analysis point of view (gold trading) is no longer our core business, so we have opted out of that. "[203]

The British *Financial Times* immediately echoed this statement loudly on April 16,

"As Keynes said, this 'savage relic' of (gold) is walking into the dustbin of history. Gold as an investment is even closer to its end when we see the esteemed Rothschild family exiting the gold market and even the Bank of France, which claims to be the most hardcore 'gold bug', having to weigh up its gold reserves." [204]

No coincidence, the silver market's big brother, AIG Group, announced on June 1 that it was withdrawing from the silver market pricing and voluntarily downgrading to regular dealer. These two things are fishy from the inside out. Are the Rothschilds really bearish on gold? If so, why not quit in 1999 when gold prices hit all-time lows, but instead quit in 2004 when gold and silver were in full swing?

Another possibility is that the price of gold and silver will eventually get out of control and once the plot to control the price of gold and silver is unravelled, the price manipulators will become the world's public enemy. If, 10 years from now, the price of gold and silver goes badly wrong, no one can blame the Rothschilds.

It must not be forgotten that the Rothschilds not only had, but still have, the most highly organized and efficient strategic intelligence network in the world, but that they hold resources of information that are beyond the reach of ordinary people. Their foresight, combined with their vast financial resources and their ability to gather and analyze information efficiently, has allowed them to shape the fate of almost the entire world for the past 200 years. It was a rather unusual thing when they suddenly announced their exit from the core business of the family that had been painstakingly running for over 200 years.

---

[203] *BBC News*, April 15 2004.

[204] *Financial Times*, "Going, Going, gold", April 16 2004.

The death knell of the dollar bubble economy

In recent times, international oil prices have soared and the London-Wall Street axis has been talking about China's economic development as the culprit, in order to stir up discontent with China and to hide the fact that the oil boom was to stimulate demand for the dollar. As a result, the rumour was not broken and a satellite that had discovered the "mega oil field" overnight was released for the mid-term elections. This is in line with the 1973 oil embargo in which they orchestrated a 400 per cent increase in the price of oil to stimulate demand for the dollar, while blaming the Middle Eastern countries for the sharp rise in oil prices.

Due to the unavoidable nature of the dollar flood, soon, the Middle East nuclear issue will heat up again, the Iranian war will eventually be unavoidable, whether Israel does it, or the United States does it, in short, provoke Iran to block the Strait of Hormuz with water mines or missiles, cutting off 2/3 of the world's oil channel, so the price of oil will easily hit the $100 mark, the world demand for the dollar will increase again, this time the main culprit is Iran. As long as the world doesn't have an "unhealthy" association with dollar issues.

Starting with the "house arrest" of gold in the 1970s, the world's securities markets and commodity markets have shown an inverse relationship. The 1970s, when the commodity markets were on fire, was also a decade of oddly poor stock market performance. The 18-year bull market in securities, which began in the early 1980s, represents an era of bearishness in commodity markets. Since 2001, the commodity market has been on a bullish journey, while the stock market, debt market, real estate and financial derivatives market have also grown at the same time. What appears on the surface to be the appreciation of dollar assets is actually the result of the explosive expansion of the debt-dollar, which all must pay interest on, and the inevitable result of this expansion of debt at a rolling interest rate is that what used to require only the addition of capacity to one tank in the commodities or securities markets was able to digest the excess dollars, and now, when all the tanks are filled with flooded dollars, they have to spill outwards.

The question is where to find such a large water tank? So the geniuses of Wall Street started talking again about the concept of unlimited capacity in the financial derivatives market. They are constantly introducing hundreds of new "financial products", not only in currencies, bonds, commodities, stock indices, credit, interest rates, etc., but also creating new things like weather gambling, when theoretically, they can sell every good or bad day of the next year on the market with a dollar label, they can also make "financial derivatives" for every hour of every day, or even every minute of every earthquake, volcano, flood, drought, pest, flu, traffic accident, wedding, etc. of the world for the next 100 years, and trade them on the financial market at real prices. In this sense, financial derivative markets are indeed "unlimited". But this argument sounds more or less like the 1999 IT bubble at its peak, Wall Street analysts vowed to assign an IP address for every grain of sand on the planet, the same people's ancestors in the "South China Sea bubble" era, but also worried about the world's money too much, no good projects to invest, so someone proposed to drain the waters of the Red Sea to see how much gold, silver and treasure buried at the bottom of the sea when the Egyptian Pharaoh chased Moses and the Jews.

While the fever is already "high" at this temperature, the financial crisis is already close at hand. Gold, the long and systematically demonized currency of "barbaric relics", the "true dragon son of heaven", like a wise man who has been through thick and thin, is not in a hurry to make a big deal of it, he just looks on with cold eyes. There is nothing the world can do about it. Denigration, ridicule, suppression, cursing, sarcasm, when the "pseudo-currency emperor" played all the tricks, gold is still glorious, while the "strong dollar" has long been the end of the strong.

The people finally saw some doorways.

In fact, in the Chinese mind, there is never a lack of intuition about real wealth. People refer to money-related activities as "gold" financing, the place where wealth is stored is called the "silver" business, and the real thing is "real gold and silver". When the people of the world realize once again that the essence of a debt currency is nothing more than a note + promise, and that the so-called dollar wealth is nothing more than "a super-exaggerated white note" and "an infinite promise of wealth", these debt white notes are never devalued forever, and the rate of devaluation depends on the greed of those who print them. The general public, completely ignorant of finance, will eventually use their intuition and common sense to choose the "Noah's Ark" where their hard-earned wealth is stored – gold and silver. International bankers "armed to the teeth" with financial derivatives will end up in the "sea of people's wars".

The stubborn and steadily rising price of gold will relentlessly drive up long-term debt interest rates in the United States, and as international bankers sell trillions of dollars of "interest rate insurance" contracts to the financial markets, guaranteeing that long-term interest rates will not rise, they will be exposed to the extreme risks created by their own greed in the event that long-term debt interest rates are pushed higher by the price of gold.

The first to be punctured by the continued rise in gold will be the titillation of the financial derivatives market – the $74 trillion (just the data reported by U.S. commercial banks) super bubble of "interest rate swaps". With only 3.5% of the GSEs in hand, the situation will be critical. The gold price will come so suddenly and violently, the interest rate fluctuations of treasury bonds will be unusually violent and concentrated, the fragile interest rate hedge of the GSEs will be the first to be breached, the $4 trillion of GSE short-term bonds will be completely illiquid within "a few hours, at most a few days", at the same time, the predicament of JPMorgan Chase, the super-players of the financial derivatives market and gold derivatives market "domination business", trying to suppress the gold price and long-term interest rate manipulators.

The financial derivatives markets that led the collapse will generate an unprecedented liquidity panic as panicked world investors join together to try to liquidate the various "insurance contracts" in their hands, and the growth base of all these derivatives: currencies, bonds, commodities, oil, stocks will be "electrocuted" at the same time, and an even larger liquidity panic will erupt in international financial markets. In order to save the irredeemable ruins of the financial market, the Federal Reserve will inevitably increase the issuance of dollars like the Yellow River broke the bank to "fight the flood and save the disaster", when the billions of additional dollars rushed to the world economic system like a tsunami, the world economy will be in chaos.

Just over 30 years after international bankers plotted to abolish the gold currency, the United States has overdrawn 80 percent of the world's savings. To this day, the United States must continue to "bleed" $2 billion in savings from the peoples of the world on a daily basis in order to keep this "economic perpetual motion" of the United States, whose debt and interest have increased far faster than the world economy can grow. The day when the "excess savings" of all countries is drained of real money will be the day of the world financial collapse.

It is no longer really a question of if it will happen, but when and in what way.

The seemingly huge dollar bubble system, its fatal point of death lies in the word confidence, while gold is the point of hitting this fate of the "one yang finger".

Summary

★The international bankers, in order to make the fractional reserve system monopolize the modern financial world and kick governments out of the money-issuing world, have done everything in their power to abolish the silver dollar and cut off the relationship between gold and the dollar, completing the monopoly.

★The fractional reserve system, combined with the debt currency system, is the culprit of long-term inflation, under the debt currency, the United States will never be able to repay the national debt and corporate and private debt, because the day of repayment is also the day the dollar disappears.

★If China stops buying billions of dollars of national debt on average every week, the U.S. economy will be in big trouble, but as exports to the U.S. shrink, the Chinese economy will also be in big trouble, the two sides have fallen into a state of "financial terror balance".

★The essence of financial derivatives is also debt, the unprecedented boom in this speculative market that has massively absorbed the astronomical liquidity created by the interest payments on U.S. debt, miraculously controlling the core inflation index that will erupt into the worst financial turmoil and economic crisis once the financial derivatives market crashes.

★Fannie Mae and Freddie Mac bonds to some extent play the function of the U.S. Treasury bonds, they have actually become the "second Federal Reserve", providing a large amount of liquidity for the U.S. banking system.

★Gold, although it is no longer the world's currency, but it has always been the biggest obstacle to restrain international bankers from robbing the world's people of wealth through inflation, when gold prices are constantly pushed away by strong market demand, central banks will rush to the front line, openly selling large amounts of gold, until the scare off investors.

★The rate of increase in debt and interest in the United States early far exceeded the growth capacity of the world economy, seemingly behemoth dollar bubble system, the fatal point of death is in the word confidence, and gold is the point of this hit the door of the "one yang finger".

CHAPTER X

The Seekers of the World

Like freedom, gold never sinks into a place of undervaluation.
—Morrill, 1878

I n 1850, London was undoubtedly the sun of the world's financial system, in 1950, New York became the centre of global wealth, and in 2050, who will claim the throne of international financial supremacy?

The history of mankind shows that countries or regions on the rise have always created great wealth with greater productivity, and in order to protect their wealth in trade from being stolen by the diluted currency of others, these regions have an inherent drive to maintain a high purity of currency, such as the strong gold pound of the 19th century and the gold-silver dollar of the 20th century, and the wealth of the world has always flowed automatically to places that protect its value. A strong and stable currency, in turn, contributes significantly to the social division of labour and the rational distribution of market resources, resulting in a more efficient economic structure and the creation of more wealth.

Conversely, when strong countries begin to go downhill, when social productivity is shrinking, when huge government expenditures or war costs gradually empty former savings, and when Governments always begin to devalue their currencies in an attempt to escape the high debt and raid the people's wealth, there will be an irreversible outflow of wealth to find other places to shelter them.

The strength of the currency becomes the earliest indication of a country's fortunes. The majesty of the British Empire was gone when the Bank of England announced in 1914 that it would stop the gold exchange of pounds. When Nixon unilaterally closed the gold window in 1971, the United States of America had reached a turning point of brilliance. Britain's national strength dissipated quickly in the smoke of World War I, and the United States was fortunate to remain prosperous for a while in a world without major wars. However, the door of the mansion, which is ostensibly decorated with flowers and oil, has been gradually emptied of its interior by a huge debt.

Historically, countries that have manipulated their currencies to try to cheat their wealth have eventually been abandoned by it.

Money: a measure of the economic world

Money is the most basic and central measure of the entire economic sphere, and its role is similar to the most important scales in the physical world, such as the kilogram, the meter, and the second, a monetary system that is in violent turmoil on a daily basis, as absurd and dangerous as the definition of kilogram, meter, and second is constantly changing from time to time.

How is an engineer who has a ruler in his hand that varies in length every day going to build a tall building dozens of stories? Even if it's repaired, who would dare to live in it?

How can athletes compare the results of competitions conducted at different venues if the stopwatch timing standards for sporting events change all the time?

What buyer would want to buy from a merchant who is selling something if the kilogram standard of weighing is shrinking every day, as if constantly shifting the weights?

One of the fundamental problems of today's world economy is the absence of a stable and reasonable monetary metric, which results in the inability of governments to accurately measure the scale of economic activity, the difficulty for companies to properly judge the rationality of long-term investments, and the loss of a secure reference point for any long-term planning of wealth by people. The role of money against the economy, under the arbitrary and arbitrary control of bankers, has seriously distorted the rational allocation of market resources.

When one calculates the return on investment in stocks, bonds, real estate, production lines, and commodity trade, it is almost impossible to account for the true return on investment because it is difficult to estimate the extent to which the purchasing power of money has shrunk.

The U.S. dollar has lost 94.4 percent of its purchasing power since 1971, when it was completely divorced from gold, and today a dollar is worth only 5.6 cents of the early 1970s.

In China, the "10,000 yuan household" in the 1980s was a sign of affluence, while the "10,000 yuan household" in the 1990s was an average urban income, and now the annual household income of 10,000 yuan may be close to the "poverty line".

Economists are only "concerned" with the level of inflation in consumer prices, but the alarmingly high level of asset inflation goes unnoticed. Such a monetary system is a cruel punishment for savers, which is why, despite the very dangerous stock and real estate markets, it will be even more dangerous not to invest.

When people buy a house, the loan applied to the bank is just a note, the bank account does not have such a large amount of money, but at the same time as the debt is created, but "created" money out of nothing, this note is immediately "monetized" by the banking system, so the money supply will immediately increase the circulation of hundreds of thousands of dollars, these additional currency issued in real time to push up the average price level of society as a whole, especially in the asset field. That's why home prices couldn't have been so high when there were no real estate loans, and the banks claimed to be trying to help people afford housing, but the opposite happened. Bank real estate loans are equivalent to overdrafting the people's income for the next 30 years, the "future" of 30 years of money to be released today together into money, such a large amount of money skyrocketed, house prices, the stock market, the debt market, is there a reason not to soar?

After overdrafting people's wealth over the next 30 years, home prices are already high beyond the reach of the average person. To "help" people can afford more debt to support higher house prices, bankers are piloting the "great innovation" of "lifetime property debt" in the UK and the United States, the UK will introduce up to 50 years of mortgage, the United States California is ready to pilot 45 years of mortgage, if the pilot is successful, a larger debt monetary increase is coming to an end, real estate will usher in a more "glorious spring", people who borrow from banks, will be tightly bound by the chains of debt for life, those who do not buy a house will end up even worse, they will end up so poor that they do not even bother to patronize the chains of bank debt. What about when the people's 50-year diet of debt doesn't feed the bankers' appetites? I'm just afraid that one day, "father's debt and son's debt", "father's debt and grandson's debt" of "intergenerational mortgage loans" will also be created.

When a trillion dollars of foreign exchange reserves make people rejoice, 8 trillion yuan must be issued to buy these "heavy U.S. white notes", and these additional currency, if fully into the banking system, will be magnified six times, thanks to the "western heaven" from the partial reserve system "Bible". Governments have the option of issuing more national debt to absorb these rapid waves of monetary growth (or central bank notes) on a limited basis, the question is, who will pay the interest on the national debt? Or "honorable" taxpayers.

When education and health care are also "industrialized", as these social resources, originally severely inadequate, become "monopoly assets" at once from public resources shared by society as a whole, how can their profits not soar in the wave of monetary proliferation?

When documents of transactions between companies become such "notes", banks "discount" them, collecting them as "assets" of the bank at a discount, while "creating" new currency.

When people swipe their credit cards, every signed piece of paper becomes a note of indebtedness, every note of indebtedness becomes an "asset" of the bank, and every "asset" of the bank becomes an additional currency, in other words, every swipe "creates" a new currency.

Debt, debt, or debt. The yuan is rapidly sliding into the abyss of debt money.

Unlike the United States, China does not have such a "well-developed" financial derivatives market as the United States to absorb these additional currencies, and these liquidity floods will be concentrated in the real estate and stock market debt markets, where there is hardly any effective means of curbing "super-asset inflation". Japan's stock market myth of the year, real estate mania, will be repeated in China.

International bankers are waiting to see another good show of the East Asian economic super bubble. Mrs Thatcher was not being alarmist or jealous when the "insiders" dismissively said that China's economy was not going to make it big, but that they knew a lot about the debt-pulling bubble economy. When the debt-currency bubble inflates to a certain extent, internationally renowned economists will burrow out from all corners, all kinds of negative news and loud warnings about China's economy will be piled all over the world's mainstream media with big headlines, while gritting their teeth and waiting impatiently for financial hackers will swarm like vicious wolves, and international and domestic investors will scatter and run in terror.

Once the dangerous twin demons of fractional reserve systems and debt currencies are released from the magic bottle, the world's polarization of rich and poor is already doomed, and debt currencies, with the high amplification of fractional reserve systems, will cause those who borrow money from banks to buy assets to "enjoy" the "benefits" of asset inflation and being held in debt, and those who believe in the traditional notion of being debt-free and debt-light will inevitably bear the heavy cost of asset inflation. With the twin brothers' monopoly on international banking "practices", savers lost any other option to protect their wealth, and the banking industry was destined to be the biggest winner.

How can the economy develop in a stable and harmonious manner under the "metric" of continued devaluation of the debt currency and the fractional reserve system, which unquestionably will result in the devaluation of this "arrears + promise" currency?

In an age where everything is "standardized", is it not odd that there are no standards for monetary metrics? When one thoroughly understands the nature of debt money and the fractional reserve system, its absurd, immoral, and unsustainable nature is exposed beyond a shadow of a doubt.

Without a stable monetary metric, there will be no balanced development of the economy, no rational distribution of market resources, which will inevitably lead to the polarization of society between rich and poor, which is bound to lead to the gradual concentration of social wealth towards the financial sector, and a harmonious society will be an unattainable pavilion in the air.

Gold and silver: price turmoil is the pin of the sea

Keynes once told a great truth:

> "Through a continuous process of inflation, governments can confiscate a part of their citizens' wealth in secret and without their knowledge. In this way, people can be arbitrarily deprived

of their wealth, and in impoverishing the majority, the minority can be enriched. "[205]

Likewise, Greenspan said in 1966,

"In the absence of a gold standard, there will be no way to protect (the people's) savings from inflation and no safe habitat for wealth. That's the secret to the fierce opposition to gold by those welfare statisticians. Deficit finance is simply a conspiracy to confiscate wealth, and gold stands in the way of this insidious process, acting as a protector of property rights. If one grasps that core point, it's not hard to understand the vitriol being directed at the gold standard." [206]

The essence of inflation is the transfer of social wealth by devaluing the purchasing power of money. In the process, those who were able to acquire the currency before the base currency was diluted became the biggest winners, and undoubtedly the banking industry was the biggest beneficiary of inflation. Secondly, the closer to bank credit, the greater the advantage, the greater the disadvantage, while those who save frugally and those who rely on a fixed income will be the biggest casualties of inflation. The division between the rich and the poor is well established in the design of the world's financial system today, with inflation achieving the theft of others' wealth without burglary by siphoning off the wealth of the majority of society into the pockets of a few!

On July 13, 1974, *The Economist* magazine published a shocking report on price statistics for Britain throughout the Industrial Revolution era. For 250 long years, from 1664 to 1914, under the operation of the gold standard, prices in England remained on a steady and slightly declining trend. There is no second country in the world today that has been able to maintain such long-running price data without interruption. The purchasing power of the pound has remained surprisingly stable. If the 1664 price index was set at 100, it was below the 1664 standard for the vast majority of the time, except during the Napoleonic Wars (1813), when prices briefly rose to 180. When World War I broke out in 1914, the British price index was 91. In other words, under the gold

---

[205] John Maynard Keynes, *op. cit.*, p. 235.

[206] Ayn Rand, Alan Greenspan, *op. cit.*, p. 35.

standard, a pound in 1914 had more purchasing power than its equivalent in 1664, 250 years earlier.[207]

The situation is very similar in the United States under the gold and silver standard, where in 1787, the United States Constitution, Chapter I, Section 8, authorized Congress to issue and define money. Section 10 makes it clear that no state shall require any currency other than gold and silver to be used to pay its debts, thus making it clear that the currency of the United States must be based on gold and silver. The Minting Act of 1792 established the dollar as the basic measure of U.S. currency, with a dollar precisely defined as containing 24.1 grams of pure silver and $10 defined as containing 16 grams of pure gold. Silver as the cornerstone of the dollar monetary system. The gold-silver ratio is 15:1. Anyone who dilutes the purity of the dollar and devalues it faces the death penalty.

In 1800, the price index in the United States was about 102.2, and by 1913, prices had fallen to 80.7. During the era of great industrialization throughout the United States, prices fluctuated by no more than 26 per cent, and during the gold standard from 1879 to 1913, prices fluctuated by less than 17 per cent. In the 113 years that the United States has been experiencing rapid production growth and the country's full industrialization, the average inflation rate has been almost zero and the average annual price fluctuation has not exceeded 1.3 percent.[208]

Also under the gold standard, major European countries maintained a high degree of currency stability at a critical time of unprecedented economic development in the transition from agricultural to industrial countries.

> ➤ The **French franc**, from 1814 to 1914, kept its currency stable for 100 years.

> ➤ The **Dutch guilder**, from 1816 to 1914, kept the currency stable for 98 years.

> ➤ The **Swiss franc**, from 1850 to 1936, kept the currency stable for 86 years.

---

[207] Ferdinand Lips, *op. cit.*, pp. 10–11.

[208] Ferdinand Lips, *op. cit.*, pp. 10.

> ➤ The **Belgian franc**, from 1832 to 1914, kept the currency stable for 82 years.

> ➤ The **Swedish krona**, from 1873 to 1931, kept the currency stable for 58 years.

> ➤ The **German mark**, from 1875 to 1914, kept its currency stable for 39 years.

> ➤ The **Italian lira**, from 1883 to 1914, kept its currency stable for 31 years.[209]

No wonder the Austrian school of Mises held the gold standard in high regard as the highest achievement of the entire Western civilization in the golden age of capitalism. Without a stable and reasonable monetary metric, it would be an unimaginable thing for Western civilization to exhibit the enormous creativity of wealth that it has displayed during the period of rapid capitalist development.

The highly stable price system that gold and silver have developed in the natural evolution of the market can make all the "genius" economic planners of the 20th century sweat. Gold and silver as money are the product of natural evolution, the product of a true market economy, an honest currency that humans trust.

The so-called monetary metrics, is not to the greedy nature of the financial oligarchy for the transfer, not to the good or bad of the government for the transfer, not to the "genius" economist's interest speculation for the transfer, history, only the natural evolution of the market gold and silver money to do this, the future also only gold and silver can bear this historical responsibility, only gold and silver can honestly protect the people's wealth and the rational distribution of social resources.

There is a popular view among contemporary economists that the increase in gold and silver has not kept pace with the increase in wealth and that under a gold and silver monetary system would lead to deflation, which is the arch enemy of all economies. This is actually an illusion of preconceptions. The "inflation justified" argument is a theoretical basis for the international bankers' concoction with Keynesians to abolish the gold standard and thus "covertly tax" the people through inflationary means, robbing and stealing their wealth

---

[209] *Ibid.*, p. 15.

without a trace. The social practices of major European and American countries, such as Britain and the United States, from the 17th century onwards, illustrate with irrefutable facts that great socio-economic development does not inevitably cause inflation, in fact, both countries completed the industrial revolution in a state of mild deflation.

The real question should be whether gold and silver are not increasing as fast as wealth is increasing, or whether they are not increasing as fast as debt currencies are increasing. Is debt money abuse really good for social development?

Debt Money Fat and GDP Weight Loss

An economic development model oriented to GDP growth is akin to a lifestyle in which weight gain is a core health task. A government policy of pulling economic growth with a fiscal deficit is like relying on hormone injections to stimulate weight gain. And the debt currency, the fat that grows out of it.

Is a person who looks increasingly bloated really very healthy?

There are only two modes of economic growth in a country, one is the accumulation of real wealth through savings, which is then invested to generate more real wealth and thus socio-economic progress, which results in the development of economic muscles, the strengthening of economic bones and the balanced distribution of nutrients in the economy. Although the effects are slow, the quality of the growth is high and the side effects are small. Another model is debt-pulled economic growth, in which the State, enterprises and individuals become heavily indebted, and these debts are monetized by the banking system, and the huge debt-money increases create a sense of bubble wealth, inevitable currency devaluation, artificial distortion of market resource allocation, and increasing polarization between the rich and the poor, with the consequence of massive economic fat growth. The potential side effects of a debt-driven economy, which relies on hormone injections for rapid fattening, although miraculous in the short term, will eventually lead to complications, at which point the economy will have to take more and more drugs, which will further deteriorate the economy's own endocrine system and cause a complete disruption of the body's ecological environment, which will ultimately be hopeless.

The first thing that comes out of debt-money fat gain is economic hyperglycemia-inflation, especially asset inflation. This economic hyperglycemia, on the other hand, has led to overcapacity in the production sector, serious duplication of construction, a great waste of market resources, the creation of a bitter price war in the production sector, depressing consumer goods prices, making asset inflation and consumer goods deflation coexist. The household as the basic unit of the economy, while being squeezed by asset inflation, is likely to be affected by employer layoffs resulting from a downturn in production, which reduces the spending power and desires of the average household and leads to the loss of vitality of a large number of cells in the economy.

Another problem caused by debt monetary fat is economic blood hyperlipidemia. When debt is monetized, money will no longer be scarce, the liquidity flood caused by increased currency issuance will pile up in every corner of society, and people will find more and more "money", but fewer and fewer opportunities to invest. Under the gold standard, the main characteristics of the stock market are that the financial structure of listed companies is solid, the company's liabilities are good, the company's own capital is sufficient, the company's earnings grow steadily, the stock dividends increase year by year, the stock market is risky, but it is a real market worth investing.

Today, the world's major stock markets are so overwhelmed by piles of debt currencies that they are severely overvalued, and almost no investors are expecting the dividends from stocks, but instead are pinning all their hopes on the expectation of rising stock prices, the so-called "boondoggle theory". By the day, the stock market is losing its investment aspect and evolving into an unusually crowded mega-casino. The situation in real estate is very similar.

The debt itself causes the walls of the economy's blood vessels to become more brittle, the crowded debt currency increases make the economy's blood sticky, the huge amounts of money deposited in the stock and real estate markets make the economy's blood vessels even more bloated, and the economy's hypertension symptoms will be unavoidable.

A prolonged state of economic hypertension will add to the burden on the economic heart. The economic heart is the natural ecological environment and social resources that people use to create wealth.

The heavy monetary burden of debt will cause an increasing overdraft on the entire ecological environment, environmental pollution, resource depletion, ecological damage, climate anomalies, frequent disasters are the snowballing interest payments on the debt currency. The polarization of the rich and the poor, economic turmoil, social contradictions, and corruption are the fines of a debt currency against a harmonious society.

When these complications of economic hyperlipidemia, hyperglycemia, hypertension, etc. induced by debt money fat coexist, the natural endocrine system of the entire economy will be in a state of disorder, with malabsorption of nutrients, severe damage to internal organs, failure of metabolism and loss of autoimmune system resistance. A headache to head, feet to feet approach would create greater drug dependence and thus worsen the endocrine system of the economy.

When we recognize the nature of debt money and its hazards, we must adjust our strategies for economic development accordingly. The old model of growth based on GDP growth, debt money and deficit finance should be transformed into a new model of accumulation-led growth centered on harmonious social development and measured by honest money.

Gradually establish a stable monetary metric system in China supported by gold and silver, expel debt from monetary circulation step by step, steadily increase the ratio of bank reserves as an important means of financial macro-control,[210] so that the profitability of the financial industry remains at the level of the average profitability of various social sectors. Only by eradicating the two persistent problems

---

[210] The term "macroeconomic control and regulation", or simply "macroeconomic control" or "macro-control", refers here to the direct intervention of the central government of the People's Republic of China to calm the overheated economy. This policy was first introduced in 1993 by Zhu Rongii, Premier and Governor of the People's Bank of China at the time. His policies included collective measures to restrain monetary policy, suppress the stock market and real estate, control inflation, lower the supply of raw materials and reduce domestic consumption. The objective was to achieve a soft landing for an economy that was growing too fast. As all these measures can greatly affect the economy and political stability, macro control has become a hot topic for economic and political observers in the People's Republic of China (source: Wikipedia).

of the debt currency and the fractional reserve system can social equity and harmony finally be guaranteed.

The process of squeezing debt out of currency circulation is bound to be a long and painful one, much like losing weight. Reducing your diet, restructuring your meals, and increasing your physical activity is indeed a bit more painful than relying on the warm comforter of a debt-money build-up.

The mild deflation that ensues is like getting up in the morning for a winter swim, a test of will and endurance. When the initial pain is gradually overcome, the flexibility of the economy will be significantly enhanced, the defense system against various economic shocks will be more robust, the ecological pressure will be reduced, the allocation of market resources will be rationalized, the symptoms of high blood sugar, high blood lipids and high blood pressure in the economy will be effectively alleviated, the natural endocrine system of the economy will be gradually restored to balance, and society itself will be more harmonious and healthy.

While China is fully opening up the financial sector, it must recognize the advantages and disadvantages of the Western financial system, adopt an open-minded attitude, abandon it and have the courage and boldness to innovate comprehensively.

All the great powers that have risen in history have made ground-breaking contributions to the development of human society. China is at this particular "strategic inflection point".

Financial Industry: China's "Strategic Air Force" for Economic Development

The status of the world's reserve currency is the highest level of currency issuance for all sovereign nations, and it represents an unparalleled authority that has universal trust. For the economy of the reserve currency country, its destiny will be beyond its borders.

People are often confused as to why China lacks pricing power in the international market. Walmart can squeeze profit margins on Chinese corporate products to the point of heartbreak, economists explain, and because it is the largest consumer and represents the largest consumer market in the United States, consumers have pricing power.

It has also been explained that Wal-Mart holds the sales channel for the U.S. market and that channel rights determine pricing rights.

What about iron ore? What about oil? Where's the medicine? Where's the passenger plane? What about Windows software? China is almost always one of the largest markets in the world, and also completely control the sales channels of the Chinese market, as the largest consumer, how can others say go up, say how much China must honestly pay?

In fact, the key problem with China's lack of pricing power is the lack of financial strategic air-holding power!

China's economic development has been dependent on foreign capital for a long period of time, and without the policy of opening up to foreign investment, China would not have the economic development it has today. But foreign investment can choose China, and equally choose India, and foreign investment can choose to enter, and equally choose to withdraw. The party that controls the right to flow the money is the true owner of the pricing power.

All companies in the world, whether they are in the top 100 or the top 500, whether they are the rulers of the automotive industry or the giants of the computer industry, have to finance themselves, and money is as indispensable to them as air and water. The financial sector is an absolute master for all sectors of society. Whoever controls the flow of money can determine the rise and fall of any business.

For international bankers, who have a monopoly on the issuance of dollar currencies, one phone call would be enough if Australia's iron ore companies needed to cut prices. Do you want financing? If it doesn't, the company will run into walls everywhere in the international financial markets. More simply, it would be to subvert the price of its stock bonds on the international stock market until the company is on its knees begging for mercy. The killer application of the financial industry is the ability to cut off the corporate "food channel" at any time in order to force rivals to take action.

The financial sector is like a country's strategic air force, and without the support of air strikes, the various industries on the ground are bound to be caught in a fierce battle with other countries, or even kill each other. It's all about low prices, resource consumption and poor working conditions.

In a word, in the international market, without financial short-sightedness, there is no right to price products and no initiative for economic development strategies.

That's why China's currency must become the world's reserve currency.

What kind of currency, then, could serve as a reserve currency for the nations of the world? The history of the British pound and the US dollar, both of which were once the world's leading currencies, as reserve currencies, is in fact the history of the rapid development of material production under the economic coordinate system built up by a stable monetary metric in the British and American domestic economies, which eventually dominated the world trade settlement system. The cornerstone of the sterling and dollar's good reputation is gold and silver. In the course of the rise of the two countries, their banking networks gradually spread around the world, the pound sterling and the United States dollar can be freely and conveniently converted into gold at the international level, much sought after by the market, and is firmly known as "hard currency". At the end of the Second World War in 1954, the United States owned 70 percent of the world's gold, and the dollar became known as the "dollar". The stable measure of wealth provided by the gold and silver standard is not only the guarantee of the rise of the Anglo-American economy, but also the historical precondition for the pound and the dollar to become the world's reserve currency.

After the world monetary system was finally decoupled from gold in 1971, the purchasing power of national currencies competed irretrievably to melt away like popsicles in the glow of gold. In 1971, an ounce of gold was worth $35, and in 2006, an ounce of gold was worth $630 (23 November 2006). For 35 years, relative to the price of gold.

> ➤ The purchasing power of the **Italian lira** fell by 98.2 per cent (converted to euros after 1999)

> ➤ The purchasing power of the **Swedish krona** has fallen by 96%

> ➤ The purchasing power of the **pound** has fallen by 95.7 per cent

> ➤ The purchasing power of the **French franc** declined by 95.2 per cent (converted to euros after 1999)

> ➤ The purchasing power of the **Canadian dollar** has fallen by 95.1 per cent

> ➢ The purchasing power of the **US dollar** has fallen by 94.4 per cent

> ➢ The purchasing power of the **German mark** fell by 89.7 per cent (converted to euros after 1999)

> ➢ The purchasing power of the **yen** fell by 83.3 per cent

> ➢ The purchasing power of the **Swiss franc** has fallen by 81.5 per cent.

The eventual collapse of the dollar system is a logical necessity, and if the debtorized dollar cannot be relied upon, then who is the world to believe that other debtor currencies can ultimately do better than the dollar?

Of all the "modern" debt currencies in the West, the Swiss franc is the strongest. The reason for the world's high level of trust in the Swiss franc is simple: the Swiss franc was 100% backed by gold and has the same credibility as gold. With a population of only 7.2 million, its central bank gold reserves were as high as 2590 tons (1990), accounting for 8% of the total gold reserves of all central banks in the world, second only to the United States, Germany, and the IMF, when Switzerland joined the International Monetary Fund (IMF) in 1992, the IMF banned member countries' currencies from being pegged to gold, Switzerland was finally forced by pressure to decouple the Swiss franc from gold, then the gold support of the Swiss franc declined year by year, by 1995, only 43.2% remained. By 2005, Switzerland had only 1,332.1 tons of gold left, which is still more than twice as much as China's official gold reserves (600 tons). As the gold support for the Swiss franc declined, the purchasing power of the Swiss franc was diminishing.

Japan's gold reserves were only 765.2 tons in 2005, not because Japan was unwilling to increase its gold reserves, but because it was forbidden by the United States to increase its gold holdings because Japan had to submit to the will of the United States to defend the dollar. World gold expert Ferdinand Lips is a famous Swiss banker who, together with the Rothschild family, founded the Zurich Rothschild Bank and ran it for many years, he founded his own bank, Lips Bank, in 1987, is the "insider" of the international financial empire. In his book *The Gold War*, it was revealed that at the 1999 annual meeting of the World Gold Association in Paris, a Japanese banker, who wished to remain anonymous, complained to Lips that the Japanese government was prohibited from buying gold as long as the U.S. Pacific Fleet remained in Japan "to protect their security."[211]

At present, China already has $1 trillion in foreign exchange reserves, and the proper use of this enormous wealth will be crucial to the future of China's national fortunes for a hundred years, which is never a simple matter of spreading financial risk. It is important for China to consider how it can win the strategic initiative in the upcoming international financial war and ultimately achieve monetary hegemony in an international "post-dollar system".

By the end of 2006, China will fully open up the financial sector, international bankers have long sharpened their knives, a currency war is imminent. This time, people will not see the guns and guns and hear the battlefield tearing down, but the final outcome of this war will determine the future fate of China. Whether China realizes it or not, and whether it's ready or not, China is already in a state of undeclared currency war. Only a clear and accurate judgement of the main strategic objectives and thrusts of international bankers can develop a proven response strategy.

The fundamental strategic objectives of the international bankers' drive into China are twofold: to control China's currency-issuing power and to create a "controlled disintegration" of the Chinese economy, ultimately removing the last obstacle to the establishment of a world government and world currency dominated by the London-Wahl Street axis.

It is well known that whoever can monopolize the supply of a certain commodity can make super profits. And money is a commodity that everyone needs, and whoever has a monopoly on the issuance of a country's currency has the means to make an unlimited amount of super profits. That is why, for centuries, international bankers have sought to monopolize a country's currency issuance by all means, by all means, by all means. Their highest calling is to have a monopoly on the world's currency issuance.

China's banking industry is several orders of magnitude worse than international bankers who have been playing with money for more than a few hundred years, in terms of financial philosophy, human

---

[211] Ferdinand Lips, *op. cit.*, p. 143.

resources, business model, international experience, technical infrastructure and supporting legal system. The only option to avoid total defeat is "you fight yours, I fight mine", never to play by the rules set by the other side.

It's a no-nonsense currency war, and there are only two ways out of war, the victor and the loser. China was either conquered by the "new Roman Empire" in this war or, in the process of defeating its rivals, it established a rational new world monetary order.

China's Financial Future Strategy: "Build a Wall, Accumulate Food, and Be King"

"Building the Wall": two defence systems, the internal financial firewall and the external financial floodwall, should be established.

With international bankers about to make a big push into China's financial hinterland, China is out of the woods. When people talk about foreign banks entering, most people focus on foreign banks competing with mainland banks for the resident savings pie, but what is more dangerous is that foreign banks will be directly involved in China's currency issuance by providing credit to Chinese businesses and individuals. Foreign banks, through the partial reserve system, will greatly promote the monetization of the debts of the Chinese state, enterprises and individuals, these foreign banks issued additional "credit renminbi", will enter the Chinese economy through bank cheques, bank notes, credit cards, real estate mortgage loans, corporate liquidity loans, financial derivative products and other ways.

If small and medium-sized enterprises (SMEs) and individuals who have suffered from decades of lending laziness by state-owned banks are as thirsty for capital as dry wood, then foreign banks, which have been so eager and generous in their services, are like a blazing fire, and it is perfectly predictable that China will be flooded with credit, and that the large amount of capital will lead to even greater duplication of efforts, aggravated by both a tightening of consumer prices and asset inflation, with the former submerging China in bitter cold water and the latter putting it on the grill. When there is severe overcapacity and asset bubbles rise sharply, the international bankers will start shearing the wool of the Chinese people. The most profitable time for international bankers has never been the day of economic collapse.

Thomas Jefferson, the founding father of the United States, had a cautionary tale:

> *"If the people of the United States finally let private banks control the issuance of the nation's money, those banks will dispossess the people, first by inflation and then by deflation, until one morning when their children wake up with a start, they have lost their homes and the continent that their fathers once explored."*

More than two hundred years later, Jefferson's warning still sounds so clear and so powerful today.

The most fundamental difference between the full entry of foreign banks into China and the previous one is that the former state-owned banks, while having the impulse to drive asset inflation to make profits, had no malicious intention or ability to create deflation to blood wash the people's wealth. The reason why China has never had a major economic crisis since its founding is that no one has the subjective intent and objective ability to create one with malicious intent, and the situation has changed fundamentally with the full entry of international bankers into China.

China's internal financial firewall is designed to prevent foreign banks from maliciously creating inflation to push up China's asset bubbles, and then pumping silver to create deflation, forcing large numbers of businesses to fail and people to go bankrupt, thus cheaply buying China's core assets at fractions or even tens of a percent of normal prices. The financial administration must strictly monitor the scale and direction of credit disbursement by foreign banks, use the reserve ratio and reserve component to carry out financial macro-control, and strictly prevent foreign banks from monetizing domestic debt in large quantities.

For foreign banks and international hedge funds such as financial hackers to join forces, but also to be more vigilant. All financial derivative contracts of companies in China must be reported to the financial administration, especially those with foreign banks, need to be doubly careful to prevent international financial hackers overseas to carry out remote non-contact attacks on the Chinese financial system, the 1990 international bankers remote "nuclear" attacks on the Japanese stock market and financial markets is not far away.

China's external financial floodwall is mainly aimed at the collapse crisis of the dollar system. Under the almost astronomical debt of $44 trillion, the United States economy is like a "river hanging above the ground" tens of meters above the ground, the huge debt compounding expenditure created by the liquidity flood, day and night impacting the increasingly dangerous river bank, to China and other East Asian countries and regions living under the "river hanging above the ground" low-lying areas have caused great threats.

China must act urgently to prepare for financial "flood relief" and "protection of people's property security". The rapid devaluation of dollar assets has long been not a prediction, but a fact that is happening every day, and the situation is still just a flood, with unimaginable consequences in the event of a "dam crash". China's huge foreign exchange reserves are already at high risk.

In the next sudden and severe international financial storm, the eye of the wind will be the already super-bubbled financial derivatives market and the dollar system, and gold and silver will be the safest "Noah's Ark" of world wealth. A substantial increase in China's gold and silver reserves has become an urgent issue.

The "broad accumulation of grain" means that the government and the people will work together to substantially increase China's official and private gold and silver reserves. All gold and silver resources in China must be closely protected as the most important strategic assets and gradually nationalized.

Internationally, gold and silver-producing companies should be acquired vigorously to supplement China's future gold and silver resources. The ultimate direction of China's monetary reform is to establish a "two-track monetary system" supported by gold and silver that is in line with China's national conditions, to achieve a stable monetary metric and complete the strategic preparation of the world's major reserve currency.

To "delay claiming the throne" means that China's own difficulties and limitations must be fully taken into account. The rise of the world's powerful countries is inevitably a result of their unparalleled capacity for innovation, which means that they are able to produce in large quantities new products and services that cannot be replaced by others, to produce in large quantities the world's leading technological and scientific innovations, and to produce in large quantities the great ideas and concepts that lead the direction of world civilization. China is still only making great progress in copying Western production technology on a large scale, and is still far from being able to innovate in terms of ideas and science and technology. Especially in the field of ideology and culture, there is a serious lack of civilizational self-confidence, and an important manifestation of this lack of self-confidence is the inability to discern the rationality and irrationality of the Western system, the lack of moral courage to criticize its obvious absurdities, the fear of trying something that the West does not have, and the lack of boldness to try to establish new world rules. All of this, is not a problem that can be solved overnight. So China can only move forward slowly.

The Road to a World Reserve Currency

A rising world power will not have only leading technology and a strong military as its solid foundation. Only when she establishes a monetary and financial system with universal credibility will she be invincible among the peoples of the world. The prestige of the world is unshakable in the midst of the fickle international climate.

Imagine if today's China and the United States simply removed the dollar as the pillar of the world's currency, even if the status of the F22 and Microsoft is still unchallenged, her position and voice in international affairs, how can she still be so easy to say and speak with one voice? Will it still be the "lighthouse the world looks to"?

China, as the star of tomorrow, will undoubtedly move forward in the process of establishing a mature and credible monetary and financial system.

Money is undoubtedly the blood of the human socio-economic organism. Those who are able to supply the blood supply to the people in charge naturally occupy the first mobile strength. What kind of "blood source" is it that people are looking for? It must be born out of a sound and complete body – the internal model of economic and civil development and the financial system – and if it is infected with the incurable "AIDS" virus of cyclical fission debt and tied to the "blood transfusion" of everyone, it will only lead to the same fate. Likewise, that "blood" should be O-shaped – i.e., with a distinctive credibility and unshakeable acceptance.

What kind of monetary and financial system is China's healthy type O "blood source" for tomorrow?

This complete and solid system should be supported by a diversified background, while the current single tactic of relying only on strong exports to exchange a large amount of foreign exchange, staring at the dollar overbought U.S. treasury bonds is becoming more and more obvious. The side-effects of an export-drawing economy are too great, and its essence is to rely on the United States to increase its debt to stimulate its own economic and social development, while the United States wants its people to be overburdened with debt. Such an outcome is effectively the ultimate lose-lose.

The specific deconstruction of a country's pluralistic and virtuous monetary and financial system is a huge and difficult task, and in this book we focus only on one scenario – the injection of gold and silver elements into the context of pluralism. The monetary system endorsed by gold and silver is a "shortcut" to the status of the world reserve currency.

Let's explore the depths of the trail, step by step, along this vision.

If the Chinese government and people ate gold on the scale of $200 billion a year, at $650 an ounce, China would be able to buy 9,500 tons of gold, the equivalent of buying all of the U.S. (8,136 tons) of gold reserves in one year. At the beginning of the battle, international bankers will be desperately trying to suppress the price of gold through financial derivatives, the central banks of Western countries may join forces to sell gold, the gold price may temporarily plummet. If the Chinese side sees through their opponent's undercard, depressing gold prices will become the most generous financial aid to China in Western history.

To know, the world's total gold mining in 6000 years only 140,000 tons, all the European and American central banks' book gold reserves only 21,000 tons, considering that in the 1990s, the European Central Bank's frenzied leasing of gold, its total household income may be far below 20,000 tons. At the current price of gold ($650 an ounce), that's just a small plate of $400 billion, and China's trade surplus is so huge that digesting $400 billion in gold reserves is just a matter of 2 or 3 years. The bullets from the European and American central banks will all be shot in a not too long time.

If China were to eat gold for five years in a row with such an appetite, the soaring international gold price would pierce the armor of the long-term interest cap on the dollar set by international bankers, and people would be fortunate to witness how the world's seemingly most powerful dollar monetary system is falling apart.

The question is not whether China can beat the dollar system with the price of gold, but whether it will. The gold price issue is a matter of life and death for the dollar, China does not really eat into the $200 billion of gold, just put out the word, the U.S. Treasury Secretary and the Federal Reserve Chairman will immediately be highly nervous.

The Taiwan issue, which has plagued China for decades, will translate into a question of whether the United States wants Taiwan or the dollar. Naturally, China can't really "go down with the United States" financially, as long as the United States offers reasonable terms, and if necessary, may be able to help the dollar.

As China gradually increases its official and private gold holdings, it can begin monetary reform, gradually introducing gold and silver into the monetary system. The gradual transformation of China's monetary system into the "Chinese Yuan" under the gold and silver standard will be a major contribution of China to the world economy.

The implementation of the "Chinese Yuan" can be carried out in phases. The first thing that could be done is to issue Treasury "gilt bonds" and "silver bonds" to settle the principal and interest on the bonds in physical gold and silver. For example, a five-year "gilt bond", with an interest rate that can be set at 1 to 2 per cent, and since the physical gold itself is the ultimate means of settling principal and interest, people will actively buy this financial product, which has a real "wealth preservation" effect.

The difference between the yield rates of "gilt" and "silver" bonds on the bond exchange market and the yield rates of the same amount of ordinary treasury bonds for the same period will be a true reflection of the market acceptance of gold and silver currencies. This important parameter will serve as a reference system for the next phase of the pilot.

The second phase of the work could allow for a restructuring of the reserve structure of the banking system. Whether foreign or state-owned banks, their reserves must include a certain proportion of gold or silver, while reducing the proportion of debt instruments in reserves, the higher the proportion of gold and silver in reserves, the higher the loan amplification factor will be, similarly, the greater the proportion of debt instruments, the lower the lending capacity. Central banks should stop discounting everything but gold and silver. This measure will strengthen the position of gold and silver in China's monetary system and increase the level of demand for gold and silver assets from banks.

The absence of gold and silver as reserves will severely constrain their ability to extend credit. At the same time, the banking system will gradually drive debt instruments out of currency circulation. Banks will also be interested in opening physical gold and silver storage escrow and trading operations to the people. The formation of a nationwide market for the circulation of physical gold and silver.

All high-margin industries in the country, such as real estate, banking, tobacco, telecommunications, oil, etc., must include a certain percentage of gold and silver in their business taxes, which will further boost the market demand for gold and silver.

In the third stage, gold and silver from the Ministry of Finance were used as full collateral for the issuance of "Chinese Gold Yuan" and "Chinese Silver Yuan" banknotes, with one yuan of "Chinese Gold Yuan" being the standard measure of China's currency and, according to China's gold and silver reserves, each yuan of "Chinese Gold Yuan" contains several grams of pure gold. "Chinese Gold Yuan" is mainly used for bulk trade settlement, interbank transfers, and large cash payments. The amount of "Chinese Gold Yuan" above a certain amount can be exchanged for physical gold at the Ministry of Finance. The "Chinese silver dollar", which can be used as a coin, contains several grams of pure silver in each dollar and is mainly used for small payments. You can also redeem the equivalent amount of Chinese silver at the Ministry of Finance for more than a certain amount of "Chinese silver dollars". The ratio between the "Chinese gold yuan" and the "Chinese silver yuan" is published by the Central Bank and adjusted regularly.

The principle of "bad coins will inevitably drive out good coins in circulation" is generally considered to have an important prerequisite, that is, the government intervenes to impose the value of bad and good coins. In a natural market, the opposite is true, and good coin necessarily drives out bad coin, because no one in the market is willing to accept bad coin.

While the Chinese Gold and Silver Chinese Yuan is in circulation, the ordinary Chinese Yuan with a debt component is still in circulation in the market. The government needs to make all taxes payable in gold and silver dollars, and the market will be free to choose between gold and silver dollars or the ordinary yuan, and the financial market will determine the ratio of gold and silver dollars to the ordinary yuan based on supply and demand. At this point, one will find that the purchasing power of ordinary RMB credit with a debt component, issued by commercial banks, will gradually depreciate compared to the gold and silver Chinese Yuan. The ratio of the two currencies in the financial markets will clearly reveal this information.

It is the Treasury, not the commercial banking system, that must ultimately control the issuance of gold, silver and Chinese Yuan, for the simple reason that wealth creation begins and ends with the people, and no private person must have a monopoly on and control over currency issuance.

While China's export boom will gradually decline as the Chinese dollar strengthens, it is actually an essential part of GDP weight loss.

As gold and silver-backed Chinese Yuan issuance grows, the Chinese Yuan is bound to become the focus of attention in the financial industry worldwide. Since the Chinese Yuan is freely convertible into gold or silver, it will be the strongest and most powerful currency in the world, and it will rightfully become the preferred reserve currency of the world in the "post-dollar" era.

Wealth has always flowed automatically to places where it can be protected and appreciated, and strong wealth creativity and a stable currency are bound to make China the world's center of wealth convergence.

Summary

★One of the fundamental problems of today's world economy lies in the absence of a stable and reasonable monetary metric. The role of money against the economy, under the arbitrary and capricious control of bankers, has seriously distorted the rational allocation of market resources.

★Gold and silver as money are the product of natural evolution, the product of a true market economy, an honest currency on which humanity depends.

★The old growth model of GDP growth, based on debt money and deficit finance, should be transformed into a new model of accumulation-led growth centered on harmonious social development, with honest money as a measure.

★In the uncompromising currency war, China was either conquered by the "New Roman Empire" or, in the process of defeating its rivals, established a reasonable new world monetary order.

★China should establish two defensive systems, the internal financial firewall and the external financial flood wall, while the government and the people together to substantially increase China's official and private gold and silver reserves, Xu Tu slow progress.

POSTSCRIPT

A few thoughts on China's financial openness

The biggest risk to China's financial opening is the lack of "war" awareness.

When discussing the risks of financial liberalization in China, most scholars and policy makers are concerned about the risks at the "tactical" level, such as the risks of foreign banks taking part in shareholding, the risks of supervision of mixed operation of financial institutions, the risks of interest rate marketization, the risks of securities market volatility, the risks of depreciation of foreign exchange reserves, the risks of real estate lending market, the risks of capital account opening, the risks of RMB appreciation, the risks of internal control deficiency of state-owned banks, the risks of financial derivatives market, the risks of Basel shock, etc. In fact, the greatest risk of financial openness comes from the "strategic" level, that is, the essence of financial openness is actually a "currency war", and the lack of awareness and preparation for war is the greatest risk to China at present!

It is extremely dangerous to interpret the opening up of the financial sector as the opening up of the general industry. Money is a commodity, and what distinguishes it from all other commodities is that it is a commodity needed by every man in every industry, every institution, in every society, and control over the issue of money is the highest form of all monopolies!

The issuance of currency in China was originally controlled by the State, and only State control of currency can guarantee basic equity in the social structure. When foreign banks enter the country, China's currency-issuing power will be in jeopardy.

The average person might think that China's currency is the renminbi, and only the state can print and issue currency, so how can foreign banks print the renminbi themselves? In fact, foreign banks do not need to issue renminbi at all to "create" a money supply. They introduce a dizzying array of "innovative" financial products and create and monetize debt instruments in various ways, which is the "liquidity" analog of money. These financial currencies have the purchasing power of money in the real economy, and in this sense, foreign banks will participate in the issuance of Chinese yuan currency.

If foreign banks "create" more RMB credit than state-owned commercial banks, they will actually be able to override China's central bank and control the issuing power of China's currency! They will have the ability and intent to maliciously create fluctuations in the money supply, thus bloodwashing the wealth of the Chinese people, first through inflation and then deflation, just like the recurring economic crises in history.

They will "encourage and support" the results of academic research in their favor by providing funds for academic research projects, they will heavily fund various social groups to influence public agendas, thus forming a powerful "mainstream public opinion" from the bottom up, they will generously support the market-oriented operation of the news media in response to society's "positive evaluation" of foreign banks, they will use high returns on investment to sway the direction of publishing institutions, they will invest heavily in the pharmaceutical industry, including the systematic demonization of Chinese medicine, and they will gradually infiltrate the education sector, the legal system and even the military system. In a commodity society, no one is "immune" to money.

Foreign banking powers will also control China's state-owned monopolies in telecommunications, oil, transportation, aerospace, and military industries through investment, after all, there is no law that states that state-owned monopolies cannot borrow and finance from foreign banks. Once foreign banks become the main providers of funds to China's state-owned monopoly industries, they will hold the lifeblood of these Chinese "core assets", and foreign banks can cut off the capital chain of these important enterprises at any time, thus leading to the paralysis of China's core industrial sectors.

Foreign banks entered China to make money, of course, but not necessarily in the conventional way.

The strategic risks of financial liberalization are far from simple as the financial industry itself; they encompass the entire spectrum of Chinese society, and the consequences of a slight slip are unimaginable. It is regrettable that the list of State-owned industries protected by China does not include the most deserving financial sector. At present, the Chinese domestic bankers and the European and American banking giants killed in the "bloody wind and rain" for more than 200 years, is not a level of rivalry at all! It's like putting a single-skinned junior in a fight with champion Tyson, and it doesn't take much imagination for people to predict the final outcome.

Since the strategic risks of financial liberalization involve the overall situation, it is no longer possible for the existing CBRC, SEC and CIRC to undertake such a comprehensive cross-industry supervision of strategic risks, and it is proposed to establish a "National Financial Security Committee" to unify the functions of the three, directly under the highest decision-making level. (b) Vigorously strengthen financial intelligence research and strengthen research and analysis on the backgrounds of personnel in foreign banks, capital mobilization and collection of war cases. The establishment of a National Financial Security Clearance (NFSC) system through which key financial decision makers must be vetted. It is important to consider "soft restrictions" on the sectors in which foreign banks can be involved. Various plans for China's sudden plunge into financial crisis were developed and regularly rehearsed.

Financial security is an area for China that requires far more close scrutiny than strategic nuclear weapons. Rushing into full liberalization before a strong financial security regulatory regime is in place is the way to go.

Monetary sovereignty or monetary stability?

Monetary sovereignty is one of the fundamental and inalienable powers of any sovereign State, which is entrusted with the responsibility of formulating monetary issuance policies in accordance with its own national circumstances. Monetary sovereignty is supposed to prevail over all external factors, including all international practices and international agreements, as well as external political pressures. Monetary sovereignty should serve only the fundamental interests of its people.

Maintaining monetary stability refers to maintaining the monetary stability of the national currency in the international monetary system in order to provide a sound and stable ecological environment for economic development for domestic industries.

At present, China's dilemma is that monetary sovereignty and monetary stability can only go either way. Preserving the sovereignty of the renminbi would face the consequences of appreciation, while pursuing basic stability in the exchange rate between the renminbi and the dollar would result in the loss of monetary sovereignty. China's current policy is to abandon monetary sovereignty in favor of monetary stability, which it has to pursue for economic development. The gist of the matter is that the Fed actually swayed China's money supply to a large extent. Since China adopts a compulsory foreign exchange system, the United States can force China's central bank to increase the issuance of base currency by increasing its trade deficit with China, which, through the amplification of commercial banks, will have a multiplier effect on the issuance of base currency, resulting in a flood of liquidity, pushing up the stock market and real estate bubble and greatly deteriorating China's financial ecological environment. In order to hedge against such an increase in monetary issuance, governments and central banks would be forced to issue additional treasury bonds and central bank notes to absorb the excess liquidity, but this would in turn increase the government's debt burden, which would sooner or later be repaid with interest.

Such a completely passive financial strategy posture is extremely detrimental to China. As long as the dollar is the world's reserve currency, China cannot get out of this situation. Fundamentally, only by promoting the re-monetization of gold can we create a free, fair and harmonious financial ecological environment for all countries in the world. In the context of the highly volatile international exchange rate markets, the economic costs to the countries of the world are extremely high and painful, especially for the countries that produce material wealth. If it is difficult to do so in one go, the diversification of international reserve currencies should also be vigorously promoted, with a split approach.

Currency appreciation and "endocrine disruption" of the financial system

If there is anyone who can serve as the antithesis of the dramatic appreciation of the currency, Japan is certainly the most appropriate candidate. Japan's long-term economic sluggishness, of course, has its own internal objective factors, but the complete lack of mental preparation for the sudden "financial war" launched by the United

States should be one of the most important factors, Japan launched the "sneak attack on Pearl Harbor" in 1941, the United States was caught off guard, while the United States nearly half a century later in 1990 in response to Japan's "financial blitzkrieg", the two sides are also equal.

Motobu Yoshikawa, author of Japan's Financial Defeat, lamented that in terms of the proportion of wealth lost, the consequences of Japan's financial defeat in 1990 were almost comparable to those of the defeat in World War II.

Japan, like China, is a typical example of a country that strives to create material wealth with one hand and one foot, and is always skeptical of the idea of illusory financial wealth. Japan's logic is very simple, their own production of high end products of high quality and low price, in the market competition is almost invincible, while the banking industry was a world-class giant, with the world's largest foreign exchange reserves and the status of the largest creditor countries and proud of the world. 1985 to 1990, Japan's domestic economy and export trade unprecedented red-hot, the stock market and real estate soared year after year, a large number of acquisitions of overseas assets, the Japanese confidence also reached an unprecedented degree, more than the United States seems only a decade away. Japan, which has no concept of financial warfare, is similar to the current optimism in China, which is still far from being as strong as it was then.

Forgetting war is as profound for yesterday's Japan as it is for today's China. From the exchange rate of 250 yen to the dollar at the time of the Plaza Agreement in 1985, the dollar depreciated dramatically to about 200 yen in three months, and the dollar depreciated by as much as 20 per cent, to 120 yen in 1987, doubling the value of the yen in just three years, which is the most important external ecological change in Japan's financial industry, and the results have shown that such an ecological change is enough to lead to the "extinction of dinosaurs".

American financial masters have long understood that forcing the yen to appreciate sharply for a short period of time is similar to forcing Japan to swallow a large dose of hormones, the consequences of which are bound to cause serious disorders in the Japanese economy "financial system endocrine". The efficacy would be even better if Japan were further coerced to maintain an ultra-low interest rate of 2.5% for up to two years. Sure enough, Japan's economy was stimulated by financial endocrine disorders and large doses of hormones, fatty tissues such as stock market real estate grew rapidly, muscle tissues in material production sectors and export industries severely atrophied, then economic hyperlipidemia, hyperglycemia, hypertension symptoms appeared as expected, and finally, the financial system suffered heart disease and coronary heart disease. In order to induce these complications more easily, in 1987 international bankers at the Bank for International Settlements developed a new special drug for Japan, the Basel Accord, which requires banks with international operations to have an equity capital ratio of 8%. And the United States and Britain took the lead in signing the agreement and then coerced Japan and other countries to abide by it or they would not be able to deal with the U.S.-British banks that hold the high ground in international finance. Japanese banks have a general problem of low capitalization, which can only be achieved by relying on off-the-books assets generated by high bank stock prices.

The Japanese banking system, which was highly dependent on stock prices and the real estate market, finally exposed its weaknesses to the swords of the United States financial war, and on 12 January 1990, the United States launched a "long-range non-contact" strategic strike against the Tokyo stock market in Japan, using a new financial "nuclear weapon", the Nikkei Put Warrant, on the New York stock market.

Heart disease and coronary heart disease in Japan's financial system could not withstand such a strong stimulus and finally suffered a stroke, which then led to a 17-year-long paralysis of the Japanese economy.

Now, almost the same prescription has been introduced to China by "enthusiastic and eager" American financial doctors, but the difference is that the Chinese economy is not as strong as that of Japan in those days, and this medicine is not as simple as hemiplegia. The bedridden Japanese are even more anxious than American doctors to see how China reacts when they drink the drug.

The bad news is that China's early symptoms are now extremely similar to those of Japan from 1985 to 1990.

Outside combat in the open

"International practice" is now a rather fashionable term, as if following the "international practice", the world will be scaled from now on, and financial openness will be as beautiful and relaxing as an idyllic pastoral song. Such a naive and rotten idea can only lead to the wrong country and wrong people.

The formation of "international practices" is entirely under the control of international bankers who have already established monopoly positions, and under certain conditions, it is very likely that a set of "international practices" will be tailored for China to completely block the survival and growth of the Chinese banking industry, which has become an effective weapon for the U.S. and British banks, which are at the high point of monopoly in the financial industry, to block their competitors.

The old Basel Accord, which succeeded in destroying the momentum of Japan's financial sector expansion, has been revamped and upgraded to the new Basel Capital Accord of 2004, and could well be used against China's banking system, thus becoming a major obstacle to China's financial sector development abroad.

Some developed countries consider that all branches of foreign banks in their countries must be fully compliant with the Basel New Capital Accord in order to continue to operate, not to mention the fact that even the home countries of these foreign banks must be compliant with the Accord, otherwise there may be "regulatory loopholes". Such a provision would undoubtedly significantly increase the operating costs of these foreign bank branches. For China's financial industry, which is just beginning to go global, it is like pulling out the bottom of a cauldron. In other words, if China's domestic banks have not yet achieved Basel's new capital agreement, meaning that their branches in the US and Europe could be restructured or even closed, there is a danger that China's painstakingly built overseas financial network could be wiped out in one fell swoop.

The rule makers of the game in the European and American banking industry, who have a huge advantage, will easily stifle the external development of China's financial industry. There is nothing more unfair than the rules of the game for China's domestic banking industry, which still has to comply with these so-called "international practices" that are so pompous that they are blocking itself. In front of an opponent who has a huge advantage and has to be tied up, the game is long overdue.

It is also rude to come and not go.

China's response has been, and can only be, "external combat under reciprocal opening". If the host country uses whatever "international practice" to block China's overseas banking branches, China will follow the law and enact banking regulations "with Chinese characteristics" to restrict or even close its banks' operations in China. Looking back on the Anglo-American journey to become the dominant force in international banking, it is not difficult to see that the establishment of an international banking network was a necessary path. Rather than just aligning China's banking industry with the international community, China's banking industry should conduct external warfare, directly acquire banks or expand branches in Europe and the United States, build its own financial network around the world, and learn from war in war. If China's banking sector is hampered in its overseas acquisitions or expansion, China may wish to follow the principle of reciprocity in handling foreign banks' actions in China.

It's better to hide money from the people than gold from the people

In the face of the prolonged depreciation of the dollar, many scholars have offered to hide foreign exchange to share the risk of loss of the country's foreign reserves. If China abandons the compulsory foreign exchange settlement system and enterprises directly control foreign exchange, although the risk of devaluation of the country's foreign exchange reserves is apportioned and the pressure on currency issuance and the appreciation of the renminbi is reduced, it will inevitably weaken the country's ability to monitor foreign exchange flows, thus increasing the overall risk of the financial system, which is not a complete policy.

Instead of hiding money from the people, we should hide money from the people. Any foreign exchange will depreciate against gold in the long run, just at a different rate. The only way to preserve the purchasing power of the enormous wealth that China has created is to turn foreign exchange reserves into gold and silver reserves. The international gold price fluctuation is actually just an illusion, see through this layer, even if its exchange rate market set off a thousand waves, China has its own tons of gold as a divine needle of the sea.

The security of the people's wealth is fundamentally protected by the fact that inflation, whether in the form of commodities or assets, cannot erode the true purchasing power of the population, which is the cornerstone of economic freedom indispensable to the construction of all societies committed to harmony and equality. After all, it is the people's labour that creates wealth, and the people have the right to choose the way they store their wealth.

Gold has the highest level of liquidity of any currency. Not only has gold been recognized as the highest form of wealth in the 5,000-year history of mankind by different civilizations, races, regions, eras and polities, but it will also play a major historical role in future societies as the most basic measure of economic activity. In the history of the world, there have been four attempts to abandon gold as the cornerstone of the monetary system and to "invent" a smarter monetary system, the first three have failed, and our world today is experiencing a fourth failure. The inherent greedy nature of mankind has doomed attempts to label objective economic activity with human subjective consciousness to failure.

The "Chinese Yuan", backed by gold, will stand on the ruins of international finance caused by excessive debt and greed, and Chinese civilization will have its own day to emerge.

United States debt implosion and the world liquidity crunch

In early 2007, a sudden liquidity crunch storm swept the world, the stock markets of various countries violently shaken, the bond market almost paralyzed, central banks have injected huge amounts of money into the banking system to save the market confidence on the verge of collapse, in August 9 and 10 two days, Europe, the United States, Canada, Australia, Japan and other central banks injected a total of $32.3 billion, is the largest global central bank joint action after the "September 11" incident. Even so, still can not contain the market panic, the Federal Reserve was forced on August 17 to suddenly cut the discount rate by 0.5 percentage points (5.75%), financial markets have finally stood firm. This is the second major earthquake in world financial markets since the first of 2007, the last being on February 27.

There is a growing consensus, both in academia and in the media, that the subprime mortgage problem in the United States was the "epicenter" of the earthquake, but the perceptions of subsequent developments are very different.

Most people believe that the proportion of subprime mortgages in the U.S. financial markets is small and limited in scope, and that the financial markets are overreacting to the violent shocks, and that the market panic will soon subside with the resolute and massive capital injections by central banks. The U.S. real economy is not in recession as a result of a massive shock. However, there are also some people who believe that so far the exposure of the subprime mortgage problem is still only the tip of the iceberg, the larger scale of the truth will gradually surface, subprime mortgage is likely to be the first domino to fall, he will trigger a series of other markets occur more intense, more destructive financial earthquake, the ultimate consequence is the world-wide excess liquidity suddenly reversed into a liquidity crunching economic boom cycle of change, in other words, the world economy's "ice age" may not arrive, unprepared economic "species" may become extinct.

Crisis replay

Let's replay in slow motion the process of international financial market shaking since the beginning of August 2007 and the Fed's capital injection tactics, we may be able to find some clues about the intensity of the earthquake.

> On 1 August, Credit Suisse warned that global liquidity "is evaporating like water in the desert" and on 1 August, two Bear Stearns hedge funds declared bankruptcy protection.

> On August 2, Michael Perry, CEO of prominent mortgage bank Indymac, exclaimed, "(MBS) the secondary market is in a panic and liquidity is completely lost."

> On Aug. 3, U.S. stocks plunged on news that asset-rating firm Standard & Poor's had warned of a Bear Stearns rating cut.

> On Aug. 4, Freddie Mac worried that more subprime loans would come up, "loans that should never have been made in the first place."

> On August 5, Reuters worried that the issue of the size of subprime loans would continue to plague Wall Street.

> On 6 August, the Frankfurt Trust Fund in Germany, "tainted" by United States subprime loans, announced a halt to redemptions.

> On August 7, Standard & Poor's downgraded its Class 207 ALT-A MBS credit rating.

> On August 8, the subprime loan problem spilled over into the ALT-A loan market, with the ALT-A loan default rate climbing sharply.

➢ On Aug. 8, the $10 billion hedge fund of Goldman Sachs & Co. lost 8 percent in a week.

➢ August 9, the European Central Bank since "9.11" for the first time since the emergency injection, the size of up to 95 billion euros.

➢ On August 9, the Federal Reserve, three emergency injections of $38 billion a day.

The Fed's three emergency injections were issued at 8:25 a.m., in the amount of $19 billion, by way of 3-day repurchase agreement (REPO), collateralized MBS bonds, at 10:55 a.m., in the amount of $16 billion, by way of 3-day repurchase agreement (REPO), collateralized MBS bonds, at 1:50 p.m., in the amount of $3 billion, by way of 3-day REPO, collateralized MBS bonds.

It is very interesting to note that all three of the Fed's emergency injections used MBS mortgage-backed bonds as repo collateral, rather than the repo agreements (REPOs) that would normally purchase "hybrid collateral".

The Fed's capital injection action into the banking system, simply put, traders in the bond market to open a loan note for its three days, and then handed to the Fed to ask to borrow dollars, as the issuance of dollars the Fed said that by virtue of the note alone can not, must be collateral, for example, the Treasury issued the best Treasury bonds, because there are government taxes as collateral, as long as the U.S. government still exists, there will be taxes, because these institutions are often guaranteed by the U.S. government. There is also Fannie Mae and Freddie Mac, two government-licensed companies issued mortgage loans (MBS), can also be used as collateral. on August 9, the market was in a panic, cash is extremely scarce, and the Federal Reserve is also particularly stubborn, saying that MBS must be used as collateral, bond dealers from their own safe deposit box to turn over MBS to the Federal Reserve, the Federal Reserve in its books of assets under the entry to receive a number of debit notes from a dealer, worth a total of $38 billion, the term of three days, mortgage for the equivalent MBS bonds, and then in the liabilities of the entry to pay cash to a dealer $38 billion, the final note, after three days, the dealer must redeem these MBS bonds, return to the Federal Reserve $38 billion in cash and three days of interest, if these three days, these MBS bonds just received interest payment, the money belongs to the dealer.

The Fed's so-called capital injections actually only have a three-day time limit (most of the time only one day), and the money will be siphoned off when the deadline is reached. Such ad hoc action is primarily intended to deal with "peak moments" in a situation of market panic, in other words, to "save the poor rather than the needy".

On a normal trading day, the Fed is all three types of bonds and rarely only one type of MBS. So why was the Fed so erratic on this day, August 9? His own explanation is that Treasuries are a safe haven and investors are fleeing that day, so as not to crowd out resources, so only eat into MBS. good media added that investors (especially foreign investors) must not misinterpret MBS bonds as no one bought them.

That last sentence is the crux of the matter, not only as the root cause of the current liquidity crunch in international financial markets, but also as the key to guiding our understanding of the entire subprime crisis. To understand why MBS is so closely tied to liquidity, we must first understand the substance of asset-based securities.

Asset securitization and excess liquidity

It is well known that various financial innovations in the world today emerged after the abolition of the "quasi-gold standard" of the Breton system in the 1970s. The reason is that under this system, the core asset of the financial industry is gold, and all money in circulation must be tested by the economic law of "paper money for gold". The banking system cannot and does not dare to produce "other people's debt" in order to create a debt currency to avoid a run on the people. Debt has remained modestly sized under the tight regulation of gold.

Under the constraints of the gold standard, inflation in the world's major countries is almost negligible, there is no hiding place for long-term fiscal deficits and foreign exchange risk is close to zero. And in just over 30 years after the dollar was decoupled from gold, the purchasing power of the dollar has fallen by more than 90 percent. What exactly is in the best interest of those in society for the devaluation of the purchasing power of the currency, or inflation? And who is the biggest loser in this huge game of social wealth?

Or was it Keynes who made it clear:

> *"By means of successive inflation, governments can secretly and unknowingly deprive people of their wealth, and in the process of impoverishing the majority, enrich the minority."*

Greenspan also said in 1966,

"In the absence of a gold standard, there will be no way to protect people's savings from being eaten up by inflation."

The Austrian school has figuratively compared the fractional bank reserve system, which is one of the root causes of inflation, to criminals "stealing and printing counterfeit money". Under a fractional reserve system, there would inevitably be permanent inflationary problems.

Inflation will have two main consequences, a decline in the purchasing power of money and a redistribution of wealth.

Money that prints more things naturally goes up in price, and anyone who has experienced Chiang Kai-shek's rampage of handing out golden vouchers before fleeing the mainland in 1949 will understand this simple truth. However, today's economics mainstream recognizes that there is no necessary link between currency issuance and price increases, and they will come up with plenty of data to show that ordinary people's feelings about price increases are wrong.

The redistribution of wealth due to inflation is not so intuitive. To put it figuratively, the creation of cheque currency "out of thin air" by banks under fractional reserves is tantamount to printing counterfeit money. The first person to get the "counterfeit banknotes" first went to a high-end restaurant to eat a meal, as the first person to use "counterfeit banknotes", the market price is still the same as before, the "counterfeit banknotes" in his hands have the same purchasing power as before. When a restaurant owner accepts a "counterfeit note" and buys a piece of clothing with it, he becomes a second beneficiary, and the circulation of "counterfeit notes" has not yet reached the level of market detection, so prices remain unchanged. But with the "fake notes" continue to change hands, and more and more "fake notes" into circulation, the market will slowly find that prices will gradually rise.

The worst offenders are those who have not even had time to see the face of the "counterfeit banknotes" and whose prices have risen across the board, and whose money in their hands continues to lose purchasing power as prices rise. That is to say, the closer to the "counterfeit money" the more advantageous people are, the farther away and later the worse luck. In the modern banking system, real estate is closer to banks, so it takes a fair bit of advantage. And people who live on pensions and save honestly are the biggest losers.

Thus, the process of inflation is the process by which social wealth is transferred. In the process, the wealth of those families who were far from the banking system was lost.

When the core concept of gold as an asset was abolished, the concept of asset was replaced by pure debt, and after 1971, the dollar was transformed from a "receipt for gold" to a "note of debt". The debt-dollar issuance, which is free from the gold bondage, is like a wild horse, today's dollar is no longer the heavy "dollar" as people remember it, but the dollar has been depreciating for more than 30 years.

As early as the 1970s, U.S. banks were buying and selling each other's real estate mortgage debt, it just wasn't as easy to buy and sell the entire loan directly. How can these claims, which vary in size, condition, time frame and creditworthiness, be standardized for trading? Bankers naturally thought of the classic carrier that is the bond. This was the world's first mortgage-backed bond, MBS (Mortgage Backed Securities), pioneered by Fannie Mac in 1970. They take many mortgage debts with very close terms and package them together into standard certificates, which are then sold to investors as collateralized certificates, with the interest income from the debt and the risk of the debt "passed-throughs" to investors at the same time. Later, the Federal National Home Mortgage Association (Fannie Mac Fannie Mae) also began issuing standardized MBS bonds.

It should be said that MBS is a major invention, just as the emergence of gold and silver money greatly facilitated the exchange of commodities, MBS also greatly facilitated the transaction of mortgage bonds, investors can conveniently buy and sell standardized bonds, while banks can quickly remove long-term, large, difficult to liquid real estate mortgage bonds from their own assets and liabilities, after eating a certain spread, and then transfer the risk and return together, and then cash to find the next person willing to borrow money to buy a house.

From a financial industry perspective, it's a mixed bag, with banks solving the liquidity problem of mortgages and investors getting more investment options, people buying homes getting loans more easily, and people selling homes more easily getting properties.

But convenience comes at a price. When the banking system was quickly freed from 30 years of mortgage lending by using the MBS bond method (usually for only a few weeks), and at the same time shifted the entire risk to society, that risk included the little known problem of inflation.

When the buyer enters into a loan contract with the bank, the bank places this "debt lien" as an asset under its balance sheet, creating an equal amount of liability, noting that this liability of the bank is positively equivalent to money. In other words, the banks created money at the same time as they issued the debt, and since the fractional reserve system allowed the banking system to create money that did not exist, the hundreds of thousands of dollars of new money that had just been "created out of thin air" by the banks were immediately transferred to the real estate companies.

In this process, banks can "legally steal and print counterfeit money" in the fractional reserve system. Real estate companies are the first to get their hands on "fake money", which is why real estate companies accumulate wealth at an alarming rate. When real estate companies start spending this "fake money", the overall upward pressure on prices throughout society will spread in waves as the "fake money" changes hands. Given the complexity of this transmission mechanism and the fact that changes in the supply and demand of social goods increase the multidimensional variables, there is also a considerable degree of lag in the monetary psychological response of society in space. In essence, the banking system's ability to amplify debt money issuance several times over due to the amplification of fractional reserves, which is fundamentally bound to greatly exceed the rate of real economic growth, is the real source of excess liquidity.

The essence of this bank currency is the "receipt" issued by the bank. On the gold standard, this "receipt" corresponds to a bank's gold assets, whereas in a purely debt-money system, it corresponds only to the equivalent debt owed to the bank by another person.

MBS has fundamentally increased the efficiency of the banking system's issuance of checking money, while inevitably creating a serious oversupply of money that would have continued to blow up the real estate price bubble had it not flooded into the crowded stock market, or worse, "leaked" into the realm of material production and commodity consumption, causing grievances about price increases.

Inspired by MBS, an even bolder idea was put into practice, which was the Asset Backed Bond (ABS, Assets Backed Securities). The bankers thought that since MBS with future fixed principal and interest income as collateral could be a hit, by extension, all assets with future cash flow as collateral could be securitized using the same idea, such assets could include: credit card receivables, auto loans, student loans, business loans, rental income from auto-aircraft plants and shops, even future income from patents or book rights, etc.

Wall Street has a famous saying that if there is future cash flow, make it into securities. In fact, the essence of financial innovation is that anything that can be overdrawn can be liquidated today.

The ABS market has expanded rapidly in recent years, tripling in size from 2000 to the present, to a staggering $19.8 trillion.

These ABS and MBS bonds can be used as collateral for loans to banks, and MBS issued by Fannie Mae and Freddie Mac can even be used as reserves for banks that can then be used by the Federal Reserve as collateral for repurchase agreements (REPOs). A currency increase of this magnitude would inevitably lead to severe asset inflation. If inflation means a quiet transfer of social wealth, then take the banks as a circle. Given the size of the loan radius, it is easy to see who has moved the people's "cheese".

Subprime and ALT-A mortgages: asset toxic waste

When most of the ordinary people's resources for real estate mortgage loans are exhausted, bankers have set their sights on the original "not ordinary" people. That's 6 million poor or discredited poor and new immigrants in America.

The U.S. mortgage market can be broadly divided into three levels: the prime market, the ALT-A loan market, and the subprime market. The quality lending market is geared towards excellent customers with high credit scores (660 or above), stable and reliable incomes and reasonable debt burdens, who mainly choose the most traditional 30-year or 15-year fixed-rate mortgages. The submarket is defined as people with credit scores below 620, lacking proof of income, and high levels of debt. The "ALT-A" lending market is a large gray area between the two, comprising both the mainstream segment with credit scores between 320 and 660 and a significant portion of high creditworthy customers with scores above 660.

The total size of the submarket is roughly around $2 trillion, nearly half of which has no fixed income credentials. Clearly, this is a high-risk market with higher returns, and its mortgage lending rates are roughly 2 to 3 percent higher than the benchmark rate.

Submarket lenders have become more "innovative" and have boldly introduced a variety of new lending products. Some of the better known are: no principal loan (Interest Only Loan), 3 year ARM Adjustable Rate Mortgage, 5 year Adjustable Rate Loan, and 7 year Adjustable Rate Loan, Option ARMs, etc. The common feature of these loans is that monthly mortgage payments are low and fixed in the first few years of repayment, and after a certain period of time, repayment pressure increases steeply. The main reasons for the popularity of these new products are twofold: first, people assume that real estate will always rise, at least for what they consider a "reasonable" period of time, and that the risk is "manageable" as long as they can get the house out in time, and second, people take for granted that real estate will rise faster than the interest burden will increase.

"ALT-A" loans are fully referred to as "Alternative A" loans, which generally refer to those with a good or excellent credit history, but who lack or have no legal documentation of regular income, savings, assets, etc. Such loans are generally considered more "safe" than subprime loans, and the profit is considerable, after all, the lender has no bad credit "history", the interest rate is generally 1% to 2% higher than quality loan products.

Is an "ALT-A" loan really safer than a subprime loan? This is not the case. Since 2003, "ALT-A" lenders have lost a minimum of rationality in pursuing this interest in the hot real estate bubble. Many lenders simply do not have normal proof of income and simply report a number themselves, which is often exaggerated, so that "ALT-A" loans are called "fraudulent loans" by industry insiders.

Lenders are also heavily involved in introducing a variety of higher risk loan products. If the no principal loan product is a 30-year Amortization Schedule to amortize the monthly payment amount, but in the first year can provide a very low interest rate of 1% to 3%, and only pay interest, no principal repayment and then the second year begins to fluctuate according to the interest rate market conditions, generally also guarantees that the annual monthly payment amount does not exceed 7.5% of the previous year increase.

Selective adjustable rate loans, on the other hand, allow borrowers to make monthly payments that are even lower than the normal interest rate, with the difference automatically counting as more money owed to the bank after repayment. The interest rates on such loans will also follow the market after a certain period.

Many "creditworthy" people who speculate in real estate for a short period of time believe that prices will only rise in the short term, and they have no time to cash out, and many "creditworthy" people use these loans to afford homes that are beyond their actual ability to pay. Everyone has the idea that you can sell the house immediately to return the loan and make a profit, or you can refinance the loan and take out the money for emergencies and consumption, even if interest rates rise quickly, and there is a last line of defense to increase the annual repayment by no more than 7.5%, so it is a low-risk investment with a high potential return, why not?

According to statistics, more than 40 per cent of total real estate mortgage loans in the United States in 2006 were in "ALT-A" and subprime products, totalling more than $400 billion, and the proportion was even higher in 2005. The total amount of high-risk mortgage loans, such as "ALT-A" and subprime loans, has exceeded $2 trillion over 200 years. Currently, the delinquency rate for subprime loans over 60 days has exceeded 15 per cent and is fast approaching an all-time high of 29 per cent, with 2.2 million "subprime individuals" about to be swept away by the banks. The "ALT-A" delinquency rate is around 3.7 per cent, but it has doubled over the past 14 months.

The dangers of "ALT-A" have been ignored by mainstream economists because their delinquency rates have so far been less pronounced than in the already "smoking" subprime market, but the potential danger is even greater than in the subprime market. The reason is that the "ALT-A" loan agreement generally "planted" two heavy time bombs that will automatically trigger the implosion of this market once the mortgage rate market continues to rise and house prices continue to decline.

The last line of defense in the previously mentioned no-principal loans, when the interest rate goes with the market and the monthly payment increases by no more than 7.5%, gives many people an "illusory" sense of security. But there are two exceptions here, and two heavy bombs, the first of which is called "Timed Reset" (5year/10year Recast). Every 5 or 10 years, the ALT-A lender's repayment amount will automatically reset, the lender will recalculate the monthly payment amount to the new loan amount, and the lender will find that their monthly payment amount has increased significantly, which is called "Payment Shock". As a result of the "Negative Amortization", many people's total loan debt is rising, and their only hope is that property prices will continue to rise so that they can sell their house and unload it, otherwise they will lose the property or sell it with blood.

The second bomb is the "loan ceiling". While one may not consider a regular reset after a few years, the "Negative Amortization" has a limit that the accumulated debt may not exceed 110–125% of the original loan amount, and once this limit is reached, it will automatically trigger the loan reset. It's a time bomb big enough to kill people. Because of the lure of low interest rates and cheaper first-year repayment pressures, most people opt for the lowest possible monthly payment. For example, if you pay $1,000 a month in normal interest, you can choose to pay only $500, and the other $500 interest difference is automatically added to the principal of the loan, which accumulates at such a rate that the borrower will be "maxed out" before hitting the 5-year loan reset bomb.

If these loans are so sinister, why doesn't the Fed step in and regulate them?

Gerrard (Greenspan) did step up to the plate. And twice. The first time was in 2004, when Gao felt that the institutions offering loans and the people buying homes were too timid, because they were not yet particularly fond of the high risk adjustable rate products (Option ARMs). The American public would benefit greatly if lenders could offer more flexible options than traditional fixed-rate products," complained Gerrard. Traditional 30- and 15-year fixed-rate loans may be too expensive for consumers who are able and willing to take the risk of interest rates."

So Fannie Mae, New Century Gate, and the average home buyer got bolder and bolder, and the situation got more and more outrageous, and the prices got more and more crazy.

So, 16 months later, Gergo appeared again at a Senate hearing, this time with a frown, saying, "It's a bad note that American consumers are using these new ways of lending (referring to Option ARMs, etc.) to afford a mortgage they otherwise couldn't afford."

One may never really understand what Gogol was thinking. Yes, Gogol's words are dripping, he's saying that if the average American can afford interest rate risk and can manage that risk, they might as well use risky loans. The implication is that if you don't have it, don't make a scene. Maybe Gertrude really doesn't know the financial fortune of the American people.

Subprime CDO: Concentrated Asset Toxic Junk

Subprime mortgages and ALT-A loans, two categories of asset-based toxic junk, total $2.5 trillion. This asset toxic junk must be stripped off the asset ledger of the subprime mortgage banking system or the consequences will be endless.

How to divest? That is, through the asset securitization that we were talking about earlier.

MBS bonds, which were originally collateralized by subprime mortgages, are easy to generate but difficult to dispose of because the investments of large U.S. investment institutions such as pension funds, insurance funds, and government funds must meet certain investment conditions, i.e., the investment must be AAA rated by Moody's or S&P. Subprime MBS apparently don't even meet the minimum investment grade BBB, which makes them unavailable to many large investment institutions. It is because of its high risk, and therefore its high return, that Wall Street investment banks took a glance at the potentially high investment returns of asset toxic junk.

So the investment banks began to get involved in this high-risk asset collar city.

Investment bankers first cut "toxic junk" grade MBS bonds into pieces (Tranche) based on the probability of default, known as CDO (Collateralized Debt Obligations). The lowest-risk ones are called "senior CDOs" (seoior tranche, which accounts for about 80%), which are wrapped in gift boxes and tied with gold ribbons by investment banks. Medium risk "mid-tier CDOs" (Equity, about 10%) are also put in gift boxes and tied with silver ribbons. The highest risk is called "Common CDO" (Equity, about 10%) and is placed in a gift box with a copper ribbon. After such a dressing down of Wall Street investment banks, the previously ugly asset toxic junk immediately became glittering and glistening.

Even Moody's and S&P looked dumbfounded when the investment bankers knocked on the doors of the asset-rating firms again with beautiful gift boxes in their hands. The smart-talking investment banks talk about how reliable and insurable the "premiums" are, show data from recent years to show how low the default rate of the "premiums" is, and then show mathematical models designed by the world's leading mathematicians to show that the probability of future defaults is also extremely low. Even in the event of a default, the first to lose the "ordinary" and "intermediate", with these two lines of defense, the "high grade" is simply a solid soup, and then talk about the real estate development situation how pleasant, mortgage lenders can always do "re-lending" (Rc-finance) to come up with a lot of cash, or very easily sell the property and then shed a large profit. Living examples are readily available.

Moody's and S&P take a closer look at the past numbers, there's nothing broken, and pushing the mathematical models that represent end-time trends over and over again doesn't seem to pick anything wrong with how real estate is red-hot as we all know. Of course, the Moody's, with their instincts from a decade in the business and experience of how many recessions they've been through, understand the pitfalls behind these gimmicky articles, but they also know the stakes. If you look at the gift box "impeccable sting" from the table, Moody's and S&P are happy to do the same, after all, we are all in the financial jungle, Moody's and S&P also have to order the business of investment banks to have a meal, and Moody's and S&P also have competition with each other, you do not do others will also do, offend people not to say also lost business. So Moody's and S&P made a big splash and "Premium CDO" received the highest rating of AAA.

The investment bankers went off in joy.

Image, this process is similar to unscrupulous traders collect the waste oil dumped by McDonald's, then after a simple filtration and separation, "waste into treasure", repackaged and sold to restaurateurs for stir-fry or fried fries.

After receiving a CDO rating, the investment bankers who were the underwriters of the toxic waste went to law firms to establish a "Special Purpose Legal Vehicle" (SPV), which was registered in the Cayman Islands to avoid government regulation and taxes. The "entity" then buys the assets and issues the CDO, so that the investment bank can legally circumvent the "entity's" risk.

What are some of these smart investment banks? They are: Lehman Brothers, Bear Stearns, Merrill Lynch, Citi, Wachovia, Deutsche Bank, Bank of America (BOA) and other major investment banks.

Of course, the investment banks would never want to hold this toxic junk for the long term, and their way of hitting it is to cash out quickly. With the highest rating of AAA and the talent of investment bankers, selling a "premium CDO" is a piece of cake. The purchasers are all large investment funds and foreign investment institutions, including many pension funds, insurance funds, education funds and various government-run funds. However, the "intermediate CDO" and the "regular CDO" are not so easy. Although the investment banks have taken great pains, Moody's and S&P are also unwilling to endorse the two "concentrated toxic trash", after all, there is a "professional ethics" of the bottom line.

How do you peel off hot "concentrated toxic waste"? The investment banks went to great lengths to come up with a masterstroke – a hedge fund!

The investment banks took some of their own money and set up independent hedge funds, which then "spun off" the "concentrated toxic waste" from their balance sheets to independent hedge funds, which then bought the "concentrated toxic waste" CDO assets from the investment banks "which were born from the same root" at a "high price", which was recorded on the assets of the hedge fund as the "Enter Price". The investment banks have thus legally completed the process of demarcating the "concentrated toxic waste".

Fortunately, the ultra-low interest rate financial ecology created by the Fed since 2002 has spawned a wave of rapid credit expansion that has seen real estate prices double in just five years in such a boom. Subprime lenders can easily get funds to keep up with their monthly payments. As a result, the rate of delinquency in subprime loans is much lower than originally estimated.

The CDO market is much cooler than other securities markets, and "toxic junk" rarely changes hands in the market, so there is no information available for reference. In this case, regulators allow hedge funds to use the results of internal mathematical model calculations as an asset valuation benchmark. For hedge funds, this is a great news, after their own "calculations", 20% of the return rate is too embarrassing to say, 30% difficult to boast to other funds, 50% difficult to rank, and 100% may not be able to have exposure.

At one time, the hedge of having "concentrated assets toxic junk" CDO from gold red through Wall Street.

Investment banks are also delighted, did not expect, ah did not expect, holding a large number of "concentrated toxic trash" of hedge funds into the sought-after goods. Due to the eye-catching returns, more and more investors are asking for hedge funds, with the influx of large amounts of money, hedge funds have become the investment bankers' money machine.

The basic characteristics of the hedging fundamentals are high risk and high leverage operations. Since the hands of the "concentrated toxic trash" CDO assets are looking to inflate, if you do not make good use of high leverage also sorry for the name of hedge funds. So, hedge fund managers come to commercial banks to ask for mortgage loans, collateral is the market righteous red "concentrated toxic trash" CDO.

The banks also heard the big name of the CDO and gladly accepted the CDO as collateral and then issued loans to continue creating bank money. Note that this is the nth time that the banking system has used a portion of the same mortgage debt to "steal and print counterfeit money".

Hedge funds are 5 to 15 times more leveraged to bank mortgages!

When hedge funds get the money of the banks, back to their own investment banks to buy more CDO, investment banks then happily complete more toxic junk MBS bonds to CDO "refining", in the fast-track asset securitization, the issuance of subprime loans to the banks then more quickly get more cash to hedge more and more subprime borrowers.

Subprime lending banks are in charge of production, investment banks, Fannie Mae and Freddie Mac are in charge of deep processing and sales, asset rating companies are the quality watchdogs, hedge funds are in charge of warehousing and wholesale, commercial banks provide credit, and pension funds, government trust funds, education funds, insurance funds, and foreign institutional investors are the ultimate consumers of asset toxic waste. A by-product of this process is the global excess of liquidity and the polarization of the rich and poor.

A perfect chain of asset toxic waste production was thus formed.

According to the United States Department of the Treasury,

➢ $200 billion of CDOs were issued in the first quarter of 2007.

➢ CDOs of $31 billion were issued throughout 2006

> ➢ CDOs of $151 billion were issued throughout 2005
>
> ➢ 100 billion CDOs issued throughout 2004

Synthetic CDO": high purity concentrated toxic waste

In some cases, investment banks may also keep some "concentrated toxic garbage" in their own hands for "ethical" and investor confidence-building advertising purposes. In order to make this highly toxic asset economically viable, the smartest investment bankers have come up with another trick.

As we mentioned earlier, Wall Street's consistent thinking is to find ways to make securities as long as there is future cash flow. For now, the "concentrated toxic waste" assets in the hands of investment banks have not yet experienced serious defaults, and the monthly interest income is stable. But there's a good chance of phoenix insurance in the future. What to do? They need to find a way out of this bad outlook and get an insurance policy for a possible future default, which is the Credit Default Swap (CDS).

Before launching such an intermediate product, investment banks first need to create a body of theory to explain its rationality. They break down the CDO's interest income into two separate modules, one for the use of the funds in Naraki and the other for the cost of default risk. The default risk module now needs to be passed on to someone else, for which there is a cost.

If an investor is willing to take the risk of a CDO default, then he will get the default insurance payments that the investment bankers pay in installments, and for the investor, the cash flow from this installment of insurance payments looks no different than the cash flow from a regular bond. That's the main thing about the CDS contract. In this process, the investor who assumes the risk does not need to contribute any money or have any relationship with the insured asset; he simply assumes the risk of potential default by the CDO and receives an installment of the premium. Due to information asymmetry, the average investor's judgment of default phoenix insurance is not as accurate as that of investment banks, so many people are attracted by the superficial returns and ignore the potential phoenix insurance.

At this point, although the "concentrated toxic waste" in theory remains in the hands of the investment bank, the risk of default has been passed on to others. The investment bank has gained both face and money.

Originally, the investment bank has been "successful" up to this point, but the greedy nature of man has no end, as long as nothing has happened, the game will continue in a more thrilling form.

In May 2005, a group of Wall Street and the Financial City of London's "financial geniuses" finally "developed" a new product based on credit default swaps (CDS): the Synthetic CDO – "high purity concentrated toxic junk" assets. The genius idea of the investment bankers was to integrate the default insurance cash flow paid to the CDS pair, again in separate gift boxes according to phoenix insurance coefficients, and again to knock on the doors of Moody's and S&P. Moody's have been pondering this for a long time, and they feel badly about it. Not getting a rating is all talk. That's a lot to worry about for investment bankers.

Lehman Brothers, the world's leading experts in the field of "synthetic CDOs", and its "financial scientists" have cracked the world's most toxic "Equity Tranche" asset rating of "high purity concentrated toxic waste" in June 2006. Their "innovation" is to accumulate the cash flow generated by the assets of the "ordinary synthetic CDO" into a reserve "pool", in case of default, the reserve "pool" will start the emergency function of supplying "cash flow", this approach to the "ordinary synthetic CDO" has played a role in credit enhancement. Finally, Moody's has given this "high purity concentrated toxic waste" a AAA rating.

The attractiveness of "synthetic CDO" investment has reached a peak, it is so glamorous, any investor will have the illusion of an angel descending on earth, think about it, in the past to invest in CDO bonds, in order to get cash flow, you have to put in real money, and must bear the possible investment risk. Now that your money can be immobile and still be sitting in the stock market or elsewhere for you to continue to create wealth, you'll get a steady cash flow with some risk taking. It's a more attractive option than CDS because this investment product is rated AAA by Moody's and S&P.

No money is needed to get a steady cash flow and the risk is minimal because they are AAA-rated "synthetic CDO" products. The result is not hard to imagine, with large numbers of government fiduciary fund balances, pension funds, education funds, insurance fund managers, and a large number of foreign funds coming on board in droves, increasing the returns of the entire fund without using a penny of their funds, and of course their own high bonuses.

In addition to large funds being important buyers of "synthetic CDOs", investment banks are also looking for hedge funds with a penchant for high risk and high returns, and they have created a "synthetic CDO" product for hedge funds with a "zero coupon" (Zero Coupon). The biggest difference between it and other "synthetic CDOs" is that other products do not require capital to generate cash flow, but the fatal drawback is that all risks must be taken on a full time basis, with the possibility of losing the entire investment. The "zero-coupon bond" type of product is put into the par value of part of the funds, and no cash flow income, but wait for the CDO time limit, will be able to get the full amount of par value, but to remove the default losses and costs, this essentially similar to the option products will be the biggest risk to a "first say break, and then not mess", the hedge base of the masses up to the beginning of part of the funds invested, but in case there is no default, that can earn people hair, the "in case" the good hope of hedge funds is really impossible to resist. Of course, the investment banks are aware of the inner workings of hedge fund managers to design such "thoughtful" products. The role of an investment bank is to stimulate and exploit each other's greed while standing almost forever on its own, and it's up to the hedge fund to decide its luck.

The imagination of Wall Street financial innovation seems to be endless, in addition to CDO, CDS, synthetic CDO, they also invented CDO-based "CDO square" (CDO2), "CDO cube" (CDO3), "CDO of N-square" (CDON) and other new products. According to Fitch, the credit derivatives market reached a staggering $50 trillion in 2006. From 2003 to 2006, this market exploded by 15 times! Currently, hedge funds have become the mainstay of the credit derivatives market, with a sole share of 60 per cent.

In addition, BIS statistics show that $92 billion of new "synthetic CDOs" were issued in the fourth quarter of 2006, compared to $121 billion of "synthetic CDOs" in the first quarter of 2007, with hedge funds accounting for 33 per cent of the market. Who is the mainstay of this high purity concentrated toxic waste market? Surprisingly, the results show that it is "conservative funds", including pension funds and foreign investors, that are concentrated in the most toxic of the "synthetic CDOs", the "generic synthetic CDOs".

Asset rating company: complicit in fraud

Of all subprime MBS bonds, about 75 percent were rated AAA, 10 percent AA, another 8 percent A, and only 7 percent BBB or lower. In fact, the default rate on subprime loans reached 14.44 per cent in the fourth quarter of 2006 and increased to 15.75 per cent in the first quarter of 2007. With the inevitable unprecedented "monthly payment panic" caused by the $2 trillion interest rate reset near 2007 and 2008, the subprime and ALT-A loan markets are bound to experience higher rates of default. From late 2006 to mid-2007, more than 100 subprime lenders have been forced to close. This is just the beginning. A survey released by the Mortgage Bankers Association of America shows that 20 percent of subprime loans will likely end up in the foreclosure process and 2.2 million people will lose their homes.

On July 15, 2007, news broke that the Ohio Police & Fire Pension Fund, the third-largest pension fund in the United States, had suffered serious losses, with 7% of its investments in the MBS market. Marc Dann, the Ohio attorney general, blasted "these rating companies for making a fortune on every subprime MBS-generated rating. They continue to give these (asset toxic junk) AAA ratings, so they are actually complicit in these frauds."

To this, Moody retorted that Jane Yuk was ridiculous. "Our opinions are objective, and there's no compulsion to buy and sell." Moody's logic is that, like the critics, our praise for Full of Gold Armor doesn't mean we're forcing you to buy tickets to see the film, in other words, we're just saying, don't you take it seriously.

The investors who are so angry that they think that for such extremely complex products as CDO and "joint CDO" and the price information is quite opaque, the market trusts and relies on the evaluation of the rating companies, how can they just push the 6.2.5 and not accept it at all? Moreover, without such a rating as AAA, how could large pension funds, insurance funds, education funds, government fiduciary funds, and foreign institutional investment funds be heavily subscribed?

Everything is based on a AAA rating, and if that rating is wrong, the hundreds of billions of dollars of portfolios these funds cover are in jeopardy. In fact, asset ratings drive all aspects of the game.

Recently, two hedge funds engaged in subprime mortgages under Bear Stearns, one of Wall Street's five largest investment banks, posted large losses. In fact, long before Bear Stearns happened, many investors and regulators began investigating the pricing of assets held by investment banks and hedge funds. "The Financial Accounting Standard Board (FASB) began to require that an asset's Exil Pricc rather than the Enter Price must be calculated at "fair value". The so-called "exit price" is the market price at which the asset is sold, whereas the price currently used by investment banks and hedge funds is "imputed" by an internally designed mathematical formula. Since CDO trading is extremely rare, there is a great lack of reliable market price information. An investor who asks 5 intermediaries for CDO quotes is likely to get 5 different prices. Wall Street is interested in keeping that market opaque in order to earn high fees.

When people have money, they are all happy, but when things go wrong, they scramble to get out of the way. At this point, the usual modesty of Western society will tear off all sorts of disguises. Such is the case with Bear Stearns' relationship with Merrill.

Bear Stearns' two hedge funds were reported to have "misplaced their bets in the secondary MBS market, resulting in huge losses", and the correct reading would be that they played a role in the highly concentrated toxic "synthetic CDO" in the unfortunate default risk, and "were on the wrong side of history", and the party that passed the risk on was perhaps the investment banks, including its own family. As of March 31, 2007, Bear Stearns' two funds still controlled more than $20 billion in assets, and in early July the assets of both funds had shrunk by about 20 percent. As a result, creditors of these funds have also sought to divest.

One of the largest creditors, Merrill Lynch, has been in a rush and has announced that it will begin auctioning off more than $800 million in mortgage bonds held by Bear Stearns Fund, amid repeated unsuccessful attempts to collect money. Merrill Lynch had previously said it would not sell the assets until Bear Stearns' hedge from King announced plans to recapitalize them. Childish diva Merrill Lynch rejected Bear Stearns' proposed restructuring package. Bear Stearns' emergency plan for another $1.5 billion capital increase was not endorsed by creditors. Sekirin is prepared to sell conventional securities first, and then also plans to sell related derivatives. Meanwhile, Goldman Sachs, JPMorgan Chase and Bank of America, among others, have reportedly redeemed their respective fund shares.

To everyone's dismay, only 1/4 of the bonds at the public auction were quoted, compared to 85% to 90% of the value of the ticket. This is the best part of Bear Stearns Fund's AAA rating, if even these quality assets are going to lose more than 15%, the thought of other toxic CDOs below BRB that no one is even asking for is simply mind-boggling, and the scale of the loss will be unimaginable.

The harsh reality woke Bear Stearns and shook Wall Street as a whole. Be aware that $750 billion worth of CDOs are sitting on the balance sheets of commercial banks as collateral. Their current ploy is to move these CDO assets to an Off Balance Sheet, where they can calculate prices using internal mathematical models, without having to use market prices.

Wall Street bankers have only one belief at this point: never go to public auction on the market! Because this would expose the true price of CDOs to the light of day, one would see that the actual price of these bubble assets is not 120% or 150% of what is published in the financial statements, but most likely 50% or even 30%. Once the market price is exposed, all funds, large and small, that have invested in the CDO market will have to re-examine their asset accounts, and the huge losses will no longer be concealed and the unprecedented storm that will sweep the world financial markets will surely come.

By July 19, Bear Stearns' two hedge funds have "nothing of value left over", the huge $20 billion in assets within a few weeks went up in smoke. on August 1, Bear Stearns' two hedge funds declared bankruptcy protection.

Who exactly holds the assets of toxic junk? This is a very sensitive issue on Wall Street. It is estimated that, by the end of 2006, 10 per cent will be held by hedge funds, 18 per cent by retirement fund balances, 19 per cent by insurance companies and 22 per cent by asset management companies. And of course there are foreign investors. Since 2003, foreign financial institutions in China "grandly launched" various "structured investment products", how much has been polluted by these "asset toxic waste", I am afraid only God knows.

The Bank for International Settlements has warned that "the U.S. subprime mortgage market is becoming increasingly problematic, but it is not clear how these intersections will permeate the entire credit market." Does this "unclear" suggest a possible collapse of the CDO market? Subprime and ALT-A loans and CDOs built on top of them, with CDS and synthetic CDOs totaling at least $3 trillion or more. No wonder the Bank for International Settlements has recently strongly warned that the world could be headed for a Great Depression like the 1930s. The bank also sees a trend shift in the global credit sector's boom cycle in the coming months.

Judging by the comments of Fed officials, policymakers do not share financial market concerns about the subprime lending market and do not expect its effects to spread through the economy. Bernanke had said in late February 2007 that subprime lending was a critical issue, but there was no indication that it was spreading to the major lending markets, and the overall market still seemed healthy. Subsequently, both investors and officials shied away from the potential risk of a spreading subprime lending crisis. Avoiding the problem does not eliminate it, and the people are constantly touching the impending crisis in real life.

If the government-trusted funds of all kinds lose heavily in the asset-backed market. The consequence is that ordinary people could face $3,000 in traffic tickets every day. If the pension fund loses out, everyone ends up with an extended retirement age. What if the insurance company pays it out, the cost of all kinds of insurance will go up.

In short, the law of financial innovation on Wall Street is that the winning bankers get astronomical bonuses and the losing ones are paid by taxpayers and foreigners. And, win or lose, the inevitable consequence of the huge debt currency and inflation created by the repeated, cyclical and multiplied debts of the banking system in the "process of financial innovation" quietly divides up the wealth created by the people of the world. No wonder the world is becoming more and more divided between rich and poor, and no wonder the world is becoming more and more discordant.

Debt implosion and liquidity crunch

The U.S. subprime mortgage crisis is essentially a classic debt implosion-type crisis. Banks create money "out of nothing" while generating mortgages, not exactly what ordinary people imagine by transferring other people's savings to others, which is in fact printing future uncreated labour into money in advance and putting it into circulation. On the other hand, the central bank, in order to deal with inflation, had to cope with it by raising interest rates, the combined force of these two roles led to a gradual increase in lenders' repayment pressure, until the huge debt crushed and the default rate rose sharply, followed by a fall in housing prices, investors began to withdraw from the housing market, MBS and CDO no one asked for help, the bond market and the note market suddenly appeared liquidity tightening. This tightening and shocked the financial derivatives of the credit default swap market, a large number of fund managers who bought the credit default swap contracts suddenly found that the risk to the home of the money chain broke down, at this time, banks and investors to call the debt, panic and helplessness only to sell assets to cash the trick. Unfortunately, the direction and pattern of most investors was highly similar and the sell-off finally evolved into panic.

This is the law of debt-money-driven economic development: debt creates money, money stimulates greed, greed exacerbates debt, debt implodes, implosion triggers austerity, and austerity is recession!

The view of many analysts that subprime mortgages are an "isolated problem" and that regulation is modest compared to the overall financial market in the United States ignores the "shape and structure" of the financial market, i.e. that the residual mortgage market is not horizontally developed and independent.

From a vertical perspective, subprime mortgages exhibit a large inverted pyramid shape. The bottom of the pyramid is people about 4000 ~ 5000 million U.S. dollars will eventually become a bad debt subprime mortgage loans, and it is supporting the CDO above 750 billion U.S. dollars, and then there is a bigger 50 trillion U.S. dollars of CDS credit default swap market, CDS above and "synthetic CDO", and MBS, CDO, synthetic CDO, etc. together with the mortgage to commercial banks, to 5 ~ 15 times the new "fake money" support the liquidity of high leverage magnification. When this dangerous inverted pyramid tilts and shakes, it will also implicate the $100 trillion interest rate swap market, the largest in the financial derivatives market. Because the liquidity pan-cover reversal into a liquidity crunch is so sudden, there will be problems with MBS and long-term US Treasury financing, but once long-term interest rates continue to rise, the $10 trillion interest rate swap market will implode in a tighter market.

In terms of debt structure correlation, when the 2.2 million subprime borrowers who are heavily indebted are facing a sweeping crisis, can they be expected to pay their car loans, student loans, credit card debt and other forms of debt on time? And how can ABS bonds and other derivatives based on these debts be left untouched? These bonds and their derivatives are staggered throughout the banking system, with a high level of lenders and repeated derivation, and when a debtor goes down, it will immediately pull down a large swath of debt instruments. Millions of people fall at the same time, who can save them? Rather than "diversifying" the risks, "financial innovation" is actually creating unprecedented systemic risks on an unprecedented scale. If it is said that in 1998, when the United States long-term capital companies went wrong, the Federal Reserve also knew to inform several of the largest creditors to meet to study the countermeasures, Xing and why today's market once there is a massive and astronomical debt implosion, by dry credit default contracts are held by tens of millions of investors each other, and several over-the-counter transactions, lack of supervision, several of the nodes at the same time default, there will be a terrible "chain reaction" immediately, the whole system will be paralyzed. Image, in the phoenix risk concentration of the "traditional financial market", the risk node is huge and clear objectives, once the "bleeding" problem, the central bank doctors can quickly take effective action and decisively "stop the bleeding". And when the risks of modern financial markets are highly dispersed to thousands of institutional investors, once there is "serious blood loss", is almost impossible to cure the "diffuse bleeding", doctors have no idea where to start.

In this sense, the unprecedented capital injections by the Federal Reserve and the European Central Bank since early August 2007, which broke through the magnitude of the problem, did not overreact and, without the full force of the central banks' rescue, it is no exaggeration to say that today's world financial markets would be in ruins.

Below is the mortgage reset loan schedule released by Credit Suisse. The horizontal coordinates are for the month and the starting point is 2007 L. The vertical coordinates are the mortgage debt reset scale. From this chart, we can clearly see why the first major world corporate finance market earthquake occurred at the end of February 2007, and why the second major earthquake occurred in August, while the peak of the third major earthquake was most likely the end of 2007, and the aftershocks that followed will continue for many years.

The future of the world's financial markets will be like this

While central bankers have temporarily squashed the crisis, the underlying debt implosion graph has not eased in the slightest. The $750 billion CDO asset valuation issue in the US banking system has not yet come to light, along with the massive mortgage interest rate reset that will occur in late 2007 and 2008. By that time, the affirmation was a big earthquake. It is unlikely that foreign consumers will remain gleefully debt-ridden after successive catastrophic earthquakes.

The essence of the problem is that in an era when debt money drives the world economy, paying off or destroying debt means a contraction in liquidity. Since the demand for high returns in financial markets is difficult for real economy growth to meet, financial markets cannot even tolerate a slowdown in liquidity growth, let alone a halt and decline. But the implosion of subprime mortgage debt has already shown that Americans' overdraft capacity for the future has been depleted of its potential, and the scale of debt derivatives based on this is even greater when U.S. home loans increased by $1.9 trillion in 2006. If the performance of this massive debt instrument system declines, where does that leave my larger debt system?

As a new debt replacement, the geniuses of Wall Street are ramping up the development of a new product called the "Death Bond". The heart of the "death bond" is the reversal of life insurance payouts after a person dies. Investment banks will find people who have life insurance and they will suggest that life insurance is for someone else to spend after they die, so why not take it out now and use it during their lifetime? The proposal was a temptation to everyone, and the investment banks packaged 200 or so life insurance policies into asset-backed bonds (ABS) to sell to investors on Wall Street. An individual who sells a life insurance policy usually receives 20 to 40 percent of his or her entire benefit in cash, while an investor who buys a death bond pays this amount and continues to pay the insurance on a monthly basis until the insurer dies, after which the entire benefit goes to the investor. The sooner the insurer dies, the greater the investor's admission. So the investor is tapping the stopwatch and waiting for the insurer to die. The investment bank takes a 5% to 6% fee in the middle. That said, this market is also far from being a substitute for mortgage lending, and even at its highest level, it only generates about $19 billion a year in debt instruments, only $1/10^{th}$ the size of mortgage debt.

Another idea is to extend the maturity of mortgage debt for everyone, from an ordinary 30-year term to 40–50 years, which can also increase the size of the debt in a big way to provide sufficient liquidity for the financial market.

Without a debt system that is large enough, increases fast enough, and operates with reasonable mechanisms to replace temporarily crippled mortgage debt, there will be little power to stop the onset of a severe recession.

CHRONICLE OF MAJOR EVENTS

The first modern bank was born in 1694 when King William I granted a Royal Charter to the Bank of England.

In 1789, Hamilton was appointed by President Washington as the first U.S. Secretary of the Treasury, and he was a major promoter of the U.S. central banking system.

On February 25, 1791, Washington signed a mandate for the first central bank in the United States, valid for 20 years, to receive foreign money to buy in. The first major victory for the international bankers.

In 1800, the Rothschilds became one of the richest Jewish families in Frankfurt. Meyer received the title of "Imperial Agent" from the Holy Roman Emperor.

In 1803, Meyer made a loan to the King of Denmark in the name of the Rothschilds and rose to fame, greatly enhancing the reputation of the Rothschilds.

In 1811, the Bank of England and Nathan Rothschild became major shareholders in the First Bank of the United States, the central bank of the United States.

On March 3, 1811, the closing of the First Bank of the United States made Nathan furious to teach the Americans a lesson, and a few months later, the War of 1812 between Britain and the United States broke out, striking the United States government in debt.

The Battle of Waterloo, June 18, 1815, saw Britain defeat Napoleon's army. Nathan Rothschild was informed in advance of the war and used the British public debt to make 20 times as much money as he did, becoming the largest creditor of the British government and dominating future British public debt issuance.

In 1816, the Second Bank of the United States was born.

In November 1818, the Rothschilds simultaneously sold off French bonds throughout Europe, causing a great panic in the markets and forcing Louis XVIII to turn to them for help, eventually taking full control of French finance.

In 1818, both Solomon and his brother Carl attended the Aachen Conference to discuss the future of Europe after Napoleon's defeat, at which they befriended Metternich, and thus began frequent lending and financing to the Crown.

In 1822, the Habsburg royal family awarded the title of Baron Rothschild 4 Brothers.

In 1822, three brothers, Solomon, James, and Carl, attended the important Verona Conference, after which the Rothschild Bank received funding for the first Central European Railway project.

On January 8, 1835, President Jackson paid off the last of the national debt, the only time in history that the U.S. government lowered the national debt to zero and also generated a $35 million surplus.

On January 30, 1835, President Jackson was assassinated, but was lucky to escape.

In 1837, the second bank of the United States of America's application for extension was rejected by President Jackson, the Rothschild family controlled the main European banking industry at the same time tightened the U.S. banking, the United States fell into a serious "artificial" money in circulation drastically reduced the situation, finally triggered the panic of 1837, the economy plunged into recession for as long as five years, its destructive power is as great as the Great Depression in 1929.

On March 4, 1841, President Harrison was struck by a cold that became increasingly severe during his inaugural address and eventually died, with some historians suggesting that the president was poisoned with arsenic.

In 1843, Solomon acquired the Vitkovice Consolidated Mining Company and the Austro-Hungarian Smelting Company, among the ten largest heavy industrial companies in the world at the time.

On July 9, 1850, President Taylor died of a mysterious stomach attack.

Around 1850, the Rothschilds had amassed a total wealth equivalent to $6 billion.

By 1853, foreign capital, especially British capital, had already owned 46 percent of the U.S. federal national debt, 58 percent of state bonds, and 26 percent of U.S. railroad bonds, thus caging the U.S. economy once again.

In 1863, Lincoln had to bow to the banker forces in Congress to sign the National Bank Act of 1863 in order to obtain authorization for the third greenback issue to win the war.

On April 14, 1865, Abraham Lincoln was assassinated. The assassination is widely believed to have been a massive conspiracy in which members of the government and financial forces may have been involved.

In 1869, J. P. Morgan met with the Rothschilds in London, and the Morgan family's collaboration with the Rothschilds grew to a new level.

In 1872, Ernest Sade was commissioned by international bankers to procure the Coinage Act of 1873, known as the "Draconian Act of 1873", through bribery, making gold coinage the sole dominant currency.

In 1879, the Rothschilds became the largest creditors of the American railroads.

On March 1, 1881, Lincoln's ally, Tsar Alexander II, died at the hands of an assassin.

On July 2, 1881, James Garfield, the 20th President of the United States, was assassinated and later died.

On February 5, 1891, the Rothschilds and a number of other British bankers formed the secret organization "Round Table Group", and a corresponding organization was established in the United States, led by the Morgan family.

In 1912, Edward House published the novel *Philip Dru: The Administrator*, whose predictions of the future of the United States matched the high expectations of international bankers, and upon its publication attracted the attention of American high society.

In 1913, the Federal Reserve Bank of the United States was established, ultimately marking a decisive victory for international bankers.

On December 23, 1913, the Federal Reserve Act was passed and international bankers took complete control of the national currency issue in the United States.

On November 16, 1914, the Federal Reserve officially began operations.

In September 1915, the $500 million Anglo-French loan operation officially kicked off.

On June 17, 1917, House served as convener of the Society for International Affairs in New York, which was reorganized in 1921 as the Diplomatic Association, an organization dedicated to controlling American society and world politics.

On May 8, 1920, the Board of Governors of the Federal Reserve held a secret meeting that led directly to a credit crunch and a successful "shearing" operation against agriculture.

In 1929, the sudden and sharp decline in the supply of loans to invest in stocks on the New York money market caused the 1929 crisis, in effect a calculated "shearing" of the public by the international money moguls.

In 1930, the Bank for International Settlements was established. It is a central banker's bank, operating completely independent of governments, completely exempt from taxation in time of war and peace, and accepting deposits only from their central banks.

In 1931, Wall Street bankers convened and decided to further support Hitler.

In January 1934, Roosevelt passed the Gold Reserve Act, which positioned the price of gold at $35 per ounce, but the American people had no right to exchange it.

In 1935, a special committee headed by Senator Nye issued a 1,400-page report detailing the secrets of American participation in World War I and the conspiracies and misdeeds of bankers and arms companies in the war effort.

In 1954, the Bilderberg Club was founded, the "international version" of the American Foreign Service Association, with the ultimate goal of establishing a world government.

In November 1961, the United States and seven major European countries established the "Gold Mutual Fund", the main thrust of which was to suppress the price of gold in the London market.

On June 4, 1963, Kennedy signed a little-known Presidential Order 1110, ordering the U.S. Treasury to issue silver notes, wresting the right to issue money from the Federal Reserve.

On November 22, 1963, Kennedy was assassinated and killed.

In 1967, a 15-member U.S. team of experts completed a top-secret report examining the challenges the United States would face as the world entered a phase of "permanent peace" and its response strategies. In the same year, the Iron Mountain Report was published, shocking all sectors of American society.

On 17 March 1968, the Golden Mutual Fund Scheme came to an end.

On March 18, 1969, the U.S. Congress lifted the mandatory requirement that Fed-issued dollars have a 25 percent gold backing, an act that severed the final legally mandatory relationship between gold and dollar issuance.

On August 15, 1971, Nixon closed the gold exchange window, which was the second time that the United States had been bad to the international community, following Roosevelt's bad debt to the people at home in 1933.

On 16 October 1973, Iran, the Saudis and four Arab countries in the Middle East unleashed their "oil weapons" and announced a 70 per cent increase in oil prices, a move that had a profound impact on the world scene after the 1970s.

In January 1975, the U.S. Treasury began auctioning gold for the first time, but it was difficult to resist the buying of gold.

In 1978, David Rockefeller proposed to Jimmy Carter that one of his men, Paul Volcker, become Chairman of the Federal Reserve.

In January 1981, Reagan began his administration by asking Congress to establish a "Gold Commission" to study the feasibility of restoring the gold standard, a direct violation of the no-go zone for international bankers, and on 30 March 1981 Reagan was assassinated.

In September 1985, the finance ministers of the United States, Britain, France, Japan and Germany signed the "Plaza Agreement" in New York Square, aimed at "controlled depreciation" of the dollar against other major currencies, and the Bank of Japan was forced to agree to an appreciation of the yen.

In September 1987, the fourth General Assembly of the World Commission on Wildlife Conservation was held in the United States, and the proposal for a "world environmental bank", effectively under the control of international bankers, was presented.

On December 29, 1989, Japan's stock market reached an all-time high when the Nikkei rushed to 38915, and the Nikkei plunged as a large number of short selling options on the stock index began to take hold.

In September 1999, European central bankers reached a "Washington agreement" to limit the total amount of gold sold or leased by countries over the next five years, and news came that the gold "leasing" rate had jumped from 1% to 9% in a few hours, and that short-selling gold producers and speculators had suffered heavy losses on their financial derivatives.

On April 14, 2004, the Rothschilds abruptly announced their withdrawal from the London gold pricing system.

Other titles

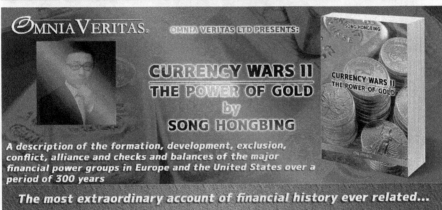

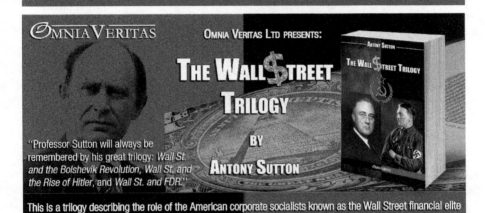
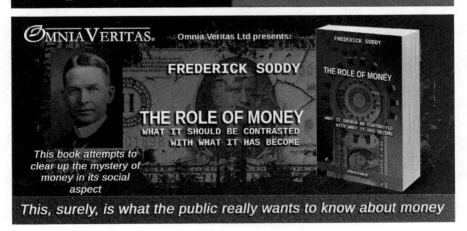

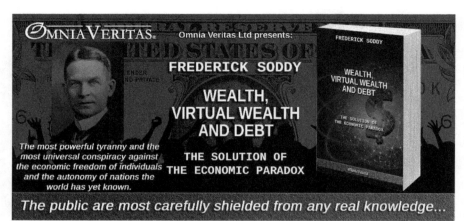

OmniaVeritas

Omnia Veritas Ltd presents:

FREDERICK SODDY

WEALTH, VIRTUAL WEALTH AND DEBT

THE SOLUTION OF THE ECONOMIC PARADOX

The most powerful tyranny and the most universal conspiracy against the economic freedom of individuals and the autonomy of nations the world has yet known.

The public are most carefully shielded from any real knowledge...

OmniaVeritas

Omnia Veritas Ltd presents:

MURDER BY INJECTION

by

EUSTACE MULLINS

THE STORY OF THE MEDICAL CONSPIRACY AGAINST AMERICA

The cynicism and malice of these conspirators is something beyond the imagination of most Americans.

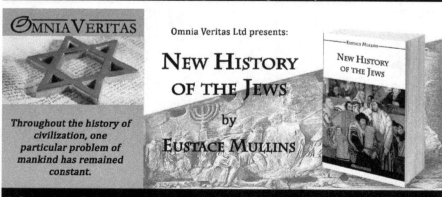

OmniaVeritas

Omnia Veritas Ltd presents:

NEW HISTORY OF THE JEWS

by

EUSTACE MULLINS

Throughout the history of civilization, one particular problem of mankind has remained constant.

Only one people has irritated its host nations in every part of the civilized world

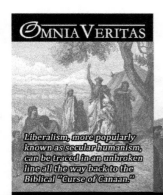

Omnia Veritas Ltd presents:

THE CURSE OF CANAAN
A demonology of history

by

EUSTACE MULLINS

Humanism is the logical result of the demonology of history

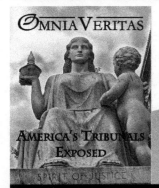

Omnia Veritas Ltd presents:

THE RAPE OF JUSTICE

by

EUSTACE MULLINS

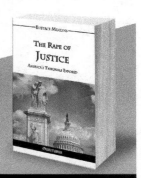

American should know just what is going on in our courts

Omnia Veritas Ltd presents:

THE SECRETS OF THE FEDERAL RESERVE

by

EUSTACE MULLINS

Will we continue to be enslaved by the Babylonian debt money system?

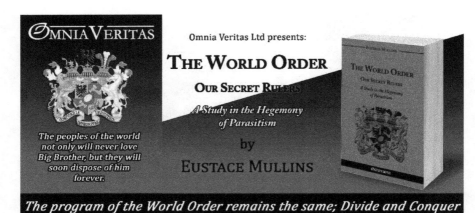

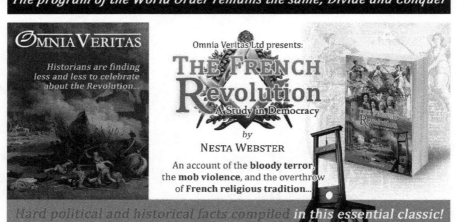